HUNTED

Book One
The Zodiac Murders

Mark Hewitt, DBA

Genius
Book Publishing

Encino, California

TABLE OF CONTENTS

For more information regarding the Zodiac Serial Killer series, please visit **zodiac.geniusbookpublishing.com**. There you can find updates on the case, sign up for periodic newsletters, and get information about special offers and our upcoming books.

zodiac.geniusbookpublishing.com

Please look for the upcoming books in the series:

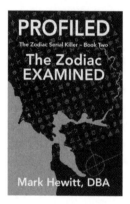

PROFILED: The Zodiac Examined
Available Now

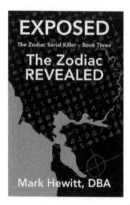

EXPOSED: The Zodiac Revealed
Releasing in fall 2018

ACKNOWLEDGMENTS

For the creation and publication of this book, I am indebted to many. I therefore gratefully acknowledge the hard work of each individual who assisted me in researching, writing, and editing of these pages.

My publisher, Steven Booth of Genius Book Company, labored night and day to get this to print. He and his team worked to fine tune my words, clarify my ideas, and offer you this book.

My family and friends have been my incomparable inspiration. Without their love and support this project would never have been completed.

Other select individuals served to impel, direct, or challenge me. These include Soren Korsgaard of Denmark, Ricardo Gomez of San Francisco, and the elusive and enigmatic Kevin DeWeerd.

Above all, glory to God in the Highest, the giver of life and the creator and solver of all mystery.

DEDICATION

This book is dedicated to Cheri Jo, David, Betty Lou, Darlene, Cecelia, and Paul. I would have liked you, and I have come to respect and admire you all. In your own way, you have each exuded your personality as engaging, vibrant, warm human beings. Typical Americans, if there is such a thing, pursuing typical American activities, you were guilty only of crossing paths with a sociopathic killer. Your tragic loss has deprived the world of so much.

Your murderer is a heinous fiend with no conscience. While future revelations may usher us toward a clearer understanding of his experience and personality, even offering up mitigating circumstances, nothing will ever justify these appalling, senseless crimes that cut short the precious lives of you who were so alive.

PROLOGUE

"This is the murderer..."

September 27, 1969

The man dressed in black betrayed no emotion as he ascended from the expansive reservoir. He knew it would be dark soon, and the heat of the day would give way to a cool, dry night. The sun continued to wane behind the tree-covered hills he was climbing. Still, he was in no hurry. He carefully made his way toward his car which was parked nearly 200 yards from the shoreline. He maneuvered his sturdy, black leather boots across the rugged terrain. Behind him, he left a horrific crime scene of senseless brutality that would haunt generations to come. It is possible he suspected—even hoped—that his actions would be discussed and debated for the next four decades and beyond.

As the man put distance between himself and the water, a young couple struggled to survive. Bryan Hartnell and Cecelia Shepard fought against the agony of a combined 16 stab wounds to their torsos. They wrestled at the water's edge with the hollow, plastic cords that bound them. When they felt it was safe, they screamed for help. They could feel their lives ebbing away in a torrential gush of blood.

Their assailant continued in a measured stride. The foot-long knife back in its wooden scabbard on his belt and a menacing handgun returned to its smooth, black holster on his other side, he trudged up the hill at a chillingly calm pace. He had just completed what would become his signature attack. He was concealed from view behind a dark, rectangular hood with eye holes that was pulled down to cover part of his chest. Across his front in white, an ominous gun-sight symbol bore silent witness to the threat posed by his weapon. Before the day was over, he would scrawl on the car door of his victims, then drive to the nearby town of Napa and boast of his carnage in a telephone call to the Napa Police Department. Before he would complete his criminal career, there would be other crimes—and other victims.

His many attacks would leave at least five dead and two critically injured across a three-year span of unprovoked violence. The assailant—who gave himself the terrifying and cryptic name, the "Zodiac"—captured the attention of the American public and the law enforcement community by claiming credit for his deeds in telephone calls, by writing missives to area newspapers, and by creating and sending ciphers that would evade decryption for decades. He wanted "front page coverage" from the papers, and gave ample evidence that he was eager to spread fear. His motivating force, the reason for the murders, appeared to be a quest to make a name for himself. He demanded fame. In his apparent aim, he was only partially successful.

For a killer who desired publicity and infamy, he could scarcely have chosen a more ill-advised time and place to ply his trade than Northern California in the year 1969. International events and local news would both conspire against the Zodiac serial killer to deny him the attention he seemed so desperate to acquire. Though he may have begun his appalling career in 1966, and killed again in December of 1968, he did not garner nationwide interest or international curiosity until the summer of 1969 with his creation of ciphers, his claim to an iconic moniker, and his use of a personal symbol.

As newsworthy as his macabre and horrific killings were, the Zodiac's deadly actions were overshadowed by the wanton and seemingly random carnage of the Manson Family in the Los Angeles area of Southern California. On two nights of bloody mayhem in mid-August, a band of antisocial and psychopathic cult members—led by the soon-to-be infamous cultural icon Charles Manson—invaded the quiet homes of two carefree families and slaughtered everyone they found. They used knives, guns, rope, and a barbeque fork. Their conscience provided no restraint. They capped their evil work with cryptic words splashed across surfaces in the fresh blood of one of their victims. Regardless of the many headlines claimed by the Zodiac, he was always the neglected younger step-brother to his media-savvy rival to the south. The scandalous scenes of horror that the Manson Family left behind could never be equaled in gore, never eclipsed in evoking the dread of a community, and never be bested in manipulating the media to spread a palpable message of fear.

The Zodiac also suffered from geography. Northern California has always seemed to play second fiddle to the southern half of its state. Maybe it was the weather. Northern California's gray, rainy winters encouraged rueful depression in some, while Los Angeles and San Diego enjoyed year-round sun and some of the most pleasant climatic patterns the planet has to offer. And publicity followed the sun. The north, with its earthy business people and pensive wine connoisseurs, appeared content to remain outside of the glow of the limelight. Instead, public attention focused its beam on Hollywood's celebrities, Malibu's pricey homes, and the tanned beach bodies to the south. If Southern California was where you went to find excitement, glamor, and a fast-paced life, Northern California was your destination for an easy retirement, a relaxing vacation, or a slow, casual lifestyle.

The Manson Family was not the only one snatching headlines from the Zodiac in the summer of 1969. National and international wires were buzzing with the interplanetary news of Neil Armstrong's first human boot prints on the moon, a story that united a nation and captured the imagination of everyone who had access to a radio or a television set. Man had left the bonds of earth. All eyes tilted skyward as Apollo 11 lifted off the launch pad at Cape Canaveral on July 16, 1969. Two of its three astronauts maneuvered the Lunar Excursion Module onto the gray pumice of the moon four days later. The very next morning, July 21, Armstrong planted the boot of his spacesuit onto the surface of earth's only natural satellite—the first time a human had found footing on a heavenly body—and declared, "That's one small step for a man, one giant leap for mankind."

Closer to home, a Utopian sociological experiment erupted on the East Coast. The Woodstock Festival in upstate New York played host to hundreds of thousands of youngsters who flocked there to watch their prized musicians. The muddy fields and availability of communal marijuana provided a counterstroke to the nerds who reveled in their space adventures and had ruled the drab 1950s. Opening less than a week after the Manson murders, the musical lollapalooza was reported on near and far. Love and peace were in the air with the fragrant scent of flowers and pot.

The year 1969 had something for everyone. The Manson Family, the Woodstock experiment, and the Apollo 11 voyage dazzled a people who had already borne witness to so much: the violence and incomprehensible death of the Vietnam War and many related conflicts, the rise of counterculture hippies with their anti-war demonstrations and their LSD, and the assassinations of presidential candidate Robert F. Kennedy and civil rights leader Martin Luther King, Jr.

With the backdrop of a new age—the cultural changes shocking even the most open minded—the Zodiac serial killer could not be expected to compete for attention. No matter how hard he tried, his failure was predestined.

Yet these same forces at work in time and geography that prevented him from achieving global media dominance may have also saved him from capture. So many other serial killers, both before and since, have been identified, apprehended, and imprisoned, if not executed. His bad luck in the pursuit of infamy may have been the boon that enabled him to remain hidden for so long, and ironically, provide him the notoriety and lasting legacy of being America's most enigmatic serial killer.

Worldwide, only Jack the Ripper, London's notorious prostitute slasher of 1888, has done more to electrify the public's imagination. American serial killers Ted Bundy, Jeffrey Dahmer, John Wayne Gacy, and Ed Gein have each in their own way startled the public with their gruesome, macabre practices. But what little remains unknown in these and other high-profile cases pales in comparison to the mysteries present in the person of the Zodiac. Following their capture, and the public's initial appetite for details, serial killers find that interest in their story eventually subsides. Once fleshed out, their motives, their bizarre actions, and the specifics of their inevitable capture become passé. By contrast, the Zodiac remains fresh for speculation. Since he was never caught, never even identified, he continues to tantalize public sensibility.

The Zodiac's clever evasion of justice was carried out despite a prolonged and concerted effort on the part of a united law enforcement community that struggled in the face of the killer's constant needling.

The investigation started out with humble beginnings, small police task force meetings that would grow over time. On Tuesday, October 14, 1969, at 9:00 p.m., Officers Ken Narlow and Richard Lonergan of the Napa County Sheriff's Department gathered with Detectives Bill Armstrong and Dave Toschi of the San Francisco Police Department (SFPD) at the Napa County Sheriff's Office to discuss similarities between murders the two departments were independently investigating. It was only one of many information-sharing sessions.

Six days later, at 1:00 in the afternoon, another event was convened at the SFPD. The investigating detectives shared what they had with each of the departments that were pursuing the murderer of cab driver Paul Stine. Soon, an office full of investigators working the case would be laboring around the clock and reaching for leads across the country.

A month later, on November 20, the Attorney General of California, Thomas C. Lynch, arranged a meeting—labeled "the Zodiac Conference" by the press—in San Francisco for 27 detectives from seven agencies to exchange information about the serial killer operating within the jurisdictions represented. This latest gathering was the most comprehensive of any previously held. As the participants proceeded to discuss each of the attacks—a couple murdered in Solano County, a woman killed on the outskirts of Vallejo, the couple stabbed on the shore of Lake Berryessa in Napa County, and a San Francisco cabby executed with a bullet through his skull—each detective and each department gave with open arms to all the others present.

A common thread running through these law enforcement summits—apart from a desperate desire to know the name and identity of the perpetrator who called himself the "Zodiac"—was an enthusiastic optimism. With each meeting, the agents were more hopeful than ever that enough information had been collected and disseminated that a capture would be inevitable. They may not have felt any closer to a resolution, but they moved forward in confidence.

What none of the participants could have known at the time was that four decades would quickly pass without the identification of the perpetrator. The case files would grow as more than 2,500 men were investigated. Theories would emerge, flourish, and then branch into multiple permutations. Officers would come and go in normal departmental turnover. All with no resolution to the case.

The initial meetings revealed that there were no shortage of clues from which to identify their quarry. Often in unsolved crimes, the only clue that investigators possess is a single crime scene—sometimes none—the evidence of unlawful behavior, and possibly a vague idea of a motive. Eyewitnesses may be uncooperative or never located. The few items of forensic value must be collected with the possibility that other investigative avenues will develop. All too frequently, even the few leads that are discovered quickly dry up, and the file goes cold.

For the case of the Zodiac serial killer, there was an abundance of evidence. But evidence of what? The files bulged with information covering multiple crime scenes, several eyewitnesses, and forensic material. It was all easily accessible. Evidence would be collected, tests run, and copious leads followed—all to no avail.

For better or worse, citizens involved themselves throughout the process, sometimes helping but more often interfering. As detectives moved through the evidence, a supportive public offered up hundreds of suspects. Each proposed perpetrator was considered, many were interviewed, but all would eventually be dismissed. Some were followed for a time—one for many years. A few didn't fit for obvious reasons, but all would defy investigators due to their dissimilar handwriting, non-matching stature, or iron-clad alibi that eliminated all suspicions.

And then the Zodiac stopped.

This raised nearly as many questions as the crime spree itself. It is thought that serial killers almost without exception continue to murder until they are apprehended, incarcerated for other crimes, or killed. Was he a rare example of a killer who reformed his ways or merely lost interest? A curious public and a duty-bound law enforcement community demanded to know who he was and why he killed.

Nearly five decades later, the police are no closer than they were in 1969 to identifying this most mysterious criminal, a serial killer who brutally murdered and then wrote taunting and threatening letters—sometimes accompanied by a curious telephone call to terrorize an already fearful public—before disappearing into the ether.

This is the story of the Zodiac serial killer and law enforcement's quest to identify and capture him.

These events could have occurred in any town or any city. Solano County, the City of Vallejo, and metropolitan San Francisco reflect America in all its forms: rural, small town, and urban, respectively. They are anywhere, or everywhere, USA. The attacks therefore could have happened to anyone or anyone's children.

For over forty years, the investigation has proceeded with no resolution. Justice has had to wait in silence, longing to have the final word. Investigators and armchair enthusiasts alike continue to seek the answers to all the relevant questions in the minutia of the crimes—for it is in the details that the murderer remains hidden.

Mark Hewitt
Santa Rosa, California

1 | RIVERSIDE, CALIFORNIA

"SHE WAS YOUNG AND BEAUTIFUL"

Cheri Jo drove herself to the library. It would be the last ride of her life.

At 3:00 in the afternoon, and again at 3:45, 18-year-old Cheri Jo Bates, a pretty Southern California brunette, telephoned Stefani Guttman, her close friend and fellow Riverside City College (RCC) student. She invited her friend to accompany her in picking up a few books from the college library. It was Sunday afternoon, and Cheri Jo, a conscientious first-year student, needed the literature to complete a class assignment. Guttman would forever regret passing on the opportunity.

Alone, Bates set out sometime before 6:00 p.m. on October 30, 1966.

Just before she left, she wrote a note for her father, with whom she lived, informing him of her destination: "DAD—Went to RCC Library."

Joseph Bates arrived home shortly afterwards and found his daughter's words. Before he departed for dinner at a friend's home, he too scribbled a note—Stefani had called and left a message. This father and daughter team communicated well and often. Joseph had phoned Cheri Jo from his friend's home at 5:00, and again at 5:15, to invite his daughter to join them for dinner, but the line was busy on both occasions. He had just missed her when he got back home around 6:00 p.m.

Joseph showered, changed his clothes, and traveled back to his friend's home. Cheri Jo would have to fend for herself.

Earlier that day, the two had celebrated Mass at Saint Catherine's Catholic Church, followed by breakfast. When her dad went to the beach at Corona del Mar with his friend to enjoy the unseasonably warm temperatures that afternoon, Cheri Jo had declined to accompany them. She had homework to complete. She also hoped to make time to compose a passionate letter to her boyfriend in San Francisco.

When Joseph finally arrived home to stay around midnight, he discovered that his message remained untouched. A feeling of worry overcame him. Cheri Jo, his only daughter, had not returned from the library.

Alarmed, he hurriedly telephoned Guttman for any information he could gather. He would call her again at 6:50 in the morning. At daybreak, he filed a missing person's report with the Riverside Police Department (RPD). He and Cheri Jo were so close, and she was usually so careful and punctual, that he refused to wait any longer. He knew something was wrong.

Something was.

At 6:30 on the morning following her disappearance, the body of Cheri Jo Bates was found face down on a dirt pathway that led to a student parking area. It lay between two old, vacant houses that had been purchased by the college in preparation for an expansion. Bates's remains were approximately 100 yards from her disabled car (one police estimate lists 200 feet instead of 300 feet, possibly a typing error). The grisly discovery was made by 48-year-old RCC groundskeeper Cleophas Martin as he operated a street sweeping machine. Cheri Jo had been stabbed numerous times, including a *coup de grace* to the neck, a slice that nearly decapitated her.

The furrowed grass in the area bore witness to a horrific struggle. Bates was fully clothed in a yellow blouse (the coroner described it as a "loose pink moderately heavy blouse"), home-made red Capris, and white sandals. She wore no sweater because she was planning to return home immediately after collecting the books—she preferred to study at home. Her arms were drawn in, and her body partially concealed a woven straw tote-bag purse beneath her, papers from which would be used to identify her. She had been beaten about the face and strangled. The autopsy would detail seven deliberate cuts to her young throat.

Born in Nebraska on February 4, 1948 to Joseph C. Bates and Irene Karolvitz, Cheri Josephine Bates lived with her father, a machinist at the Naval Ordinance Laboratory in Norco. Her only sibling, her younger brother, Michael, had joined the Navy and was stationed far from home. She could see her mother anytime, since she too lived in Riverside, having divorced Cheri Jo's father. The family, which had been intact at the time, had moved to California eight years prior to the attack. A family of four, through divorce and a military assignment, had become a household of two.

Her parent's divorce and her brother's absence did not hold Cheri Jo back. She was even-keeled, dedicated, and determined. A full-time student at RCC, she still found time to do typing and other clerical work for Riverside National Bank. She was well liked by her friends, but more importantly, she was respected by them. Never given to erratic impulsiveness, her word was her bond. Everyone who knew her knew that she was as dependable and prompt as she was loyal. Her creative flair never resulted in periods of irresponsibility. She was generous and kind, and always seemed to have a smile on her face. She had no shortage of date requests from the many men drawn to her gregariousness. She was planning a career as a flight attendant. An official at the Ramona High School where Bates had been a cheerleader described her as bright and very popular with both boys and girls during her high school career in Riverside.

Riverside, California, the town where Cheri Jo and her family had lived for almost a decade, was founded in 1870. Named for the Santa Ana River on which it sat, it became the county seat in 1873 when Riverside County was established. No permanent settlement had occurred at the site prior to this time, but the area was well known to the local Native Americans, who had over the years built many temporary dwellings there. The Spanish first arrived in the region in 1774.

Once established as a permanent town, and seat of the county, Riverside became known for the Washington Navel Orange, a popular variety of seedless orange. It boasted large settlements of Chinese and Korean workers, possessing one of the largest Chinatowns to be found in California. It played host to NASCAR racing and other track events at the Riverside International Raceway that operated from 1957 to 1989. When it finally closed, the raceway's buildings and track were dismantled to make way for a shopping mall.

In the 1960 census, the town boasted a population of 84,332. Cheri Jo Bates would never again be counted among the cities' residents, however. She had been murdered in cold blood.

ᝣ

The 1960s in California was a tumultuous decade. As far as American history, only the 1860s with the Civil War offered more social and cultural upheaval. One consequence of the free love and rebellion was a large number of serial killers spawned in the turbulence of the 1960s and 1970s. They may have emerged on the scene as a result of widespread interpersonal alienation, the increased number of absentee parents, or merely the nebulous but palpable angst that permeated the culture. Whatever the cause, the surge of a "new" type of criminal was notable and alarming. At the time of Bates's death, no one realized that a lone murder in Southern California was the opening salvo of a deadly spree, and the beginning of a decades-long mystery. It was a one-off event when it occurred, and it seemed unrelated to other contemporary crimes.

The crime in and of itself was high profile, and the community felt an urgency to find its resolution. In the usually safe town of Riverside, murder was rare. Riverside Police Chief L. T. "Curly" Kinkead quickly assigned seven officers. They were ordered to drop their current projects and apply themselves full time to the murder investigation. Detective Sergeant Gren was assisted by six detectives: Dick Yonkers, Earl Brown, Wayne Durrington, Cliff Arons, Curtis Best, and Bob Walters. These investigators would in turn be supported by full-time detectives assigned to the case by the District Attorney's Office, and additional detectives from the Coroner's Office. On the first day of the investigation alone—the day Bates's body was discovered—24 officers put in a total of 133 man hours of effort.

And this was only the beginning. The first month recorded a total of 30 different law enforcement agents working the many facets of the murder case.

Gren, Brown, and Yonkers preserved the integrity of the crime scene and began to search for clues, even as students began to flow past on their way to class. Many stopped to stare.

Subsequent investigation revealed that Bates had checked out three books on the U.S. Electoral College system from the RCC library at approximately 6:00 p.m. When she returned to her lime green Volkswagen Beetle, parked on a city street near the library at 3680 Terracina Drive (the address of college), she was unable to start the vehicle. Apparently, not realizing the damage that had been done to her car, she turned over the engine again and again, enough to drain the battery. Three library books lay on the passenger seat of her car; the keys remained in the ignition.

Under greater scrutiny, it was evident that someone had deliberately tampered with Miss Bates's 1960 Volkswagen. Riverside County Sheriff's deputies Jack Reid and Jack Elms, who located Bates's car on the morning after her disappearance, noted that the distributor coil and condenser had been torn out, according to one source, and the coil wire dislodged from the distributor socket. A few greasy fingerprints and palm prints that dirtied the driver's door must have come from whomever had disabled the car. Both windows were rolled down. The passenger door was ajar, suggesting to detectives that her assailant may have been in the vehicle with her. Detective Captain Irvin "Irv" L. Cross of the Riverside Police Department (RPD) ordered the vehicle towed to the police station to be examined.

Dr. F. Rene Modglin, a pathologist on contract with the Riverside County Coroner's Office, began his preliminary autopsy right at the spot Bates lay. He had been called at home at 7:15 in the morning by Chief Deputy Coroner William J. Dykes and notified of a possible homicide. Dykes called again at 8:30—this time to Modglin at work—ordering him to proceed to the site. The pathologist arrived just after 9:00 a.m. Based on the temperature of Bates's liver, and the corpse's stage of rigor mortis, he tentatively estimated that the girl had been killed at 10:30 p.m. That estimate would be modified following a more extensive study of the body.

The detectives gathering clues soon learned that Cheri Jo may have announced her passing.

A woman who lived in the vicinity reported that she heard a scream the previous evening between 10:15 p.m. and 10:45 p.m., followed by a second, muted scream, and then two minutes later by the sound of an older car roaring to life. This information was described in the newspapers as originating from an anonymous caller, who at the time of the sounds did not think them important enough to contact the police. Whether these were related to the violent attack was never established.

The screams could have come from someone unwittingly stumbling across the body in the dead of night, or by someone unrelated to the crime. If they had been made by Bates, and denoted the time of the attack, investigators were left to wonder what Bates was doing between 6:00 p.m. and 10:15 p.m., especially in light of the fact that she could not start her car and may not have shown herself to her friends in the library, which shuttered for the night at 9:00 p.m. The police believed that the screams coincided with Bates's death, but would not confirm this without corroborating evidence.

Authorities transported the body to Acheson and Graham Mortuary, where Modglin performed a complete autopsy. Those present included: Detective Gerald H. Dunn, Detective Earl T. Brown of the RPD, Investigator Jim Lesseigne (Riverside County District Attorney's Office), Michael J. Reilly (Riverside County Coroner's Office), and Mr. Scotty Hill, an embalmer at the mortuary. The pathologist ruled it a death due to hemorrhage of the right carotid artery. Fingernail scrapings suggested that the victim had struggled against a white, male assailant.

Bates weighed 110 pounds. The doctor noted her green eyes and brown hair. Her blood type was AB positive, and tested negative—as expected—for traces of drugs or alcohol. He recorded, among many other abrasions and wounds, a 2-centimeter oblique laceration to her upper lip, numerous petechia in the skin of her forehead, and an area of dark blue-gray discoloration of the skin of her left cheek and chin. He removed from her stomach the roast beef that had been cooked and eaten by Bates on Sunday, evidencing between two and four hours of digestion. He now set the time of death to a range of time between 9:00 p.m. and 1:00 a.m., but an even earlier time would be stated in a future document.

During the preliminary procedure, still at the crime scene, Modglin found a clot of blood with four sandy-brown hairs attached to it. They were on the base of Bates's right thumb, and provided a most intriguing potential forensic link to her killer. Analysis conducted by the Trace Evidence Unit of the Federal Bureau of Investigation (FBI) in 1999 revealed that the hairs did not match exemplary hairs taken from Bates. The killer may have deposited the clot during the mortal violence.

The wounds on her body revealed that the friendly coed had been attacked with a small knife whose blade measured only three and a half inches by a half inch, possibly a pen knife or a small kitchen implement. She had been stabbed numerous times in the chest, once in the back, and slashed across her neck. Investigators had on their hands a homicide caused by multiple stabbing and slashing wounds of the abdomen and neck—inflicted with a sharp instrument or knife. Despite having no eyewitnesses and no firm time of attack, they remained hopeful that enough clues were present to identify and convict the person or persons responsible. They wanted the case solved.

They wanted it solved quickly.

Detectives Bob Walters and Earl Brown of the RPD used a metal detector to search the area of the crime scene for a murder weapon. None was found. An investigation of the library also proved fruitless. Walter Seibert was one of a few of Cheri Jo's friends who was at the library from 7:15 p.m. to 9:00 p.m. None of them saw Bates, whom they knew and would have noticed, according to the police report. Bates's friends did report that they saw four men in work clothes sitting on a fence across from the spot where Bates's car was located. One newspaper reported that Bates had been seen studying at the library until its close at 9:00 p.m. *San Francisco Chronicle* reporter Paul Avery later wrote that "numerous witnesses" had observed Bates in the library though none had spoken to her.

The Press, a local Riverside newspaper, carried two stories about the attack on the day after Bates was found. In the first, information about the discovery of a body was shared with the public. Bates was identified by name, and her father's name and address were listed, the naïve standard of an innocent time, "Joseph Bates 4195 Via San Jose." The article noted that the area of the crime had to be roped off because students were beginning to arrive for classes. Officer J. Walters was pictured looking for clues. In a separate picture, Officer Ben Castlebury interrogated librarian Harry Back and reference librarian Winifred Turner about the library's hours of operation. The story noted that officers carefully circumnavigated the pathway, preventing the destruction of any forensic material, until it had been processed.

The second article, titled, "Father waits in vain for daughter's return," told the heart-wrenching story of Cheri Jo's dad. By Monday morning, Joseph knew that a body had been found at RCC, and that Cheri Jo's Volkswagen, with California license plate PNA-398, had been discovered nearby. Police didn't say anything to him at first, but he suspected that the remains were those of his only daughter.

The police eventually notified him of what he already knew. He was now very alone.

ల౧

On Tuesday, Gren informed reporters that the detectives had interviewed 75 people, but still had not solved the riddle: "So far we have drawn a blank." He asked for public assistance from anyone who had seen Bates before her demise, hoping that knowledge of her movements and activities of Sunday night would aid the investigation.

Tips flooded in. Everyone wanted to help, it seemed. When the public was told of the small blade that was used against the popular, young coed, telephone calls came in from people all over town who had located just such a knife. On November 14, the campus gardener raked up a small knife on the college grounds. Unfortunately for the investigation, it had no dried blood on it and the size was wrong.

It was reported that one witness had seen Bates as she drove toward the library on the day she went missing. A 1965 or 1966 bronze-colored car, possibly an Oldsmobile, had been observed following her. No one else could confirm the sighting, and no such vehicle was ever positively identified.

Riverside Police Chief Kinkead revealed on Wednesday that nearly 125 citizens had been interviewed by police, who were working the murder case around the clock.

In the aftermath of the attack, RCC illuminated and provided open space at the spot the crime had occurred. Facing pressure from the community, it moved up its schedule to install mercury vapor lights on the campus between Terracina Drive and Fairfax Avenue.

The few pieces of physical evidence found at the scene of the murder intrigued investigators. A heel print in the soil from a military shoe, sized between 8 and 10, appeared to come from her attacker. It was identified as a B.F. Goodrich waffle design, a men's four-eighths inch washer-type half heel. At first it appeared that the shoes that made the impression originated in England. Subsequent investigation indicated that they were sold only to federal prison industries at Leavenworth, Kansas, where they were cobbled with leather into shoes for the U.S. government. The pair that made the impressions in the soft ground could have been purchased at nearby March Air Force Base, a Strategic Air Command base. Shoes bearing the identified tread patterns were also available to other government agencies, including prison administrations.

A man's Timex watch, with the fastener on one side of the watch torn off, may have also been deposited by her attacker. It had a white, stainless steel face and no serial number. Located ten feet from Bates's body, with its hands stopped at precisely 12:24, the watch may have been pulled from her killer during the struggle. It was later determined that the watch had been purchased from the PX at an overseas military base. This resulted in the interrogation of 154 airmen stationed at March Air Force Base—all those who took classes at the college.

The Timex was sent on Thursday to the California Bureau of Criminal Identification and Investigation (CII) in Sacramento, and subjected to many tests by a private company in San Diego. A summary of the crime five years later indicated that the police were convinced that the watch belonged to her murderer, but they also knew it could have been totally unrelated to the attack or purposefully placed by her attacker as a false clue. If it was worn by Bates's killer, the police had one more piece of information about him: he had a seven-inch wrist. The watch was dotted with white paint spatter, an intriguing potential clue to its owner's identity.

The investigation also turned up a discarded cigarette butt near the site of the murder. Law enforcement never determined whether it was related to Bates's death, or was deposited by someone totally unconnected to the case. The police soon realized that they did not have much concrete evidence from the site of the murder, but would have to somehow move the case forward nevertheless.

℀

A murder investigation usually begins with a careful evaluation of the crime scene. It proceeds with a comprehensive study of the victim, and then continues outward in ever-expanding concentric circles of the victim's social relationships. A crime scene analysis, an integral part of any investigation, makes two important assumptions stemming from what is known in criminology as the Locard Transfer Principle, articulated by Dr. Edmund Locard: "every contact leaves a trace." The first assumption is that when anyone commits a crime, he or she will inevitably leave something of him- or herself behind at the scene, such as a head hair, fingerprint, or trace fiber. It is not possible for someone to inhabit a place without leaving some evidence of the visit, however small. The question is whether scientific investigative means are available to record and document the evidence before it is destroyed or contaminated.

The second assumption is a corollary: every perpetrator of a crime takes something with him or her from a crime scene, whether it be microscopic traces of the environment, such as soil, vegetation, or water samples; some portion of the victim, such as bodily fluids, a hair, or clothing fibers; or something brought to the scene by the victim or someone else. If a suspect can be identified soon enough, evidence of his or her presence can be preserved and presented in a court of law.

In an investigation, the crime scene evidence may aid investigators in developing the rudimentary beginnings of a profile. The police want to know what type of person might feel comfortable operating in such an environment, and what about the scene itself may have led to the crime. Since the scene can reveal what is likely or possible for the criminal behavior, a good investigator will linger, attempting to understand as much about it as possible.

While the investigators in 1966 lacked many modern investigative techniques, they were able to develop a rough profile of their suspect.

Criminal profiling is as old as investigation. It is an attempt to describe as accurately as possible what is known or can be inferred about an unknown offender. It will incorporate eyewitness reports and any details of the perpetrator's known physical properties in an effort to eliminate suspects so that law enforcement can focus its attention on a smaller set of likely candidates. Psychological profiling—the activity that attempts to describe the psychological makeup of the offender from the crime-scene evidence—dates back to the 1950s. It was unavailable to the investigation at the time of the murder, however, and would not gain widespread acceptance until published papers on the subject began appearing in reputable journals in the 1970s.

The investigators dutifully took a close look at Bates's life. Victimology, the study of the victim of a crime, often provides clues as to what happened, and why it happened. If the victim is present in some high-risk category—such as a drug-using prostitute or a known member of a violent gang—an analysis of the risks may suggest a motive for the killing. A victimology may also indicate who was responsible, or at least the type of person who should be considered. A low-risk victim, such as a well-liked member of the community who does not engage in unlawful behavior, may suggest that the killer may be closer to home—an intimate friend or a spouse.

The police were confident in their assessment that Cheri Jo was very low risk in her actions and lifestyle. She did not move in violent crowds, break the law, or use drugs. Her victimology did not suggest a motive for death. In only one respect was she at an elevated risk at all: she was young and attractive. Eyesome females run an increased chance of violent death at the hands of lovers, ex-lovers, and wannabe lovers in all-too-frequently-played-out scenarios of fatal revenge, spite, or misdirected passion.

The Riverside police were well aware that most murder victims are known to their killers. Frequently, the perpetrator is a friend or family member. It is an early step in any investigation to examine and, if possible, clear all close associates. Murder is a deliberate and hostile act, usually having at its root a soured friendship, a broken family tie, a failed business partnership, or love affair gone wrong. The overwhelming majority of murders of young women are committed by boyfriends, husbands, or men who once filled these roles.

Cheri Jo *was* dating at the time of her death. According to newspaper reports, her exclusive partner, Dennis Highland, had left the area to attend San Francisco State College after studying at RCC. The weekend prior to her death, Cheri Jo had joined Highland's parents on a trip to visit him at the Northern California campus. The trip went well by all accounts. Cheri Jo and Dennis were very much in love. Highland was questioned and cleared quite quickly. He was far away from Riverside at the time of the murder, and had no apparent motive to kill his girlfriend even if he had been in the area.

Early on, in the initial fog of the murder, two friends of Cheri Jo's told police that their friend had gone to the library to meet her boyfriend. Further investigation eliminated this possibility. Captain Cross reported on Thursday that the information was based on hearsay, and was incorrect. By this time nearly 200 people had been questioned.

The Tiger Times, the RCC newspaper, in a story published five days after the attack—"Police Still Lack Clues in the Murder"—noted that the police had no suspects. The tentatively held theory was that the killer disabled Bates's car, then waited for her in one of the driveways on Terracina Drive. The paper indicated that Bates "put up a tremendous struggle" in her valiant, but ultimately unsuccessful, attempt to survive. It also reported that there was an increase in students who dropped night classes—but added that, according to John Matulich, the Dean of Admissions, this may have been prompted by other factors, including a drop-class deadline.

Exactly two weeks after the murder, according to several sources, the police staged a reenactment of sorts. They invited everyone who had been at the library on the night that Bates was killed to reassemble. Participants were told to wear the same clothes they had worn, park in the same space in which they had parked, and sit at the same desk they had occupied that night. Each of the 65 participants was questioned and asked to give a statement as to what they had seen and done a fortnight earlier. Further, the men were fingerprinted and asked for a lock of their hair. (The color of the hair found on Bates's thumb was initially withheld from the public.) Everyone willingly agreed to the requests to help locate Bates's killer.

Through the reenactment, it was concluded that Bates, or a woman who looked like her, had arrived at the library at 5:40 p.m. and waited until it opened at 6:00 p.m. Captain Cross announced that the police sought a 1947 to 1952 Studebaker with light-colored oxidized paint. One had been seen by students at 7:00 p.m. on the night of the murder, but it had not been present for the reenactment two weeks later. Also, police were looking for a heavyset man with a beard. He too had been observed at the library, but had failed to return.

By December 1, no strong suspect or suspects had been developed. Many people brought to the attention of law enforcement had been investigated. One man moved south immediately following the murder. Further investigation eliminated him from suspicion. A mental patient at a nearby State Hospital reported that he might have killed the petite beauty. He was found to be subject to delusions and hallucinations—and not responsible for the murder. Because the attack closely resembled an April 1965 stabbing of another coed in a spot not far from where Bates was found, investigators moved quickly to find the assailant of the earlier violence. The 19-year-old was cleared as soon as he was located. He was still serving time for that attempted murder when Bates was stabbed, and therefore could not have been responsible.

Investigators carefully analyzed the evidence. Drops of dried blood found in a driveway suggested that the killer had returned to Terracina Drive after completing the injuries to Bates. It was also possible that Bates was stabbed at or near her car, and then shed these drops as she fled for her life to the promise of safety among the abandoned homes. Captain Cross initially speculated that the victim had sprinted from the library, noting that scuff marks were found in the gravel along the driveway. His suspicions were revised with the discovery of footprints leading to the crime scene that suggested instead that Bates had gone willingly, unaware of what awaited her, as a lamb to the slaughter. The right window of Bates car was partially open, leading investigators to wonder whether she had been approached at some point in the ordeal from the passenger side of her vehicle.

The odd condition of her car puzzled investigators. Through interviews, they learned that she loved her vehicle, and worked very hard to pay for it. She never left it, they were told, until it had been carefully locked and its windows dutifully rolled up. They could not account for the unlocked doors, the unrolled windows, and the key thoughtlessly abandoned in the ignition. They speculated that she knew her attacker and was comfortable enough to let her guard down and leave with him.

This was reinforced by the knowledge that Bates was afraid of the dark. Because that Sunday was the first day of the return to Pacific Standard Time, the city was dark at 6:15 p.m. Investigators believed that she would only have ventured between the two dilapidated campus homes with someone she highly trusted.

⁊

As the Riverside Police Department strove to understand what had happened to Bates and locate a perpetrator, the idea of a serial killer was never considered. This was a single murder, unconnected to any other crime at this point. Additionally, the term "serial killer" would not be coined and in common use for another decade or so. Only traditional motives for the killing were explored because those were all the categories that existed in the minds and training of investigators. In 1966, they had no other arrows in their investigative quivers.

Murder for financial gain was quickly eliminated when Bates's purse was located under her body, its contents including cash completely undisturbed. Investigators also ruled out a sexual attack, because the girl's clothing was unmolested and no semen or other evidence was present to suggest such a motive. They considered and rejected other common motives, and were left wondering whether it was a drug-related murder, a revenge killing, or a spur of the moment attack committed by a perpetrator in a psychotic fit of rage. Further investigation failed to reveal any known enemies, or any hint of a drug or organized crime connection in Bates's life.

A few fingerprints were collected and sent to CII in Sacramento on November 4, specifically the Latent Fingerprint Section. The file became latent case #73096. Further analysis would eliminate all but four fingerprints and three partial palm prints, which were never matched to anyone. On November 9, a preliminary report was filed with the Riverside County District Attorney's office, and nail scrapings, vaginal smears, and hairs from the base of Bates's right thumb were processed for analysis. Despite the physical evidence, the investigation soon sputtered for a lack of motive, any real suspects, or a single eyewitness. The police were left to scratch their heads at this most mysterious, senseless killing.

One fact regarding the murder seemed clear. If Bates's attacker planned to kill her, he was a novitiate in murdering with a knife. The three and a half inch by half inch blade was not nearly sufficient for a clean and efficient kill, and it allowed his victim to put up a noble struggle. If he were to murder again with a knife, he would know to bring something larger—much larger. If the attack was unplanned—perhaps an intended sexual assault that got out of hand, or the perpetrator impulsively reacted with violence to some unexpected psychological trigger—and knowing what we now know, perhaps the killer enjoyed his first taste of blood and made the decision that this would not be his last.

The murder investigation, case #352-481, would eventually go as cold as Bates's lifeless body. No one could be found who had a reason to kill the young coed, and Bates did not engage in any high-risk behaviors that would suggest a motive. Friends and family members were questioned and cleared. Not only were the members of her closest circle not responsible, no one seemed to know by whom or for what purpose their much-loved Cheri Jo was murdered.

૭૭

The Confession letters

The investigation reignited one month after the killing with the arrival of two letters. On November 29, an unstamped envelope addressed to the Homicide Division in Riverside was removed from the collection box in the main post office at 5:00 p.m. The block lettering, done in heavy felt pen, was likely a disguise of the true handwriting of its author. Inside, the RPD found their copy of the Confession letter. The very next day, a Riverside newspaper, *The Daily Enterprise* (today publishing as *The Press-Enterprise*), received an unstamped envelope with a separate copy of the Confession letter.

Efforts to locate the identity of the typewriter used in the creation of the letters proved negative. The two letters were carbon copies revealing a common original that was typed, single spaced, and used short sentences and minimal punctuation (only periods and commas). The letter type most closely resembled a font coming from a portable Royal typewriter, likely a Merit Pica 508, its specific font-type an elite Canterbury shaded. The original from which the copies were made never surfaced. There may have been two originals. Whoever had killed Bates wanted the police and the press to know details of the attack, he wanted them to know it was he who had placed a phone call, and he wanted others to know that he would kill again.

Either that, or some hoaxer wanted to claim credit for an unsolved murder. The police had to consider every possibility. Whatever their source, the letters had to be investigated. In detail and tone, they sounded like authentic communications from Cheri Jo's killer. If the claims were sincere, whether the letters came from Bates's killer or not was immaterial. Someone had sent terrorist-like threats and used the federal postal system to communicate these, both of which were felonious activities. The writer had underscored his message by providing it in duplicate.

Typed in all capital letters, the Confession letter read as follows:

```
                    THE CONFESSION
                    BY_____
```

SHE WAS YOUNG AND BEAUTIFUL. BUT NOW SHE IS BATTERED AND DEAD. SHE IS NOT THE FIRST AND SHE WILL NOT BE THE LAST. I LAY AWAKE NIGHTS THINKING ABOUT MY NEXT VICTIM. MAYBE SHE WILL BE THE BEAUTIFUL BLOND THAT BABYSITS NEAR THE LITTLE STORE AND WALKS DOWN THE DARK

ALLEY EACH EVENING ABOUT SEVEN. OR MAYBE SHE WILL BE
THE SHAPELY BLUE EYED BROWNETT THAT SAID NO WHEN I
ASKED HER FOR A DATE IN HIGH SCHOOL. BUT MAYBE IT WILL
NOT BE EITHER. BUT I SHALL CUT OFF HER FEMALE PARTS
AND DEPOSIT THEM FOR THE WHOLE CITY TO SEE. SO DON'T
MAKE IT TO EASY FOR ME. KEEP YOUR SISTERS, DAUGHTERS,
AND WIVES OFF THE STREETS AND ALLEYS. MISS BATES WAS
STUPID. SHE WENT TO THE SLAUGHTER LIKE A LAMB.SHE DID
NOT PUT UP A STRUGGLE. BUT I DID. IT WAS A BALL. I
FIRST PULLED THE MIDDLE WIRE FROM THE DISTRIBUTOR.
THEN I WAITED FOR HER IN THE LIBRARY AND FOLLOWED
HER OUT AFTER ABOUT TWO MINUTS. THE BATTERY MUST HAVE
BEEN ABOUT DEAD BY THEN I THEN OFFERED TO HELP. SHE
WAS THEN VERY WILLING TO TALK WITH ME. I TOLD HER
THAT MY CAR WAS DOWN THE STREET AND THAT I WOULD GIVE
HER A LIFT HOME. WHEN WE WERE AWAY FROM THE LIBRARY
WALKING, I SAID IT WAS ABOUT TIME. SHE ASKED ME "ABOUT
TIME FOR WHAT". I SAID IT WAS ABOUT TIME FOR HER TO
DIE. I GRABBED HER AROUND THE NECK WITH MY HAND OVER
HER MOUTH AND MY OTHER HAND WITH A SMALL KNIFE AT HER
THROAT. SHE WENT VERY WILLINGLY. HER BREAST FELT VERY
WARM AND FIRM UNDER MY HANDS, BUT ONLY ONE THING WAS
ON MY MIND. MAKING HER PAY FOR THE BRUSH OFFS THAT SHE
HAD GIVEN ME DURING THE YEARS PRIOR. SHE DIED HARD.
SHE SQUIRMED AND SHOOK AS I CHOKED HER, AND HER LIPS
TWICHED, SHE LET OUT A SCREAM ONCE AND I KICKED HER
HEAD TO SHUT HER UP. I PLUNGED THE KNIFE INTO HER
AND IT BROKE. I THEN FINISHED THE JOB BY CUTTING HER
THROAT. I AM NOT SICK. I AM INSANE. BUT THAT WILL NOT
STOP THE GAME. THIS LETTER SHOULD BE PUBLISHED FOR ALL
TO READ IT. IT JUST MIGHT SAVE THAT GIRL IN THE ALLEY.
BUT THAT'S UP TO YOU. IT WILL BE ON YOUR CONSCIENCE,
NOT MINE. YES I DID MAKE THAT CALL TO YOU ALSO. IT WAS
JUST A WARNING. BEWARE...I AM STALKING YOUR GIRLS NOW.

CC. CHIEF OF POLICE
ENTERPRISE

The Confession letter's unusual use of the word "that" to describe
Bates—rather than the grammatically correct "who"—would much
later suggest that its writer may also have penned a strange follow-up
letter that repeatedly made this same grammatical error. It is not out
of character for a callous murderer to describe his victim as an inanimate object.

If the Riverside police believed the letter writer and anticipated additional killings by the same perpetrator, they still did not suspect that they were up against a serial killer because the phrase did not yet exist. The only qualifier of the word "murderer" for investigators in 1966 was that of "mass murderer," used to describe anyone who kills more than one person in a single incident, for any reason and under whatever circumstances. But the killer would kill again, and write more letters, and make more telephone calls. Finally, years later, he would cease his campaign of terror. All this would be completed before Bob Ressler, of the FBI's Behavioral Science Unit (BSU), would coin the term "serial killer" in the 1980s to distinguish those who kill repeatedly (three or more instances) across expanses of time (often called a "cooling-off period") from other types of murderers.

The phrase "serial killer" would in time have to be further qualified to differentiate organized serial killers (those who premeditate and bring tools and instruments of their trade to the murder) from disorganized serial killers (those who utilize whatever is available at the scene). There are other kinds of "serial" killers as well, such as paid assassins, gang killers, spree killers, and other types who repeatedly commit murders. Investigators attempt to discern two things about a serial killer: how they physically conduct the murder, and what mentally drives them to commit the murders including the psychological effects of the act of murder on the serial killer themselves. With this information, investigators can begin to unravel the killer's modus operandi, and with luck identify them before they kill again, or at least use their analysis in prosecuting the alleged killer.

Entire volumes have been written on the science of behavioral analysis. It is beyond the scope of this work to recreate what other authors have already so admirably written on the subject.

℮⁎

The Confession letters, so called because of the title centered across the top of the page, were postmarked Riverside, California, and delivered despite their lack of postage stamps. The press copies were eight inches wide by unknown length since the top and bottom of the letters had been torn off by the writer for reasons unknown.

The police attempted to identify the letter's author. Even when typed—a clever means of disguising any handwriting idiosyncrasies—letters can be traced to their creators. Typewriters have a unique signature that can yield a match for investigators who check the height of individual characters, distinctive wear patterns, or other unique characteristics of the specific letters. The writer of the Confession letters apparently anticipated this: he sent only carbon copies of the typed original, possibly a fourth or fifth copy produced by a multilayered sandwich of papers and carbon sheets. The text was therefore difficult to read, and virtually impossible to link to a specific machine.

Though titled "THE CONFESSION," the text of the letters would more aptly be described as a narration of events infused with the promise of additional killings. The only "confession" present was a taunting braggadocio. The killer was apparently proud of his work, and looked forward to repeating it.

The motive behind Bates's death, according to the letters, was revenge because of "BRUSH OFFS" she had apparently given the killer "DURING THE YEARS PRIOR." This provided for the killer—in his eyes—a reason to kill not only Cheri Jo, but any other women he might choose. He promised to choose more.

The police quickly accepted the authenticity of the letter. They felt strongly that the wording could only have come from the responsible party. By November 30, the RPD advised that they had reviewed news releases, and none of them had mentioned the disabling of the middle wire of the distributor. Also, other points in the letters suggested to them that the writer was the killer: the manner of the murder was correctly described in the Confession letters, as was the mention of a phone call to the police. His quote, "ITS ABOUT TIME," may even have been a veiled reference to his lost watch. As late as October 20, 1969, the RPD sent a memo to the Napa County Sheriff's Office, attention Captain Donald A. Townsend, declaring, "The person who wrote the confession letter is aware of facts about the homicide that only the killer would know. There is no doubt that the person who wrote the confession letter is our homicide suspect."

The argument would have been forensically bolstered had a piece of the blade been left at the crime scene. The letter writer had claimed that his knife had broken during the struggle, but no piece was located in or around Bates. In a follow-up report, investigators noted that if the responsible knife was ever discovered, it *might* have a piece missing or be broken. The police could not independently confirm the killer's claim. The police could also not confirm that a telephone call had been placed by the killer, another specific claim made in the letter.

When a string of murders were perpetrated hundreds of miles away in Northern California, including a few that seemed related to the attack on Bates, the connection was eventually made. Some investigators became convinced that Bates's death was just one in a series that included: the murder of a couple outside Vallejo; two attacks on two other couples that would each leave a woman dead and a male survivor; and the brutal slaying of a cab driver. However, not everyone believed that the serial killer who would come to be known as the "Zodiac" was responsible for the death of Cheri Jo Bates. Many lists of the killer's victims omit Bates, or relegate her to a list of possible victims. Such skepticism won many followers due to the unique aspects of the October 1966 attack. Bates was alone, she was killed by a slice to the jugular with a knife, the murder occurred in Southern California, and the follow-up letters were more poetic than the matter-of-fact style the killer known as the Zodiac would later employ. The Zodiac's future actions and communications would seem borne of a different mind, in the opinion of many.

Despite the differences that exist between the murder of Bates and the future killings of the Zodiac, the similarities strongly suggested to some investigators that Bates's murderer was in fact the same man who would in time terrorize the San Francisco Bay Area. The modus operandi (MO) may have changed, as they often do between the kills of a serial killer, but to many the criminal signature clearly linked the events. Not only did the killer's actions during and after the attack match those of future murders (the behavioral details), ample internal evidence—details found within the letters themselves—demonstrated that the writer also penned the known Zodiac letters that would threaten the people of Northern California just a few years later.

The behavioral attributes of the killer surrounding the attack that would link him to additional murders included writing taunting letters, sending multiple copies of nearly identical letters, placing a telephone call in connection with a murder, communicating with the authorities through the U.S. Postal Service approximately four weeks following an attack, and bragging to the police and the press through his mailings. Sending almost identical copies of a letter to more than one recipient was a rather unique activity. Bates's killer would do this twice, with the Confession letters (2 times) and the Bates letters (3 times, discussed below). The Zodiac would perform this action following attacks in Vallejo just three years later. While the killer claimed in the Confession letters to have made a telephone call in regards to the murder (which remained unconfirmed), the Zodiac would actually call two times in post-attack behavior, and write about one of these conversations. The timing of the Confession letter—almost exactly four weeks after Bates's murder—would be the length of time between an attack and a letter, or series of letters, on at least three occasions surrounding Zodiac attacks. The killer's action of drawing the police and the press into the drama of the murder, with plenty of taunting, was another stunt the Zodiac would perform repeatedly.

Additionally, many of the writer's unusual literary traits would follow him in future missives. Even though later communications would never be as poetic or contain the grammatical flourishes of the Confession letter, the use of specific language, grammar, spelling, and punctuation would identify the same hand at work. The Confession letters contained the unusual word "TWICHED," incorrectly spelled with the second "T" omitted, as though the writer could not spell the word or wanted investigators to believe that he could not. The killer would do the same in 1970 using the word "twich," without a second "T." Where the Confession letter writer began a sentence with the word "Yes," with no accompanying punctuation following the word, he in a future letter would do the same. The Confession letter writer advised that the letter be published "FOR ALL TO READ IT." He would later request the publication of numerous letters and parts of letters. Similarly, future communications may have incorrectly used ellipses (a series of periods) without an accompanying space, just as was present in the Confession letters. Bates's killer twice started sentences in the Confession letter with the words, "I AM," a trait that would nearly become a staple of Zodiac mailings.

In another most compelling similarity, the Confession letter writer compared a sex act to an incident of violence—and found in favor of the violence, noting that her breast felt warm in his hand, though only one thing was on his mind. This was exactly the same sentiment expressed by the Zodiac in the solution to the three-part 408 cipher that would be composed in 1969, in which he claimed that killing was "more fun than getting your rocks off with a girl."

There are several possibilities that explain the similarities. The Bay Area killer had read about, studied, and attempted to copy someone else who was responsible for murdering Bates; two killers had independently stumbled upon an incredible coincidence of astronomical proportion; or one murderer was responsible for the Confession letter (and evidently the death of Bates) and additional murders in Northern California. There is also the faint possibility that two killers operated, as some have hypothesized, one in the north and one in the south, the one in the north writing all of the communications, and thereby claiming in Bates a murder he did not commit. However, as details will bear out, this is in the view of many a highly improbable occurrence.

In 1971, the serial killer commonly known as the "Zodiac" would claim Cheri Jo's murder as his own, calling it his "[R]iverside activity." He did this only after an article appeared in *The San Francisco Chronicle* reporting on the connection between that murder and the Bay Area killings. The Zodiac may have been admitting to the crime merely because the series had been made public, and he was acting on a desire to regain control of the flow of information. He would add, "There are a hell of a lot more down there," referring to other supposed murders for which he was responsible in Southern California.

From first receipt of the Confession letters, the authorities in Riverside believed that their creator was in fact the killer. The narration of events outlined in the communiques had the feel of a murderer re-living his encounter, and the description of the small knife and the wounds to her head, throat, and neck would corroborate with the autopsy details. Though it was possible that someone close to the investigation could also have possessed enough knowledge to create such missives—even if the writer of the letters was not a cop, he could have overheard a conversation somewhere or picked up the knowledge in any number of ways, such as befriending the family of an officer—the RPD at the time held the opinion that the writer was responsible for the death of Bates.

The RPD also believed the motive stated in the Confession letter, and began a search in earnest for a spurned love interest. This would prove to be a firmly held belief on its part, a dogma that would continue to petrify over the years.

The FBI was ushered into the case to evaluate the letters. The field office in L.A. requested that the FBI laboratory do an examination of the Confession letters, making the request in an airtel dated December 1, 1966, which was received two days later.

An "airtel" was in essence an internal memorandum and was often used as a cover letter to describe the contents of a package of documents. More urgent messages were sent via teletype directly to the receiving location. The use of airtels was inefficient and was later replaced by more effective means of communication. But in 1966, they were in common use by the offices of the FBI.

Responding on December 22 to a letter sent by the RPD on the first of that month, the Bureau presented its professional analysis of the Confession letters, opening FBI file #9-46005-1. After a consultation with U.S. Attorney John F. Lally in Los Angeles, it notified Riverside that extortion could not be considered because no specific targets were named or clearly identified. As requested, the FBI searched its anonymous letter file to find similar threatening communications. Nothing of use was found, and the Confession letter was added for future reference.

In their correspondence with the FBI, the RPD shared some of their progress on the case, including the fact that there were no suspects, that they believed that the murder occurred around 6:00 p.m., and that the killer was likely also responsible for the letters.

❦

The Bates Letters

At the six-month anniversary of the Bates attack, probably in response to newspaper coverage of the crime, three more letters arrived. These short, eight-word notes, each written on a single piece of ordinary, lined, loose leaf binder paper, provided little new information to the authorities. Two of the letters declared in mostly block lettering "BATES HAD TO DIE THERE WILL BE MORE." They were addressed to the RPD ("Riverside Police Department, Riverside, Calif") and the Daily Press ("Daily Press, 3512 14th Street, Riverside, California). Joseph Bates, grieving father of the deceased, received a nearly identical iteration that was in title case (addressed, "Joseph Bates, 4195 Via San Jose, Riverside, California"), "She Had To Die There Will Be More."

At the bottom of the letters sent to the police and press, a small symbol, appearing to the police to be a Z with a flourish, was centered as though it were an identifying signature. The marks may have been used to distinguish these two notes from the alternate version of the letter sent to the victim's father (which replaced the word "Bates" for the more appropriate word to the father, "She"). The squiggles have also been interpreted by some as a numerical 2 and a numerical 3, both later altered to look similar to one another, making them originally function as page differentiators—the letter to the victim's father being an unmarked first page.

Each of the three envelopes bore 2, four-cent Abraham Lincoln stamps, and was postmarked April 30, 1967. It would not be for more than three years, on November 16, 1970, that Sherwood Morrill, the State of California's Questioned Documents Examiner, identified the Bates mailings as having come from the same author of numerous Zodiac letters that had been sent in 1969 and 1970. At the time they were received, the RPD wondered what, if anything, these notes could add to the case.

ↄ⅃

The Desktop Poem

Earlier—sometime in December of 1966—a custodian at the RCC library, while stowing furniture in a separate storage room, discovered a desk whose soft plywood surface had been defaced with a poem. The desk was likely available to students in the library around the time of Bates's murder. Its doggerel, if tied to the killing, was only obliquely related.

The prose went as follows:

```
cut.
clean.
if red/
clean.
blood spurting,
    dripping,
    spilling;
all over her new
dress.
oh well.
it was red
anyway.
life draining into an
uncertain death
she won't
die.
this time
Someone'll find her.
just wait till
next time.
    rh
```

Etched with a blue ball-point pen, the words appeared to describe the unsuccessful suicide attempt of a woman wearing a red dress. The only real relationships to Bates's murder were the poetaster's references to death, to cutting, and to blood. Bates did not wear a red dress on the night of her demise. The poem may have carried no connection to the case at all.

The desktop message was signed at the bottom by the initials "r" and "h," interpreted by some to be the initials of the killer of Bates. The letters could also have been a reference to blood typing, which distinguishes a blood's "rh" factor. At the time of the murder, the president of RCC, where the murder occurred and the poem was discovered, was R.H. Bradshaw, another possible reference to the two signatory letters. Even "Robin Hood" had to be considered as the correct interpretation of these initials.

Because of its possible connection to the murder, the tabletop poem was dutifully collected and preserved by the police for its future forensic value, along with the entire surface of the desk. It would re-emerge in time as an important piece of evidence when Sherwood Morrill of the FBI matched its lettering to future Zodiac letters. At the time, however, the tabletop and the three Bates letters were not considered to be real evidence in the case. They were presumed to be the product of a copycat or hoaxer—or possibly two—and were promptly filed away.

Dated November 1, 1967, just past the one-year anniversary of Bates's death, an unusual letter, signed "with hope, Patricia Hautz, Fellow Student," arrived at the desk of the editor of the Press-Enterprise. The typed page referenced a previous article in the newspaper, the writer suggesting that another story about the boy responsible for the killing could be "more rewarding." It could cause others to think about the lives of their own children, the note suggested. "Are we laying the blueprint for another killer?" is a question the writer hoped might be brought to mind by such an article. Not only was there no "boy" to report on, no Patricia Hautz could be located, leading to suspicions that the note was tauntingly authored by the killer.

The mysterious writer was never publicly identified. If the letter was a hoax, it was a puzzle to the police as to why someone might compose and send it. If Bates's killer himself was responsible for the effort, perhaps he had a message to convey, or he hoped that the public would take something instructive away from his brutal attack. Many years later, one journalist laid claim to locating a Patricia Hautz, now living under her married name, who admitted to writing notes to editors around that time. Though she provided handwriting samples that could be compared to the Hautz letter envelope, her claimed desire for anonymity prevented any public confirmation of authorship. In other words, though the missive remains an enigma, it may have been an innocuous letter to the editor.

Nearly three years later, on October 20, 1970, the RPD sent a letter to the Napa County Sheriff's Office, attention Captain Donald A. Townsend, as a follow up to a telephone conversation that was conducted three days earlier. In it, Sergeant H. L. Homsher of the Detective Division outlined his reasons for believing that the Bates murder was directly related to a series of killings in the San Francisco Bay Area. Even though Riverside was a long way from the Bay Area, there appeared to be a sufficient number of similarities to investigate whether there was provable linkage between the two cases: a common criminal signature and a similar modus operandi, possible evidence that the same killer was responsible for the entire collection of murders. Of particular interest were the similarities between the attack on Bates and a subsequent attack at Lake Berryessa that had occurred in September of 1969. Both involved the damaging or defacing of a Volkswagen automobile, both ended with a knife attack, both involved the murder of a woman, and both led to the subsequent taunting of the police with notes and possibly a telephone call.

Latent fingerprints lifted from Bates's car were eventually compared by the FBI to prints that were collected from the Volkswagen Karmann Ghia at Lake Berryessa, but they provided no match. The Bates prints were never identified or matched to anyone else either. They remained with the FBI, file #32-27195. The RPD letter included several enclosures: two reproductions of the Confession letter, a photo of the envelope received by the press, a photo of the envelope received by the police, and two photocopies of envelopes after having been processed for prints. A copy of the letter was additionally sent to the San Francisco Police Department (SFPD) Chief of Police. The entire package was signed by Sergeant H. L. Homsher, with the letterhead backing of L. T. Kinkead, the Riverside Chief of Police.

❧

The death of Cheri Jo Bates became the focus of renewed attention in 1982, Riverside officials expressing confidence that the case would soon be resolved. In a press release on May 20, the RPD reported in response to substantial pressure put on it by the press and the public that in November, 1981 new information had come to light. Accordingly, four investigators had been assigned to the case full time. They would be tasked, the press release notified, with interviewing numerous people and re-examining all the physical evidence available.

The RPD denied that there was a connection to other cases in Northern California. The detectives expressed an awareness of an individual who was being considered by the SFPD, and adamantly maintained that the Riverside suspect was not responsible for additional murders to the north, nor was the man being investigated in the Bay Area responsible for Bates's murder. Any speculation and creative reporting could hamper successful prosecution, the press release warned, and any media reports that linked the murder of Bates to the killings in the Bay Area were outdated.

The RPD promised a thorough investigation for 90 days before anyone would be charged, a sentiment that was to prove overly optimistic and unnecessarily confident. No one was charged after 90 days; no one was ever charged. Due to privacy concerns, and the fact that the suspect was never arrested, the RPD never publicly shared his name.

Nevertheless, some members of the RPD remained convinced that they had identified the perpetrator but were merely unable to gather sufficient evidence to bring the case to trial—and that he was not responsible for any Northern California activity. No credible evidence against their suspect ever leaked out of the department, and no follow-up was ever provided to the 1982 press release. However, the department's dogmatic stance would be challenged less than two decades later.

In 2000, mitochondrial DNA testing was conducted on the blood clot discovered on the base of Bates's right thumb. The resulting sequence was compared to mitochondrial DNA testing done on blood drawn from the RPD suspect. There was no match. The RPD's suspect was not the origin of the biological material deposited on the victim.

✃

Services for Cheri Jo were conducted at St. Catherine's Catholic Church in the sanctuary that she had visited with her father just hours before her death. Detectives observed the attendees, while police photographers captured faces on film.

Cheri Josephine Bates was laid to rest on a misty hillside at Crestlawn Memorial Park into which she was interred on November 4, 1966. Twenty years later, her body would be exhumed and cremated, and her ashes scattered at sea.

The man responsible for her death would not remain so quiet.

2 | SOLANO COUNTY

"the boy was on his back with his feet to the car"

On the bitterly cold evening of December 20, 1968, the killer struck again. He resurfaced more than 400 miles to the northwest, just outside of Benicia, in an unincorporated area of Solano County, part of the larger San Francisco Bay Area of Northern California.

Despite the lack of eyewitnesses to the crime itself, the investigators could pinpoint in time the attack at Lake Herman Road through statements made by those who had been in the immediate area at the time of the attack. Not only did the citizens report on what they had seen as they drove past gate 10, the entrance to the Benicia Water Supply Pumping Station—the scene of the crime—some of them reported on the actions and movements of others, and thereby corroborated one another's statements. If each of the statements given by people in the vicinity is to be believed, there was only a six-minute window of opportunity, between 11:14 p.m. and 11:20 p.m., in which the perpetrator callously shot and killed two teenagers in the roadside turnout.

Stella Medeiros, formerly Stella Borges, a 32-year-old Vallejo mother, was the first to observe the carnage. Close to noon on the day before Christmas, she gave an interview to Detective Sergeant Leslie "Les" Lundblad of the Solano County Sheriff's Office, the seasoned lead investigator of the dual homicide. She described the events that led to her discovery of the ghastly crime scene four days earlier.

She explained to Lundblad that on the evening of Friday, December 20 she had returned from Oakland at about 10:50. When her mother called to ask her to pick up her 13-year-old son at a show, she did not stop to take off her coat. She left her home, which was on the other side of the street from her parents' house, to retrieve her son. A glance at the clock told her it was ten minutes past eleven. She, with her mother-in-law and young daughter in tow, entered Lake Herman Road. Driving cautiously, she covered the serpentine 2.7 miles to the crime scene in about four or five minutes. Medeiros estimated that they arrived at the pump house entrance on Lake Herman Road at 11:14 or 11:15, though it was determined at the interview that her watch was one minute fast. She added that she observed no vehicles going in either direction.

As she reached the gravel alcove which served as a small parking lot off to the south of Lake Herman Road, an entrance to a dirt roadway that led toward a county pump house, her headlights picked up a vehicle. She told Lundblad that she observed a boy who looked as though he had fallen out of the open door of his station wagon. A girl, adorned in an elegant purple dress, was collapsed on the far side of the lot, facing the road.

Stillness pervaded the scene. There were no other cars parked nearby.

Medeiros raced farther along Lake Herman Road. She achieved speeds between 60 and 70 miles per hour. At the horrific sight of the bodies, she needed to gather her composure. She knew she had to report the incident to an officer in the sleepy town of Benicia. When she found a police car, she honked her horn and flashed her lights until she received the attention from Officer Daniel Pitta of the Benicia Police Department (BPD) that her ordeal warranted.

Pitta corroborated Medeiros' statement, reporting that he first observed her at 11:25 p.m. He quickly responded, and with his partner for the evening, BPD Officer William T. Warner #12, he arrived at the scene three minutes later.

In 1969, Lake Herman Road was a desolate, rural road that connected the tiny town of Benicia with Vallejo, its larger neighbor to the west. It remains quiet and undeveloped to this day. One end is located just east of Vallejo, where it joins Columbus Parkway. The other end is in Benicia Township, six miles to the east. Most long distance drivers will circumnavigate the stretch by steering to the north or the south of Vallejo, the indirect highway routes providing much quicker transit through the area. To locals, however, Lake Herman Road provides an often convenient, if meandering, back route.

Its six-mile length still has no street lights in the second decade of the twenty-first century. It is a very dark, out-of-the-way, corridor. It sees infrequent traffic, especially at night. In the 1960s, amorous couples came to rely on its seclusion for late night "necking." The entrance to a pumping station, a gravel turnoff to the south of Lake Herman Road bordered by sharp turns and a steep hill, was a particularly popular lovers' lane. Couples knew they could linger there in relative privacy, far from the prying eyes of parents and the local police. The lot itself, only a handful of yards wide and directly in the line of sight to eastbound traffic, offered scant privacy from anyone who drove past, but if the occasional car did happen by, everyone knew why the couple was parked there, and they were left alone. Sometimes, groups of students would congregate. It was a fun, enticing hangout, well known to all who attended either Hogan High School or Vallejo High School, the two secondary educational institutions in Vallejo.

Police officers were also aware of the location. They knew cars would assemble there and understood the attraction that brought the young people. A county worker made daily checks on the pump house, driving the length of the dirt road to ensure that nothing nefarious was occurring at the property owned by Solano County.

Formed in 1850, Solano County comprises seven jurisdictions, including the towns of Vallejo and Benicia, as well as some unincorporated regions. The county was incorporated in 1850, marking the founding of the county. It hosted the California state capital for nearly 13 months in 1853 and 1854.

The town of Benicia, the southernmost part of Solano County, was founded in 1847, and named for the wife of General Vallejo,

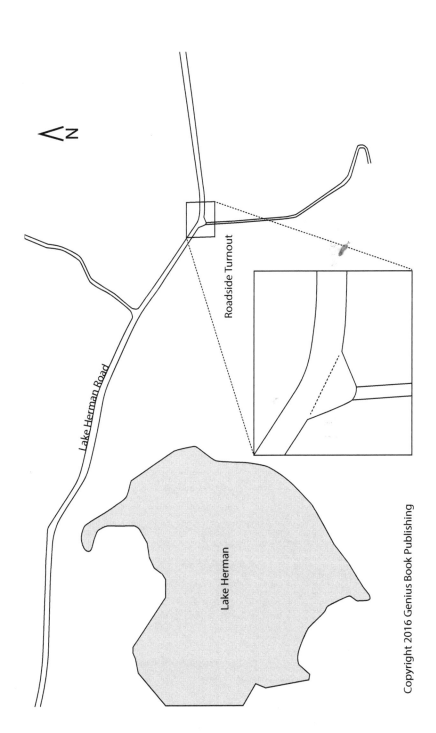

N

Lake Herman Road

Roadside Turnout

Lake Herman

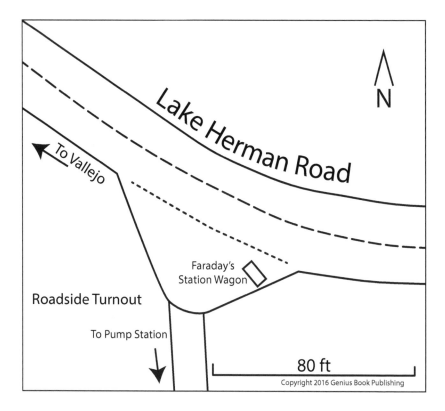

the region's top military man and first landowner. In 1852, with the opening of the Young Ladies Seminary, it boasted the first woman's college west of the Rocky Mountains. The Seminary's name was later changed to Mills College, and was in time relocated to Oakland. In the 1960s, the town saw dramatic changes, including the closing of the Benicia Arsenal of the U.S. Army, which occurred from 1960 to 1964, causing a disruption of the economy, at least until growth was made possible into the former property of the Arsenal. The completion of the Benicia-Martinez Bridge in 1962 transformed the lick-spittle village into a convenient suburb of San Francisco, causing a surge in population to around 5,000 by 1968.

Pitta, upon arrival at the scene, noted a young female lying face down. Next to her in the gravel a large volume of blood was flowing to the north of her motionless head. She had obviously expired. To the west, a dark-haired young male lay face up, blood pooling around the back of his skull. An A1 ambulance arrived, alerted by a code 3—an emergency requiring lights and siren—and the male was transported to Vallejo.

Solano County Coroner Dan Horan was summoned to care for the remains of the girl. Pitta notified the Solano County Sheriff's Office, requesting an investigator and a Sheriff's unit.

At 11:52, Deputy Sheriff Russell T. Butterbach and his partner, Deputy Wayne Waterman, both of the Solano County Sheriff's Office, reached the scene of the crime. They observed several police units that had arrived before them. Officer Pitta, Lieutenant Little, and Officer Warner were poring over the scene. A reporter from the Fairfield Daily Republic, Thomas D. Balmer, following the scoop, was trying to capture some useful photographs and any stray details about the breaking story. He would later report that he took pictures from "a discrete distance" once the coroner arrived at the scene and carefully lifted the blanket.

Deputy Sheriff Butterbach's regular partner had been unavailable that evening. Waterman, typically stationed at the jail—the starting assignment for all new officers—had asked Butterbach for permission to ride along. The patrolman was more than happy to have the company.

Earlier in the evening, the two were assigned to scout for the blue truck of a man who had gone fishing at Lake Berryessa and had not returned home. They were ordered to search Lake Herman Road for the missing vehicle. As soon as they entered the road, however, their car was reassigned to visit the Hells Angels headquarters on Warren Street in Benicia. After about 30 to 40 minutes there, Butterbach recalled years later, they learned that a shooting had occurred. When they returned to their patrol car, they were notified of a double 187 (murder) on Lake Herman Road, and raced to the scene.

Pierre Bidou, a detective with the BPD, with his partner for the night, served the search warrant on the Hells Angels. They confiscated about a pound and a half of marijuana, a rather large bust for 1968. As Bidou and his partner headed back to the Sheriff's Office to drop off the seized drugs, they passed the Lake Herman Road pumping station entrance. The site of the future crime scene was deserted. The actors in the macabre drama that would play out in just a few minutes had not yet assembled. When the officers finally arrived at the office parking lot, they heard the BPD call: a possible shooting with victims on Lake Herman Road. They turned around immediately and headed back. By the time they arrived on the scene, there was already a police sergeant as well as a marked patrol car present.

Butterbach and Waterman surveyed the scene. They observed a 4-door, 1961 Rambler Station Wagon with a dark tan over light tan paint scheme, sporting California license plates DTL-962. The front of the car pointed in an easterly direction. At 28 feet 6 inches behind the vehicle—an initial police report incorrectly stated 10 feet; another provided an estimate of 10 yards—the body of young woman lay motionless on the ground.

Years later, Bidou would state that he took her pulse. It was an unnecessary task. It was obvious that she was dead.

The lifeless girl would be identified as Betty Lou Jensen, a 16-year-old Caucasian female, born July 23, 1952. Her remains were partially covered with a gray wool blanket, because the police wanted to protect any evidence and modestly conceal the victim from the press and the public. Her face and head were awash in blood. Next to the body, a large amount of blood was pooling.

Despite passing her sixteenth birthday in July, Betty Lou was, in appearance and action, still a chubby-cheeked child. Her sweetness and innocence made her a most tragic victim. At five feet three inches and 115 pounds, the round-faced brunette had only had two previous "relationships" with young men prior to meeting Faraday. These innocent bonds consisted merely of talking together and walking the hallways at Hogan High School, where Jensen was a junior. David was her first serious boyfriend, and her time with him on December 20 was her first real date.

A native of Colorado, the ingénue was an honor roll student, and always dedicated to the task at hand. She was hoping to earn a generous art scholarship to pursue her talents in a variety of artistic media. Her many friends described her as caring and kind. Warmth radiated from her bright blue eyes. She was a member of the Pythian Sunshine Girls. She welcomed the input of others, often seeking advice from her friends and her older sister and only sibling, Melodie. She resided with the other members of her family at 123 Ridgeway Court in Vallejo.

On the cusp of adulthood, Betty Lou had become secretive about some aspects of her life—nothing sinister, just a growing independence. Prior to that evening, her parents did not know that she had begun dating. Whether from embarrassment or not wanting her parents to meddle in her affairs, she kept her relationships quiet. She had also begun to experiment with cigarettes.

Butterbach and Waterman observed a chalk outline on the ground, on the passenger side of the station wagon. The newly created shape, laid down by Warner, represented the point of collapse of David Faraday. A large pool of blood was present by the right front door of the station wagon, extending from where the young man's head was outlined. Bidou would later state that when he first arrived at the scene, he could see Faraday's breath in the cold evening air, because the young man was fighting to live.

David Arthur Faraday, a 17-year-old senior at Vallejo High School, enjoyed music and friends. He had a ready smile that complemented his dark brown eyes and dark brown hair. His long face was horse-like, his mouth perhaps too large for his other features. Whatever he lacked in physical beauty, however, he more than made up for in charm.

He was a fun-loving, easy-going teenager who had recently discovered girls. He had just started to date Jensen, whom he met on a committee to decorate the Pythian Castle for a music festival. Once the two found each other, they were quickly an item.

Born October 2, 1951, and originally from San Rafael, California, Faraday resided at the small suburban home of his parents at 1930 Sereno Drive. The family had been in Vallejo for only three and a half years. Faraday possessed a firm confidence that had served him well during his years as an Eagle Scout, a member of Explorer Post 209. Recently, he had won the prestigious "God and Country" award—the highest honor in scouting—for his hard work.

His accolades did not end there. He was active in school government. He was Lodge Chief of the Order of the Arrow for Napa, Solano, and Lake Counties. He served in the Knights of Dunamis, was active in the Presbyterian Church, and participated as a member of the staff of the Silverado Area Council Camp.

In addition to all of his committees, he found time for athletics, competing on the wrestling team. He was planning for a career as a teacher. His interactions with his three siblings—16-year-old Debra, 15-year-old Robert, and the youngest, Stephen, at 13—no doubt aided his gregariousness and helped hone his leadership abilities, attributes that Jensen likely found both alluring and attractive.

Butterbach and Waterman found small caliber casings littering the ground. Upon closer inspection, the officers noticed that the vehicle had also been violated. There was a bullet hole in the rear window on the right side, just above the chrome stripping on the lower portion of the window and slightly off center to the rear of the vehicle. Another bullet had entered the station wagon just above the center of the right rear passenger window. A lady's white fur coat lay undisturbed on the left side of the rear seat. Realizing the gravity of the situation, and his own limitations as a mere patrolman, it was at this point that Butterbach contacted his office to summon the sober-sided Detective Sergeant Lundblad.

The eerie quietness of the scene belied the horrendous violence that would, in a few short hours, rock the community. Butterbach and Waterman ordered Butler and his camera out of the area until Lundblad and the coroner gave permission for the press to approach.

At the arrival of Coroner Horan and Dr. Byron Sanford of Benicia, Jensen was pronounced dead at the scene by Sanford. The subsequent autopsy, conducted by pathologist S. Shirai, revealed that a bullet had pierced her heart, traveling right to left, penetrating both atria. Another bullet had penetrated her liver. Still another, her right kidney. The cause of death would be reported as "multiple bullet wounds to the chest and abdomen with hemorrhage." So severe was the damage that immediate attention from a modern, twenty-first century trauma center would not have been able to save her.

The autopsy noted that Jensen's body exhibited five entrance wounds on the right side of her back. Two holes on her front—one at the left breast area and the other on the lower right side of the waist—revealed that some of the shots had penetrated and then exited her body. When the mortician removed her clothing, a .22 caliber bullet fell down from her panties, where it had apparently been trapped.

The gun must have been held at a distance from Jensen, since only the uppermost wound had any accompanying gunpowder residue—and that hole had only a single grain.

The veteran Lundblad—described by *The San Francisco Chronicle* and Examiner as "the graying, husky officer in charge"—would later report that he received a telephone call at midnight. He was notified of a possible slaying on Lake Herman Road. He was also informed that Sheriff's deputies, Coroner Horan, and representatives of the BPD were standing by at the scene. Upon his arrival, a few minutes past midnight, he learned that Faraday was en route to the hospital by ambulance. Jensen was dead and was awaiting transport to Colonial Chapels, a funeral home in Vallejo.

Taking control of the mix of officers, Lundblad ordered Butterbach and Waterman to follow the speeding ambulance and get a statement from Faraday.

The two-vehicle convoy arrived at Vallejo General Hospital, 601 Tennessee Street, at 12:23 in the morning. When the officers found the nurse on duty, Mrs. Barbara Lowe, and requested permission to see the patient, she informed them that Faraday was dead on arrival (DOA), having been pronounced at 12:05 a.m. by a Dr. Siebert. Their work at the hospital was far from over.

Butterbach and Waterman inspected Faraday's remains. It became apparent that the victim had been shot in the upper portion of the left ear with a small caliber bullet, which penetrated both his ear and his head. They noted a large lump on the right cheek, and the hair on the left side of his head was matted with blood. Blood was present on his hands and on the sleeves of his shirt. They also noted his clothing.

For the evening, the deceased young man had worn brown corduroy pants—a Levi brand—black socks, tan leather shoes of a rough texture, and a Timex wristwatch with a chrome case and band. His left front pants pocket held 85 cents: three quarters and a dime. His left hip pocket had a black comb. Though there was nothing in his right hip pocket, his right front pocket concealed a white handkerchief and small bottle of Binaca breath drops. He grasped a class ring—which was made of a yellow metal and topped with a red stone—by the tips of the ring and middle fingers of his left hand, a cadaveric spasm that refused to relinquish its property. Butterbach was particularly interested in this piece of jewelry. It appeared to him as though someone had attempted to take it away from the victim who even in death held it tight.

The officers received Faraday's small, black wallet from nurse Lowe. It contained several ID cards, including a Social Security card and a driver's license. They also received a brown leather belt. When Butterbach called Sergeant Cunningham to have someone come to the hospital to take photographs of Faraday's body, Deputy J.R. Wilson obliged.

Not long after midnight, Lundblad learned that the male was DOA. He spent some more time at the crime scene, and then proceeded at 1:38 a.m. to Colonial Chapels, where he learned that the female had five bullet holes in the right side of her back, three of which had emerged from her right side. The coroner described the entry holes as placed in a "remarkably close pattern."

Faraday's lifeless body was transported to Colonial Chapels as well. The coroner noted and recorded other details of both victims. Faraday's body had one bullet hole in his left ear that proceeded into the back of his head. The ear had a dark area that appeared to be powder burns, indicating that the shot was fired at close range. The coroner recorded that the young man had worn black socks, low cut brown "fruit boots," white cotton shorts, a white cotton t-shirt, a light blue boy's long sleeve shirt (size 20), and brown corduroy trousers. On her final evening, Jensen was attired in black strap shoes that were now blood-stained, a blue and white padded bra showing blood stains on the left side and on the straps, full panty-type hose, pink and white cotton panties, and a purple dress with a white collar and cuffs that was thoroughly stained with blood. A Christmas broach adorned the dress's white trim.

Back at the entrance to the pump house, Lieutenant Little created several sketches of the death scene, gathering and recording relevant measurements. One drawing showed the final resting place of the .22 caliber shell casings, including one that had ejected so far that it was recovered 20 feet away from the body of the female, and in a different direction than the one in which she had fled. It noted that her head pointed almost exactly east and just slightly to the north. Later, these sketches would be enhanced and refined by the witnesses who claimed to have observed the victims, some before the attack, as well as from Stella Medeiros who saw them soon afterwards.

Little also photographed the area. A search for a weapon in or around the vehicle proved futile, ruling out a murder-suicide. Because the ground was frozen solid under a reported 22-degree temperature, no footprints were found. Also, no visible fresh tire tracks were observed at or near the entrance to the road. One deep heel print was located among some brush, behind a fence that ringed the pump house. The investigators noted that the brushy growth was the only area offering a potential sniper any semblance of cover, if indeed that is how the attack unfolded, with the killer lying in wait. The car was carefully dusted for fingerprints.

ℰᴕ

In early January, the Solano County Sheriff's Office sent the following items away to the CII at the Office of the Attorney General in Sacramento for further analysis:

- One damaged bullet removed from Faraday's head during the autopsy.
- Two bullets removed from Jensen during her autopsy.
- A bullet found in the underpants of Jensen that appeared to come from her lower back through her body, emerging under the waistband elastic of her panties.
- Five shell casings found at the scene by Coroner Dan Horan, which were turned over to Lundblad at the scene.
- Four shell casings found at the crime scene by Sergeant Silva of the BPD, and turned over to Detective Sergeant Lundblad at the mortuary.
- A damaged bullet recovered in the top of the 1961 Rambler, the vehicle registered to David's mother, Mrs. Jean Faraday.
- A damaged bullet recovered in the 1961 Rambler, having entered the right rear window and become lodged in the floor mat on the left side of the cargo area.
- A bullet recovered near victim Jensen along the blood-strewn path of her attempted escape route. It had apparently entered her back, emerged from the center of her stomach, and fallen to the ground without passing through her dress.
- Jensen's white-trimmed purple dress bearing five holes in back and one in the front, heavily stained with blood.

Butterbach and Waterman left the hospital for Colonial Chapels, completing the two-minute drive at 1:38 a.m. They remained there until 4:30 in the morning. The initial search for clues was wrapped up at about 4:00 a.m., Butterbach later estimated. Because the murders had occurred within the Solano County Sheriff Department's jurisdiction, its office would head up the investigation. The BPD would have to accept the position of second fiddle and provide any assistance needed, despite being the first department on the scene.

Officer Butterbach, much to his surprise and amusement, received a telephone call later that morning in which he was invited to conduct the investigation into the murders with the more seasoned Detective Sergeant Lundblad. Butterbach, a mere patrolman, had become a detective by fiat. Together, the two would run down leads, collect evidence, and attempt to answer all relevant questions about the crime, especially the burning question of who was responsible for this despicable act.

Years later, Bidou acknowledged the limitation of the investigation, as though he wished that he could have done more. The officers at the time simply did not have the experience, with so few people being murdered in the area. In fact, there had been none in the previous five or six years. Their first concern was for the welfare of Faraday, of course. Only secondarily did they apply themselves to gathering evidence.

Besides, the state of forensics was limited in 1968. Law enforcement officials did not have the benefit of today's knowledge or the ability to collect and analyze hairs, fibers, soil samples, and other types of trace evidence.

Bidou would also express a belief that he was just minutes from the crime scene when the murders occurred. He did not recall passing any other vehicles as he made his way to Benicia on the night of the murders, a fact which he related to the Sheriff's Office. Probably what transpired, he later opined, was that the killer had driven from Vallejo, where he would not have crossed paths with Bidou's police car, though Bidou admitted that they did take a bit of a short cut when traveling to Benicia, which may have prevented him from encountering the perpetrator.

༄

Just before 5:00 in the morning, Deputy Vehrs of the Solano County Sheriff's Office received a telephone call from Lieutenant Colonel Verne M. Jensen, the grief-stricken father of Betty Lou. After 27 years of service in the army, Colonel Jensen had retired in 1963, and was now employed in San Francisco as a supply officer for the General Services Administration, an agency of the federal government tasked with managing real estate. The sleep-deprived family man was still in a state of shock. Despite his pain, he wanted to share some potentially important information for the investigation. He and his wife, upon hearing that their daughter had been shot, had called their Vallejo home from Mare Island and received a piece of provocative news. Their daughter, Melodie, Betty Lou's 24-year-old sister, informed them that on December 20, Betty Lou had confided in her that Richard "Ricky" Burton, a friend of Betty Lou's, had threatened the now-deceased girl. Dutifully, Vehrs took down the information and promised that Sergeant Lundblad would contact them later in the morning.

The lead detectives were back at the pump house entrance soon after daylight. While the two were rechecking the crime scene to see if anything had been overlooked in the darkness of the previous night, they were approached by Bingo Wesner, a rancher who lived on the Old Borges Ranch, not far from the Humble Oil Company property. It was 8:00 a.m. Wesner told the officers that he tended sheep in the area east of the Benicia Pumping Station, and that while he was checking the area around 10:00 p.m. the previous night, he noticed a white Chevy Impala sedan that was parked by the south fence at the entrance to the pumping station. At about the same time, he also observed a red Ford flatbed pick-up truck with wooden sideboards in the area. He did not see a Rambler station wagon. Wesner's observations would prove particularly helpful to the investigation in corroborating the statements of other witnesses during the creation of a timeline.

The officers eventually left the scene to embark on a series of interviews with the victims' friends and immediate family members.

They hoped to uncover a motive for the puzzling double murder, ultimately expecting to identify the responsible "who." They knew that finding the reason behind the carnage, the "why," might suggest a pathway to a suspect. For now, the event was a mystery, and many of the early police reports filed in the case reflected law enforcement's bewilderment: "no apparent motive."

Soon after 9:00 in the morning, they met with Sharon, one of Betty Lou's closest friends. The Hogan High School student was brought to the officers' attention by Betty Lou's mother, Virginia, who knew of her daughter's close relationship with the 16-year-old. Sharon explained that David and Betty Lou had come to her house at approximately 8:20 the previous evening, and had remained there until 9:00 p.m. At that time, as she walked the couple to their car, they gave no hint to her of where they were headed. She stated that she herself had attended a party held at 254 Frisbie Street from 10:30 until after 1:00 a.m., her mother supplying for the detectives the precise return time of 1:10 a.m. Sharon related that Betty Lou had "gone steady" with a mutual friend named Ricky from December 1 until December 14, though they had only talked around school and had never actually gone out on a date. As far as Sharon knew, Ricky did not drive and did not own a gun.

At 3:45 that afternoon, Lundblad and Butterbach met with Verne and Virginia Jensen at their cozy suburban home, which was just a couple of rooms on a tiny lot. Before speaking with Betty Lou's parents, the officers interviewed Melodie, Betty Lou's older sister, to question her about the threats her sister had received prior to her death. She told them what everyone who followed the troubling case would soon discover: the night she was killed, Betty Lou was on her first date.

Melodie had been the one who had suggested that Betty Lou introduce David to her parents. Earlier that day, at about 6:00 p.m., the now-deceased girl had confided to her sister that she was afraid of a friend named Ricky because he had threatened to tell her parents that she smoked and was having dates. Ricky told Betty Lou that he was going to beat up David, and something about brass knuckles.

Acting on her sister's advice, Betty Lou brought David home about 8:00 p.m. to meet her mom and dad, Melodie continued. The couple, with the permission of her parents, then left with the stated intention of attending a gathering at Hogan High School, and a party to be held afterwards. She noted that Betty Lou was expected home no later than 11:00 p.m.

Melodie also shared that on December 20, in the afternoon, David had gone over to Hogan High School to have some words with Ricky. Apparently, while they were talking, a Mr. Grove came upon the scene unaware that anything was taking place. There was no physical conflict, but David realized that he was in a place where he should not have been since he was not at his own school, and promptly left.

Melodie added that her sister would often say to her, "Close the blinds. Ricky is spying on me." Apparently, her younger sister did not want to be in the house with him peeking around outside. Several times Betty Lou's mother had noticed that the gate to their home's backyard was open. The family suspected it was left in that condition by Ricky, but no one actually saw him on their property.

The officers then turned their attention to Virginia. Ruefully, the grieving mother told the detectives that the grisly evening had been Betty Lou's one and only date. The parents had first met David at approximately 8:00 p.m. Virginia explained that the couple's plans were to go to a festival at nearby Hogan High and attend a party afterwards. The Jensen's were unaware of the address of the party. Virginia stated that Betty Lou had promised to be home by 11:00 p.m.

Virginia provided the officers with phone numbers that were listed in a small book among Betty Lou's possessions. She then began to speak of a classmate of Betty's who had been providing their daughter with much unwanted attention. Betty Lou was convinced that she was being spied on and had insisted that the curtains of the house be drawn. Ricky was known to call the house at any time after 3:00 p.m., the close of school. He would call every fifteen minutes, and this happened many times. Sometimes Betty Lou would speak with him; other times, she would cut him off. Virginia was unaware of any boyfriend—other than David Faraday—that her daughter had had. She referred them to two of Betty Lou's best friends, Sharon and Dian, evidently unaware that the officers had already spoken to Sharon.

At 4:39 p.m., Lundblad met with Dian to take a statement. Dian shared that she had ridden home from school with David and Betty Lou about four times. Her take on Ricky was much less ominous than the detective had heard from others. He and Betty Lou were good friends, she told the officer. David had told her that Ricky had seen him in the halls of school on Friday, December 20, though he never said what time it was. She stated that Ricky, a person who had piqued the interest of the officers, did not drive, at least as far as she knew. She never heard of anyone being bothered. Ricky was merely an old flame, in her opinion.

Dian added that Betty Lou had been going with Ricky for the two weeks before December 14, at which time her friend had met and developed a crush on David. Betty Lou had only walked the halls with Ricky at school, but for the past two weeks she had been ignoring him. Dian shared that Betty Lou had been "going" with another student, Bob, for a short time before she went steady with Ricky. She suggested that Lundblad also speak to Alice, another friend of Betty Lou's, who might add additional details about the social life of her slain friend.

Lundblad and Butterbach met with Brenda, another classmate of Betty Lou's, at 5:15 p.m. She had heard around school that Ricky was merely "using" Betty Lou and that, according to Betty Lou, he called her all the time. Brenda had never seen him out at night and did not recall ever seeing him with a gun. She noted that Ricky did not have any close friends. He spent time with a brother-in-law who drove an old, blue car with chipped paint, and hung out at the Jumping Bean on Springs Road. A friend of Brenda's thought she had seen Betty Lou talking to a boy named Jeff at Castlewood the previous night.

The thorough investigation revealed that there was no festival scheduled at Hogan High, and the couple never attended any of the three area parties that *did* take place. Instead, they visited Sharon's home, the best friend of Betty Lou's, arriving at about 8:30 p.m., Sharon estimated. There was talk of going to San Francisco, but no specific plans were mentioned.

☙

The detectives applied a great deal of time and energy to the investigation of Ricky Allen Burton. They did so because Betty Lou's mother had identified him as a person who "bugged" her daughter, because interviews with his peers had indicated that he was somewhat odd, because as a former boyfriend—and possible jilted lover— he had a motive to harm his former girlfriend and her new beau, but mostly because the police had so few good leads to pursue. David and Betty Lou were by all accounts good kids. They had no enemies, and none of their actions appeared to have invited their attacker's wrath.

But Ricky was easily eliminated from suspicion. He possessed an unimpeachable alibi: at the time of the killings, he was in the presence of his family and some family friends, including a Mare Island military police officer. The investigators nevertheless thoroughly examined Ricky's movements the day of the attack until they were fully satisfied that he was in no way responsible for the murders.

The lead investigators first met with Ricky on Saturday morning just after 11:00. Because Betty Lou's parents had identified him as a person who bugged Betty Lou while she was attending school, the officers decided to advise him of his Constitutional Rights. It had been legally necessary since a Supreme Court ruling in 1966. The officers didn't want to risk having key pieces of evidence thrown out of court, should Ricky make any self-incriminating statements. The so-called Miranda warning advised him of his rights under the Fifth Amendment of the Constitution of the United States of America, that he had the right to remain silent, that what he said if he did speak could be used against him in a court of law, and that he had a right to an attorney—one would be provided to him if he could not afford his own. That relatively recent ruling was not yet a part of popular culture, so Ricky could not be expected to be familiar with it, but in any case, it was required to legitimize their interrogation of him. Ricky said that he understood his rights and wanted to speak with them so that he could aid the investigation in any way possible.

The 16-year-old told the officers that he "went with" Betty Lou for two weeks. He spoke to her on the telephone often, the last time being Thursday afternoon, about 4:30. He had not attended school that day and had called her to find out what had occurred in his absence. He had also inquired about her weekend plans.

Concerning Friday, December 20, the date of the attack, he said that after school he visited his sister's house in Vallejo where he remained from about 4:15 to 5:00 p.m. His mother picked him up and brought him home afterwards. He had a TV dinner for supper. He went to the Gallenkamp's store between 7:00 and 7:15 p.m., and then returned home again for the night.

At home that evening, he watched the 1964 movie called *A Global Affair* starring Bob Hope, he told the officers. Also present for the viewing of the film were his mother, his father, his sister, his brother-in-law, and a father-and-son pair, who were friends of his father. Ricky reported that the movie lasted until approximately 10:45 p.m. His father, now living separately from his mother, left the gathering at 10:55 p.m.; his father's friend and *his* son—also named Ricky—left around 10:55 p.m. as well. His brother-in-law, Larry, remained behind and chatted with his wife, Ricky's sister Janette, until they left around 11:30 p.m.

Ricky stated that when he went to bed, only he, his sister Diane, and his mother were present at the house. He climbed into bed around 11:30 p.m. as his radio played. He awoke at 8:30 a.m. Saturday morning. He was not aware of the shooting until his mother called him at his job at the family business, Sylvia's Auto Wreckers, after she had heard from the officers who were now interviewing him. Ricky explained that he earned two dollars per week in allowance, provided that he worked in the yard and cleaned up the laundry room. He was not allowed to go out at night after 9:00 p.m., especially on weeknights. He did not usually go out on weekends, he added.

Upon further questioning, the officers learned that Ricky's mother owned a maroon-colored Grand Prix, which he did not drive. He admitted that he had had problems with the law when he was caught burgling the previous summer, for which he had been assigned to a probation officer. He recommended that the detectives speak to his friend, Darryl, who lived on Cherrywood Street.

Lundblad and Butterbach had already spoken with Ricky's mother, Mrs. Mary R. Burton, at 9:30 that morning. They had contacted her after hearing what Betty Lou's parents had said about Ricky. She had informed the detectives that her son was with his father at Sylvia's Auto Wreckers on Napa Road. In attempting to detail her son's whereabouts the previous evening, she had recounted his activities almost exactly the same as they would later hear from him: he had of been let out of school at 3:00 p.m., went to his sister Debby's home until about 4:00 p.m., returned home at 5:00 p.m., and went to Gallenkamp's to be fitted for a new pair of shoes that were to be a present to him from his brother-in-law. When he returned home from Gallenkamp's, he remained home all evening. Those who spent the evening with him—celebrating his sister's birthday with cake and coffee—were his father; his mother; his sister, Diane; his sister, Janette; Janette's husband, Larry; and two family friends. Together, they watched *A Global Affair* with Bob Hope, a movie that ran from 9:00 p.m. to 11:00 p.m. Ricky's mother reported that her estranged husband had left at 10:55 p.m.; the family friend subsequently left at the end of the program. Ricky had gone to sleep at 11:30 p.m.

To confirm the story they had received from both Ricky and his mother, the detectives interviewed Ricky's father, Donald, on December 28 at noon. He essentially reiterated what Lundblad and Butterbach had already heard, that he was present at his estranged wife's house on December 20 to celebrate his daughter's birthday. He explained that his own birthday was on December 22, so the gathering was actually a joint party. When he arrived at 7:00 p.m., his son, Ricky; his daughter Janette; and his son-in-law Larry were there already. His friend from Mare Island, and *his* son, also named Ricky, arrived later. Ricky Burton received a call about 8:00 or 8:30 p.m. After this, there were no calls, and no one came to the house that evening, Mr. Burton reported. They enjoyed cake, coffee, and a Bob Hope special, *A Global Affair,* on television.

Mr. Burton did not like the show, and left before it was over, at an estimated 10:15 or 10:30 p.m., he thought. He told the officers that he was the first to leave. He added a few items of note. Ricky did not own a gun, nor did he have access to one. He wasn't allowed to drive, even though he was entirely capable of doing so. Mr. Burton eagerly gave the detectives verbal permission for his son to be polygraphed. At the conclusion of the interview, he expressed his concern for a newspaper article that appeared to mention his son, though, admittedly, it did not name him.

To further confirm the story, the next day at 4:30 p.m., Butterbach and Lundblad questioned the friend of Ricky's father, who was a police sergeant with the Mare Island military security force. The sergeant confirmed for them that he was a guest at the Burton home on December 20. He had been invited with a telephone call for cake and coffee. He had also received a note from Mr. Burton, but had not seen it until after receiving the telephone call that invited him. He attended with his son, Ricky, and arrived at the Burton residence just after 8:00 p.m. Donald and his wife were present. So were their daughter Diane, their daughter Janette, and her husband Larry. Ricky Burton, the apparent suspect in Betty Lou's murder, was definitely present, the sergeant insisted.

The sergeant confirmed earlier reports that they watched "Global Affair" with Bob Hope on channel 5, from 9:00 p.m. to 10:45 p.m. There were no phone calls; there were no visitors. At no point while he was there did Ricky leave the room for more than a couple of minutes. He reported that he left with his son 5 or 10 minutes after the show was over. Mr. Burton had departed about 30 minutes earlier. When he and his son left, he noted, Mrs. Burton, Larry, Janette, Diane, and Ricky were still there. He observed that Ricky Burton had been sitting on a chair, later moving to the couch. He had no knowledge of any guns in the house. He estimated his departure at between 10:50 and 10:55 p.m.

The investigation into Ricky Burton seemed to have run its course. The detectives were convinced of his strong alibi for the evening of the double murder that they were investigating. But if he wasn't responsible, they wondered, who was?

ও

At a quarter past 8:00 the morning after the murders, Lundblad and Butterbach took a statement from James A. Owen, a local resident who had read a story about the shooting in the newspaper, and had contacted the Sheriff's Office. Owen, a retired Air Force enlistee who was an employee of Humble Oil in Benicia, had been driving to work the previous evening for his graveyard shift when, at 11:20 p.m. he estimated, he passed the entrance to the pumping station. He observed two cars parked side by side, about 10 feet apart. His description of the station wagon—a 1955 or 1956 boxy wagon with neutral colors—matched the Faraday vehicle. The other car was to the right and abreast of the station wagon, which the officers surmised must have belonged to the attacker or attackers. Owen could provide little information about the other vehicle, except that it was dark in color with no apparent chrome. It was mid-sized, neither large nor compact. He saw no other people or activity in the area.

The officers reviewed Owen's movements of the night. He was certain that he left home at 11:00 p.m. The trek from his home to the scene of the crime would have taken him 19 minutes. His clock was observed to be 5 minutes fast. Together, these facts would place him at the scene of the crime at precisely 11:14 p.m., just a few minutes before Medeiros would discover the bodies beside pools of blood, making him the second eyewitness to provide a bookend to a very narrow window of opportunity for a double murder.

Owen advised the officers to speak with one of his co-workers who also worked the graveyard shift, who lived in the apartments at the end of Springs Road. He may have seen the cars as well. When Butterbach telephoned Owen the next evening, however, the officer learned that Owen had already spoken to his co-worker, and the co-worker had not driven to work via Lake Herman Road the previous night.

Intrigued by the importance of what Owen had seen, Butterbach and Lundblad re-interviewed him on the day before Christmas, just after noon. He again told them that he had seen two cars parked at the entrance to the pumping station on the previous Friday night. This time, he added that he may also have heard the sounds of the attack. Driving east from Vallejo, after having left home at approximately 11:00 p.m., he said he noticed two vehicles parked 3 to 4 feet apart—closer than the 10 feet apart he claimed the day after the attack—sitting side by side. He observed no one in or around the cars. As he drove past, about one quarter of a mile beyond the gate 10 entrance, he thought he heard a shot even though his car radio was playing softly. He added that another vehicle had passed him just before he arrived at the location of the attack. The other car was driving in the opposite direction toward Vallejo. Unfortunately for the investigation, Owen could provide no description of the vehicle that had passed him on Lake Herman Road.

The detectives could only speculate about the witness's changing story. Was he embellishing his memory with a repeated recounting of his experience to his friends and family? Why did the distance between the cars narrow over the course of a few days? Did he manufacture the memory of the sound of the gunshot?

Approximately 24 hours after the attack, Officer G. Meyring, #298 of the Vallejo Police Department (VPD), entered the Solano County Sheriff's Office with some potentially important information for Butterbach. He repeated what he had heard from a Vallejo resident, a 14-year-old boy named Stan. The boy and a friend, a student from Solano College, were driving toward Blue Rock Springs on Columbus Parkway the previous night. The two had noticed that two cars, a blue 1963 Chevy Impala with two occupants and a blue, 2-door, hard-top Oldsmobile 88, had turned off Lake Herman Road onto Columbus Parkway, heading in the direction of Blue Rock Springs.

Because the time stated was 10:30 p.m., more than 30 minutes before the attack commenced, this sighting was in all probability inconsequential to the investigation. Nevertheless, this information, like everything else, was filed away for future reference. The investigators knew that criminals sometimes injected themselves into a case, or provided false information to give themselves an alibi, so the details of this report—including information on the two who reported it—were carefully recorded.

At 4:30 on Sunday afternoon, December 22, Lundblad and Butterbach interviewed a man who felt that he might have important information about the crime. William Crow had read a plea in the local newspaper asking for witnesses to come forward. He called the Solano County Sheriff's Office to describe his experience.

The report, written up some time later, noted that Crow and his girlfriend were in the area of the crime scene between 9:30 and 10:00 p.m. on the Friday night that Faraday and Jensen were murdered. Crow was testing his girlfriend's car and adjusting the motor. While they were parked by the pumping station entrance precisely where the murders occurred, a blue car, possibly a Plymouth Valiant, drove west down Lake Herman Road from Benicia toward Vallejo.

The blue car stopped in the middle of the road, the report continued, after just having passed Crow and his girlfriend. The car's reverse lights came on and began to back up toward them. Fearing a confrontation—the car appeared to pose some kind of threat—Crow took off with his girlfriend at his side. He raced east toward tiny Benicia followed by the strange blue car driving at a high rate of speed. The other car did not gain on them. When Crow turned off into Benicia, the strange vehicle proceeded straight ahead.

When exposed to the report many years later, Crow was surprised at what he read. Apparently, the officers had not heard him correctly, or had failed to accurately record what he had told them, he maintained.

He highlighted the few omissions and errors that he perceived. The girl was merely a friend, and not a girlfriend, he explained. Though he knew the sheriff who wrote the report, Crow noted that the officer never shared his writings with him, nor followed up on it with a later interview or any additional investigation. No one interviewed his friend even once about the odd event. Additionally, the reporting officer used the word "they" to describe the occupant(s) of the other vehicle, but should have used the more correct "he."

Crow denied saying that there was only one person in the car. What he reported was that he was unable to see whether the driver was alone. It was dark out, and the area provided no artificial illumination. He could not see into the passenger side of the car. He had said that he had seen a Caucasian driver, only noting that it was someone he did not recognize. He had not seen him long enough—just a couple of seconds at most—to get a good look at him. (Accordingly, he declined the chance to review suspect photographs many years later, insisting that the exercise would be fruitless.)

Further, the word, "Valiant" was not used by Crow at the time of the attack and the subsequent interview. What he had shared with the officers, he claimed, was that he observed round brake lights that came on once the vehicle had passed them at the pump house entrance. That word was the reporting officer's interpretation of what Crow had said, he surmised. The officer must have been aware of the shape of Valiant taillights to interject that.

Crow, still living only a few miles from the site many years later, admitted to periodically visiting the crime scene. He remained convinced that he had encountered the assailant. The time, place, and menacing stance of the blue car all led him to believe that the driver soon returned and carried out the dastardly attack on Faraday and Jensen.

Late Sunday afternoon, Lundblad and Butterbach were at the Faraday residence, 1930 Sereno Drive, in Vallejo, to meet with Joe, a friend of David's. The Faraday home was large for Vallejo in 1968, consisting of numerous rooms on a single level spread across an over-sized lot. Joe was direct: he knew of no one who considered David an enemy. He then described for the officers how David had met Betty Lou about a week previous at the Pythian Castle. (The Pythian Castle in Vallejo was the home of Lodge #7 of the Knights of Pythias, an international, non-sectarian fraternal order, established in 1864 It was the first fraternal order to be chartered by an Act of Congress, formed to heal the Civil War wounds between the North and the South, promote amity, and relieve suffering.) The couple became acquainted while decorating the hall for a social event, a meeting that sparked a mutual interest, led to a budding relationship, and ulti-mately resulted in two deaths. Joe reported that on Friday, December 20, the young couple was with him at the house of a friend named Daniel (one police report identified him as "David," obviously con-fusing his name with that of the murder victim's). David and Betty Lou arrived at about five o'clock, and did not say where they were headed when they left about an hour later.

Concerning Ricky Burton, Joe was very dismissive. He told the officers that their suspect was just a big talker with no close friends. The officers would later learn that Ricky was alleged to have told Daniel that he had his mother's car and was going out Friday night. They found no evidence from Joe to support this.

Joe was thanked for his time as the officers turned their attention to Mrs. Jean L. Faraday, David's mother, who worked in the Passenger Reservations Department at Travis Air Force Base. She told the offi-cers that she did not know, nor had she ever met, Betty Lou. The girl had only been dating her son for a very short time, she explained. She also did not know of any enemies that her son may have had. She recounted the final hours of her son's life for the officers.

On the night of the attack, she recalled, at 7:10 her son had driven his sister, Debbie, to a meeting of the Rainbow Girls, a masonic organization, which was held at a rented room at the Pythian Castle on Sonoma Boulevard. He returned at 7:20, only to depart again ten minutes later. She had given him $1.55, all in quarters and dimes. (Based on the crime scene details, evidently 70 cents had been spent, stolen, or misplaced between the time David received this gift from his mother and the 85 cents had been recovered from his lifeless body.)

When the officers questioned 16-year-old Debbie Faraday, she informed them that she heard from David that he and Jensen were headed out to Lake Herman Road because a bunch of kids were going to rendezvous there that night. She stated that she knew who some of the kids were, but was unable to contact them by phone for the officers. She promised that she would get in touch with the kids and subsequently let the officers know the details of her conversations.

The officers caught up with David's friend, Daniel, at 9:30 Sunday night. The 16-year-old who attended Hogan High School acknowledged knowing David and Betty Lou, and hosting them at his house the previous Friday. He had seen David drive Betty Lou in the station wagon 4 or 5 times in the previous two weeks. He said that on Friday they were at his home from 5:00 to 6:00 in the after-noon, listening to songs from his record collection. Neither David nor Betty Lou had said where they were going when they left.

Daniel expressed his dislike for Ricky, complaining of the boy's big mouth. He tried to avoid him where possible, he admitted. He told the officers that he was walking by Ricky's house on Friday, December 20 while Ricky was at the curb washing his mother's car, a maroon Pontiac Grand Prix. The radio was playing. At that time Ricky had said that he was going to go out in his mother's car on Friday night, flashing the keys as evidence that he both could and would. Daniel was not aware of any firearms in Ricky's possession. He had never seen him drive a car, but had seen him the previous summer riding around with a friend named Scott in a green Ford pick-up, a model from a year between 1951 and 1954. He suggested that the investigators speak with Scott, who now lived in a large brown house at the end of Falcon Drive.

The officers took note of what they heard and departed.

❦

Earlier that afternoon, Lundblad received a telephone call from Officer Warner of the BPD. Warner had been contacted on the phone by Mrs. Peggy Your, a woman who lived with her husband, Homer, on West "L" street in Benicia and worked at Mr. Ed's Drive-In Restaurant. (A July 1969 VPD report identified Peggy Your's home as a pink house on the frontage road, a mile north of Lake Herman Road, between Benicia and Cordelia.) Your had told Warner that her husband was employed by the Frederickson Pipe Company, which had a contract to lay new underground pipes in the Lake Herman Road area. That contract brought the couple to Lake Herman Road on the evening of December 20.

Your reported that on the night of the murders she and her husband, with their children, upon returning from Sacramento, were checking on pipes and equipment at the construction site along Lake Herman Road. At about 11:00 p.m., with Homer at the wheel of their 1967 gold Pontiac Grand Prix, they arrived near the scene of the pumping station, continued along Lake Herman Road down to the bottom of the hill, turned into the Marshall Ranch to make a U-turn to go back to Benicia, and passed the pumping station area once more.

Both times that the Yours passed the spot that would in just a few minutes become the site of a grisly double murder they spotted a Rambler which was parked to the left of the gate pointing east toward the field. It did not move between sightings. A young couple nestled in the front seat. The boy sat in the driver's seat, the girl resting her head on the boy's shoulder. When the lights of the Your's car first illuminated the Rambler, the boy immediately put his hands on the steering wheel of the car as though he feared that the police were approaching.

Peggy added that they were not the only ones present in the area that night. After they had turned around at the entrance to the Marshall Ranch, she and her husband had seen a red pick-up truck with wooden sideboards parked in the field about 25 feet in from the road. Two Caucasian adult men were in the truck, one about 25 to 30 years of age, wearing a hunting jacket and a stocking-type hat or cap over his head and carrying a three-cell flashlight. Peggy reported that they did not pass any cars as they drove along Lake Herman Road, and only the Rambler was present at the entrance to the pumping station at 11:00 p.m.

The investigation was starting to develop. The officers now had some promising leads and some useful information about some residents' activities on the night of the attack. Lundblad checked the times and distances reported by the Yours, and sketched out a preliminary timeline of their movements. The two men who the Yours had seen at the entrance to the Marshall Ranch had already been identified as two raccoon hunters by Deputy Villarreal. Lundblad and Butterbach had interviewed them at 9:22 on the evening after the attack in the hopes that they had seen something useful to the investigation. There was also the very real possibility that they were responsible for the shooting.

Frank Gasser, the older of the two at 69 years, lived at the Gasser ranch, north of the Goodyear station. He and his friend, 27-year-old Robert Connelly, an employee of Pacific Gas & Electric, had been looking for raccoons the previous evening—the night of the attack—from 9:00 p.m. until about 11:00 p.m. At approximately eleven o'clock, the younger man looked at his watch—it may have been five or ten minutes before the hour—and decided to head back to the truck, a trek along the creek that would have taken them three to four, or possibly five, more minutes. They were just about to depart in the truck when a gold Grand Prix appeared.

The hunters estimated that they left the Marshall Ranch at 11:05 p.m., or a few minutes after the other car departed. They too noted the light-colored Rambler parked in the entrance way to the pump house, but believed that its location was to the southwest of where it was eventually found. They added that they observed a white, 4-door hardtop 1959 or 1960 Chevy Impala parked in that lot at around 9:00 p.m. when they first arrived. Also at that time they saw a truck emerge from beyond the gate. This addendum would corroborate the statement given by Bingo Wesner, who was in that white truck, and had reported seeing the parked Impala and the red truck transporting the raccoon hunters.

Butterbach and Lundblad met again with Connelly five days later. Because there was a discrepancy, possibly just a misunderstanding, arising from the first interview, he was asked to provide a more detailed explanation of his activities that night. His description of the location of the Faraday vehicle did not agree with that of the Yours. Additionally, being present in the area that night while in possession of a weapon made him more than a witness. He was now a suspect. Thursday afternoon, he retold his story with added detail.

He explained that he had gone to Frank Gasser's ranch that evening about 6:00 p.m., departing several hours later with Frank. They passed the pumping station entrance about 9:00 p.m., and parked inside the Marshall Ranch area. Once out of their red truck, the two men followed the creek toward the pump station. As they approached the Dotta ranch, still from a distance, they noticed some commotion. All the lights were on, but they could not determine the cause of the noise. Then the dogs treed a raccoon in an oak tree near the pump station. He said they shot the animal with a .22 long barrel revolver, but never shared what happened to the creature.

Connelly stated that he recalled looking at his watch at this point and noticing that it was close to eleven o'clock, possibly 5 or 10 minutes before eleven. He and Frank made the ten-minute trek back to their truck. They were only at the truck for about 5 minutes when a vehicle approached (evidently the Yours) and then turned around and headed back toward Benicia. Approximately 5 minutes later, they departed in his truck, a 1959 red pick-up with white wood sideboards—actually, cattle guards. They drove back to the Gasser ranch, heading toward Benicia. They passed only one car along the route.

Connelly insisted that the Rambler had been parked on the south side of the pump house entrance area. It had to have been between 11:00 and 11:15 p.m., he estimated. He explained that he spent the next hour at the Gasser's, and then left the area on Highway 12, through Jamison Canyon, heading home. He estimated his arrival at his house at about 12:30 a.m.

He then reluctantly admitted to having an automatic rifle on the evening of the attack. The officers advised him of his Constitutional rights under the Fifth Amendment because he was in the area of the murder and had in his possession at the time an automatic rifle which he previously denied having with him.

Though his firearm was confiscated in exchange for a receipt, it was not the gun the officers were seeking. Rifle testing in the Sheriff's

Office by Range Master George Parks would in time eliminate it as a suspect weapon. Connelly noted that Gasser also owned an automatic rifle, but that he did not have it at the house. Gasser apparently did not leave guns at the ranch because of recent thefts in the area. Connelly suggested that the detective speak with Harlan, a friend of Frank's, who may have had possession of it.

The detectives quickly became aware of some differences between the details given by the Yours and those offered by the raccoon hunters that required some clarification.

On Friday afternoon, December 27, Lundblad telephoned Peggy Your to establish the time of her departure from Sacramento and her time of arrival in Vallejo. With no direct witnesses to the crime, he hoped that he could more firmly establish the time of the attack through careful scrutiny of the people who were in the area that evening. Your maintained that she had left Sacramento between 10:00 and 10:15 p.m. Her husband was driving which meant that they drove the speed limit or slower; he always obeyed the traffic laws. She estimated the time of arrival in the Benicia area, off Highway 12, to be approximately 11:00 p.m. They then drove the three to four miles of Lake Herman Road at a slow pace as he checked the pipes and equipment carefully laid out along the side of the road. To clarify her earlier statement, she noted that the Rambler at the entrance to the pump house was facing the fence, the rear section facing directly west toward Vallejo. A check of her clock's accuracy revealed that it was in fact 7 minutes fast. Lundblad reasoned that, as a result, her time of arrival at the pump house entrance would be closer to 11:00 p.m. than 11:15 p.m.

The following spring, on March 22, Butterbach re-interviewed the Yours. Possibly some additional information, or a closer examination of the timeline, raised some suspicions about what the couple had previously told the officers. There seemed to be some discrepancies between witnesses—or some misunderstandings—so the couple was separated and interviewed individually. Maybe nothing would come from another look, but as leads in the case were thinning out by this time, it was worth a try.

Homer was questioned first, at twenty past five in the afternoon. He told Butterbach that on December 20, between 11:00 and 11:20

p.m., he was driving west on Lake Herman Road. He turned into the path that led to the Marshall Ranch. Once off the road, he spotted a red pick-up truck with wooden sides about 30 feet in from the road. A man standing by the truck shined a flashlight into their vehicle. Because Peggy had spotted another man with a gun, she shouted to her husband, "Let's get out of here!"

Homer was adamant that his wife had not spoken to the man with the gun. That night, she had in her possession an unloaded .38 special, he maintained. The shells were in his pocket. He proceeded to show the officer the guns he owned: a 2-inch .38 special Smith & Wesson, serial #55246, and a Remington 12-gauge automatic shotgun, serial #248011.

Peggy was interviewed at 7:15 p.m. Her information did not contradict her husband's story, but did contain more detail than her first statement given the previous December. She again told Butterbach that they had been returning from Sacramento between 11:00 and 11:20 p.m. Because her husband was employed by a construction company doing work in the Lake Herman area, he wanted to check on the pipes which had been laid out in preparation for installing and burying them in the side of the road. The couple was driving west on Lake Herman Road and noticed two Caucasians, a male and a female, seated in a Rambler, facing east, at the entrance to the Lake Herman pumping station. When the headlights hit the Rambler, the male sat up. This, the officer noted, was different than what she had said in December when she stated that he put his hands on the wheel. Despite the fact that it was a very cold night, there was no frost on the station wagon that Peggy could observe that might have obscured her view.

Continuing with a more elaborate version of essentially the same story she had told in December, Peggy explained that her husband had driven past the pump house entrance and turned right into the Marshall Ranch. As the car approached the ranch gate, she observed a tall, white male adult who was dressed in dark clothing. He was standing by the left side of their car (where her husband was sitting in the driver's seat) about six feet away. He was holding a long-barreled weapon. A red pick-up with white wooden sides was parked about 40 feet ahead of their car. An old man exited the pick-up and shined a flashlight into the Your's vehicle. At the sight of the man dressed in black, and particularly his weapon, she told her husband that there was a man with a gun standing by the car and to get the hell out of there. Peggy stated that the man stood motionless. He did not point the gun, but he stared at them. They turned the vehicle around and escaped east on Lake Herman Road.

When they passed the pump station entrance again, she continued, at about 11:15 or 11:18 p.m., the Rambler was still parked in the same spot. She kept looking back, she explained, as they drove slowly along Lake Herman Road because she was afraid of the two men near the red pick-up truck. They saw no lights behind them, not from the pick-up or from any other vehicle.

They did encounter another vehicle, farther along Lake Herman Road, at the entrance to the Humble Oil property, Peggy added: a long, dark-colored car. A security guard was leaning over talking to the driver. The dark car had a long speedometer indicator light that emitted a greenish glow and gave the men an alien appearance.

Butterbach asked Peggy if she had a gun in the car that night, and whether she or her husband had pointed it at the man near the red pick-up, saying, "My gun is bigger than yours." Peggy admitted that she had a .38 special with a small barrel in her possession that night. It was lying on the rear seat of their car. It was not loaded, however, as Homer had the shells in his pocket. She insisted that they did not point the gun at the man, nor say anything to him.

∽

On Monday December 23, at 2:00 in the afternoon, a funeral for David Faraday was held at the First Presbyterian Church of Vallejo, the Reverend James O. Hulin officiating. A private internment of David's cremated remains followed at Tulocay Cemetery in Napa. Friends were invited to call at Colonial Chapels.

Betty Lou's funeral, a Christian Science service, had been held at the Colonial Chapels at 11:00 that morning. The reader was High Martin Niemoller. Jensen's classmates served as pallbearers. She was privately entombed at Abbey Memorial Gardens.

✧

The Yours and the raccoon hunters were not the only people to drive past gate 10 that evening. On December 23, Lundblad took a statement from Helen, a young Vallejo woman. She and her boyfriend, a sailor, driving in a brown and white 1956 Ford station wagon, covered the length of Lake Herman Road and spotted the victim's car at the pump house entrance at approximately 10:15 p.m. Helen immediately recognized Jensen, a former classmate. She noted that the station wagon was parked facing the gate. When Helen and her boyfriend passed by the pump house entrance a second time, having driven to the end of the road and back, she again saw the Rambler. It was facing the field this time, its front a little to the side. Helen also reported seeing a bright yellow foreign car parked near the area where the attack occurred. There were two Caucasians within, a male driver and an unknown passenger.

Even as the venerable Lundblad carefully took the statement, there was a problem. The first time Helen had spoken with him, she had claimed that the Rambler was backed into the pump house entrance, facing neither the field nor the gate. When he later realized this discrepancy and wondered about it, Lundblad telephoned her, and arranged that on December 28 she would bring her boyfriend down to the station to clarify the exact position of the Faraday vehicle that evening.

Late afternoon on Monday, December 23, Butterbach sat down to record important statements received through several phone conversations that day. In one, a man named Louis called to report information he had received from his wife. According to Louis, his wife's girlfriend was dating a volatile "Latin-type man." The girlfriend split up with the man to return to her former boyfriend, who drove a Nash station wagon that roughly fit the description of the Faraday's Rambler. Butterbach was told third-hand that the Latin-type man was a very jealous person, and could be responsible for the attack through a case of mistaken identity. Perhaps he believed the driver of the Rambler was dating his former girlfriend, and was responsible for the end of his relationship with her.

On the afternoon of December 24 at 1:15 p.m., Lundblad and Butterbach met with Sharon's mother, the close friend of Betty Lou's. Sharon's mother reported to the detectives something she had heard about David, something that may be related to his killing, and something she had to get off her chest. She had heard from her daughter that a boy named Mark was speaking about an incident at the Pancake House on Tennessee Street. She recounted the second-hand story that Faraday was about to turn someone in to the authorities for "pushing grass" (selling marijuana), and that that someone had threatened Faraday.

In an unrelated point, she heard from her daughter that Betty Lou had mentioned plans to go to San Francisco on the night of December 20. The officers immediately discounted this. The distance to San Francisco, and the time required to drive there and back, most likely excluded the possibility. Nevertheless, the detectives committed themselves to checking out the details of all the information they received.

In the initial days of the investigation, the officers remained upbeat about their prospects for solving the case. Lundblad was quoted on December 24, "We expect to have an answer before very much longer."

The lead detectives of this most mysterious case attempted to sneak in a short, but well needed, break for Christmas. They desired to celebrate with family, open gifts, and catch up on sleep. Instead, Lundblad spent the day reviewing statements and evidence. He went over their findings with Sergeant Jack Oller, an investigator in the Fairfield Office of the Sheriff's Department. All too soon, any break was over and the detectives were again gleaning from the community what little scraps of information they could find.

Detective Lundblad visited Hogan High School on Thursday, December 26 at just after 11:30 in the morning. He was met there by Principal Lee Y. Dean, Sharon (who had shared locker #1003 with Betty Lou), and Sharon's mother. His intent was to collect any notes or personal property of Betty Lou's, perhaps retaining something that would move forward the investigation into her murder. Nothing found in the locker was of evidentiary value. Pencils, textbooks, and articles of clothing were given to the principal, who was free to pass them along to the deceased woman's family.

Sharon revealed to the detective that her friend also had a private locker in gym class, an alternate location where personal items could be stored. Mr. Dean promised to examine this locker too, but likely not until Monday at the earliest because, surprisingly, he did not possess a pass key for that area of his school.

Later examination of Jensen's private papers brought to light an ominous note which appeared to be in Betty Lou's handwriting (especially when compared to other material that was obviously in her handwriting). The note, found in the last page of a binder and retained for evidence, read as follows:

```
DO YOU KNOW A KID NAMED RICHARD BURTON?
I WAS GOING WITH HIM, UNTIL 2 DAYS BEFORE
THE INSTALLATION. HE STILL PHONES ME, AND IS
THREATENING ME TO KEEP AWAY FROM DAVE.
HE SAID IF HE'S EVER CLOSE ENOUGH TO DAVE, HE WOULD
PUNCH HIM ONE IN THE TEETH. I TOLD HIM TO LEAVE ME
ALONE, IF HE KNOWS WHAT [IS] GOOD [FOR] HIM.
```

❧

In early January, prior to the resumption of high school classes, Principal Dean called the detectives to report that Betty Lou's gym locker contained only shoes, hair spray, and an archery score card. Nothing that would assist the police.

Upon examining Jensen's note and considering other information gathered, Lundblad decided to speak again with 16-year-old Ricky. His alibi may have been iron-clad, but he now had a clear motive—and was at least accused of making threats to one of the victims. The detectives had to consider the possibility that he might know more about the attack than he was admitting. A meeting was arranged for December 28 at 1:00 p.m. at the Sheriff's Office.

Ricky arrived at the appointed time with his parents. He was read his Miranda rights once again. Once again, he expressed a desire to waive his rights and speak with the detective in order to do all he could to aid the investigation. By all outward appearances, he had nothing to hide.

He was confronted by a statement that his acquaintance, Daniel, had shared with the police that he, while washing his mother's car, displayed the car keys and bragged that he was going out Friday night. Calmly, Ricky explained that he wasn't sure exactly what day it was—he washed the car a couple of times a week—but it could have been Wednesday or Thursday. He denied saying that he was going to get the car Friday. He did acknowledge that he had surreptitiously taken the car on a previous occasion but that he had been found out by his mother.

He also denied having seen Faraday on Friday. He claimed that he never made any threats to his face, though he may have told Betty Lou that he would tell her parents that she smoked, but only because he did not approve of it. When shown Betty Lou's note from her notebook, he was surprised she had written it. He acknowledged that it was her handwriting. He was not upset by what he saw, and shrugged it off by saying that he could have made the remark about punching Faraday during a telephone conversation with his former girlfriend.

Lundblad urged Ricky to clear his name by taking a polygraph examination. Ricky asked what the results would reveal if a person were nervous, as though he were trying to buy time. The officer said that an operator would explain the procedure. The accused young man agreed to take the test, and his parents gave their consent. Arrangements would be made, he was told. He would be notified. The next morning, however, Ricky's father telephoned and reported that his son had decided not to take the examination. He explained that Ricky was just too nervous. Besides, they all knew that he was innocent. He was obviously home at the time, a fact to which many witnesses could, and did, attest.

❦

On December 27, Lundblad and Butterbach met with an upset young couple from Napa. Their tale was provocative, and provided another possible lead for the investigation into the attack that occurred seven days earlier. Larry, aged 20, and his wife, Linda, who was 18, sat down with the investigators at 11:00 in the morning to recount their experiences from the previous night. While Larry was at work at a Standard Oil filling station on Imola Avenue—he worked the night shift from midnight until 8:00 in the morning—he was visited by a former neighbor, named Pete, who had once lived in the same apartment complex as the couple. The time was 1:45 a.m.

Fifteen minutes later, the detectives were told, Pete showed up at the couple's home. Linda let him in, since he was known to her and her husband. Once inside, Pete asked her, "What would you do if I raped you?" Thinking quickly on her feet, she responded that she would pound on the wall and her neighbor would telephone the police. Changing tactics—if there was indeed any plan behind his actions—Pete asked Linda if she was happy. Upon learning that she indeed was, he complained, "Happy people piss me off." He confessed to her that he had been fighting with his wife and was planning to go to Vallejo. He also stated that he intended to move back to Redding because all the people in the area were stabbing him in the back and, after the knife was in, twisting it.

Pete remained in the apartment for about 45 minutes, Linda estimated to the officers. After he left, she heard someone walking around outside, but she did not look to see who it was. The couple could not recall Pete's last name, but knew that he drove a blue 1952 Chevrolet coup. He also had a 1955 cream- and maroon-colored Buick. He owned a rifle and a pistol, but she did not know the calibers. She *did* know that he carried a fishing knife in his pocket.

The couple provided a rough description of their strange guest: about 28 years of age, five feet eleven inches in height, jet black hair, and acne pits on his face. They also shared that he served as helper on the day shift at Kaiser Steel.

Lundblad detailed Butterbach to drive to Kaiser Steel with Larry to attempt to identify Pete's car in the company parking lot. If possible, they would also try to collect any information about him that they could from other employees.

A Vallejo woman, named Jean, contacted Sergeant Lundblad that same day. Though she was hesitant to provide a statement, she offered that her three children, ages 18, 16, and 14, and a 17-year-old boy who lived with them, had made comments that they knew who was responsible for the killing. The woman admitted that it was probably a guess from no more than speculation. Nevertheless, the person responsible, according to the youths, was named "Gary." The woman could offer no concrete proof, nor any additional facts.

Like so much other vague information provided to the department, this would be filed for future use. No one knew when a minor detail would break the case, but everyone shared the belief that something in the voluminous, and ever-growing, file would eventually cough up the criminal.

Also on December 27, Lundblad took a statement from a gunsmith at Al's Sport Shop who had been contacted by Lundblad to provide information on certain types of self-loading revolvers and pistols. Based on the evidence available, the gunsmith suggested that the fatal shooting could have been carried out with a type of Ruger that had a tube magazine and carried from 12 to 15 rounds, depending on the ammunition used. He offered to provide any help he could to the department as it labored to identify the responsible weapon.

The next morning, Lundblad and Butterbach met with George Parks, the Range Master assigned to test any seized weapons to determine whether they were associated with the attack. He told the officers that by means of test firings he was able to eliminate three guns that had been provided to him: Connelly's Marlin automatic rifle; James A. Owen's Ruger automatic rifle, serial number 138577; and a Remington automatic rifle, model 550-1, owned by another man named James.

The CII later concluded that an exact match with a particular weapon would be difficult, if not impossible, since the copper coating on the slugs made the rounds too hard to accept a clear impression of the barrel's rifling pattern, and prevented the identification of a unique pattern of lands and grooves. But many firearms could and would be eliminated.

Though many guns were present in the area of the attack, none that came to the attention of law enforcement was ever linked to the assault on Faraday and Jensen. Forensic analysis eliminated all the weapons that were tested. Apparently, the gun that was used to kill the couple had left the immediate area and was as elusive and mysterious as the person who had fired it.

Tests of rifling marks on the slugs—6 right-hand grooves, land to groove ratio of 1:1+; groove width approximately .056, and land width approximately .06; semi-circular firing impression at 12 o'clock, and small ejector markings on the shell casings at 3 o'clock; somewhat-visible, faint ejector markings at 8 o'clock—revealed that the weapon could have been a J.C. Higgins model 80, a High Standard Model 101, or some other .22 caliber semi-automatic pistol, as opposed to a rifle, and categorically eliminated any model of revolver, since they do not leave ejector markings. (Mel Nicolai, in a 35-page California Department of Justice report written on January 22, 1971, shared that criminologist David Q. Burd of the CII linked the shooting to a J.C. Higgins model 80 automatic pistol.) The ammunition was identified as .22 caliber Super X copper-coated long rifle rounds, the knowledge of which would later become one among several pieces of information by which the perpetrator would later identify himself in letters to law enforcement as the one responsible for this attack.

Because there were no eyewitnesses to the attack itself, the investigators had to rely on crime scene evidence to reconstruct exactly what had happened. Shell casings found scattered about revealed that 10 shots had been fired at the scene, though only 8 of the slugs could be accounted for: 1 in Faraday's skull, 5 fired through Jensen's back, and 2 discovered lodged in the station wagon. The other 2 missing rounds evidently represented misses on the part of attacker, or possibly 1 or 2 warning shots fired into the air.

Initially, one of the bullet holes in the station wagon was misidentified as being the product of a .38 caliber weapon. This led investigators to falsely conclude that there were two guns—and possibly two shooters—at the scene. Subsequent analysis confirmed that only one gun was responsible for all 10 shots.

∽

The investigators reviewed the details of the actual attack. Between the time that the mid-sized, dark car, lacking in chrome, was spotted by Owen at 11:14 p.m. and the time that Medeiros found the victims outside the car at 11:20 p.m., the officers theorized that the killer had exited his vehicle, commanded or threatened the couple to leave the station wagon, and fired the deadly shots before fleeing the scene. The bullets recovered from the interior of the car may have been an attempt to force Faraday and Jensen to leave the relative safety of their vehicle. The rather close scatter of shell casings to the right of the station wagon—and the 28-foot-long trail of blood from the car to Jensen's collapsed body—suggested that the killer did not move very far from his own car parked next to and paralleling the Faraday car before the deed was done and he was back on the road.

It appeared to investigators that Faraday had been shot first, possibly at the moment he stumbled out of his vehicle. But it was not an obvious conclusion. Jensen could have then been fired upon first as she fled between the cars, attempting to gain some distance from the killer's weapon. It is also possible that the killer coerced the couple to stand outside the car, and even spoke with them. "Possibly they were ordered out of the car," speculated Lundblad. Whether the couple and shooter exchanged words, and whether Faraday and Jensen were given a few seconds to stand in the last moments of their lives, were known to the killer alone. The shot to Faraday's head appeared to investigators to be an effort to subdue the stronger of the two victims, and was the violence that instigated Jensen's flight.

The condition of the station wagon also suggested some details about the attack and its aftermath. The officers arriving at the scene found the passenger front door open. The other three doors, and the tailgate, were closed and locked. The front seat was set back so the couple could recline. The seat position may have prevented the raccoon hunters from observing the teenagers within the car as they passed the Rambler just after 11:00 p.m. It may somehow have been related to the attack as well, the couple's sudden emergence possibly startling and angering their attacker.

The investigators were left to speculate on the activities of Faraday and Jensen between 9:00 p.m. when they were last seen by Betty Lou's friend, Sharon, and 10:15 p.m. when they were first spotted at the attack site by former classmate Helen and her boyfriend. The couple spent some money, or Faraday somehow parted with some of the change given to him by his mother.

The officers astutely noted that even if the attacker had some compelling reason to attack the couple—and no obvious motive emerged—he would not have known where to find them. This suggested a random attack on victims not known to their killer, possibly the impulsive action of a trigger-happy assailant, Faraday and Jensen just happening to be at the wrong place at the wrong time.

Substance abuse appeared to play no part in the attack. No alcohol or narcotics were found at the scene or were revealed in the course of the autopsies. The two victims merely wanted to be alone and enjoy the intoxicating power of love when their lives were suddenly and brutally extinguished.

What was absent from any scenario created in the minds of the investigators was any kind of rational motive. On the first page of the main murder report, the officers marked in clear letters, "no apparent motive." Lundblad at first believed that the killer's intention was to sexually molest Jensen, but investigators were able to eliminate robbery and sexual assault quite quickly. They initially considered that the couple had been followed to the location, but then discounted that possibility. Subsequent investigation did nothing to reveal or clarify the killer's reasoning. Lundblad described it as a "senseless murder." The act was perhaps carried out by a demented person. By Sunday night, 24 hours after the attack, investigators were already theorizing that the killer was unknown to the victims.

In early spring, in an attempt to assure the public that progress was being made in the by-now-slow-moving investigation, and to allay its fears, Detective Sergeant Lundblad answered questions that became a story in the local paper on Sunday March 30, 1969. He informed readers that his department had spoken to over 100 people in the course of the department's work, filing reports on more than 50 of them, many of the individuals being interviewed more than once. The file of reports had grown to over four inches thick, plus many items were collected in a "fairly sizable evidence locker."

Lundblad did not reveal all of his cards, however. He retained enough pieces of information so that if someone were to confess to the crime he would know quite quickly whether the person had been at the scene or not. He worked on the case every day, he noted, and had received assistance from many sources.

But he hadn't yet found the clue that would lead him to the killer.

The case, V-25564 #9, by itself achieved a high profile status, becoming one of the most infamous unsolved cases in California at the time. Numerous law enforcement agencies contacted Lundblad to offer assistance, and he was grateful for the support that he received from numerous agencies in the vicinity of his department, including the VPD, BPD, Napa Police Department, Napa and Sonoma County Sheriff's Offices, and the Fairfield PD.

The community also rallied around the investigation. When Lundblad requested all the small caliber weapons owned by the residents living in the vicinity of the attack be tested, he received good cooperation. Jim Gaul, a Hogan High student, spearheaded a Jensen-Faraday reward fund drive. He, together with students from both Vallejo high schools, planned fund raisers in the hopes of collecting $1000 in reward money toward the arrest and conviction of the person or persons responsible for the appalling double murder. The students planned to canvass businesses, make door-to-door neighborhood requests, sponsor car washes, and host candy sales. If the money was unclaimed after one year, they decided, it would convert into memorial scholarships.

In time, leads became dead ends, and new sources of information dried up like the brown, grass-covered hills in a Northern California summer. As winter disappeared under the new life of spring and spring warmed to a hot, dry summer, investigators and the public alike began to wonder whether this crime would ever be solved. There was no known motive, no eyewitnesses, and the forensics that were gathered yielded few hints as to who had done this and why.

A pattern would emerge only after the killer attacked again.

3 | BLUE ROCK SPRINGS PARK

"the boy was also shot in the knee."

By the time the fourth of July rolled around, the odd event on Lake Herman Road the previous December was no longer on the forefront of the minds of most Solano County residents. It had become less and less relevant as life in the area returned to normal and the murders receded in history. Though the gruesome, unsolved attack left many unanswered questions, no one anticipated it would be repeated.

Then the killer returned.

Just before midnight on a day in which many Americans had enthusiastically celebrated the founding of their country with boisterous picnics and loud, colorful parades, 22-year-old waitress Darlene Ferrin slowed her brown Corvair and entered the Blue Rock Springs parking lot, just east of Vallejo, and stopped at the low, curving stone wall that marked the back of the lot. The two were only a couple of miles from the spot where Faraday and Jensen had been murdered six and a half months earlier. As she conversed with Michael Mageau, the slender 19-year-old who sat beside her, a mysterious vehicle entered the darkened lot and eased up behind them.

Believing that a police officer was approaching, the two foraged for identification. The driver stepped out onto the macadam and calmly walked to Ferrin's passenger window. He carried a large flashlight. Without speaking a word, he began shooting at the couple with a handgun, striking Mageau first, then Ferrin. The attack was sudden and brutal. Michael scrambled into the back seat, his lanky limbs akimbo. He became a moving target. Darlene recoiled as the bullets entered her side. Blood began to pour freely from her wounds.

The gunman casually headed back toward his car. He was distracted from his departure by the sounds of life—a piercing scream from Mageau. Realizing that his shots had not been entirely successful in his murderous efforts, he returned to the passenger side of the Corvair. Darlene suffered two more rounds; Michael thrashed around in a vain attempt to avoid the two additional bullets fired at him. As the helpless victims bled, their attacker slipped behind the wheel of his car and disappeared into the darkness.

Though numerous police officers and an ambulance would soon rush to the scene, Darlene would not survive. Michael lived, but would never be the same. He was irreparably damaged, and began his new life with multiple surgeries and a long rehabilitation. Nothing would remove the indelible scars.

The killer had re-emerged in less than seven months, striking only a few miles away from the Lake Herman Road scene of his previous brutality. It was another shooting attack on another couple in another lover's lane area. Terror quickly spread, infiltrating every corner of the normally quiet community.

The City of Vallejo was no stranger to drama. Located on the northeast shore of San Pablo Bay, it was named for General Mariano Guadalupe Vallejo. It was once home to several Native American tribes, until 1843, when along with a much larger area, it was deeded—84,000 acres in all—to General Vallejo, the regional military officer and first land holder. In 1850, the General proposed a new city that would contain state capital buildings, a university, and botanical gardens. Originally slated to be called Eureka, the town's title was changed to Vallejo, and its present site was chosen for its military and strategic value: the Napa River flowed through the city until it became the Mare Island Strait. It didn't hurt that on a clear day San Francisco was visible from the hilltop. It was designated the first capital city of California, and drew important officials from near and far. When the general failed to supply adequate facilities—the participants sat on barrels in leaky rooms—the gathering was moved to Sacramento after only 11 days of meetings. Business convened in 1853 only long enough to move the official capital to Benicia, a neighboring village named for General Vallejo's wife. Once the capital was relocated, the legislature voted to establish the naval shipyard on Mare Island, a partial payment or indemnification for the loss of the business that its presence would have induced. The shipyard served the area until 1996.

Today, Vallejo, whose motto is "the city of opportunity," is a bustling, twenty-first century city—the tenth largest by population in the Bay Area, and forty-ninth largest in California—with its own commerce and tourist attractions, such as Six Flags Discovery Kingdom (a large amusement park) and the Mare Island Museum. In 2012, it boasted more than 116,000 people, a population that had held steady for 20 years. Also known as "Valley Joe," "V-town," and "the V," Vallejo made national news in 2008 when it filed for bankruptcy. Burdensome contracts had become unsupportable when the weakening housing market led the nation into severe recession. It was the largest city in California to declare bankruptcy until Stockton followed suit in 2012.

Vallejo has produced some notable citizens, including major league baseball players, major league basketball players, major league football players, actor Raymond Burr, and numerous rap musicians. The 1970 census measured the population at 66,733. Despite its diminutive size at the time, it would forever be remembered as ground zero for the attacks of the Zodiac serial killer, even though the December 20, 1968 and July 4, 1969 murders were not the killer's first, even though he would not return to attack in Vallejo, and even though the murders occurred before the killer adopted his infamous moniker.

The citizens of Vallejo responded to the unprovoked attack:

At 12:10 a.m., a woman telephoned the offices of the Vallejo Police Department (VPD) to report that two juveniles were being shot. Nancy Slover, the on-duty dispatcher, VPD #355, took the information, later describing the caller as an agitated and excited

Caucasian female in her late teens. The report was passed on to the radio operator on duty, who Slover later recalled as being unsure of which unit to send to the scene. All of the patrolling officers were currently on assignment.

Also at 12:10 a.m., Officer Richard Hoffman of the VPD, a young assignee to Juvenile Detention, dressed in plain clothes and riding unit #130, received a radio call alerting him that two teenagers were being shot at the Blue Rock Springs Park, to the east of downtown Vallejo.

He had just driven through the popular parking lot in his unmarked vehicle at approximately 11:55 p.m., a mere 15 minutes before being summoned—or was it "30 minutes or so" prior to the call as Hoffman maintained many years later?—and had seen no cars or people. The park had been closed and there were no young people fighting or drinking as he suspected there might have been on the warm and sultry Fourth of July evening. He headed back to the park, following closely behind unit #119, which had also been notified of the assault.

Blue Rock Springs Park, so named because of the famous sulfur springs that turned rock formations an attractive blue, was a popular park by day, just as it continues to be into the twenty-first century. It was frequently bustling with activity. Families would grill meat and engage in relaxed summertime recline, or play on its green lawns. After dusk, it became a popular lover's lane. With few inhabitants around the barren parking lot, in a region that had not originally been incorporated into the City of Vallejo, it made an attractive, secluded rendezvous for young lovers. VPD Sergeant George Bawart claimed that often there would be four or five cars parked quietly in the dark.

Unit #119, VPD Officers Meyring and Lindemann, while en route to the Blue Rock Springs Park, observed a gray, 4-door 1963 hardtop Cadillac with a California license, CXB-890, approaching from the direction of the park. The car was only traveling at 20 miles per hour, as if it were stealthily attempting to creep away from a shameful act. Thinking that its occupants may be involved in the shooting, or as witnesses to a crime at the very least, the officers made a U-turn on Columbus Parkway, just east of the Blue Rock Springs

Golf Course, and pulled over the car. A man named Andy emerged from behind the driver's wheel. He was immediately recognized by Hoffman as the young officer drove past. Unit #119 continued the stop by demanding identification from the Cadillac's occupants.

Nineteen-year-old Andy dug for his driver's license. He asked the officers, "Is this about the guy laying down back there?" In what was certain to raise suspicions, he had been at the scene of a shooting, noticed Mageau stretched out on the ground writhing around in agony, and had departed without offering aid.

The officers carefully searched the Cadillac, and though no weapons were found, Andy and his 19-year-old passenger, Betty, were eventually booked on suspicion of murder. The young couple was turned over to Sergeant Kenneth Odiorne and taken in for questioning; the Cadillac was impounded and transported to the VPD by Bob's Tow Service. Andy and Betty would suffer the distinction of being the only two people ever arrested for any of the crimes committed by the serial killer later known as the "Zodiac."

While Unit #119 tended to the Cadillac, Hoffman continued on to Blue Rock Springs Park, thus becoming the first officer on the scene. Hoffman took note of what he saw as he entered the parking lot: Ferrin's car, a brown, 2-door, 1963 Chevrolet Corvair Coupe, with its head and taillights on and its left turn signal flashing, front and back. Drawing nearer, he realized that the Corvair's motor was not running. The ignition was in the on position and the transmission was in first gear with no hand brake engaged. The radio was softly playing popular music, an ill-suited requiem. The passenger door was agape. Mageau lay in anguish on his back outside the door. He was perpendicular to the car, gesturing for assistance. He was "shot to pieces," the officer would later recall.

Ferrin's coupe, with Mageau beside it, sat in the park's main parking area, less than 100 feet from Columbus Parkway. Blood was gushing from Mageau's mouth. He had also been shot in the neck and chest. A wound was apparent on his left lower leg. He was moaning in great pain. Looking through the open passenger-side window, Hoffman, aided by a flashlight, observed Ferrin in her blue and white slack-dress slumped away from him against the driver's side door. He could see from that angle that she had incurred three gunshot wounds, two on her upper left arm and one on her right side a few inches below her armpit. A copious amount of blood spatter dotted the car's interior. Darlene's breathing was weak and shallow. She attempted to say something like, "I" or "my," but there was only unintelligible mumbling. A few minutes later, Hoffman checked for a pulse, but couldn't detect one. VPD Sergeant Conway arrived next. He viewed the crime scene and called for an ambulance and an investigator. He was then sent by Hoffman to provide aid to Unit #119: to tell the officers to detain the gray Cadillac, place a hold on its occupants on suspicion of felony, and search the vehicle. Conway returned within a few minutes. He approached Mageau as Hoffman tended Ferrin. Attempting to question Mageau, who was obviously in a great deal of pain, he could only determine that the unknown assailant who had not spoken to his victims was a young, Caucasian male, driving a brown vehicle, alone. This description was quickly relayed to all units.

When VPD Officer Doug Clark arrived—he had been on patrol and had heard the 12:10 a.m. radio call—he attempted to administer first aid to the victims until the ambulance arrived, assisting Hoffman and Conway. The spot where Mageau lay was outlined for future reference. VPD Detective Sergeants Edward "Ed" Rust and John Lynch and Sergeant Odiorne entered the scene before the ambulance.

Rust had also heard the first radio call at 12:10 a.m. He had asked his partner, Lynch, the older detective of the plain-clothed pair, whether they should respond. Lynch thought it was a concern over mere fireworks, and suggested that they ignore the news. A few minutes later, when a second call confirmed the initial report, Rust, who had been steering the unmarked car that general direction, made haste to the park.

After Conway briefed the officers present, the investigation was assigned to Rust and Lynch. Rust took the opportunity to circle the victim's car and peer into the driver's side window, which was, like the passenger window, also rolled down. Many years later, the earnest detective recalled that he could see Ferrin's blue eyes through the narrow slits of her "flickering" eyelids, as though she were trying to open her eyes. (One police report listed Ferrin's eyes as "green," probably confusing them with Mageau's green eyes.) He felt her weak pulse as he asked her what had happened. Only mumbling or a moaning sound could be heard: he could distinguish no real words. As he struggled to hear her, she passed out. He circled the car to check on Mageau and then returned to Ferrin, who was still unconscious. Her breathing was shallow. He again checked her pulse, and again found it weak.

When the Solano ambulance finally arrived, Ferrin was placed in the back, followed by Mageau. The two gunshot victims were rushed to Kaiser Hospital in downtown Vallejo.

Hoffman rode along to gather information, though neither victim spoke during the trip. As an ambulance attendant administered CPR to Ferrin, Hoffman noticed that a small piece of material in the victim's brassier fluttered with each breath she received, alerting him to the fragility of her health. One or more bullets had perforated her lungs; her condition was grave.

As the ambulance hurried away from the scene, Rust peered into the back seat of the blood-bedashed vehicle and discovered Darlene's black and green handbag, a quilt-pattern leather drawstring purse, behind the driver's seat. It held a mere thirteen cents. He rustled for her driver's license in an effort to identify her.

In the inside door panel next to where Darlene had sat, he noticed a bullet hole, one-half to one inch in diameter. He would later order VPD ID Technician John Sparks to dig for a slug. He found papers in the glove compartment. Because the car was registered to J. Ferrin of 930 Monterey Street, the female victim was incorrectly identified in the newspaper the next day as J. Ferrin.

Hoffman had earlier placed Mageau's wallet on the back right fender after he had identified the male victim. Rust later deposited the purse and wallet in room 28 at the Vallejo Police Station. On July 7, Lynch passed the purse with its contents—some personal papers and thirteen cents—to Deputy Coroner Bill Braker.

In an initial search of the parking lot crime scene, Hoffman collected seven empty brass shell casings, all found on the right side, within a few feet of the victims' vehicle. Rust located two additional casings on the right rear floorboard of the car. He noticed a misshapen copper-jacketed slug that fell from Mageau as he was moved. It was not bloody and had no skin on it. The place from where it had been recovered—on the ground where Mageau's back had been—similarly had no blood. Two additional slugs were recovered from inside the Corvair, one in the driver's side door panel and one on the seat after Ferrin was removed. From inscriptions and marks on the base of the casings, the bullets were identified as Winchester Western 9mm Luger (parabellum) rounds ejected from a semi-automatic pistol. All shell casings and slugs were retained and placed into evidence.

There was some confusion over the exact number of shots fired. One or more of the bullets may have struck both victims, or there were shots that the police could not account for from Mageau's testimony and the nine shell casings collected. A police report speculated that at least one casing may have been removed from the scene by the killer, possibly unintentionally. There were a total of nine shots that the investigators could account for, but the assailant may have fired more than that. Eight bullets were eventually recovered.

Rust traveled to the hospital. He found Hoffman, who was assigned to conduct an interview with Mageau if at all possible. But the patient would not be made available for more than a day and a half, surgery and pain management placing higher on the hospital's list of priorities than investigation.

At the scene, Odiorne called for a tow truck to spirit Ferrin's car to the Vallejo Police Station. Prior to the vehicle's removal, ID Technician John Sparks—who had been detailed at 2:00 a.m. by Lieutenant Allbrighton to search the scene, dust for prints, and take photos—captured a total of nine photographs of the car's interior and exterior to be developed later. He considered dusting the car for prints at the scene, but decided that it would be preferable to do this part of his job in the protected confines of the department building. He followed as the tow truck made its way to the Police Station, ensuring that no one tampered with the evidence.

The ambulance reached the hospital at 38 minutes past midnight. Dr. Bordy declared Ferrin dead on arrival (DOA) from catastrophic internal injuries and a fatal loss of blood. The murder became VPD case #243146.

At 1:15 a.m., Odiorne entered the Vallejo Police Station to interview three teenagers who had stumbled upon the crime scene and had alerted the police. The youths told their story, and then each provided a written statement.

Lynch sped to the hospital, spoke to Dr. Bordy, and at 3:30 a.m. proceeded with Sparks to Twin Chapel Funeral Home, where Ferrin's body had been transported, to continue gathering evidence. Sparks captured a total of six photographs of Ferrin's remains. Coroner Dan Horan handed Ferrin's blood-stained clothing to Lynch—one pair of blue shoes, one blue-and-white flowered slack dress, one pair of white panties, and one white brassier—to be tagged and placed into the evidence locker.

The short, scabrous life of Darlene Ferrin had reached its conclusion.

In life, Darlene was a petite, blonde-haired extrovert. At a mere five feet, four inches and 128 pounds, her warmth toward others far outsized her stature. Born Darlene Elizabeth Suennen in Oakland, California on March 17, 1947, she at times had a strained relationship with her family members, which included four sisters and two brothers. But she never lacked for companionship. She had little patience for theories and concepts. Darlene's world was people, and she knew many. Her antennae to her environment were her relationships. She navigated the emotions and drama with comfort and ease. Because she was so sociable and friendly, she attracted a wide circle of friends and acquaintances. Many craved her upbeat friendship and enthusiastic attention. When she was with women, she frequently ended up at the Coronado Inn. She often took men to the Blue Rock Springs Park.

Only 22, she had the responsibilities of a much more seasoned adult pulling at her from all directions. She juggled these as best she could, but if she could not keep up with all of the needs of others, her attitude remained, *oh well; that's life*. Ferrin shouldered the weight of many demands in her short life, but seemed to wear them as an ill-fitting dress. She bore them willingly, but never very well. She was a sister, a wife, a daughter, a mother to a young child, and an employee. Still, she found time to spend with friends—many friends. Already on her second marriage, she nevertheless felt the pull of fun and the carefree lifestyle. She hung out with girlfriends when she could. She socialized with men outside of her marriage—many men—and this caused her problems. Dean, her husband, learned about many of his wife's liaisons at his job as an assistant cook at a restaurant named

Caesar's Palace, his wife's "friendliness" the fodder for concern if not ribbing.

Because of her many male companions, her behavior was unusual and noteworthy. Mageau would later claim that while some people called her derogatory names, he never considered her in anything but positive terms. To him, she was "nice" and "kind." If any of her relationships with men became sexual trysts, she was discrete. She left no conclusive evidence that she ever cheated on her husband. Mageau only reported kissing and hand holding.

Nevertheless, her second marriage began to exhibit the same trouble as her first, short-lived, marriage, which both began and ended abruptly. Investigators learned from her parents that Darlene left home after a family dispute on November 25, 1965, the year she graduated from Hogan High School. She had met James Phillips in August of that year, after his discharge from the Army. The couple lived together before marrying in Reno on New Year's Day, 1966. For months, Phillips had no job, and lived off any meager earnings that Darlene provided for the couple, which included work in San Francisco.

Darlene's parents did not hear from their daughter again for almost a year, until October of 1966, when the couple came to live with them. Phillips claimed that he owned a newspaper in the Virgin Islands, where the couple said that they had spent the previous five months. He also intimated that he had been an undercover agent for the U.S. Army. Darlene's mother discovered that her son-in-law had no money, no job, and no income. Mr. and Mrs. Suennen soon tired of watching him mooch off of their daughter, so he was given an ultimatum: get a job or move out.

Phillips quickly found employment with *The Daily Republic*, Fairfield's newspaper, as an assistant editor. Just as quickly, however, he left, just as he had abandoned other jobs. Though he only had a high school education, he was very intelligent, his IQ measuring 138. Mrs. Suennen later thought that he had worked for *The Daily Republic* for about three weeks. In truth, he was there for only five days, January 6-11, 1967, and did not return. Following his departure, several people called the paper to inquire about him—mostly regarding money owed to them—but he gave no forwarding address when he and Darlene left the area for Pennsylvania.

When the couple returned to Vallejo a couple of months later, the marriage was not going well. Darlene had finally adopted her parent's view of her husband. She suspected he was bad for her, but she needed to arrive at that conclusion for herself. She realized that she had so many friends—and an easy time making more if needed. If she wanted another husband, she knew that too could be arranged. Phillips had become an anchor that was a drag on her social life. Darlene made the decision to travel to Reno and file for divorce.

In testimony in divorce court, Darlene cited emotional and physical abuse from her husband. She claimed that he used four letter words frequently, and because of his penchant for knocking her around, her health was adversely affected. She felt nervous and had difficulty paying her medical bills from three hospitalizations. On June 2, 1967, the divorce decree of the young, ill-matched couple was final. The judge granted Darlene's petition without incident.

Phillips claimed that he did not want the divorce, but neither did he contest it. He moved to San Francisco, and had no contact with Darlene except to sign divorce papers. Darlene's mother told the police that two of her family members recognized him sitting with a pregnant woman in the back row at Darlene's funeral, but she herself had not seen him, and he had no contact with family, not even at the funeral.

Following her divorce, Darlene quickly married Dean Ferrin. But she could not stop running around with other men.

Darlene's proclivity to date provided fertile ground for suspects— and speculation. Anyone who participated in an intense, emotional relationship with her may have had motive enough for murder. All of her friends had to be considered by law enforcement officials, and it took much time and effort on their part to untangle her relationship past as best they could. When her history began to emerge, some people called her names, like "whore," as though her behavior merited her murder. Those who knew her well did not share the sentiment.

One of her later suitors was Gordon, a 21-year-old sailor. On September 1, he stopped into Terry's Waffle Shop, Darlene's place of employment at the time of her death. There he learned of her murder. He was on leave from the Naval Submarine School in New London, Connecticut, after being released from the Naval Schools Command

Nuclear Power School in Idaho Falls, Idaho. He discovered that the Vallejo police wanted to speak with him. He headed immediately to the police station, and was openly cooperative.

He provided a statement to Rust. He told the investigator that he met had Darlene in December of 1968 while she was working at Terry's, the restaurant on Magazine Street at Interstate 80, where Darlene was known as the chatty, outgoing server. Single at the time, and on leave from the Navy, Gordon had traveled to visit his family in Fremont, California. From there, he drove to Vallejo and made Darlene's acquaintance.

About a month after that introduction, Darlene planned a trip with friends to San Francisco. Gordon tagged along, and got to know her as the two walked along the beach. Over the next few weeks, she and Gordon would meet up regularly. Sometimes he would drive her home from work in the early hours of the morning.

At the end of January, or early February, 1969, he picked her up at 1:00 a.m., went to the Blue Rock Springs Park—a favorite location of hers—and then took her home at 1:30 or 2:00. Darlene insisted that he come in and meet her husband. After some persuasion, he reluctantly agreed to the awkward encounter. He thought Dean friendly on their first and only meeting, when her husband took a break from painting his home to meet him.

Gordon explained to Rust that he felt free in flirting with Darlene only because he was not in a relationship at the time. His knowledge that she was married, however, was a constant reminder to him that there were limits to his advances. He soon found Darlene clingy and desperate to get out of her second marriage.

The next, and last, time that Gordon saw Darlene was one or two days before his leave ended and he was required to travel back to Idaho Falls. He went out dancing with Darlene and some friends to San Francisco. Or was it Oakland? Gordon could not recall which. Wherever it was, Dean did not join them, but was fully aware that Gordon was going along, ostensibly as Darlene's date. Gordon brought Darlene home at 1:00 a.m., and even met her parents who were babysitting her daughter that night.

It was on this final "date" that Darlene confided in Gordon that her marriage felt like bondage. She wanted out, and hoped that he would take her along when he returned to Idaho and his nuclear training with the military. He dissuaded her, pointing to the best interest of Deena, her child. She had a stable home, which he could not afford to provide. Bobbie, a friend of Darlene's, would later claim that Gordon promised to send money so that Darlene could eventually leave Dean and move to Idaho Falls. Gordon denied that there were any such plans. Later, in Idaho, he did receive two or three letters from her, but he never replied. He called her when she requested it in one of the mailings. She told him over the phone that she thought she was pregnant. When in the next letter he learned that she had been in the hospital, Gordon suspected that she had gotten an abortion somewhere.

Darlene had become too demanding, Gordon told Rust. She requested that he visit her in May during his next leave. He decided against it. He *did* travel to the Bay Area, but only to be with his family. He kept his distance from Vallejo. He didn't even call Darlene to say he was on the West Coast. Gordon explained that he had decided not see Darlene again, realizing that the relationship meant far more to her than it did to him.

Evidently, the magic was gone. Darlene would remain in Vallejo to face her responsibilities, and in just a few weeks' time, her demise.

✑

At the hospital, Dr. Jantzen attended to Mageau who had been transferred to the Intensive Care Unit (ICU) in critical condition. The hospital staff hurriedly removed his clothing, which curiously included far too many garments than the weather would suggest. He had on three pairs of trousers, one t-shirt, three sweaters, and one long-sleeve buttoned shirt. Why he was so attired on a hot July evening in Northern California would raise suspicions among the police. Hoffman received these garments and transferred them to the evidence locker at the Vallejo Police Station.

The medical staff provided Mageau with sedatives which would eventually enable him to descend into a recuperative sleep, at which time the necessary operations could be performed on his damaged body.

By 8:25 p.m., surgery on Mageau was finally complete. Dr. Jantzen passed to Detective Lynch a slug that he and Dr. Black had removed from the patient's leg. It had been marked by Black and placed in a glass bottle with some liquid. The container was labeled and deposited in the ID property room evidence locker. It was not until Sunday afternoon at 3:00 p.m. that Doctor Scott acceded to Rust's request to be given a chance to interview Mageau, and even then only for a short time because the patient would soon succumb to the effects of additional sedatives. Rust eagerly took the opportunity to question an obviously medicated patient.

Born with his identical twin brother on October 29, 1949, Michael Renault Mageau was 19 at the time of the attack. Like his brother, he sported black hair. He had green eyes and a slender frame. Measuring an even six feet in height, he weighed a mere 170 pounds, in his opinion an embarrassingly light weight for such a tall young man. It was his shame in being skinny that prompted the layers of clothing he wore that night, he would explain. He was attempting to fill out his physique for any who would look at him. Darlene knew of his layering and joked with him about it, he later claimed.

Despite graduating from Hogan High School, Mageau lacked strong ambition. He had no shortage of imagination, however, which he demonstrated as an intrepid teller of tall tales. He worked for his father as an exterminator at Doyen Pest Control Service, a career that would be cut short by the attack.

The subsequent investigation revealed that Mageau's past was not squeaky clean. Rust had checked police records at 4:30 a.m. and found no information relevant to the attack, but there was a file on Mageau. He had been arrested for petty theft at the Purity Store on Springs Road the previous September 6. At that time, he had given a false name to police, that of William James Janssen. The police had found on him an ID with the address of 1214 Oakwood, Apt. 12. The police file, #214080, contained a five by eight inch photo of the young delinquent. There was nothing else in the files under his name or the alias he had provided in 1968. An FBI report on Mageau finally arrived at the VPD on August 29, but provided little additional information.

Lawlessness was by no means a pattern in the young man's life; he kept out of trouble for the most part. Though Darlene had at first been afraid of him, Michael was easily able to justify this to investigators. He had told her that he was wanted in New York City. It was just an immature ruse to impress a pretty woman. He later described joking with her, telling her that he was a gangster like Warren Beatty.

Before he drifted off into a drug-induced stupor, Mageau responded to as many of Detective Rust's questions as he could. From the short answers offered—Mageau's tongue was severely injured and his jaw was broken—Rust was able to piece together many of the details of the horror that had occurred that night in the park on the outskirts of Vallejo:

Mageau and Ferrin's contact that day began at four o'clock in the afternoon, Mageau explained haltingly. Darlene telephoned and suggested they attend a movie in San Francisco. The initial plans were for her to pick him up at his house, 864 Beechwood Avenue, at 7:30 p.m. These plans were scuttled, however, when she didn't arrive. Darlene called at 8:00 p.m. to say that she had to take her 15-year-old sister, Christine, to the Miss Firecracker contest, an annual Vallejo gathering sponsored by the Chamber of Commerce. *The Vallejo Times-Herald* reported that because Christine was a runner up in the contest, she was invited to ride in the boat, the Genora, that night in the Mare Island Channel lighted boat parade. The Genora won first place. Darlene agreed to go to his house as soon as she was done shuttling her sister. She called at 10:30 p.m. to say that she'd be over shortly.

Ferrin drove along Georgia Street to travel from her home on Virginia Street to the Mageau residence, ominously covering some of the same pavement traveled by Faraday on his way to pick up Jensen six and a half months earlier.

Ferrin finally arrived at 11:30 p.m., or shortly after, by Mageau's recollection. Both of them were hungry because neither had had any dinner. They departed Mageau's parents' house, and after a short jog in the road, turned left, or west, at Springs Road. Darlene wanted to talk to Michael about something, but she never got the chance to share her information—or even mention the topic.

Abruptly, Darlene turned the car around, performing a U-turn near Mr. Ed's Restaurant at 1339 Springs Road, and headed east. Neither would eat that night. They drove to Blue Rock Springs Park at Mageau's suggestion. Once they arrived, Darlene turned the car off and extinguished the headlights. The radio remained on, playing the music they enjoyed.

In the park, as the couple entered, there were three vehicles present. This is what Mageau maintained in later interviews. Another possibility is that these cars entered the lot just after the couple arrived, as Detective Rust would report from his bedside interview. Firecrackers exploded and some rowdy young people joked and carried on, their voices elevated. Soon, the three cars left, only a few minutes at most after Mageau and Ferrin had arrived. The couple sat alone in the quiet of the parking lot.

Shortly after that, a vehicle coming from the direction of Springs Road pulled into the lot, stopping behind and to the left of Ferrin's brown Corvair. It approached as close as six to eight feet. Its headlights went dark. Michael asked Darlene if she knew the person who had approached them so closely in an otherwise vacant lot. She replied, "Oh, never mind." Mageau was not sure whether she knew the driver, or she simply did not want to talk about the car, whoever its occupant. He had often chided her about her wide circle of acquaintances.

The shape of this newly-arrived car looked similar to a Corvair, according to Mageau, not unlike Ferrin's. He could not see its color; he did not get a good look. The car remained in place for about one minute, and then the driver—the only person in the car as far as he could tell—drove off at high rate of speed toward downtown Vallejo.

It—or maybe it was an entirely different car that only looked similar to the one that had just left—returned about five minutes later, coming from the direction of downtown Vallejo, where it had previously departed. Later, Mageau wasn't sure if it was the same car or not.

This time, the strange driver maneuvered his car behind and slightly to the right of their vehicle, as close as five feet. The speed of the departure, the menacing stance behind the couple's car, and the similarity of size and shape led Mageau to suspect that the second car was in fact the same one they had just seen. Whether it was the return of the other vehicle or not, this second car posed an imminent threat.

As it approached, the couple believed it was a different vehicle. They thought that a police unit was now behind them so they readied their identification cards. They may have concluded that the police had arrived in response to the exploding firecrackers. The couple may have considered it part of the weekend ritual of parking in a secluded location only to be hustled away by a concerned police officer, a familiar dance between teenagers and the police in the 1960s. The illumination of a brilliant spotlight seemed to confirm the couple's suspicions that they were being accosted by law enforcement.

A man stepped out of the vehicle and made his way to the passenger side of Ferrin's car. No words were exchanged. No warning was provided. As the man neared, Mageau heard muffled sounds, possibly from a gun with a suppressor (more commonly known as a "silencer," which does reduce the sound of the shots, but not as much as is generally believed). Many years later, Mageau described the sounds as similar to firecrackers: "pow, pow, pow, crack, crack, crack," or something approaching the sound of a BB gun.

Pain ripped into Mageau as a bullet struck his neck. The gunman fired again and again without speaking a word. Mageau felt as though the shooting went on and on for a long period of time. As the shots continued, he found his way into the back seat, half diving, half falling.

Once he was satisfied that the passenger had received a sufficient number of wounds, the stranger turned his attention to Ferrin and repeatedly shot her several times as well. Then he casually walked back in the direction of his car.

Mageau yelled in searing pain or yelled at his assailant. On hearing his victim, the shooter returned to the open window. Years later, Mageau would explain that he had managed to hoist himself up while still in the back seat. The stranger fired some more: one shot in Mageau's back and one in his left leg. He aimed and fired two more bullets into Ferrin before returning to his vehicle.

The two victims were in rough shape. Mageau said something to Ferrin, but got only a moan in response. He fumbled around to escape the car, but discovered that the inside door handle was broken. He reached outside the car to unlatch the door and let himself fall. As he collapsed to the ground, he saw the gunman back his car around and then drive out of parking lot, heading back toward Springs Road at what his victim described as a "high rate of speed." Mageau saw only the rear part of the car, which he noted was similar in shape and color to that of Ferrin's, possibly a lighter shade of brown. The car bore California license plates whose specifics he could not read.

Mageau struggled in his bed to describe for Rust the events that followed the shots.

Approximately 8 to 10 minutes after the attacker departed, three "hippy" types, two males and a female, approached at a distance in a car. Mageau pleaded with them to come over to help. The girl told him to lie still as they went for help. He estimated it was another 5 to 10 agonizing minutes passed before an officer in an unmarked car arrived.

Mageau described his attacker as between 26 and 30 years of age, five feet eight inches, and heavyset with a beefy, not muscular, build. He estimated that the man who shot him was between 195 and 200 pounds, but not blubbery fat. He had short, curly, light brown hair—almost blond. He wore a short-sleeve blue shirt, but Mageau could not tell whether it was light blue or dark blue. Because he only saw the face from a side view, he was unable to give useful specifics that would lead to the creation of a composite picture. He did note that his assailant had a large face with no facial hair and no glasses. The large face was the only unusual attribute he could recall. It was dark so he did not get a good look.

When Rust pointed out that the police had discovered him with the car lights on, Mageau explained that Darlene had turned them on after the attack to draw attention to her emergency. He couldn't remember if he had asked her to do so. She may have been flashing them for help. He may have been the one who flashed the lights, he admitted. He couldn't recall.

As the hospital interview wound down, Mageau added a few additional remarks. He said that he could think of no one who would want to do this to him. He didn't think Darlene was a target, either. If Darlene had an enemy, she would have told him, he was certain. Petty jealousies were her only problems with other people.

Michael Mageau descended into sleep, and Detective Rust quietly left his hospital room.

A few weeks later, still in the hospital recuperating, Mageau would share additional details with the press. He explained that while the flashlight was first illuminated from within the strange car, causing them to believe that it was a police officer, the light was soon extinguished—only to be relit when the gunshots erupted and the man was standing beside him. The stranger's headlights remained on throughout the attack. Mageau described the assailant's vehicle, suggesting it could have been a 1958 or 1959 Ford Falcon, brown or bronze in color. Its body was similar in shape to Ferrin's 1963 Corvair. This time, he explained that the attacker's car had departed from the parking lot with speed enough to scatter gravel, but it did not burn rubber or squeal tires. This additional information, which later became part of a story in *The San Francisco Chronicle* in August, may not have been exactly correct, Mageau admitted. His nervousness and his weakness from a month in critical condition in an ICU made him uncertain about the specifics of his experience. He believed that what he shared was more of an impression.

℃℧

At 12:40 a.m., less than one hour after the sound of the gunshots, the telephone rang again at the Vallejo Police Station. The killer had not yet completed his evening of terror. Because the 911 emergency phone system had yet to be conceived of, the caller had dialed the operator and requested that his call be transferred to the police department. Nancy Slover answered, as she always did, "Vallejo Police Department."

The caller recited the following message:

"I'd like to report a double murder. If you will go one mile east on Columbus Parkway to the public park, you will find the kids in a brown car. I shot them with a Luger. I also killed those kids last Christmas. Good-bye."

According to one police report, the man started his words instead with, "I want to report a double murder..." Another quoted, "I called to report a double murder..."

Slover, the young police dispatch operator who fielded both this call and the initial one about the shooting, later attempted to relate as much information about the conversation as she could for VPD Captain L. Wade Bird. She wrote out her description of the caller's voice in detail, noting that she had heard no trace of an accent. It was even and consistent, soft but forceful. It was mature, and the caller did not stop until he had completed his message. When she tried to wrest from him additional information—she had said something like, "Yes, we have a reported shooting in that area. I still need your name and location."—he merely spoke louder to cover her voice. She related that his words sounded as though they were read, or at very least, well-rehearsed. His voice struck her as monotone, completely devoid of any emotion. Years later, she would add that she could not detect any slurring from drug or alcohol intoxication.

The sign-off was very troubling to the youthful dispatcher. His "good-bye" appeared to be a taunt drawn out in a deeper and slower voice. She would later describe the sound as eerie and lacking in feeling. When first spoken by the killer, it gave her chills. She was left with a "scary-type creepy feeling from the call."

Slover attempted to patch in the desk officer on duty. Though she connected the line, the caller hung up before anyone else could hear him. He dropped off suddenly, just as he had when attacking Mageau and Ferrin in the Blue Rock Springs parking lot. He disappeared as quickly and surely as he had after shooting Faraday and Jensen on Lake Herman Road the previous December.

Upon receiving reports of the taunting call, the VPD set about finding its origin. Mrs. Johnson of Pacific Telephone and Telegraph (PT&T) contacted the VPD at 12:47 a.m. Betty Main, also of PT&T, had traced it to a pay telephone at Joe's, a Union 76 service station located at the corner of Tuolumne Road and Springs Road. It was not far from downtown Vallejo; it was even closer to the Vallejo Police Station the man had called. Main's supervisor forbade her from providing any statement to the police.

Sergeant Conway rushed to the phone booth. He was met there by unit #122, Officers Agenbroad and Peach. But the caller had absconded. Conway patiently waited until ID Technician Waricher arrived to gather any evidence that the scene would yield.

Sergeant Odiorne also visited the booth that night. After traveling to the hospital and learning that Ferrin was deceased, he had directed Waricher to the location. It was later confirmed that the Union 76 station had been closed at the time of the telephone call, having shuttered for business that evening at 8:25.

The assailant and his victims were not the only witnesses to the shooting at Blue Rock Springs that night. The son of the park's caretaker, 22-year-old George Ronald Bryant, who worked at the nearby Selby Smelter, was attempting to sleep at his home at the park, a mere 800 feet from the spot of the attack.

Around midnight, after flipping over his pillow, he was lying on his stomach looking out the window in lieu of sleep. All the house lights were on. He heard the young people with their firecrackers as if foreshadowing the gunfire to come, but he could see nothing. He was then jolted by the sound of a gunshot, followed after a pause by another shot, then a series of rapid shots. These, he observed, were much louder than the firecrackers he had heard. A car exited the lot at what he described as "super speed," with squealing tires that burned rubber. The July 6, 1969 edition of *The Vallejo Times-Herald* quoted a detective sergeant, "[Bryant] heard the car take off at a high rate of speed, peeling rubber and cutting corners." Bryant was too far away to capture any visual details of the shooter or the car, and was uncertain of the direction the car departed.

Initially, he believed that the shots were from more powerful, louder fireworks and took no action. He contacted the police less than 24 hours after the murder with the few details that he could provide, agreeing to accompany officers to the park to recreate the scene to the best of his ability the night after the attack.

❧

One victim dead, another seriously wounded and in critical condition. This unexpected and unexplained act of violence set in motion a police investigation that would in time engage the entire VPD, and draw it into contact with numerous other police departments throughout California, as well as the FBI in Sacramento, San Francisco, Los Angeles, and Washington, D.C. At first, it appeared a unique event, not connected to any other known crimes. That changed with the assailant's telephone call. The brutality of the two Vallejo-area events, coupled with the possibility—or inevitability—

of more carnage, mobilized the department. Investigation is the duty of law enforcement, and the VPD set about performing that task to the best of their ability. With great personal sacrifice, and the aid of the forensic technology of the day, the officers did an admirable job of collecting the scant evidence, amassing the facts, and running down many, many leads in the effort to preserve life and balance the scales of justice.

At the scene, even before the arrival of the ambulance, Detectives Ed Rust and John Lynch were selected to head up the entire investigation. All aspects of the Sisyphean labor would be directed by, and coordinated though, these two dedicated professionals. They had no idea, as they settled into the work, of the personal and professional costs that this case would exact from them, or of the pitifully few answers that their years of work would produce.

The scene was processed. Officers Cruz and Guerra made a detailed sketch of the area, which would provide an exact layout of the car and victims for anyone unable to visit the crime scene before it was dismantled. They captured an excellent representation of the park with its circular stone wall, precise measurements between Ferrin's car and all relevant landmarks, and the exact location that Mageau was found as he struggled to survive on the gravel next to the vehicle.

Fire Captain James O'Gara and Fireman Williams arrived with a fire unit to illuminate the area in a search for physical evidence. With the limits of technology of 1969, not much was found. By 2:00 a.m., with no additional results, the search was called off by Lieutenant Allbrighton. Darlene's coupe was impounded and towed to the Vallejo Police Department by AAA to be dusted for prints and to retrieve any bullets or other evidence.

Deputy Villarreal informed Rust that he had been at the scene just before midnight, and had observed a blue Ford Sedan parked near to where the Corvair eventually stopped. Because he had been summoned away on another call, Villarreal explained, he did not get a chance to speak to its occupants or observe anything else about the vehicle. He did not see Ferrin's Corvair or any other car.

A police unit was sent to notify Mageau's parents of the shooting. No one was present at 864 Beechwood Avenue, the home of Michael and his father, when the unit arrived, even though the house lights were on, the television was blaring, and the front door unlocked. Michael, eager to spend time with Darlene, had apparently left in great haste. Another unit was dispatched to notify Dean Ferrin, Darlene's husband, at the couple's home, 1300 Virginia Street.

At 2:35 a.m., Dean entered the Vallejo Police Station, accompanied by his employer, William "Bill" Leigh. Rust had arrived at the station at 1:15 a.m., after the officer had made a quick trip to the hospital and a visit to the phone booth used by the killer.

Dean, who knew only that Darlene had been shot, became visibly distraught when he was gently told that his wife was dead. He related that he last saw her at about 10:30 p.m. when she left Caesar's, 315 Tennessee Street, with her sister, Christine. The agenda she was following, according to Dean, called for her to drop her sister off at their parents' home, deliver the babysitters to their homes, and then return home herself. She never had a chance to follow through on these plans.

Leigh added that he spoke on the phone to Darlene at about 11:30 p.m. and requested that she find some fireworks for a party to be held at the Ferrin's house once he and her husband were done with work. Darlene had agreed. When the two men finally arrived at Dean's home at 1:30 a.m., Darlene was not there. Dean noted that he had received two "hang-up" telephone calls as they waited for her.

Odiorne interviewed Christine at 3:15 that morning about her deceased sister. She corroborated the information that Ferrin and Leigh had shared. She added that she and her sister had also stopped at Terry's, Darlene's place of employment, on the way to 1300 Virginia Street. While there, Darlene had only interacted with a couple of her co-workers. Christine acknowledged that she knew Michael Mageau, but that she didn't know anything specific about him.

Later, in August, Christine described for the VPD a man who had once come to the door asking to speak with her sister. She estimated the stranger's height at five feet eight inches, and his weight to be 165-170. He appeared to be around 30, with dark hair and casual clothing. He drove a late model, blue, hardtop Pontiac GTO. She had reported at that time that if she had heard his name, she couldn't remember it. For Odiorne, she could offer no additional information about her sister, or anyone who would want her killed.

Meanwhile, at the Twin Chapel Funeral Home, Dr. Shirai removed two copper-jacketed slugs from the lifeless body of Darlene Ferrin, one from her right second rib, the other from between the left seventh and eighth ribs. He marked these and personally passed them on to the VPD which was tasked with collecting all relevant evidence. The skilled Contra Costa County Pathologist conducted the autopsy, concluding that any of the four bullets that struck her—two that had passed through her and two that were removed from her—could have been fatal. Once shot, she never had a chance.

At 8:00 the morning after the attack, Sparks lifted two partial prints from the right door handle of Ferrin's car. He was preparing to do the work at 4:45 a.m., but was interrupted by Allbrighton who told him that he could go home for a couple hours of sleep and return to the work later in the morning.

He also collected two additional slugs, one from the driver's side door and the other from the back of the driver's seat. These were tagged and placed in the evidence locker. Two weeks later, VPD Captain Bird sent all the gathered slugs and shell casings by registered mail, #41991, to Sacramento to be reviewed by the California Department of Justice, specifically the CII.

Rust and Lynch returned to the crime scene at 6:55 in the morning, hoping to find evidence missed by previous searches. They found none. While they scoured the lot, Darlene's sister, Linda Doris Del Buono, arrived with her husband, Steven. She provided the detectives with the names of a few of Darlene's closest friends.

Ferrin's other sister, Pamela, would later offer the police an intriguing lead. On August 18, she told VPD Sergeant Jack Mulinax that while babysitting for Darlene several months before her sister's death she had received an unusual telephone call from a man asking to speak with Darlene. Pamela thought his name was David, but this may have been fed to her by the officer. The strange caller demanded to meet with Darlene as soon as possible. Upon hearing of the call, Darlene told her sister that she wanted nothing to do with the man, and to just forget it. She never elaborated on her relationship with the caller, nor explained her desire for distance from him.

Detective Rust gathered the two girls who were the Ferrin's babysitters for the evening of the attack, having learned of their identities from Bill Leigh, Dean's employer. Pamela, aged 15, and her 14-year-old friend, Janet, met him at 6:45 p.m., July 6, in room 16 of the Vallejo Police Station. With their protective fathers present, the two girls reported their experiences.

Pamela was the actual babysitter of Darlene's daughter, 18-month-old Deena. This was the first time she had sat for the Ferrins, though she had met Darlene prior to that night. Janet had joined her only to keep her company during the evening. The two girls had been picked up at 7:00 p.m. by Darlene's father. Christine was along for the ride. The sisters left the Ferrin home at 7:45 p.m., telling the two girls that they were going to the festivities downtown and that they would be back at 10:00 p.m. Darlene explained that when she returned she was going to go to San Francisco. She did not tell them with whom or why. When Darlene called the house around 9:00 p.m., she was told of a phone call she had received from a female—and was instructed to go to Terry's Restaurant. Darlene returned home at 11:30 p.m. or shortly before, according to the girls. She now said that she was not going to San Francisco, but would host a small party later that night when her husband got home. She announced that she was leaving to buy fireworks, and would be back by 12:30 a.m. After cleaning up the house a little, she left at 11:40 p.m. That was the last time the girls saw her.

At approximately 1:30 a.m., according to the babysitters, Dean Ferrin arrived home with some friends. He wasn't worried about his wife's absence, explaining that "she's always late." Dean took the girls home shortly before 2:00 a.m., and was apparently going right back home. The babysitters could add nothing more to the investigation, and said that they were not close to Darlene. Both were thanked for their assistance.

Another babysitter of the Ferrins, a girl named Karen, provided a provocative statement when she met with investigators. Though Karen was not present on the night of the attack, she related her experience of sitting for Darlene and Dean on a previous occasion. She reported that while babysitting for them in February or March of that year—they were living at 560 Wallace at the time—she looked out of the window at about 10:00 p.m. and noticed a Caucasian man sitting in a white American sedan. She observed that he remained in place for a couple of hours, but had left by the time Dean returned home, shortly after midnight. Karen estimated the man to be middle-aged. She had only gotten a glimpse of him when he either lit a cigarette or illuminated an interior light.

Karen shared this information with Darlene the next night as her employer put on makeup in the bathroom, Karen told the investigators. Darlene had responded, "I guess he's checking up on me. I heard he was back from out of state. He doesn't want anyone to know what I saw him do. I saw him murder someone." Karen heard a short name, possibly with only three or four letters, and a last name that was nearly as short. She could not reproduce it for the investigators. Karen recalled that Darlene seemed genuinely fearful of this man, who had evidently also checked up on her at Terry's Restaurant.

The officers were intrigued by this lead. They suggested that Karen be hypnotized in an attempt to recover any hidden memories of the man. When they approached a hypnotist, they inquired as to whether the short name could be recovered, or any additional information about this man who may have attended a painting party at the Ferrin's residence in May of 1969. The hypnotist was equivocal about the likelihood of success.

A session with a hypnotist was eventually scheduled, and Karen was able to provide some additional facts. She described the stranger she had seen out of Darlene's window as a heavyset, middle-aged, white male with a very round face, and curly, wavy dark brown hair. The white sedan had a large windshield. She recalled a phone ringing, which suggested to the hypnotist that Karen might have been afraid of testifying in court (and therefore subconsciously she refused to remember anything more about him). Regarding the painting party, Karen recalled being present and caring for Darlene's daughter, Deena. When three unidentified young men arrived for the party, Darlene felt very uncomfortable with them and eventually left, but not before advising Karen to stay away from them.

❦

The investigation into the shooting brought the VPD into contact with many of the victim's friends and relatives.

Judith, a 25-year-old friend of Darlene's, went to the Vallejo Police Station to provide a statement on July 6. She described an argument that she had witnessed between Darlene and her husband, Dean. Following a movie that she and Darlene had attended, Darlene had wanted to go hang out at the Coronado Inn, but her husband had refused to take her. This set off a heated exchange. Judith chose not to intervene. The family spat drove a wedge between Darlene and Judith, the latter choosing to see less of her former friend in the future, though she used to be very close to Darlene when they worked together at Terry's restaurant.

Michael Mageau's parents, Robert and Carmen Mageau, submitted to interviews, but could not offer much additional information. Carmen was approached by Detectives Rust and Lynch at her ex-husband's home, 864 Beachwood Street, just after midnight on July 6. When she had initially heard of the shooting the day before, she had traveled with her two sons—Michael's twin, Stephen, and a younger son—from her home in Southern California.

As far as his parents knew, Michael had no enemies. His father Robert, age 43, was given a preliminary interview when he went to the Vallejo Police Station at 9:00 a.m. on the morning following the attack. He had stayed at the Kentwig motel the previous night. Rust and Odiorne had the unenviable task of informing him that his son had been shot and was in critical condition at the hospital. At the time, Robert had agreed to inform his ex-wife and other sons about the shooting, after which he rushed to the hospital to check on Michael.

Robert was interviewed again that night at 8:00 at the Vallejo Police Station. He reported that Darlene telephoned the house daily, sometimes more than once a day. He received many of these calls and dutifully passed the phone to his son. Darlene had called several times on the day of the shooting, but he was unaware of how they had finally gotten together that evening. Though he had never met his son's friend in person, Carmen had, and approved of her.

When twin brother Stephen was questioned, he informed Rust and Lynch that he had lived in Los Angeles from February until June of that year. He had moved back to Vallejo at that time, only to return to Los Angeles three weeks prior to the attack. He stated that he chose to reside with his mother because he didn't get along very well with his father. He acknowledged that many people were aware of Darlene's love of the Blue Rock Spring Park, a place she had gone with many men. He emphatically added that his twin had no enemies. Michael would have said something to him if he had.

Rust interviewed Darlene's co-workers on July 6. He was ushered into the restaurant's office by Marlin, the manager, who brought several of the restaurant's employees, one at a time, off the floor to speak with the officer. Bobbie was first.

Bobbie stated that she and Darlene were good friends. On the night of her death, Darlene had worked until 4:00 p.m. and then had gone home. Later, at 10:30 p.m., Bobbie reported, Darlene and her sister, "Chris," had come into the restaurant. They had only spoken for a few minutes. Darlene had promised to return to talk about something—nothing important as far as she could tell. Darlene and her sister left shortly before 11:00. Bobbie was certain that her friend had spoken only to other waitresses. When pressed, she could think of no one with a motive to harm her friend. She knew that Darlene had many male friends, but did not think that any of them posed a threat to her. She recalled the name of Warren, a man who had given her and Darlene a ride to work one day.

Rust then spoke with an older woman, a waitress named Evelyn. She described her contact with the deceased as a sort of mother/daughter relationship. Evelyn knew that Darlene had many boyfriends. Darlene had confided to her that she thought Dean didn't love her anymore, and that the marriage was just about over. After hearing this, Evelyn noticed that Darlene spent more time with other men. Though Evelyn knew that her friend and co-worker went out with many guys, she was sure that none of them was a serious relationship and that Darlene had had no problems with any of them.

When Rust spoke to Lois, the third waitress that day, he heard a familiar theme: Darlene had many male friends but that none of them was a danger to her. Lois only knew one of the men who came in with his brother, both of whom worked in pest control (apparently Michael and Steve Mageau). Rust then spoke with the manager last and learned that Darlene had worked there since April of 1968. Marlin too was aware that Darlene ran around with many men.

The three waitresses shared with Rust that a man named George Waters wanted to date Ferrin, but she did not want to go out with him. To them, he seemed bitter and gave her a hard time. They reported that Waters was jealous and became visibly upset when Darlene did not pay him enough attention. She was friendly toward him only to keep him at a distance. They described him as short and stocky with black hair.

George Waters was identified as a part-time bartender who sometimes worked at the Elks Club (though very sporadically, according to Myra, the Elks' office manager), as well as Casa De Vallejo, Kentwig, and the Fireside—all Vallejo bars. Born in Manila, the Philippines, George was not a citizen of the United States. He was a promising lead for police, his name having been raised by other people in Darlene's circle. Some described him as the only person who truly sparked fear in Darlene. One of Darlene's sisters explained that he was attracted to the now-deceased woman and craved her attention, but that the interest was not reciprocated. He had often visited Terry's Waffle Shop when the bars closed at 2:00 a.m. He welcomed Darlene's friendliness, and frequently drove her home at the end of her shift. Sometimes, according to Waters, she even called him for rides *to* work at Terry's, a fact confirmed to police by Dean Ferrin. He had once purchased a faded red 1951 Ford pick-up truck from the Ferrins, but had only met Dean on that one occasion.

Eventually, Waters' actions took on a sinister edge. Darlene related her concerns to Mageau, and he shared these with his twin brother, Steve, who never met the man. She related that Waters had threatened to rape her or "get into bed with her one way or another," but she had been able to defuse the situation, and he eventually left the apartment. Steve told Lynch that he and his brother had not taken the claim too seriously at the time.

In addition to the faded red truck (described by some as pink), he owned a brown car, possibly a Corvair. The possibility of a brown Corvair instantly seized the attention of the investigators who sought a vehicle of similar size and color: the one that was driven by Ferrin's murderer. On July 7, Lynch sent a teletype to CII in Sacramento requesting all information about Darlene's fear-evoking friend. The reply came back: "No Record."

Further investigation revealed that Waters had worked at Kaiser Steel. On July 7, Odiorne telephoned an employee of the company and learned that Waters had been laid off on June 13 and was residing in Yountville, some 23 miles north on Highway 29. Odiorne immediately contacted the Napa County Sheriff's Office (NCSO) to arrange for an officer to escort Officer Blair and Odiorne to the correct Yountville address.

NCSO Sergeant Munk marshalled the two VPD officers to Waters' house, in front of which they found a 1964 maroon Pontiac with California plates, MGW-681. By a radio call, they learned that it was registered to a George Waters. While the officers were observing the home, a man matching Waters' description exited and approached the Pontiac, in which he drove off. Odiorne requested that Munk follow up on this lead by speaking with neighbors and uncovering all that he could about the man's cars, his friends, and anything else relevant to the investigation. Munk agreed and asked Odiorne to contact him at 8:00 p.m. the following evening.

Dean Ferrin acknowledged that he had met Waters once, and only once, when he sold the stocky man his truck. He had no reason to believe that the truck buyer was involved with his wife. Leigh knew him a little better, explaining that Waters had often pestered Darlene when she lived at an apartment near him. He would hang around, apparently attempting to "pick her up."

But Waters was old news. When questioned by Lynch and Rust on July 11, he admitted to flirting with Darlene, whom he called "Deedee," but denied ever threatening her. He had met her around the beginning of the year. He said he teased her, sometimes to the point where she became angry. By the time of the attack, however, he was married and had no contact with her—and he claimed he never became involved with her because he knew she was married. He was now employed as a bookkeeper and office manager in St. Helena. He had worked at the Pastime Club in Benicia from January until he quit on March 9. He started a job at Kaiser Steel where he received 12 weeks of training as a boilermaker, but was immediately laid off at the end of the orientation. He denied ever owning a Corvair, and had never driven Darlene's to the best of his recollection. He had, over the previous year, owned the faded red 1951 Ford pick-up that he purchased from the Ferrins, a 1956 Chevrolet blue over white, and a maroon 1964 Pontiac.

His alibi checked out. During the day of July 4 he had managed a girls' team in a baseball game sponsored by the Napa Police Department. Afterwards, he had gone home for a nap and then had attended the fair in Calistoga, returning home at 7:00 p.m. He had seen fireworks at the Veteran's Center with his wife that night, and had arrived home to stay at about 11:30 p.m. He maintained that he had not seen Ferrin in a month and a half, not since the day he had taken his wife, Judith, to Terry's Restaurant. On that occasion, even when he kidded her, she was kind of quiet. He denied owning a gun or going to Blue Rock Springs at any time with her.

☙

Three days after interviewing the staff at Terry's Waffle Shop, Rust and Lynch caught up with Phyllis, another waitress at Terry's, at 8:30 in the evening. She did not know Darlene well, but thought that a customer named Steve resembled the description of the killer. To Phyllis, Steve appeared to act strangely. He had a mother with mental problems, and Phyllis believed that he had bought a 9mm pistol, something he had mentioned to her. She described him as five feet eight inches and heavyset with light brown hair.

Twenty-four-year-old Steve was eventually cleared. When he was interviewed in Room 28 at the Vallejo Police Station by Rust and Lynch at 9:00 p.m. on July 13, he admitted to possessing firearms—a Ruger .22 magnum pistol and a .30-30 rifle—but denied ever owning a 9mm, either pistol or rifle. His alibi was solid. With his cousin Gary and two of Gary's friends, he had traveled on July 3 to Antelope Creek, 200 miles north of Vallejo, and remained in the area until Sunday, July 5.

Darlene parents, Mr. and Mrs. Leo Suennen, were interviewed by Lynch and Rust on the evening after the attack. They related that their other daughter, 15-year-old Christine, had been at Caesar's, Dean Ferrin's place of employment, at approximately 10:30 p.m.

Their information matched what Dean and his employer had reported: that Darlene left then, planning to take her sister home, go home to retrieve the babysitters, take them to their respective homes, and then return home herself. The deceased victim's parents noted that Darlene had been afraid of Mageau because he had initially represented himself as a wanted man from New York City. Mageau had later admitted to Darlene that it was just a story to impress her.

At 3:35 p.m. on the afternoon of July 7, Dean's parents, Arthur Jay Ferrin and Mildred Louise McCarty, visited the VPD to report to Lynch that they had received hang up telephone calls around 1:30 a.m. on the night of attack. All they heard at the other end of the line was heavy breathing. They were certain that someone was there. Even though the investigator plied them with questions, they were unable to add anything to the investigation.

Earlier that day, Captain Bird jotted down a note for Lynch. Peggy Your, the woman who had passed the Lake Herman Road crime scene minutes before the December 20, 1968 shooting, had called. She shared that she knew a man, named Bob, who matched the description of the Blue Rock Springs Park assailant.

&

On the afternoon of July 8, Detective Rust re-interviewed two of the three young people who had found Mageau and Ferrin at the park and had first reported the shooting. Even though they had already been spoken to, and had supplied written statements, Rust wanted to ensure that the information that had been provided to him was correct. He also hoped to dislodge a few new nuggets of evidence.

Roger and Jerry gave him corroborating information, the same story they had shared earlier. 19-year-old Debbie had been driving a brown Rambler with her two 17-year-old friends, the boys told Rust. Together they had been downtown for the Independence Day festivities. At around 11:00 p.m., they began to search for a friend of Roger's. They wandered for a while, ending up eventually at Blue Rock Springs Park hoping that they might find her there. They traveled along Columbus Parkway from Interstate 80—often referred to at the time, according to an officer, as "the back way" to the park.

They saw no other vehicles as they traversed the two miles from the Interstate to the park.

They arrived at the main parking lot at midnight or possibly shortly before and noticed a brown Corvair with its lights off. As they discussed whether or not to approach, thinking that Roger's friend might be inside, the car's lights lit up suddenly. The teenagers thought that the vehicle was preparing to leave the lot when the sound of screaming pierced the night. Debbie maneuvered her Rambler by backing it up so that she faced the Corvair with her headlights, and turned on her high beams. It was then that they noticed Mageau lying perpendicular to the vehicle out of which he had fallen. He was rolling around on the ground. Debbie drove closer.

Jerry sprinted to the victim to offer assistance, "Are you all right?"

"I'm shot; the girl's shot. Get a doc." Mageau cried out.

"All right, we'll get one." Jerry promised. Mageau told them to hurry. Roger had jumped out of the car and heard the exchange. They all saw Mageau, but none of them had looked in the car or noticed Ferrin.

Jerry offered to wait with the victims for emergency aid to arrive, but was talked out of it by Roger and Debbie. The three teenagers hurriedly drove to 938 Castlewood Road, Jerry's home in Vallejo, to telephone the police. As they exited the park, turning left on Columbus Parkway and heading toward downtown Vallejo, the only other vehicle they saw was one that had turned onto Lake Herman Road and was already too far away for them to make any kind of identification, or even estimate its speed.

Though they had done their duty, and had notified the police of what they found, the youths were unsatisfied. They were not convinced that the call had been taken seriously, and were afraid that someone might think it a hoax, the boys told Rust. They decided to pile back into the car and race to the home of Bob, Debbie's brother-in-law, who was a police officer. Nervous energy propelled them. Once there, they telephoned again to summon aid, only to discover that the VPD had already found the vehicle. They traveled next to the VPD to provide oral and written statements to Sergeant Odiorne.

To Rust, the three youths could offer no additional information. They had had no other conversation with the victims, and Mageau had shared nothing about the gunman or the gunman's car. They promised to contact the department if they recalled anything else or any other information became available.

ᗉᐧᔕ

Further investigation provided an additional list of Ferrin's many friends. A man named Lee had brought items for her from Tijuana. Bobbie, a blonde woman who worked with her at Terry's, chatted often with her. Bobbie in turn alerted police to Richard, who was slender, six feet tall, and drove a white Cougar. Dean's cousin, Sue Ayers, was fond of Darlene and cultivated a respectful interaction. None of Darlene's numerous friends and acquaintances could be tied to the attack, and none of them had any idea why this tragedy had happened or who was responsible.

ᗉᐧᔕ

A self-proclaimed hippy psychic, who had been dishonorably discharged from the Army, traveled from Chicago to San Francisco, and then Vallejo, to offer his help to law enforcement. He had no connection to the area or the case. He would not be the only citizen to attempt to inject himself into the murder investigation. After doing his own investigating and receiving psychic "vibrations," he advised the detectives to take a close look at Darlene's first husband, James Douglas Phillips.

But the officers didn't need prompting. The VPD was already exploring the possibility that Darlene's first husband was responsible for the shooting.

Born in Los Angeles, May 13, 1944, Phillips, who also went by the name James Douglas Crabtree, had been abandoned at the hospital by his birth mother. He was adopted by a couple bearing the name Phillips. After his foster father—a California Highway Patrol (CHP) Officer—was killed in 1968, he began to use his last name from birth.

Lynch contacted Phillips' foster brother and learned that James, who went by "Jim," had been in the Army and had married a German girl with whom he had a daughter. In fact, that marriage may or may not have been dissolved. Jim caused trouble with the Army, which led him to be confined to the stockade in the Presidio in San Francisco. Jim had been discharged dishonorably after he had gone on a hunger strike.

The foster brother knew that Jim was living on a ranch in the Watsonville/Santa Cruz area—a large hippie commune—and was wanted for writing bad checks in Watsonville, and also in the Reno/ Tahoe area. He believed that Jim was also involved with illegal narcotics, and recommended that Lynch contact Judge Dan Reynolds of the Central Valley Justice Courts in Central Valley, California, to inquire about his foster brother's background.

Lynch wrote the judge a letter. Captain Richard Welch of the Redding Police Department returned a call to Lynch, and promised to collect some of Phillip's handwriting by researching a previous check-writing case.

On January 23, 1970, Mulinax, who would eventually inherit the Ferrin murder case from Lynch, re-interviewed Mrs. Suennen. He desired to learn what she had told the psychic that led him to declare that Phillips was responsible for Darlene's murder. If she had provided information about Phillips that implicated him in the murder, he wanted to know. She could offer the officer nothing new, however. She admitted that she did not spend time around her daughter's first husband. He had emotional problems, she believed, because she had heard that he had been treated for them. She made it patently clear that she did not like Phillips, but had no information that linked him to the murder.

That same day, Mulinax attempted to gather information on Phillips at *The Daily Republic* in Fairfield. No employment records were found, and very little was known about him by those who worked there. The business manager promised to forward any federal tax forms he had filled out, if they were located. When Mulinax contacted the Fairfield Police Department, he learned that there was an outstanding warrant dating to December 4, 1967 for a James Donald Phillips, a photocopy of prints, and a mug shot. He concluded that these likely did not match the James D. Phillips he sought: the mug shot pictured someone much older and without glasses.

Three days later, Mulinax placed a telephone call to Special Agent Mel Nicolai of CII, leaving a message requesting information from his files on James D. Phillips. He asked that it be forwarded to him with a mug shot and rap sheet, if found. Nicolai returned the call the next day and shared the suspect's current address. Mulinax had received the mug shot and rap sheet in the morning mail.

On January 28, 1970, Mulinax made the long drive to picturesque Santa Cruz with Deputy District Attorney Charles Meyerherm. Once there, the two liaised with Lieutenant Gangloff, in charge of the Investigation Division at the Santa Cruz County Sheriff's Office, and Detective George Foster. The Santa Cruz records revealed that Phillips had been booked on January 19 on traffic warrants. Phillips had quickly posted a bail of $390 cash and had left. Mulinax opted to wait to confront the suspect until after his scheduled court appearance on February 2. Instead of searching for the man, he made plans to return to the area and collar him at a time and place he knew he could be found.

While waiting for the days to pass, Mulinax, together with Detective Chuck Hess, approached the District Attorney's Office in Fairfield on January 29, and had Chief Deputy District Attorney Neal McCaslin draw up the necessary Declaration of Affidavit, with bail set at $10,000, an amount that Mulinax was certain that Phillips could not produce. It was signed by Judge Curtis G. Singleton and retained by Mulinax. In the interest of due caution, he also met with Ferrin's mother earlier in the day to confirm that the photograph he possessed was indeed Darlene's ex-husband, the correct James D. Phillips, aka Jim Crabtree.

When Phillips appeared for his hearing at the appointed time on February 2, Mulinax was present, along with VPD Officer Zander, to arrest the fugitive on the warrant from Fairfield. He was taken into custody as he left the building. His common-law wife, Shirley, and his infant son, Jacob, were also present, and taken in a separate car to the Santa Cruz Sheriff's Office. The officers informed Phillips that he was also being investigated for murder, and read him his Constitutional rights under the Fifth Amendment.

Phillips readily agreed to cooperate, and answered everything posed to him. Shirley was questioned at the same time in another room and confirmed the details he told the officers. He denied any knowledge of his ex-wife's murder, and consented to a search of his home. After he was transported to Vallejo, he provided handwriting samples, was photographed standing—both front and profile shots were taken—and questioned further. Sparks collected finger and palm prints. It became readily apparent to the officers that Phillip's writing did not match anything from the letters collected in the case. Samples were nevertheless forwarded to the CII for further examination.

When he was formally questioned in room 28 of the VPD at 3:00 p.m., Phillips explained to the investigators that he had met Darlene in the Haight-Ashbury district of San Francisco in August of 1965 following his discharge from the Army. They wed after living together for a while, but the marriage was doomed from the start because Darlene was inclined to run around with other men. They lived a gypsy existence, he noted. Phillips admitted to owning a 1963 Corvair, which he had purchased in October of 1966 or 1967—he couldn't remember which—for $90 down with a balance of $210. He had gotten rid of it three months later because he was unable make the payments. He had left it in a public lot in Los Angeles, and telephoned the registered owner to go and retrieve it. A search of his home 20 miles outside of Santa Cruz produced nothing incriminating.

Phillips denied ever saying that if he couldn't have Darlene no one could. The truth was, he told them, that he was not too concerned when she terminated the relationship. He had gone to Mexico for a couple of weeks and had spent a weekend with Darlene in San Francisco following his return. It was there that they had decided to part ways, he explained, since nothing remained to keep them together. He then wandered the country being part of the "social revolution" with the "hip generation." He met Shirley, his current muse, in January of 1969, and lived with her in San Francisco for a few months. They moved to Santa Cruz after they became disenchanted with the San Francisco scene. Shirley had become pregnant in May, and her father had bought them the house in which they now lived, paying $11,000 in cash for it.

Jim had heard the story of the couple shot in Vallejo, he told the investigators, but had not immediately associated it with his former wife. He did not know that Darlene had remarried and changed her name to Ferrin. He recalled that on July 4, the date his ex-wife was shot, he had gone to a hippy encampment in Boulder Creek to listen to some music. He had spent that evening at home. He had no transportation at the time; their truck was inoperative.

During the tense questioning, Mulinax noticed that Phillips wore thick glasses that did not appear in his mug shot. The suspect could not see without them, unlike the assailant in the Blue Rock Springs Park on July 4 who, according to Mageau, wore no eyewear. Jim explained that the Santa Cruz officers had asked him to remove his glasses for the photograph when he was arrested on traffic charges.

On February 3, Detective Mulinax confidently concluded that Phillips was not involved in any way in the murder of his ex-wife and turned him over to the Fairfield Police Department on their warrant.

With Phillips cleared, the investigation now had to look elsewhere for promising suspects. Questions loomed large: Where had the murderer gone and why had he killed?

ဢ

In addition to the psychic, many citizens, some trying to be helpful, others apparently drawn to the case on other motives, approached the VPD with names and stories. Everyone, it seemed, had their suspicions, or thought they knew who was responsible for killing Darlene Ferrin and wounding her friend, Michael Mageau.

On July 9, Officer W. Barber took a statement from a Vallejo resident named Odell. Odell had been driving around town with his two-year-old son in a convertible MG with the top removed on July 4, and had noticed a woman who he thought resembled Darlene. He noticed her while he was stopped for a couple of minutes at a stop sign near Terry's Restaurant because she was wearing a white uniform, which stuck out to him. Odell noted that a brown, sporty 1963 Corvair was backed into a parking space. Behind it, parked lengthwise, was a faded gray, two- or three-year-old van with a slanted windshield. He was unsure of the make, but was certain that it wasn't a Chevrolet or a Volkswagen. A six-foot-tall, Caucasian man, standing across from the woman at the rear of the Corvair, was talking with her. She had the hood of the Corvair raised and appeared to be showing the man the motor. Odell described the tall man as approximately 30 years of age with a heavy upper body. His hair was combed straight back, the sides of which were Champaign white, with darker streaks running through the light hair on the sides.

One suspect brought to the attention of the VPD had purchased a box of 9mm Winchester Western bullets from the Solano Gun Shop less than two weeks before the attack. When confronted, he admitted that they were for a friend in San Francisco who was on parole, and was therefore not able to buy his own ammunition. Detective Lynch cleared both the purchaser and the parolee of involvement in Ferrin's death.

Lynch was tasked with following up on an anonymous letter received by the VPD, which he did with Sergeant Kramer. The note explained that a badly rusted and beat up brown Corvair was getting a new, bright green paint job at a local Mobile station on the corner of George Street and Monterey Street. The car's owner, the writer had added, was 25 years of age, fat (well over 200 pounds), sloppy, strange acting, and living with his parents. When Lynch and Kramer inquired at the station, they learned that the 1963 Corvair could be started without a key. However, oil pooling under it revealed that it had not been moved after 11:00 p.m. on July 4, the owner having parked it in front of his house at a slight angle after seeing fireworks in Vallejo. "Patrick," the subject of the letter, was actually 23, did not own a gun, and did not know Darlene Ferrin.

Another anonymous letter pointed an accusatory finger at a short, heavyset 22-year-old who lived in a pink house on the north shore of Lake Herman. Lynch obtained the suspect's mug shot from the Sheriff's Office and shared it with Mageau at the hospital to see if it would jar loose a memory. Mageau dismissed the possibility that the man pictured had attacked him. To the best of his knowledge, he said, the man was not the shooter.

On August 23, a teenager named Penny entered the Benicia Police Department and cautiously placed a note on the counter. But there was no evidence that the man whose name was written on the piece of paper—Perry, later identified by the nickname "Rocky," a tugboat cook—was in any way connected to Ferrin's murder.

The principal and vice-principal of Springstowne Middle School in Vallejo were concerned that a former student of theirs, named

Christopher, was responsible for the attack at the Blue Rock Springs Park. Captain Bird sent Mulinax to investigate. On September 29, the administrators related that the former student had an anti-social attitude, and had had no contact with members of the opposite sex. He had been dominated by his mother, who had died in the past year. He was now living with his father and brother in Vallejo. Once when he was a junior high student, he had repeatedly banged his head against the side of a building. He had lost a cap off one of his teeth in gym class, and was exceedingly worried about how his mother would react. He had to be restrained by teachers in that incident. On another occasion, he had attacked a smaller student who then punched him in the face. Following the retaliation, he had become sullen and withdrawn. Christopher had a high IQ, was five feet ten to six feet tall, and had greasy-blond hair. The administrators added that he matriculated into Hogan High, Mageau's school, after completing studies at Springstowne.

Mulinax drove to Christopher's residence and noticed two cars parked in front. One of these, a blue, late model, 4-door Ford sedan, reminded him of the car Villarreal reported seeing at Blue Rock Springs Park just before the attack, then described as a blue 1967 Ford sedan. Mulinax requested license information from the Department of Motor Vehicles on both vehicles present at Christopher's residence.

Mulinax and VPD Sergeant Thacker spoke with a vice-principal at Hogan High School to continue following up on the lead. Though teachers encountered problems with his parents and he was a loner, Christopher had not gotten into trouble following his graduation from junior high. He was not popular, but gave no indication that he could be responsible for violent acts. His IQ had been measured at an astonishing 175.

The VPD even received a tip by Western Union Telegram, addressed to Chief of Police Jack Stiltz. It was clear from the details offered that no follow up would be productive. None was ever initiated.

An employee of the Bay City Paper Box Company in Oakland contacted the Alameda Police Department with information about a former co-worker, named David, who resembled a composite, and was known to be a marijuana and LSD user. This information too was funneled to the VPD so that the lead could be pursued.

∽

The park continued to be a focus of police attention. No one knew whether the assailant would attack the same place again. Because the two Vallejo area attacks had occurred only miles apart, there was great fear that the gunman would indeed return, and no one knew when or where. The VPD conducted a stakeout at Blue Rock Springs Park on October 18, but no credible suspects were developed. A greenish-grey Chevy Station Wagon approached the bait vehicle at 2 a.m. The five foot eight-and-a-half inch, 145-pound driver who was stationed at Treasure Island explained that he was on his way to Lake Berryessa and had merely stopped to request directions. The surveillance brought them no closer to solving the case.

Ballistics similarly provided few clues to the identity of the attacker. The slugs and shell casings that had been collected revealed that Ferrin's killer had used 9mm Winchester Western bullets, a common size and brand of ammunition. The list of potential 9mm semi-automatics did little to narrow any pool of suspects or provide fresh leads. Though he had claimed in the telephone call to the VPD to have used a Luger, an examination of the rifling on the bullets indicated that the killer could have shot while holding a Browning, Smith & Wesson, Star, Astra, Llama, Neuhausen, Zebrojoka, Husqvarna, or Esperanza.

The investigators even had difficulty pinning down the exact time of the attack. It was so close to midnight that it was uncertain whether it actually took place on Saturday, July 4 or Sunday, July 5. *San Francisco Chronicle* reporter Paul Avery, in an August, 1971 summary, placed the attack at 12:05 a.m., likely based on the fact that the first call to the VPD had occurred at 12:10 a.m. Special Agent Mel Nicolai's California Department of Justice report similarly placed the shooting on July 5. It is equally likely that the killer first struck just before midnight, based on Mageau's recollection of time, the killer's own words in future communications, and the unknown amount of time between the shooting and the arrival of the three youths who made first contact with the police: they did not telephone the VPD until after they had left the scene and traveled home. However, if the babysitter's statement that Darlene did not leave home until 11:40 p.m. is correct, the attack may have occurred at or just after midnight, when taking into account Mageau's description of his activities following Ferrin's arrival at his house and the apparent timeline created by these events.

As a result of the telephone call from the killer that linked the two Vallejo-area crime scenes, the police reluctantly concluded that there was a maniac on the loose. The local police started running patrols around all lovers' lane areas for the next few nights in an effort to stop what appeared to be a pattern. The two Vallejo-area attacks were separated by only two to three miles as the crow flies, the distance by road not terribly much farther.

☙

Detective Lynch paid a follow-up visit to the hospital on July 28 to re-interview Mageau, hoping that the surviving witness could provide additional details or identify the perpetrator from department photographs. Investigators often schedule additional interviews because those affected by a crime are often too emotional right after the event and need the opportunity to get their thoughts in order. Also, Mageau was sedated for the first encounter with police, possibly affecting his memory. Unfortunately, the patient could offer no new information, and did not recognize anyone in the VPD mug shot books that were presented to him.

☙

Michael Renault Mageau moved to San Pedro to live with his mother following his release from the hospital. He wanted to put distance between himself and his father, with whom he had a strained relationship; between himself and the site of his near-fatal attack—and between himself and his assailant. Whoever he was.

In late September, Mulinax, with the approval of Captain Bird, sent Mageau a selection of additional suspect photographs with the hope that that the victim would identify his attacker. Mageau returned these from Southern California with a note. He was unable to recognize anyone in the pictures he had reviewed.

The scourge of Solano County also had his reasons for departing the town, albeit unknown, never to attack there again. But he was not finished with his wanton acts of bloodlust.

Not by a long shot.

He would first introduce a new side of himself to an outraged public. The Bay Area would never again be the same.

4 | THE CIPHER SLAYER

"In this cipher is my iden[t]ity."

As the residents of Northern California slogged through the sultry days of July, 1969, there was little to differentiate the serial killer who was now active among them. The soon-to-be-named Zodiac had not yet distinguished himself from the killers who preceded him, nor from the many who would follow. He killed with a knife, but so had London's infamous Jack the Ripper in 1888 (though by this time, the Zodiac's Southern California connection was not known; some would never acknowledge it); he attacked with a gun, but so would pudgy New York City resident David "Son of Sam" Berkowitz, later in the 1970s, and many others; he corresponded with law enforcement in taunting missives, but Dennis Rader, the notorious and sinister BTK (Bind, Torture, Kill), would do the same with the Wichita, Kansas Police Department in the 1980s. And many believe that Jack the Ripper boasted with letters to the press in the late 19th century. Any similarities that the Zodiac may have had to other serial murderers both past and present would, however, be eclipsed in his next series of mailings in which he deposited pieces of a mysterious cryptograph.

On the last day of July, three nearly identical letters were sent from the killer to three Bay Area newspapers: *The Vallejo Times-Herald, The San Francisco Chronicle,* and *The San Francisco Examiner.* Postmarked in San Francisco and affixed with either two or four Roosevelt 6-cent stamps, the handwritten, 2-page letters informed the respective editors that the murders of December 20 and the murder on July 4 were indeed the product of one individual, just as was communicated via phone to Dispatcher Nancy Slover at the Vallejo Police Station earlier that month. *The Times-Herald* letter was posted with four stamps rotated to make Roosevelt appear to look up toward the top of the envelope. *The Examiner's* letter had two stamps similarly affixed. *The Chronicle's* letter also had two stamps, but with Roosevelt this time tilted downward.

The murderer, unidentified and still on the loose, would forever distinguish himself by including one-third of a cipher in each of these letters. Each envelope contained a separate page—roughly a third the size of a sheet of standard letter-sized paper—on which were written symbols arranged in 8 rows of 17 columns, for a total of 136 characters per page. The 408 symbols of the three pages gave rise to the cipher's popular name, the "408," as well as the FBI's label, "Z408." The symbols included letters of the alphabet, backward letters of the alphabet, mathematical signs, flag or semaphore figures as if borrowed from a Navy manual, and a few variants of circles including a crosshair circle that resembled a gun sight. A search for the origin of these ubiquitous symbols did not produce any investigative progress, except to suggest that the person responsible for selecting them may have had a connection to the Navy and may have received training in the field of encryption.

By this time, 5 mailings had been sent by the killer: 2 identical Confession letters, followed by the 3 similar Bates letters. These 3 new missives were nearly identical, though for the first time he provided his message on more than a single piece of paper. Each letter was two pages in length (two sides on a single sheet), and supplemented with the smaller sheet of coding. The variation among the new mailings was more apparent than among those for either the 2 Confession letters or the multiple Bates letters.

Of the new mailings, *The Chronicle's* appeared to be written first; *The Examiners'* second and copied from *The Chronicle's* letter; and

The Times-Herald's, the messiest and most corrupted of the three, third, apparently reproduced from *The Examiner* letter rather than from *The Chronicle*'s. The creator had provided a contemporary use for textual criticism common in the study of Shakespeare and manuscripts of the Bible.

The intentions of the new letters were clearly laid out for all to see. The writer's first order of business was to prove that he was, indisputably, the person who had committed the two Vallejo-area attacks. He may have felt that his claim to Dispatcher Nancy Slover and the Vallejo Police Department (VPD) was unconvincing. He would, therefore, provide absolute proof that both attacks were orchestrated by one person, and that he—and he alone—was that man. To that end, he listed information that, apart from the police, only he knew. Unless the writer was a police officer, or had been privy to the investigation of the Lake Herman Road killings and the murder of Darlene Ferrin, *he* was the killer.

With proof of his identity established, the killer's next goal in writing was apparent in his demand. He wanted front page publication of the pieces of the cryptograph he had sent. If the newspapers refused to promulgate his creations, he threatened, he would carry out additional killings. No one in the San Francisco Bay Area at the time realized that the murderer had already threatened in his correspondence in Riverside—which at this point had not yet been linked to the Northern California attacks—to kill, again and again, whether or not any demands were met.

He wrote the following to *The Chronicle* (with some variations in wording to *The Examiner* and *The Times-Herald*):

```
Dear Editor
This is the murderer of the
2 teenagers last Christmass
at Lake Herman & the girl
on the 4th of July near
the golf course in Vallejo
To prove I killed them I
shall state some facts which
only I & the police know.
Christmass
1 Brand name of ammo
```

```
Super X
2 10 shots were fired
3 the boy was on his back
 with his feet to the car
4 the girl was on her right
 side feet to the west
4th July
1 girl was wearing paterned
slacks
2 The boy was also shot in
the knee.
3 Brand name of ammo was
Western
Over

Here is part of a cipher the
other 2 parts of this cipher are
being mailed to the editors of
the Vallejo times & SF Exam
iner.
I want you to print this cipher
on the front page of your
paper. In this cipher is my
idenity.
If you do not print this cipher
by the afternoon of Fry. 1st of
Aug 69, I will go on a kill ram-
Page Fry. night. I will cruse
around all weekend killing lone
people in the night then move
on to kill again, untill I end
up with a dozen people over
the weekend.
           [crosshairs symbol]
```

The three 3-Part letters were processed by local police departments for latent fingerprints, after which they were delivered by car to the VPD, who then submitted the pieces of cipher to the cryptographic unit of the U.S. Navy Radio Station at Skaggs Island, which is situated near Vallejo. Naval intelligence would take a crack at solving the cipher. In one of its many communications, the Sacramento Field Office of the FBI notified Washington, D.C. of the emerging crisis in its jurisdiction. It stated that it was not actively investigating

1. TIMES HERALD 8/1/69

2. CHRONICLE 8/1/69

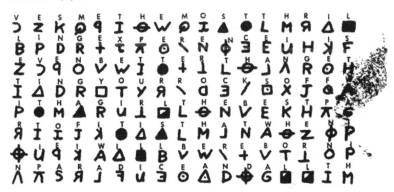

3. EXAMINER 8/1/69

the murders, but was ready and able to support the VPD and the Solano County Sheriff's Department who were conducting concurrent investigations. Latent prints in the case were labeled #A-10042 and added to the new FBI file #9-49911.

The FBI Field Office in Sacramento had first opened as a separate unit in 1966 to relieve pressure from the San Francisco and Los Angeles offices during a reorganization of sub units. Prior to September 25, 1966, the Sacramento office was a small satellite of the San Francisco Field Office. Located at 2020 J Street, the branch of 57 agents would grow in size and scope as more white collar, missing person, and serial killing cases were added to its workload. Despite its growth, the office often seemed to suffer the shame of being a mere step-child to its much larger neighbor in San Francisco.

The "signature" at the bottom of each of these letters, the crosshairs symbol (which was also present as a repeated symbol within the cipher), puzzled authorities when the letters were turned over to them from the respective news outlets. It appeared to be a gun sight or target of some sort, the writer using it to sign off on the letters as an implied salutation or casual signature. The depths of its significance to the killer would not become apparent until the arrival of his next taunting letter and the commission of his next pernicious attack.

The prose of this new letter was quite different than those that had preceded it, leading to questions years later about whether the Vallejo killer was actually responsible for the Riverside letters or the 1966 murder of Cheri Jo Bates. While the Confession letter flowed smoothly across its words, and displayed flowery, almost poetic, language, the 3-Part letters were matter of fact and to the point. They were specific in their demands, horrific in their claims, and detailed in their threats. The writing was messy; letters were haphazardly placed in uneven rows across the page. It was not typed like the Confession letters, and its contents were not splashed across the page in large block printing as had occurred in the three Bates letters. The penmanship and grammar suggested that the writer had little experience writing and a poverty of education. It was a juvenile script and terseness that might be expected from a prison inmate or an elementary school child. Could it actually have been created by the same author who three years earlier had typed, "SHE WAS YOUNG AND BEAUTIFUL... SHE WENT TO THE SLAUGHTER LIKE A LAMB... HER BREAST FELT VERY WARM AND FIRM..."?

Upon receipt of the letters, the editorial boards of the three newspaper organizations began to discuss whether or not they should each publish what they had received. Each paper had to weigh the threat of public disruption against the citizens' right to know. The promise of increased newspaper sales was always a carrot dangling in front of the editors, a temptation offering to tilt the scales. Because the letters themselves threatened the murder of as many as a dozen innocent people if they were not published by August 1—a deadline only hours away—the pressure was great. If a newspaper refused to print what it had, it could arguably be responsible for a murder spree—not to mention the withholding of a threat which many in the public would want to receive in fair warning. And any paper that did not publish could in time lose market share to a paper that did. As unpleasant and distasteful as capitulating to the demands of a serial killer may have appeared, it promised to aid the media in its quest to add readers, sell newspapers, and create a huge news story that would soon metastasize into a media feeding frenzy.

The killer had stumbled upon a publicity extravaganza, which he used to forge a working relationship with the press. Each would get what they wanted. The killer was successful in what he apparently hoped for: that under pressure from a threat of violence and from the need to compete with the other news operations, his symbol arrangements would indeed be published as he demanded. The papers in turn received fascinating copy space for their readers. The 3-Part 408 cipher was therefore a stroke of advertising genius.

In and of itself, it was a tantalizing news story. Who wouldn't want to know more about a murderer who wrote in a mysterious alphabet which if successfully deciphered would lead to the identity of the killer, as suggested by one of the letters that included the additional, taunting sentence, "in this cipher is my iden[t]ity." This was a made-for-media story that promised to place each of these papers squarely in the middle of the violence, the story and, therefore, history as it unfolded. If the cipher was published, any solution would be attempted, and possibly found, in the presence of the media, providing the organizations extra incentive to herald it.

And if the cipher was to be solved, the more eyes that saw it the better.

How and when to publish remained a question for each paper. Newspapers, which are competitive by nature, always eager to get a scoop or an exclusive, were now forced to cooperate, all the while casting a suspicious eye on one another.

This media version of a Mexican standoff was resolved quite quickly when all three papers acceded to the writer's demands. The cipher parts were printed, but they did not all appear on the front page or by the deadline, as their creator required.

If the killer had hoped to extend his range of publicity, he was immediately successful, as the story achieved national status. It was not exactly the 1969 equivalent of going viral, but the news of an unusual killer spread outside the Bay Area and beyond California. If the killer had hoped to extend the length of his publicity campaign, he was similarly successful because his letters and actions would continue to be studied for at least the next four decades, providing him an infamy that he apparently craved.

The Vallejo News Chronicle published *The Vallejo Times-Herald*'s piece on Friday, August 1, on its front page, noting that the letter had been sent to Gibson Publications, owner of both *The Times-Herald* and *The News Chronicle*. It published all three parts of the cryptograph in its August 4 edition, printing also the killer's "cover letter" in the hopes that someone might recognize the unusual script. *The San Francisco Chronicle* published its piece on page 4 on Saturday, August 2, past the deadline and off the paper's first page. *The San Francisco Chronicle* and *The San Francisco Examiner* published all three cipher pieces on the front page of the Sunday Chronicle-Examiner, the joint publication of the two papers.

However successful the murderer was in having his cipher published, he must have realized the danger he faced in dipping his toe in this new pool. Each tidbit of information he shared would place the investigation one step closer to his capture. An intricate and complex cipher certainly revealed something of its creator. The drawing up of the cipher evidently required a large investment in time and not a little skill. While the cipher itself—and its subsequently found solution—did not demonstrate the expertise of a professional cryptographer, as someone in the military or in the field of computer science might use to build a career, it did indicate that its author had at least rudimentary familiarity with the concept of cipher-making, not a widespread experience in most communities. Some training or exposure was obvious.

The makeup of the mailings and the information contained in the three letters similarly revealed details of the killer's character, if not his identity. What exactly they communicated, investigators struggled to understand.

As a result of his use of cryptographs, and his history of murder, the killer was dubbed the "Cipher Slayer" in *The Lodi News Chronicle*, and later in *The San Francisco Chronicle*. An alternate name also appeared in *The San Francisco Chronicle* on September 30, "the Code Killer." Either of these titles would effectively distinguish this murderer and provide him notoriety. However, he was evidently unsatisfied with a media-invented moniker. In his very next letter, sent less than a week later, the killer would identify himself in a name that would guarantee not only newspaper articles, but numerous magazine covers, a shelf of books, multiple movies, and an enduring legacy. His More Material letter, received by *The San Francisco Examiner* in early August, began, *"This is the Zodiac speaking,"* a proclamation that would set a major population center on edge for years to come, the phrase becoming his tagline and a title for many of his future letters.

The killer's name the "Zodiac" and its associated crosshairs symbol—which the Vallejo newspaper identified as "what appeared to be a sketch of the cross-hairs in a telescopic rifle sight"—helped launch an effective advertising campaign that would rival that of any large corporation. Companies embrace and cherish familiar logos and key phrases to comfort customers and educate society about its products. The killer from instinct, experience, or sheer brilliance (or some combination of the three) was able to pull off a large-scale publicity blitz, and earned media on a grand scale. He provided murder instead of a product, used the currency of fear in place of money, and manipulated a compliant press in lieu of an advertising budget. The public was powerless against the emergence of this new macabre brand, its message so palpable, its memes so virulent.

Accordingly, the introduction of ciphers into the Zodiac murder campaign also induced many members of the public to become actively involved in the case. Some attempted, however half-heartedly, to solve the cipher. It was not an easy task. The killer did not indicate which of the three sheets contained the first part, or the second, or the third; did not suggest whether there was as a one-to-one (homophonic) correspondence from cipher symbol to English letter; and did not confirm that the symbols were to be read left-to-right and top-to-bottom. Many quickly tired of the exercise, possibly doubting that there was any solution to be found. Some citizens began to notice family members or acquaintances who had written symbols or codes, and cast a suspicious eye in their direction. Leads regarding the possible association of the cipher symbols to astrology began to trickle in to the VPD, each of which had to be pursued.

VPD Detective Sergeant John Lynch followed up one such tip. A 47- to 49-year-old former patient of Napa State Hospital who loved to hunt became a suspect after an anonymous caller brought him to the attention of the police. He was very large in stature, and he liked to create poetry and write about killing and religion. Investigation proved that the man was actually younger than the tip suggested. Though he had been arrested in Alameda several times, and often went by another name, he was not the Zodiac.

A woman turned in her ex-husband who was known to sign notes with a crosshairs symbol. Lynch received a sample of the man's handwriting from her, and learned that he was a hippy who lived in San Francisco. His present address was unknown. He had been arrested in San Mateo County for grand theft and armed robbery.

When another woman noticed books on astrology in the apartment of a mentally ill friend named Sharon, she reported the husband to the VPD. She explained to the police that the man, named Tommy, was known to beat her friend, especially during sex; believed in the afterlife; and was expecting his wife to be his slave in the "hereafter." Sharon, who had spent time in the Napa State Hospital, had often complained that her husband was impotent and needed an artificial penis to perform sexually. He also allegedly attempted to kill his wife by leaving open the gas burners in their home without igniting a flame. He owned many books on astrology as well. Working as a pipefitter on the swing shift at Mare Island, he did not work weekends, when the Zodiac had struck. Detectives collected his employment forms for handwriting analysis. His neighbors reported that he had few visitors, none that were women, and that he was gone most weekends.

Tommy's fingerprints were located and sent to the FBI laboratory in Washington, D.C. on October 1, 1970. The reply came the next day: no match was found with any prints collected in the murders being investigated.

The VPD received a telephone call from Arkansas regarding Tommy. On October 3, Sergeant Brown of Hot Springs reported that the now-divorced Sharon, who was going through a state of mental breakdown, was speaking to her father about her ex-husband. Brown had acquired his information from the father. Sharon was claiming that Tommy had killed a girl, called Olivia, as well as Olivia's child, in June or July of 1968. They were shot with a .30-30 rifle and buried in a Vallejo backyard, according to Sharon. The details were not entirely clear as Sharon had many relapses into incoherent states of mind. She also related that her ex-husband, on several occasions, mentioned the Blue Rock Springs Park.

Sergeant Nilsson re-contacted the original informant and learned that Tommy had dated several women while married to Sharon, but that her friend did not know an Olivia. He received information from Officer Husted that Melodie, a young woman who had been living with Tommy, was in juvenile detention. Upon follow-up at the juvenile hall, Nilsson learned that 17-year-old Melodie had lived with Tommy the previous four months. She did not know an Olivia either, and had never seen guns in her boyfriend's possession. She denied that he was abusive or violent in any way, affirming that he had a normal sex drive. She stated that he never studied astrology, nor wrote cryptograms, though he *was* interested in his own Zodiac sign. No connection between Tommy and the murderer's cipher was ever established.

A Redding couple approached the VPD to alert it to a very distant relative, named Norman, who they thought was a mafia hit man and might have been responsible for the Zodiac killings. He had written them a letter in which he claimed to be a killer for the mafia, was in serious trouble, and needed their immediate help. Though they had never met the man, the couple brought in letters written by the suspect, as well as two pictures of him. John Markey of the FBI traveled to the station and took over this piece of the investigation. The SFPD compared Norman's fingerprints against those they had on file with the FBI, without establishing a match. The letter the couple had received was forwarded to CII in Sacramento for a handwriting comparison with the Zodiac's letters. But nothing they found could tie the man to the killings.

The public preoccupation with the Zodiac case was just beginning. Individuals and couples—sometimes even small groups—began to contact the VPD with all manner of advice and an assortment of suspects. Numerous perfectly innocent people became persons of interest simply because they appeared to have something, however remote, in common with the killer. The VPD received information about mental patients, homeless drifters, braggarts who made bold claims, people who wrote in codes, relatives who acted oddly, and acquaintances who engaged in gallows humor.

Law enforcement officials received numerous handwriting samples. Many armchair detectives tried to connect someone to the careless scrawl of the 3-Part letters; others attempted to tie an acquaintance's suspicious activity, or interest in astrology, to the crimes. The detectives faithfully investigated all promising leads, but no one brought to their attention was found to be responsible for the gruesome spree that was unfolding before them. Several suspects had illegal firearms in their possession, however, and were promptly arrested.

On August 7, Lynch was pressed into service by Captain Bird to travel to Vacaville to investigate an 18-year-old former foster child, named David, who had emotional problems. When upset, belligerent, or angry, David was reported to just sit and stare, or draw cryptograms comprised of strange symbols. His former foster parents (whose duty had ended in February of 1969 when their charge was emancipated at 18 years of age) described him as someone in regression who couldn't discuss his problems, and who ran with a crowd that dabbled in drugs. His probation officer added that he was wanted in Vacaville for bouncing a $20 check. Lynch learned that after his brother was killed in Vietnam, David had been in the Vallejo area for the funeral, shortly before Christmas of 1968. He had formerly lived in Benicia. He drove a Honda and owned a rifle—possibly a .22—which he received from his brother. His former foster parents reported that he had been going downhill since his brother's funeral and the advent of the Zodiac murders. Lynch received samples of the man's handwriting and some of his encryptions. Though he had bragged to others that he had met Betty Lou Jensen and found her pleasant to talk to, he was eventually cleared of any involvement in her murder.

This former foster child was only one of many individuals whose unusual actions tantalized investigators. Sergeant Conway received a telephone call from a lieutenant at the South Lake Tahoe Police Department about another potential suspect. Conway was informed of a restaurant cook who had a "hang-up" about knives. He had aroused suspicions when he left a jocular note in a milk truck, signing it "Zodiac."

The VPD was called upon to inspect some gray, spray-paint graffiti on Scandia Road near Highway 12. The scrawl said simply "Zodiac sucks and kills." Mulinax was detailed by Captain Bird to investigate. The writing was not similar to the script of the Zodiac's, and was dismissed as useless to the case, probably produced by some mischievous kids. Nevertheless, photographs were taken and brought back to the station with a follow-up request that they be developed.

A toll-taker at the Carquinez Bridge, named James, claimed to know who the Zodiac was, but was waiting for a reward to be offered before turning him in to the police. His boasts were overheard by co-workers and reported to the police, who had two more suspects to investigate: the man accused by the toll-taker and James himself.

More than one citizen dropped a tip on a suspicious distant relative. Many cranks called or visited with useless information, a trend that would continue for decades. Many who had no connection to the case found themselves turned in by ex-wives, ex-girlfriends, relatives, and neighbors. This penchant that all these helpful citizens had for offering up suspects cost many investigative man-hours. It brought to the attention of the authorities much of the dark underbelly of society at that time: those that joked inappropriately about the attacks, others who claimed to know something, people who had serious mental issues, many who were prone to violence (some of whom had recently returned from service in Vietnam), and more than a few citizens with an unwholesome interest in the macabre.

Even Darlene Ferrin's mother proclaimed that she had once seen James Phillips, her daughter's first husband, draw up some kind of code.

❦

On August 11, an anonymous letter arrived at the Vallejo Police Station, addressed to VPD Detective Sergeant Lynch. Postmarked August 10 in San Francisco, it contained a three inch by five inch card from some "concerned citizen," who wrote in part, "I hope the enclosed key will prove to be beneficial to you in connection with the cipher letter writer." It provided the key for the ciphers, a correct list of which letter of the alphabet each symbol represented. Included, curiously, were several possible alternate solutions to some symbols, indicating that several of the symbols had more than one interpretation. On August 16, the Sacramento Field Office of the FBI, realizing that the note could have been generated by the killer, sent a letter to the FBI in Washington, D.C. with the request that the note be scoured for fingerprints.

The FBI letter was sent as an airtel—which is to say, not very urgently—the reply to which came on August 21. No watermarks or indentations were found on the strange mailing. The FBI laboratory did note that the typewritten card had distinctive features, including letters with errors, that would aid in the identification of the specific machine used if the typewriter were ever located and its striking heads examined. Regarding the enclosed cipher key, the lab declared that not only was the information useful, but it represented a "substantially accurate key," providing a "generally valid decryption." The three pieces, the envelope, the card, and the white sheet containing the key, were dutifully numbered and entered into the FBI files. One latent palm print was recovered from the envelope.

But the solution to the mysterious cryptograph was not new news.

The VPD was aware that the cipher had already been broken. Three days before the anonymous letter, the VPD had received a 6:35 p.m. telephone call from George Murphy of *The San Francisco Chronicle* indicating that two private citizens, Don and Bettye Harden of Salinas, had contacted the paper with a solution to the cipher. The Hardens—he, a history and economics teacher at North Salinas High School, and she, a home-maker—were avid fans of puzzles and word games. They had decided to spend a few days wrestling with the encryption, eventually solving its mysterious riddle through brute force, imagination, and patience.

The Hardens suspected that a narcissist like the Zodiac would talk about himself, even beginning his message with some kind of boast. The avenue that provided them success was a search for four letter combinations that would represent the word "kill," a crib which they expected would be present numerous times in the solution. One of the many combinations of words they experimented with was, "I like killing..." With these few symbols solved, and a great deal of trial and error applied to the rest of the pages, they were finally able to achieve the solution in an estimated 29 hours of work.

Harden noted several strategies that were employed to throw cryptographers off track, including multiple symbols used to represent the most common letter of the alphabet, "E," possibly intentional misspellings, and a few coding errors.

Upon hearing news of the solution, Lynch drove to *The Chronicle* to retrieve from Murphy the work sheets the Hardens had sent. He also called the Hardens to inquire about their effort. He placed so much trust in the couple that when the August 11 key card arrived in the mail, he sent that information along to the Hardens to enable them to compare the new information to the solution they had generated.

The Sacramento FBI Field Office sent the Harden's solution, contained within a newspaper clipping of *The Vallejo Times-Herald's* August 9 article, to FBI Headquarters. The FBI in Washington, D.C. responded on August 19 with a letter that included a correct interpretation of the 408 cipher, all spelling and coding errors corrected. The CIA and the NSA, a secretive joint venture of the Defense and State Departments, had each separately verified the Harden's solution. The report noted that one word was missing: after the word "the" and before the next words "I have killed," at least one word (such as "people" or "kids") had been omitted, making the wording somewhat awkward:

I like killing people because it is so
much fun. It is more fun than killing wild
game in the forest because man is the most
dangerous animal of all. To kill something gives me the most thrilling experience. It is even better than getting your
rocks off with a girl. The best part of it
is that when I die, I will be reborn in
paradise, and all the [ ] I have killed
will become my slaves. I will not give
you my name because you will try to slow
down or stop my collecting of slaves for
my afterlife.

The complexity of the encryption was apparent. Many letters of the alphabet had more than one symbol attached to it. The more a letter was used in the English language, it seemed, the more symbols its creator used to represent that letter, suggesting that its creator had some familiarity with letter frequency within the English language, and the methods of decoding that are based on an analysis of letter frequency.

But there was more. Some of the letters in the final solution had more than one interpretation. While the Hardens provided a single solution for each symbol of the cipher, the mysterious three inch by five inch card indicated that some of the symbols had more than one solution. There was no difference in the message of the cryptograph, however. To achieve the Harden's interpretation, a reader had to assume that the coder was a sometimes clumsy speller, misspelling at least one word per line, often more. The anonymous letter writer put the cipher's author in a better light: his spelling and encoding was not quite as bad, if you provide additional letters for some of the symbols.

The Harden's work was checked by Dr. D. C. B. Marsh, a mathematician at the Colorado School of Mines, and head of American Cryptogram Association. He was impressed not only by the effort that the Hardens had put into the decryption, but also by the coder. He noted that the cipher had been "drawn by somebody who knows his business." The arrangement of the ciphers was also confirmed, the pieces being ordered as follows: *The Vallejo Times-Herald* cipher was first, *The San Francisco Chronicle* was next, followed finally by the piece sent to *The San Francisco Examiner*.

The final 18 symbols, possibly containing no useful translation and merely inserted to fill out the last line, became the following:

EBEORIETEMETHHPITI

Helpful citizens attempted to understand or translate these spare letters. The following re-arrangements of the 18 characters were supplied to the police. Whether any of these was the intent of the coder could not be determined:

THE TIP I'M ROBERT E EEEE
ROBERT EMET THE HIPPIE
BEFORE I MEET THEM I PITY THEM

Lynch reported that the police were checking into all Robert Emmets, hippy or otherwise. It was noted that Robert Emmet was the name of an Irish revolutionary patriot who was executed in Ireland in 1803 for his part in leading a rebellion.

An anonymous letter from Palo Alto suggested that the final 18 letters represented a telephone number with a digit missing, but no such listing was ever located.

A tip came in to the VPD from the Stanford Research Center in Menlo Park at 1:55 p.m. on August 10. The idea of "slaves for the afterlife" may have originated in South East Asia, particularly among the Mindanao of the southern Philippines, the caller suggested.

❦

The More Material letter
In response to the 3-Part letters with their encrypted sheets, the Vallejo police came up with a deviously clever tactic, and took action in the early days of August. It would not be until many years later, and much research by the FBI's Behavioral Science Unit (BSU) into the minds of serial killers, that researchers would be able to appreciate the ingeniousness of the VPD, and the panacea upon which it had

stumbled. Seeing that the writer had demonstrated a need to prove his involvement in the case, the officials decided to measure just how far the killer would go to prove himself. Besides, as long as he was writing, he was not killing, and as long as he was communicating, he was apt to make a mistake and share something revealing. At a press conference held to discuss the letters, Vallejo Police Chief Jack E. Stiltz raised suspicions that the writer was in fact not the killer, and demanded more proof. He pointed out that someone could have picked up the stray details of the attack by visiting the crime scenes, or by eavesdropping on an officer. He asked the perpetrator for more information and questioned his claims, indirectly also challenging him to demonstrate his knowledge and superiority. He invited the killer to "write more facts to prove it." All three papers that had received a piece of the cipher—*The San Francisco Examiner*, *The San Francisco Chronicle*, and *the Vallejo Times Herald*—published articles mentioning the police chief's comments. Like the press conference, the articles requested another letter with more details. The chief's comments waved a red cape in front of an angry bull.

The VPD had stumbled upon a brilliant strategy to draw the Zodiac out of hiding. Whether they were conscious of their cleverness or not, they were engaging in activity that would become standard practice for the BSU in the 1980s. Commenting on the case years later, former FBI profiler John Douglas believed that the Zodiac could have been enticed to gravesites on anniversaries of the attacks, or to official meetings convened around the subject of the killings. The Vallejo officials had responded as if they had been coached by the BSU and attempted to elicit more prose from their quarry.

It was deceitful for the authorities to claim that they did not believe the author of the 3-Part letters. In truth, they did—or they should have. He had provided so much information that could be known only to the killer (or to someone with intimate, inter-police-department information) that they could be certain of his boasts. He didn't just declare himself responsible, as would seem sufficient for most threatening authors, but went into great detail about what he knew and what he saw.

The effort put forth in the creation of the complex cipher revealed someone emotionally invested in the multiple mailings. He had diligently worked to convince authorities that he was the one and only, the *bona fide*, killer. Perhaps he was trying just a little too hard.

Stiltz's brazen gambit—if that is what it was—worked. Many criminals could be expected to pass on the bait. They would simply notice the trap, or they would decide that they had already provided enough proof. If the police could not understand what he had shared, they would never accept any amount of verification. But the Vallejo-area murderer bit. A couple of days later, another letter addressed to *The San Francisco Examiner* revealed that the author felt compelled to write again.

In a three-page letter, the More Material letter, his longest to date, the killer provided additional information about the two Northern California attacks. In excruciating detail, he added further proof of his involvement. He labeled one section "Last Christma[s]," and another "July 4:". Unfortunately, nothing that was provided led to any one individual; however, more data on how the perpetrator thought and how he organized his ideas was now available for scrutiny. The police had finagled from him three more pages of information that could someday expose the brutal murderer: his handwriting could be recognized by a co-worker, his vocabulary could be familiar to someone in the public, or his phraseology could trigger a memory.

The killer opened the new letter with the creative and menacing tagline that would become his iconic phrase, "*This is the Zodiac speaking.*" Along with the additional details of the Vallejo-area murders, he provided braggadocio regarding a penlight gun sight that he claimed to have used on December 20, and corrected information he had read from *the Vallejo Times Herald.* (He claimed that he left the Blue Rock Springs Park in a quiet manner so as not to "draw attention" to himself.) He also queried whether his cipher had been "cracked."

He wrote the following:

```
Dear Editor
This is the Zodiac speaking.
In answer to your asking for
more details about the good
times I have had in Vallejo,
I shall be very happy to
supply even more material.
```

By the way, are the police
haveing a good time with the
code? If not, tell them to cheer
up; when they do crack it
they will have me.
On the 4th of July:
I did not open the car door, The
window was rolled down all ready.
The boy was origionaly sitting in
the frunt seat when I began
fireing. When I fired the first
shot at his head, he leaped
backwards at the same time
thus spoiling my aim. He ended up on the back seat then
the floor in back thrashing out
very violently with his legs;
that's how I shot him in the
--
knee. I did not leave the cene
of the killing with squealling
tires & raceing engine as described
in the Vallejo paper..I drove away
quite slowly so as not to draw
attention to my car.
The man who told the police
that my car was brown was a
negro about 40-45 rather shabbly
dressed. I was at this phone
booth haveing some fun with the
Vallejo cops when he was walking
by. When I hung the phone up
the dam X@ thing began to
ring & that drew his attention
to me & my car.
Last Christmass
In that epasode the police were
wondering as to how I could
shoot & hit my victoms in the
dark. They did not openly state
this, but implied this by saying
it was a well lit night & I could
see the silowets on the horizon.
Bullshit that area is srounded

```
          --
by high hills & trees. What I did
was tape a small pencel flash
light to the barrel of my gun.
If you notice, in the center
of the beam of light if you aim
it at a wall or celling you will
see a black or darck spot in
the center of the circle of
light aprox 3 to 6 in. across.
When taped to a gun barrel,
the bullet will strike exactly
in the center of the black
dot in the light. All I had to do
was spray them as if it was
a water hose; there was no
need to use the gun sights.
I was not happy to see that I
did not get front page cover-
age.
[crosshairs symbol]
NO ADDRESS
```

The More Material letter arrived at the offices of *The San Francisco Examiner* on August 4, 1969, and was turned over to the VPD that same day. The accuracy and detail of the information in the letter convinced Lynch that the writer was indeed the killer. In an airtel to the FBI in Washington, D.C., the Bureau's field office in Sacramento noted that it did not have an ongoing investigation in progress, nor did the San Francisco FBI Field Office. On August 6, in cooperation with VPD, Sacramento submitted to the FBI laboratory in the nation's capital the original More Material letter plus three copies of the 3-Part letters. The VPD had already checked the 3-Part letters for fingerprints, and requested in conjunction with Sacramento the same of the new letter. Further, considering that the cryptograph had not yet been deciphered at this time, the FBI was asked to check the significance of the encryption, and compare the new letter to all other threatening letters in the FBI's extensive files.

Receiving the pages and envelopes of the four letters on August 8, the FBI numbered 15 separate documents. When the lab reported the results on August 12, the three pages of the More Material letter were granted the first 3 document titles in the case, Qc1, Qc2, and Qc3. The FBI lab searched for indented writing—which sometimes is found on anonymous letters when some other page has been written on while the letter is underneath—but found none. A watermark was identified within the More Material letter, the words "FIFTH AVENUE" pressed into its pages.

On August 29, the Latent Fingerprint Section of the FBI notified the VPD that two latent prints had been lifted from the letter, one from page two and one from page three. Additionally, through the stationery's unique watermark, they identified the paper used as stock sold at Woolworth stores. None of this information led to any suspect, the paper being available nationwide, and the fingerprints—possibly even deposited prior to the writer obtaining the paper—not matching any on file.

The details embedded within the letter were investigated, particularly the claim that a "negro" had witnessed the telephone call. Whether the writer's description of the potential eyewitness was based in fact—and future letters would contain falsehoods, and a claim to have left "false clews" to have law enforcement "run all over town"—remains a point of debate. The police set about finding an African American who had witnessed events and may have fit the killer's description. None was ever found, so the vain search by overtaxed law enforcement agents may have been the point of the possibly empty words.

☙

In the early days of August 1969, the world was the killer's oyster. He had taunted the public with two crime scenes in the Vallejo area—as well as a still-unconnected death far away in Riverside. He appeared proud and eager to boast of his achievements in letters to the police and press. He had claimed credit for the Vallejo attacks, identifying himself with a crosshairs totem and a mysterious, ominous name, the "Zodiac."

The terror he induced throughout the North Bay was complete; his infamy had spread beyond the Bay Area in news reports as far away as the East Coast. All that anyone knew was that a killer was active: identity, unknown; total number of victims, unclear; motive and future, unfathomable. He was certain to have been relishing the notoriety that he apparently craved.

The citizens of the Bay Area were discussing his attacks; more than a few hobbyists were wrestling with his cipher (which was also being studied by several law enforcement agencies and the Navy); and the fear of him hung over the North Bay like a dark cloud. The people of the region were dancing to a tune the Zodiac had composed.

But any success that he may have been celebrating was about to come crashing down like a house of cards during a West Coast earthquake. Within two weeks of its arrival, the cipher had been solved, the lack of specifics contained within—including the apparent absence of his promised identity—disappointing readers and law enforcement alike. The publicity obtained from the cipher began to wane. Then the cipher's creator was suddenly and completely overshadowed by the most infamous criminal in American history.

കൂ

On the night of August 8, 1969, a small group of disheveled hippies dressed in black gained entry to a luxurious Topanga Canyon property that was once the home of music producer Terry Melcher, son of the legendary actress Doris Day. With urgency of purpose, three drug-addled miscreants burst into the Southern California house and herded its four occupants into the living room. The residents were bound, threatened, and terrorized. One hippy lingered outside to keep watch.

"What do you want?" the bewildered captives repeatedly asked.

One of them tried to run. Another slipped out of a poorly-conceived towel restraint and fled in the other direction. The captors began to use the gun and knives they had brought to the scene as two of the captives headed toward the safety of the lush green yard.

Within minutes, all four residents were brutally murdered in a frenzy of stabbing, slashing, and gunshots. The intruders quickly made their way down Cellio Drive and escaped into the night. But these were not the first deaths for which the troop was responsible.

The hippies had already executed a teenager in a car who had moments before stopped in to visit an acquaintance at the guest house. Total dead: five. Before leaving, one of the killers—a young female—gathered some fresh victim blood on a cloth and wrote the word "WAR" on the outside of the front door.

The next morning, the newspapers screamed the horrific event in huge headlines. Leading the story was the senseless and violent murder of Sharon Tate, an actress with a fast-rising star and the wife of famed movie director Roman Polanski. Also dead were coffee heiress, Abagail Folger; hair stylist to the stars, Jay Sebring; and friend of Polanski's, Voytok Frykowski. The dead teenager was identified as Steven Parent who had at the time of his murder had just attempted to sell a clock radio. Tate was eight months pregnant with Polanski's child.

But the savages weren't done.

That night, just after 1:00 a.m., the same four, with three additional conspirators, targeted the suburban home of Leno and Rosemary LaBianca in the "City of Angels" neighborhood of Los Feliz to continue their mission of mayhem. After the couple was tied up, they were stabbed and slashed to death with knives and a barbeque fork. Someone carved the word "WAR" into Leno's chest. Again gathering victim's blood, the killers wrote "Healter Skelter," on the refrigerator door, "Death to Pigs," on a wall, and "Rise" on another wall. Charles Manson, quasi-crime boss and leader of what would become the world's most notorious cult, had struck in Southern California. These seven disgusting deaths in two frenetic and gruesome nights were not the family's first murder victims.

And they would not be their last.

The news of the attacks sent Los Angeles into an uproar. Among the rich and famous, those who could afford it left town or upgraded their security measures until questions were answered and the deaths resolved. Some traveled to Europe, others to homes in other parts of California or other states. Those who did not flee bought weapons. Gun sales shot up; ammunition flew off the shelves.

The reality of not knowing what was happening served to intensify the threat. Headlines from coast to coast captivated citizens who had already survived the most amazing news stories of the 1960s. The

Manson murders stunned a nation already familiar with the violence of war in Vietnam, protests on campus, riots across the nation, and the political assassinations of John F. Kennedy, Robert Kennedy, and Martin Luther King Jr. People around the globe, those who had just weeks earlier had celebrated Neil Armstrong's walk on the moon, now had to come to terms with an unseemly side of America.

Everyone soon heard of the massacres.

By December 1, most of the Manson conspirators were in prison on unrelated charges. Investigation into the two attacks had finally concluded that both events had been perpetrated by the same group. When one of the members began to openly brag about details of the crimes to fellow inmates, authorities were soon notified. Through a great deal of hard work and a little bit of luck, the crimes were solved. A press conference was hastily arranged to relieve the emotional pressure of uncertainty on the area's residents and law enforcement officials. The Manson Family was formally introduced to a fearful and appalled American public.

Over the ensuing two years, the planet was entertained by leaks emerging from the ongoing investigation, by the drama of a trial—the then longest in California history—and by the colorful words and actions of "The Family," headed by the charming and charismatic Charles Manson. The comments, anecdotes, and film footage became a nightly news mainstay for not only the Los Angeles area but the nation as well. The press and public couldn't get enough of the flamboyant and outspoken counter-culture cult leader, cum crime boss, whose guru-like pseudo-wisdom and bizarre antics would be reported on almost daily.

The Zodiac serial killer had been overshadowed by a much more horrific trail of carnage, carried out by a more successful attention-seeking assailant, and perpetrated in a more celebrated and public city. The key advantage enjoyed by the Manson Family in garnering attention appeared to be the celebrity attached to their crimes: not only the rich and beautiful people they killed—including the ascending actress Sharon Tate—but also the rock and roll group, the Beatles, whose songs were quoted on LaBianca's refrigerator door and walls, and Hollywood, the famed city of international attention that lay in close proximity to the crime scenes and the trial.

If the Zodiac serial killer was to compete for attention, press coverage, and newspaper headlines, he'd have to take on the notorious Manson Family with its epic violence and keen eye for publicity. He could best them with several possible strategies. He could copy them, improving on some of their ideas, or develop tactics they had not employed. He could prove himself smarter and more creative than the ragged band of hippies to the south.

If the Zodiac chose to emulate the Manson Family, he could leave a message on an inanimate structure; he could adopt cool, hippy "hip" lingo in future communications; he could make reference to the Beatles; he could attack a major population center; and he could even strike in Southern California—or strike within Southern California *again*. As details played out, the Zodiac would attempt all of these. He may have been directly influenced to do so by the total and widespread attention granted to Charles Manson and his insane antics within the Manson Family.

∞

As August, 1969 drew to a close, no one knew who had butchered actress Sharon Tate, killed her unborn child, and murdered the others gathered in her home. And no one knew the purpose of the apparent senseless brutality. In this time of uncertainty and unanswered questions, the serial killer to the north would fight to regain his momentum, to express his dominance over the Bay Area and beyond, and attempt to reestablish his short-lived status as America's preeminent boogeyman.

5 | LAKE BERRYESSA

"Sept 27-69-6:30
by knife"

The Zodiac struck next on Saturday, September 27 in Napa
County on the shore of Lake Berryessa, along Twin Oaks Ridge,
on a mound jutting out into the water that is sometimes today
referred to as "Zodiac Island."

Victims Bryan Hartnell and Cecelia Shepard had no plans to
go to Lake Berryessa that afternoon. In fact, they had no intentions
of being together until they noticed each other during lunch. They
were among the 300 or so young people crammed into the student
dining hall of Pacific Union College (PUC) in the small community
of Anguin. Bryan was enrolled at PUC; Cecelia had been a student
there the previous school year, and was returning for a brief visit. The
couple had dated in the past, but had since firmly decided to remain
friends and not lovers.

Like Mageau and Ferrin twelve weeks earlier, Hartnell and
Shepard initially planned to explore San Francisco, a round trip that
would have taken them at least two hours. Also like the couple shot
at the Blue Rock Springs Park, they altered their schedule so that
they ended up at a remote, rural spot for the purpose of spending

some time alone. The Lake Berryessa event was, in many respects, a repeat performance of the drama at Blue Rock Springs. Hartnell and Shepard confronted the brutality of the same ruthless killer who would again murder a beautiful, young woman and leave a youthful male friend fighting for his life.

Born July 1, 1949, in Walla Walla, Washington, 20-year-old Bryan Calvin Hartnell was tall and slender with an enthusiastic smile and an earnestness that was admired by all who knew him. He hailed from Troutdale, Oregon, the western gateway to the Historic Columbia River Highway, the Mount Hood Scenic Byway, and the Columbia River Gorge. He felt at home in the rugged terrain of Northern California where he could explore new landscape and enjoy panoramic views reminiscent of home. Majoring in sociology, in 1969 he was a second-year PUC student. He would later attend the McGeorge School of Law and relocate to Southern California to set up his practice. He was well liked and had a large circle of friends at the college, including those in the same year with the same major and many from other graduating classes studying a variety of other subjects. Intelligent and studious, he was eager to please and very willing to help others. The morality taught at PUC, a Seventh Day Adventist college, played a prominent role in his life.

Bryan and Cecelia traveled first to the tiny town of St. Helena, a 20-minute trek down the winding highway south of Anguin. They stopped at a rummage sale where Bryan collected an old television for his dormitory room. After paying for the TV and loading it into the passenger seat of his 1956 Karmann Ghia, he realized that there was now no place for Cecelia to sit in his cramped, two-seat vehicle. Cecelia agreed to wait as he delivered the TV to his room at Newton Hall.

Upon Bryan's return at 2:00 p.m., the couple took note of the time. It was now too late to make the long trip into the city. Bryan had pressing responsibilities back at college that evening so the couple decided instead to drive up to Lake Berryessa, the man-made reservoir north of Napa.

Named for the first European settlers in the Berryessa Valley, José Jesús and Sexto "Sisto" Berrelleza, and later Anglicized to Berryessa, Lake Berryessa was created by the Monticello Dam whose construction began in 1953 and was completed in 1958. The reservoir was not completely filled until 1963, at which time it became the largest lake in Napa County. Unfortunately, the lake's creation claimed some of the finest agricultural soil in the nation—as well as the town of Monticello, which had to be abandoned to all but scuba enthusiasts.

Today, the lake encompasses 20,000 acres—measuring 15.5 miles from north to south, with a width of 3 miles—and supplies fresh water and hydroelectricity to the northern San Francisco Bay Area. The surrounding region has become a popular recreational area, supporting such activities as fishing, pleasure boating, swimming, picnicking, bird watching, hiking, and bicycling. To the southeast, near the Monticello Dam, there is a large hole used to release water during heavy rains. In 1997, a woman died after being sucked into the 72-foot, open bell-mouth spillway.

Quiet after Labor Day, the lake no longer bustled with summertime revelry. It was remote and secluded, set back from the busier highways of the area: 101 to the west and Interstate 80 to the south. The area was far enough off the beaten path that it was relatively free of murders, often several years passing between them. 1969 recorded an unusually high number of homicides for the Lake Berryessa region, however, notching near double digits.

The couple finally departed St. Helena midafternoon. They made their way to Knoxville Road, the two-lane highway that wove through the hills to the west of Lake Berryessa, and from which they could admire the oak trees and other vegetation that surrounded the lake. As they drove to the north, they began to look for a place to park, preferably near one of the many pathways to the water. Hartnell later recalled that as they approached the area from the south he noticed a car in the first turnout. He drove on, seeking seclusion, until he found a vacant parking area, the second or third turnout. He shut off his car.

Though the two had chosen amity over a romantic bond with one another, and she had relocated to Southern California, there was deep warmth and caring between Hartnell and Shepard. Without question, each would gladly make profound sacrifices for the other.

The couple gathered their belongings for the stop—including a plaid blanket and a deck of cards—and made their way along a path that would lead them to the water's edge. After carefully stepping over a foot stile, they navigated the narrow dirt trail and descended until they encountered an unpaved road which originated at a service entrance for park vehicles. Bryan and Cecelia were now halfway between Knoxville Road and the shoreline.

Cecelia Ann Shepard, "Cece" to her closest friends, was a petite beauty with a warm smile. Two years older than Bryan—she was born on New Year's Day in 1947 in Nuzzid, India—she similarly had a wide circle of friends and was well liked by her classmates. The lithe, 22-year-old woman had just completed her year at PUC that spring and was savoring the next chapter of her life: completing her bachelor's degree at U.C. Riverside in Southern California. She had traveled up north from Loma Linda the previous day with a girlfriend to pick up some items she had stored that spring at her former school. She also wanted to check in on friends and re-live some of the many joyous memories she carried from the region. The trip was not designed for her to meet up with Hartnell, but once the two began chatting in the dining hall, she made ample space in her schedule to spend the afternoon with her former boyfriend.

Continuing to follow the path, the couple skirted a tree-covered hill and made their way toward an oblong stretch of land which jutted left, paralleling the length of the lake. In some wet winters, water covered the narrow strip that connected the mainland to the elevated promontory, making their picnic area a sometime-seasonal island. Despite the heat of September, and the high demand for water in Northern California, Bryan noticed that they were crossing a temporary spit. They had entered Twin Oaks Ridge and set foot on a grassy peninsula that would in time be labeled "Zodiac Island."

They spread their blanket near one of three large oak trees and stretched out to enjoy the shade, the spectacular view of the lake with its ragged surrounding hills, and each other's company. They would remain in their idyllic surroundings for an uninterrupted 45 minutes of pleasant conversation. Then their lives would be altered forever as a serial killer completed his Northern California hat trick of carnage.

ɞ

At 8:20 that evening, Detective Sergeant Harold Snook, "Hal" to his friends, a time-tested veteran, received a telephone call from his headquarters, the Napa County Sheriff's Office (NCSO). An ambulance had been sent to Lake Berryessa in response to a report of a double stabbing, he was told. Snook requested that Detective Sergeant Ken Narlow and Detective Sergeant Richard Lonergan be called to the scene. He also ordered a police unit to secure the integrity of the site.

Immediately, NCSO telephoned Narlow and Lonergan at their respective residences, and notified them of the brutal knife attack on the shore of Lake Berryessa. They were told that the two victims were due to arrive at the Queen of the Valley Hospital in Napa, and that they should immediately proceed there to begin their investigation. By these calls, the two were effectively assigned the case.

Just after 8:30, Narlow entered the hospital, followed 11 minutes later by Lonergan.

Before his partner arrived, Narlow was informed that the unknown assailant responsible for the attack had used a telephone booth at the Napa Car Wash, on the corner of Clinton and Main Streets, to phone the Napa Police Station. The address was 1231 Main Street. The call was similar to the one the Vallejo Police Station fielded a mere twelve weeks earlier. Snook, who had just arrived at the hospital a few minutes after Lonergan, now rushed to the intersection to process the phone booth for clues.

At 7:40 p.m. on the night of the attack, Officer David Slaight of the Napa Police Department (NPD) received the unusual telephone call. He had been on patrol that evening, and as a rookie, the affable, young cop was required to man the phones during meal breaks. Dutifully, he had returned to the station to answer calls so that others could eat. Already aware of the attack at Lake Berryessa, he initially thought that some park ranger who was out of radio contact had pressed this caller into service to provide the Police Department with an update. Slaight heard a young-sounding, male voice, possibly from someone in his early 20s, calmly state,

"I want to report a murder, no a double murder. They are two miles north of park headquarters. They were in a white Volkswagen Karmann Ghia."

When the caller paused, Slaight interjected, "where are you now?" He wanted to know the exact location of the man who he thought was calling on behalf of a ranger so someone could be sent for an update.

The caller ignored the question and continued in a barely audible voice, "I'm the one that did it." At that, the line went silent.

Once again, the Zodiac serial killer had attacked a couple in a remote area and then made a taunting telephone call to the police. Once again, he had traveled to a location a few blocks from a police station to place the call using a public pay phone. The killer was following some twisted criminal blueprint, or he was repeating an activity that had been successful for him in the past.

Slaight, suddenly aware of the call's significance, telephoned the operator on another phone line, and asked if it was possible to put a trace on the call that he had just received. The operator promised to keep that line open, informing him that the caller had used a ten-cent pay phone. In speaking to the operator, the stranger had refused to identify the number from which he was calling. She told Slaight that the prefix of the telephone number was 255.

Years later, Slaight would explain how he located the telephone. As he listened to the line, he heard the sounds of some traffic passing by and some voices, possibly women. He had difficulty hearing very well because he was in the process of calling the Sheriff's Office on another line to report the call, and his own radio was hissing in the background. Nevertheless, he could tell that the receiver had not been returned to its cradle at the conclusion of the call. When someone from the Sheriff's Office—it may have been Slaight himself, he admitted—sent out a call to patrolling officers that the attacker had called from a pay phone with a prefix of 255, and that it sounded as if the telephone receiver had not been hung back up, a local reporter who had been listening on a police scanner moved into action. (The Napa Register reported on September 29 that it was Pat Stanley, the News Director at KVON Radio, and he was at the Sheriff's Office when the call was broadcast.) He drove around looking for a phone booth with its receiver dangling. When he discovered it on Main Street, he shouted into the booth, thus alerting Slaight.

Snook reached the telephone booth, as directed, just a few blocks from the Napa Police Station, at 8:50 p.m. Already present at the scene were Officer Eric Ronback and Reserve Officer Donald Stanley, who had both carefully protected the perimeter. Snook was informed that the assailant was not there, nor had any car left evidence of its presence, such as rubber skid marks or tire tread marks. No one had approached the officers while they were there, and no footprints were observable on the blacktop. There was also no evidence that anyone had fled from the booth in a hurry.

Snook observed the scene of the call. The telephone booth stood on the south wall of the car wash on Main Street. The folding door was on the south side of the booth. The phone within the booth was situated on the north corner of the east wall, with its receiver dangled directly under and to the south of the phone unit (in front of it). The openings of the receiver faced east.

Snook captured color photographs. He lifted 35 latent prints, carefully numbering them from 1 to 35, photographing four of them, numbers 29 through 32, prior to lifting them. He noted that water beads were present for three hours after he had arrived. The phone's number was recorded, 255-9673. Snook did not leave the site until 11:49 p.m.

The ambulance bearing the victims hurried into the hospital parking lot at the same time that Snook had arrived at the phone booth, two Piner Ambulance Company employees in attendance, Earl and Robert. To Narlow, the victims appeared to be in critical condition: Shepard was in a coma, and Hartnell spoke only in short bursts. Within five minutes, both Narlow and Lonergan were dismissed from the hospital entrance so that the emergency personnel could attend to their patients.

Two skilled physicians had been assigned the care of Hartnell and Shepard, though one of them had not yet arrived.

Narlow learned that Shepard's best friend was named Judy. Once outside the emergency room, the officers contacted the Chief Security Officer at PUC to gain assistance in contacting her. Upon hearing that she had left the college that afternoon, Narlow put out an APB (all-points bulletin) around the City of Napa and the County of Napa for her yellow Datsun.

At precisely 9:37, the officers were given permission to speak with Hartnell, who had been taken to the x-ray room for a better look at his injuries. Because his partner had been called away to the telephone, Lonergan conducted the interview alone. It was clear to the detective that the patient was in a great deal of pain, and was beginning to show signs of shock. The officer listened carefully to the information that was offered.

Hartnell related that he and Shepard had been approached by a gun-wielding man wearing a black ceremonial-type hood that was square on top. He guessed that the assailant weighed 200-250 pounds, a heavyset guy. After being tied up, the two victims were stabbed with a long knife that had been slipped out of its sheath. The assailant wore dark clothing: a dark jacket and dark pants. The knife had a black handle and was possibly homemade. The handgun appeared to be an automatic, but being unfamiliar with the specifics of guns, the victim was unable to offer anything more definitive. Hartnell was overcome by his body's response to his wounds—shock was eclipsing his will to assist the police. He quit speaking as if he was turning his attention to the process of healing. A more complete interview would be conducted the next day by Detective Sergeant John Robertson of the Napa County Sheriff's Department.

Narlow and Lonergan left for the Sheriff's office at 10:15 p.m., but not before assigning Deputy Sheriff Allen Brambrink and Deputy Sheriff William Munk to remain at the hospital to provide security for the victims until other arrangements could be made. No one knew whether their assailant, or someone else, would initiate a second attack at the hospital. The deputies were also assigned the task of receiving any clothing or other evidence as it was released by the hospital. Brambrink would soon be spirited away to provide security at the crime scene through the dark of night until the first signs of daylight.

Narlow's APB was successful, and Judy was soon located and brought to the Napa County Sheriff's Office (NCSO). She told Narlow and Lonergan that she was from Sun Valley, California.

Because she had been with the couple that afternoon, she was able to provide the investigators with information on the events that led up to the strange attack. She was with the victims when they left PUC at one o'clock for the rummage sale in St. Helena. She had last seen them at two o'clock in the afternoon. At that time, she told the officers, she believed that the couple was headed for San Francisco. She knew nothing of any plans to go to Lake Berryessa.

The lead investigators next traveled to the attack site at Lake Berryessa, arriving at six minutes before midnight. They found the scene guarded by uniformed officers under the control of Detective Sergeants Dave Collins and Ray Land of the Napa County Sheriff's Department. Years later, Narlow would relate that there was not much of a scene to secure by the lake since a warden had gathered the discarded clothing, the blanket, and other items and bunched them all together. Trying to be helpful, he had inadvertently contaminated evidence in the case.

Collins and Land briefed Narlow and Lonergan.

Recalling events years later, Collins guessed that he had been informed of the double stabbing at Lake Berryessa at 6:15 p.m. Further investigation placed the time of the stabbing at an estimated 6:15 p.m., and Collins' being notified sometime later. In his report for the State of California, Special Agent Mel Nicolai of the CII, who had been assigned to assist the Napa County Sheriff's Office by Supervising Special Agent Ken Horton, recorded that Collins was notified at 7:13 p.m. Collins was on the northeast side of Napa. Immediately, he contacted his partner, Land, who was in St. Helena. They each sped to the scene, arriving at the lake at almost the same time, about 30 minutes after first notification of the crime.

The four officers observed a white 1956 Volkswagen Karmann Ghia with a black vinyl top bearing Oregon plates parked by the side of Knoxville Road, near the entrance to a path that led to the attack site. On the passenger door, scrawled in black ink, a message from the killer taunted the investigators. The detectives were shown footprints and tire tracks believed to have been left by the assailant. They waited for the arrival of police photographer Sergeant Tom Butler and criminalist Detective Sergeant Hal Snook to collect and preserve the physical evidence.

As they waited, the lead detectives learned from Park Ranger Dennis Land that there was a locked gate one-half mile south of the victim's car which opened to a service road that snaked down toward the water. It crossed the path that Hartnell and Shepard had used to get down to beach. The detectives unlocked the gate, followed its roadway, and found footprints where the footpath traversed the service road, halfway between the crime scene on the beach and Hartnell's car on Knoxville Road. These prints matched those beside the car in the lot, so they decided to secure the area and wait until daylight to hunt for additional footprints. Somebody relocked the gate.

Detective Snook finally appeared at the lake twenty minutes into the next morning, having spent three hours processing the Napa telephone booth. He took careful measurements of the scene. The placement of Hartnell's car was established at seven-tenths of a mile north of Park Headquarters (not the "two miles" quoted by the caller). Fifteen feet north of the car Snook noted a stile for traversing the barbed-wire fence that separated the parking area from the pathway to the shore.

The footprints found from the stile to the side of Hartnell's Karmann Ghia, apparently left by the attacker, were thirteen inches long and four and one half inches wide. At the heel, the shoeprints measured three and one quarter inches in width. The heel that made the print was three and one seventh inches in length. The prints revealed a parallel tread pattern on both the heel and the sole inset which was three-quarters of an inch from the edges.

Butler photographed the shoe prints. A plaster cast was created from one them, and a photo was taken of Snook pointing at it (it led away from the foot stile in the direction of the car).

Snook noticed that the assailant's car had left tire impressions about 20 feet to the rear of the Karmann Ghia. One set was photographed and a cast was made. The impression nearest the fence was four and a half inches in width and evidenced a parallel tread design. Butler photographed it; Snook made a cast of it. The impression that lay the farthest from the fence was five and a half inches in width with a straight, one-eighth inch tread design in the center of a herringbone design on either side, consisting of three approximately one-sixteenth-inch treads between two approximately one-eighth-inch treads. This was also photographed by Butler and cast by Snook. Narlow would later comment on the mismatched treads, suggesting that they evidenced an older vehicle. The distance between the inside left tread and the inside right tread measured 52 inches, making the effective distance between the wheels—measured from the center of one tire to the center of the other—precisely 57 inches.

Butler took general photos of the scene, including the car's passenger door which had been defaced with some intriguing writing. The perpetrator had apparently, using a black felt tip pen measuring three-sixteenth of an inch at its tip, written his soon-to-be iconic crosshairs symbol above the following:

```
Vallejo
12-20-68
7-4-69
Sept 27-69-6:30
by knife
```

Latent fingerprints numbering 36 to 43 were lifted from the car and taken into evidence. The vehicle remained locked and showed no signs of tampering or attempted entry. Initially, Narlow kept secret the details of the car door writing from the general public. When a photograph of the scrawl was later disclosed, the last line, "by knife," was obscured from view with tape and a piece of brown paper. The NCSO wanted to withhold some information in order to challenge any future confessions. The media and public immediately began speculating on the contents of the concealed information, drawing fallacious conclusions. The NCSO attempted to calm public fears by announcing that the final line did not in fact contain a date on which the murderer planned a future attack.

The killer had claimed credit for his work. It was another attack by the Zodiac, connected by the words written on the car door to the two Vallejo-area crime scenes. The incident would be investigated as one of a series, but it would also need to be investigated in its own right. Perhaps this was the scene at which the killer's identity could be established. He may have had a connection to one of these two victims or the area now scarred by the violence. Or perhaps this wasn't a Zodiac attack at all. It may have been some other killer wanting to throw off investigators and lead them to fallaciously conclude it had been committed as part of the series.

&

Snook received from Detective Narlow several items, including one multi-colored blanket, one army type field jacket, and several lengths of white plastic clothesline (with a hollow core). Snook locked these in his car for transport to the Napa County Sheriff's Office. Narlow had previously taken into evidence the following items from Park Ranger Dennis Land: a blanket, a pair of men's shoes, a wallet belonging to Bryan Hartnell, one pair of eyeglasses, and a deck of playing cards. A few additional items were passed between the two, including numerous strands of white hollow plastic line cut into various lengths on which there appeared to be some blood staining.

The pieces of clothesline that were turned over to Snook for preservation as evidence in time would be subjected to numerous tests, including blood typing and DNA recovery. Forty-two years would elapse before technology would enable the NCSO to conduct "touch" DNA analysis. Law enforcement was never able to extract any useful forensic evidence from them, however. Only Hartnell and Shepard were shown to have had contact with the cords.

After Snook took the moulages of car tire tread marks, with Narlow and Lonergan assisting, Lonergan drove Hartnell's vehicle to the park's maintenance shop building, having acquired the keys from Hartnell at the hospital. The car was secured for the evening with the help of Ranger Land.

The following day, the car would again be moved, this time from Park Headquarters at Lake Berryessa. The vehicle was towed to Biava Motors in Napa, a company with which the NPD frequently conducted business and the site of Napa County's corporate yard. The vehicle's several items were inventoried, including a girl's red coat, a pair of girl's shoes, one tool box with tools, and one bank book belonging to Hartnell. Snook carefully removed the passenger door with its graffiti and booked it into evidence.

A vehicle report created after the car was impounded revealed that it was not well maintained. Overall, it rated a "fair" evaluation, and all four tires were in poor condition due to excessive wear. The spare was not any better. The interior had no clock, no air conditioning, and no heater. The report described the flivver merely as "drivable." Curiously, the registered owner was listed in a police report as a Bruce L. Christie.

Narlow and Lonergan traveled back to the turnout on Knoxville Road that had once contained the vehicle and waited for Deputy Sheriffs Allen Brambrink and Mel Fechter who were assigned security of the area. At 3:00 a.m., the lead detectives finally headed to their respective homes to catch a few hours of rest before continuing the investigation. The following weeks would see many nights of scant sleep for the investigators who devoted almost every waking minute to this case. This tragic and horrible event had entered their bailiwick. For Narlow, it would be a gnawing concern, not only during his career in law enforcement, but throughout his lengthy retirement, to his death at age 80, 41 years later.

࿐

On the morning following the attack, Detective Robertson met with Cecelia's parents, 48-year-old Robert Hiland Shepard and his 46-year-old wife, Wilma Dolores Shepard, both living in Loma Linda, in Southern California's San Bernardino County. Cecelia's friend, Lori, who had driven with her from Loma Linda that weekend, was also present for the questioning. The parents told Robertson that their daughter had been threatened by Gary, a 21-year-old senior at PUC, when she started dating Bryan back in 1968.

But Gary was not a good suspect for the assault. Not only was he slight in build—far too petite to be the masked attacker—but he was also well known to Bryan who would have immediately recognized his voice and physique. Personal jealously of Hartnell did not appear to be the motive for the attack.

Nevertheless, Robertson followed up on this lead. A sergeant from Oakland called him two days later, saying that he had been in contact with a friend of Cecelia's, named Madeline, a first year Mills College student who knew Gary. The Sergeant wanted to know whether or not Gary was a prime suspect. He promised to call back if and when Gary made contact with Madeline.

Cecelia's parents could provide no other motive for their daughter's predicament, but offered the names of numerous people known to her, including Gwendolyn, who had attended PUC two years earlier; Edward, a former PUC student who worked for a mortuary in Lodi; Eleanor, the dean of students; and Jerry, a current PUC student. Lori was unable to offer a single reason for the assault on her friend.

That afternoon at 12:30 p.m. Robertson interviewed Hartnell. Shepard had undergone surgery earlier in the morning and was unavailable to talk. She persisted in a coma. Both victims remained in the ICU, Shepard in critical condition; Hartnell's condition had been cautiously upgraded to serious. A heavily sedated Hartnell gave a statement that was recorded, and later transcribed by M. Feurle.

Bryan explained that he and Cecelia had known each other for some time, were good friends, and that Cecelia had come to area for the weekend with Lori to visit some friends. The two girls were due to drive back south on Sunday, September 28.

After enjoying each other's company over the din of clacking plates and elevated voices at lunch that day, Bryan asked Cecelia (because they used to be good friends and had dated two years prior), "Well, are you doing anything special this afternoon?"

"Why?" Cecelia replied.

"I don't know. We could go out and either go for a walk, go to San Francisco, or you know just…" At that, they made plans to drive to San Francisco together. Though Bryan's current girlfriend was back home in Washington, he did not believe that he was betraying her. This was just a casual get together, a social meeting of friends, he convinced himself.

By the time Bryan and Cecelia got done picking up a few things in St. Helena and carting around a couple of people, it was too late to make it into San Francisco and be home for the evening worship service, Hartnell explained to Robertson. They made a decision at that time to drive up to Lake Berryessa.

Bryan had a favorite spot. Unfortunately, he was unable to locate it and stopped where they did simply because it was as good a place as any other. The parking area was deserted.

Recounting the minutes leading up to the attack, Hartnell explained that the couple walked down to the water, about a quarter mile from the parking area on Knoxville Road, and had selected the shade from a large tree on the peninsula from which to look at the bucolic scenery. There were two trees that he noticed, one of them large that spread out. They selected the shade from the tree that was most northerly situated. Once reclined, they began to reminisce about old times. They talked for about 45 minutes.

The first indication that the couple was not alone came from him. As they chatted—Hartnell explained to Robertson from his bed—he heard some leaves rustling and asked Cecelia if she could see anything, because she had her "specs" on (Hartnell was also facing the other direction). "See what the big deal is," he commanded.

"It's some man." Cecelia replied.

"Is he alone?" Bryan inquired.

"Yeah." Shepherd kept watching him until she told Bryan that he had gone behind a tree. Hartnell wondered out loud why the man did that, asking whether he was taking a "leak."

"Keep looking. Tell me what happens." Hartnell ordered.

Years later, he would explain that he was lying on his back with Cecelia resting her hands on his chest. They were reclining on the blanket in such a way that she could observe events back from the shore while he gazed across the water. His later description of events differed somewhat from what Robertson recorded during the hospital visit. In 2007, Hartnell said that it was Shepard who first reported the presence of the man. She was obviously distracted from the conversation, he would explain, causing him to ask what was going on.

Hartnell later elaborated that he thought that the stranger was far off in the distance, beyond and across a nearby cove, at least 1,000 feet away. He found the information about the man's presence interesting, but nothing of great urgency. His misconceptions about the man's location seemed confirmed when Cecelia reported that the stranger had slipped behind a tree. Hartnell, aware that the adjacent peninsula was undeveloped and therefore had no bathroom facilities, believed that the man had ducked behind a tree to relieve himself—not something that particularly worried him. Yet Cecelia continued her inattention to Bryan, something he found annoying.

Suddenly, Shepard noticed the stranger emerge from behind the tree whose shade they were enjoying. She squeezed his arm and shouted, "Oh my God, he has a gun!" (Hartnell's version years later would be, "Oh my God, he's got a gun!") The assailant was pointing a black, automatic pistol as he walked briskly toward them.

It would not be until 2007 that Sergeant Collins would relate what Cecelia had reported to him on the day of the attack as they rushed her to the hospital. The stranger was 200 to 300 yards away when she first spotted him, she had said to Collins. He made his way toward the couple until he was only 75 to 100 feet from them. Then he stepped behind a tree that was a mere 50 to 75 feet away, where he donned a black hood. In a 2007 interview, Collins shared Shepard's description of her attacker, though the information never made it into his report: the hooded stranger was an overweight, bulky, 190 to 200 pound, Caucasian man with brown hair who was five feet, eleven inches or six feet tall. Collins would sheepishly explain that he saw no need at the time to include this information in a police report.

Hartnell described for Robertson his recollection of the suspect's odd appearance. He was wearing a black ceremonial hood made of cloth, covering his head and shoulders, almost to his waist. (He would later characterize the garment as an "overlay" or a "dickey.") On the top of the hood, the four corners made it roughly the size and shape of a brown paper grocery bag.

The hood was ingeniously devised. On the front of the assailant's chest was a crosshairs symbol, three or four inches in diameter—four inches in diameter Hartnell would estimate years later. Even though the assailant wore clip-on sunglasses to cover the eye apertures slit into his hood—appearing to be affixed to the hood and not to glasses underneath—some dark brown, combed hair was visible.

At the time of the attack, the outfit meant nothing to Hartnell. He assumed it was some disguise used only to hide his appearance, possibly something obtained at a costume shop. The crosshairs symbol also carried no meaning for him, though he noted that it was proportional, possibly machine made, and not merely scrawled haphazardly. The stranger wore a dark blue, cotton windbreaker, the type on which the collar can be turned up, and dark blue or black, old-fashioned-style pleated suit pants. He may have had something in the pouch of his jacket. Hartnell could not remember anything about the stranger's shoes or whether he had gloves on his hands.

From the sound of his voice, Hartnell estimated that his attacker was between 20 and 30 years of age. Because it was often difficult for him to guess the height of others, he estimated that the stranger was anywhere between five feet eight inches to six feet tall. He also had difficulty estimating the weight of the man. Sometime later, he would question his estimate because he was not certain of the man's clothing. If he wore a jacket with a lining, Hartnell later reasoned, he might have been thinner and lighter than the original estimate, but he guessed the man's weight at between 225 and 250 lbs. He noted that the man was a sloppy dresser. His stomach may even have been hanging out and over his trousers.

The hooded man walked briskly toward the couple but did not run. He spoke with some kind of drawl, Hartnell suggested, but not a southern drawl. It was oddly familiar to him. He could hear it in his mind but was unable to replicate it. Also, there was something about the cadence. He described it as a moderately pitched voice that was neither high nor low. In a later interview, he described the voice as slow and measured, a very distinctive tone—with a precise cadence. He could not detect any foreign accent.

The man did not appear to be well-educated, a point about which Hartnell was certain. However, he did not feel his attacker was illiterate either, just from a lower class of people, especially suggested by his clothing.

The ridiculousness of the situation was one of the first things that struck Hartnell when he saw the costumed stranger approach with a gun. Bryan had only 75 cents in his possession, and here he was being held up at gunpoint. He even considered his good fortune: he could experience a hold-up for a very low cost. He recalled that he said to his attacker, "I don't mean to call your bluff, but wouldn't you rather be caught on a stealing charge than on a homicide?"

"'Well, just don't start playing hero on me. Don't try to grab the gun.'" Hartnell quoted the hooded man to Robertson.

In a separate report for the NCSO, Hartnell did his best to recall the conversation that had occurred between the assailant, Cecelia, and Hartnell himself, attempting to recreate the dialogue verbatim. The following quotes are Hartnell's exact words from this report:

Cecelia was the first to speak. "What do you want?"

As the hooded man began to cover the distance between himself and the couple, he pointed the gun, which he was holding in his right hand, toward them.

"Now take it easy—all I want's your money. There is nothing to worry about—all I want is your money." The man began, trying to put Bryan and Cecelia at ease.

Bryan spoke up at this point. "O.K.—whatever you say. I want you to know that I will cooperate so you don't have to worry—whatever you say we'll do. Do you want us to come up with our hands up or down?"

This may have been going more smoothly for the man in black than he ever guessed it would. In his pre-attack planning, he may have considered many possibilities like a chess player anticipating the moves of his opponent. If they screamed, he'd have to order them to shut up. If they ran for the safety of the trees, he could shoot them—or possibly just return to his car and drive off. If they asked questions or argued, he would have to reason with them or threaten them. Their compliance was as much as he could hope for, and may have caught him off guard.

"Just don't make any fast moves—come up slowly," he ordered.

"But we don't have any money—all I have is 75 cents." Bryan explained, possibly laughing.

"That doesn't matter—every little bit helps." Here the hooded man paused. His attack may have been progressing so easily that he almost didn't know what to do next. Even though the couple never asked, he felt obligated to explain himself. "I'm on my way to Mexico—I escaped from Deer Lodge Prison in Montana, Deer Lodge. I need some money to get there."

The light was fading. By 6:00 p.m., the sun had ducked beyond the hills to the west. Lake Berryessa remained aglow from the sun's radiance on the ridge across the lake and from the indirect rays emanating from the bright blue sky. Darkness would engulf the recreation area soon after 7:30; by 8:00, the welkin would be black.

It would get cold at Lake Berryessa overnight, with temperatures dropping into the 50s. Still, for the trio, it was a pleasant, near-room-temperature dusk.

Bryan attempted to be helpful. "You're welcome to the money I have, but isn't there something else I can do for you? Give you a check or get some more?" Years later Bryan explained that he was just trying to help the man in any way he could. Even though this stranger was training a gun on him, Hartnell felt compassion. He was cooperating with the stranger and expected him to reciprocate the kindness.

Bryan's offer of assistance may have surprised the assailant. In all of his preparations, he may never have expected his victims to become helpful, even offering to aid him in his quest for money.

"No," he said weakly. As Bryan would soon discover, the man with the weapon was never really interested in cash.

Taking charge of the conversation, Bryan offered more assistance. "I can give you my phone number and you can call me."

There was no reply.

"I want to get in contact with you." Bryan continued. "I am a sociology major and maybe I can even offer you more help than you think you need."

"No," the bemused man reiterated. He had become an automaton. He may not have been sure how or when he should regain the upper hand in the conversation. He had ceded control, and it likely bothered him. He had brought a gun, a knife, and some rope to the scene to give him the power that he probably lacked in other areas of his life. Kind words from a helpless victim had completely wrestled away from him any illusion of control.

Unintentionally, Bryan may have added to the insult. "Well, is there any other thing you need?"

"Yes." The hooded man seemed to have found a way to save face, all the while continuing to accede to the leadership of his victim. He could deflect the grilling by Hartnell if he could make new demands. "One more thing—I want your car keys. My car is hot."

Once again, the man with the gun had control of the conversation. Nevertheless, he again felt the need to explain and defend his request. While his car may or may not have been stolen, it was not true that he wanted Hartnell's car keys. He would never take them with him, just as he would leave behind the 75 cents, untouched. These were props, as if used in a movie, soon abandoned because they had served their purpose of disguising the faux robber's true intentions.

Bryan reached into his pockets. In the stress of the situation he had forgotten where he had stowed his keys. He patted his front pockets, then his back pockets. He explained to his attacker, "I guess in all the excitement I don't remember where I put them. Let's see. Are they in my shirt, in the ignition, on the blanket…?" The many words may have allayed Hartnell's anxiety, but may have also served to frustrate his attacker.

Hartnell changed the subject as he continued to search. "On T.V. movies and in an article in the *Readers Digest* they say that thieves rarely keep their guns loaded. Is yours?"

Responding slightly excitedly, the man blurted, "Yes, it is!" As if to explain himself and his ferociousness, he calmly added, "I killed a couple of men before."

"What? I didn't hear you." Bryan challenged. The hood was difficult to hear through, or maybe the man beneath it spoke too softly.

"I killed a couple of guards getting out of prison. And I'm not afraid to kill again." By elaborating on his past, the gunman may have been hoping to instill more fear in a young man who was more chatty and helpful than afraid. (When Narlow later contacted the Montana State Prison located in Deer Lodge, Montana, he learned that no such escape had occurred and no guards had been killed.)

Cecelia interjected at this point. "Bryan—do what he says."

"Now I want the girl to tie you up." Strangely, the hooded man spoke only to Hartnell, maybe because Bryan was so talkative, but maybe because he felt intimidated by his female victim. The assailant pulled some lengths of pre-cut, hollow clothesline from his back pocket and passed them to Cecelia.

Hartnell years later clarified this point. At the time, he felt that he could get the gun away from the hold-up man if he could get just a little closer, Bryan being the taller of the two. As Cecelia tied loose knots around his wrists, he suggested the idea to her. She responded with obvious fear and didn't want him to try anything dangerous. He heeded her request since her life would be at risk as well as his if he were to attempt to snatch the gun.

This decision may have cost Cecelia her life. But not necessarily. Bryan also noted that the hooded man stepped back a few paces and kept his distance from that point on, never giving him a real chance to reach for the weapon.

Hartnell continued to talk. "This is really strange. I wonder why someone hasn't thought of this before. I'll bet there is good money in it."

The cloaked stranger said nothing.

"What was the name of that prison?" Hartnell continued his friendly banter, attempting to draw out the mysterious man.

Again, the hooded man said nothing.

"No really, what did you say the name of it was?" Hartnell insisted.

Possibly feeling obligated, the gunman now responded grudgingly, "Deer Lodge in Montana."

Cecelia, fighting back her nervousness, loosely tied the hands of her former boyfriend. The stranger approached and tightened the cords that bound Hartnell, and then tied Shepard's hands behind her back. If there was additional dialogue here, Bryan could not recall it. It may be lost to history. The next words he remembered occurred after the couple's wrists were tightly bound.

"Now I want you both to lay face down so I can tie up your feet." The assailant demanded. Either the grammatical error in his words was inserted by Hartnell and the stranger actually said, "*lie* face down," the stranger did not know the proper use of the word "lie," or he wanted Hartnell to believe that he did not know proper grammar.

"Come on—we could be out here for a long time and it could get cold at night," Hartnell objected strenuously as darkness encroached. He considered the prospect of remaining out by the lake, through the descending temperatures, until they would invariably be discovered by Sunday picnickers. The cold would be uncomfortable, but the real annoyance was the inconvenience of remaining there for hours.

"Come on—get down." was all the man said, insistently.

Bryan was not done arguing. His amiable attitude had elicited facts as a poker player cajoles his opponents into conversation for advantage. He knew he could question and object without being shot. He continued to speak in an effort to finagle concessions.

"Listen, I didn't complain when you tied our hands, but this is ridiculous!"

"I told you…" The man tried to cut Bryan off.

"We aren't going anywhere—Anyway, I don't think that it's necessary." Bryan may instead have said, "Aw, come on—we don't want to." He couldn't remember which statement more accurately represented his actual words.

The man pointed his pistol at Hartnell. "I told you to get down!" (To Robertson, Hartnell quoted the man, "Get down. Right now!")

Hearing the seriousness of the demand and feeling the threat of the gun, Hartnell and Shepard acquiesced. They lowered themselves to the ground and lay on their stomachs. The hooded man wasted no time in using additional cords to bind their legs. Then he began to hogtie them like two expendable sheep at a rodeo.

Hartnell spoke again to continue humanizing the victims in the eyes of their assailant. "Your hands are shaking. Are you nervous?"

"I guess so." The hooded man laughed in a relaxed manner. The conversation may have been calming to him too.

"Well, I suppose that I'd be nervous too." Hartnell attempted to make a connection with the man who was binding him. It wouldn't matter. "Now that all is said and done, was that gun really loaded?" Hartnell may instead have said, "Now that everything is all said and done, could you show me that your gun is loaded?" He still suspected that no bullets were involved in this attack, still did not comprehend the extent of the threat to their lives.

"Yes, it was!" the attacker claimed. Hartnell thought his words may instead have been, "Sure, I'll show you."

In one final act of responding to Hartnell's numerous requests, the man proudly displayed the gun, removed the magazine, and demonstrated that in fact the gun was loaded by showing him a full magazine. He then returned the magazine to the weapon.

Then, without speaking, he put the gun back into its holster hanging from his belt, and with his left hand drew a 12-inch bayonet-style knife from a scabbard, also hanging from his belt. Crouching down, he thrust the blade into Hartnell's back.

In his interview with Robertson, Hartnell provided some additional information that did not appear in the transcript of the dialogue he provided the NCSO. To Hartnell, the assailant had also said, "Okay. Lay down. I've got her tied down."

Hartnell also summarized the event in a joint interview he conducted from his hospital room on October 7 with the Napa Register and the radio station KVON. To the media, he claimed, "I tried to keep the conversation as light as possible." He also acknowledged that he had "tried to maintain the psychological advantage over the hooded man." He told the media that he had asked a lot of questions, but the man refused to answer most of them.

Hartnell described for Robertson the events following the dialogue. After he saw the man put away his gun, he turned toward Cecelia to say something to her. Suddenly, without any warning of what was happening, he was struck. He may have seen a flash of the knife as it was being drawn. He couldn't remember. The knife now slid into the flesh of his back, again and again. He described the sound as, "CHOMP, CHOMP, CHOMP, CHOMP."

In reaction, he made guttural sounds as though he were unable even to scream at the way the appalling events were unfolding.

When Cecelia turned to see why he was making the odd noise, she almost fainted. She became hysterical and began to yell.

Bryan, realizing his predicament, resigned himself to dying. With 6 stab wounds deep into his back (not the 10 or the 12 that *The San Francisco Examiner* would later report, nor the "dozen" mentioned in *The San Francisco Chronicle*), he was certain that the only outcome for the two was that of murder victims.

Still, he wanted to live, so he feigned death. It was his only hope against the unprovoked brutality.

After stabbing Hartnell, the knife-wielding man turned his attention to Cecelia, who was by this time screaming uncontrollably. She had seen what had happened to her friend and knew exactly what awaited her. Frantically, she began to twist and turn against the ropes that held her in place. Thrusting with grunts of exertion, or sexual release, the assailant stabbed her 10 times (and not the 24 times *The Examiner* would report or the "more than 20 times" reported by *The Chronicle*), 5 times in her back, and then 5 in her front when she attempted to roll away from him, including 1 thrust to her groin area and 1 that pierced her left breast. Bryan would describe the attack on his friend as "some kind of frenzy," adding that the attacker "went hog-wild." Years later, he would explain that he had watched the start of the attack on her, but had turned away. He couldn't bear to witness what was happening.

Bryan described the knife to Robertson. It was sheathed in a case that might have been made of wood, and hung on the right side of his belt on the front of his trousers. It appeared to be a bread knife in size and shape, approximately 12 inches long, and three-quarters of an inch wide. The handle was hardwood, with two brass rivets. There was also some cotton surgical tape with a width of approximately one inch wrapped around the knife's handle.

Hartnell also clarified a few points, including the fact that Cecelia had tossed Hartnell's wallet toward the attacker as she was tying him up. He described his attacker's gun holster as a shiny, smooth, and black, not a weave pattern.

Their attacker departed after the stabbing. Hartnell sensed that he was being observed so he held his breath and continued to play dead. He did not hear the man make his way back up the path toward Knoxville Road. The assailant took neither money nor keys. He had been with the couple about 15 minutes in total, Bryan estimated.

Turning to Cecelia when he felt it was safe to do so, Bryan began to share. He told his friend that he did not intend to make a death-bed conversion, but wanted to speak about some things before he died.

Hartnell provided Robertson some of the personal information that flowed between the two ill-fated friends. Later to the media, he confided that he and Shepard "needed the psychological and spiritual encouragement."

∽

In addition to taking a statement from Hartnell, Robertson was also tasked with determining, if possible, the type of gun and brand of ammunition that had been present at the scene. Because Hartnell had observed the stranger's handgun, and had gotten a glimpse of the bullets when his attacker removed the magazine, investigators hoped that he could describe—and even clearly identify—what he saw. Unfortunately, Hartnell's information was of limited use, even though he tried to describe for Robertson the shape and size of the bullets and the specifics of the handgun. Drawing pictures and explaining details provided little additional information.

On the Wednesday morning following the attack, Robertson brought 10 different models of handguns to his hospital room, including a Luger automatic 9mm, a Browning automatic 9mm, and a Colt automatic .45. Hartnell, who was utterly unfamiliar with guns, was not sure whether any of them resembled the assailant's weapon. He did state that he thought the model that most closely represented what he saw was the .45 caliber steel-blue pistol. The handguns were cataloged and photographed by Sergeant Butler and Deputy D. Bush.

Robertson returned that afternoon with a collection of 10 sample bullets of various size and design. Hartnell selected a .45 caliber brass bullet with brass casing as what he possibility saw, but he said that he could not be absolutely certain whether this was exactly like what he had seen in his attacker's possession.

☙

From his hospital bed the day after the attack, Hartnell provided Robertson with details on the minutes after his ordeal:

The couple attempted to wriggle free of their bindings. Hartnell explained that Shepard was too weak to move her hands—and therefore unable untie him—but he was able to loosen her knots with his teeth. Though she pulled one hand free of the cords, she was too upset to aid him. He remained immobilized.

As they struggled, the couple noticed a boat with two people in it that was circling the waters. They yelled to the occupants for help. Bryan desperately rocked back and forth to gain their attention as if he were dodging bullets. The boat approached the shoal in front of them; the engine shut off. After about 15 minutes (the driver of the boat would later estimate only 2 or 3 minutes), its engine roared to life and it slipped away.

Hartnell would elaborate on the situation in an interview years later. In the effort to gain emergency assistance, he had set to work calling across the water, and found a specific position at which he felt the sound of his voice carried. A couple of boats passed by—as many as four or five—possibly thinking that the couple was playing or joking, or simply unaware of his cries over the sound of their motors. A fishing boat, passing between the couple and a nearby island, stopped to observe. The boat moved closer. Someone shut off the engine. The couple tried everything they could think of to cajole the boat's two occupants to come to their aid. Soon, the boat started again and, like the others, it too departed.

About the same time, Hartnell told Robertson, Shepard suggested that she try again to loosen her former boyfriend's cords. With much effort, she was able to release one of his hands. (Years later, his story would omit Shepherd's offer and provide an abbreviated, "I felt her hands on my bindings…") He quickly untied both of his hands and then released Shepard. They were free of the attacker's cords, but they were not yet in the clear.

Hartnell still believed that he was dying. He felt his consciousness drain from his body, as someone might experience the descent of a fall. When the bottom never came, he began to think that he could survive. As he considered his fate, he thought of his parents and their Christian faith: his father was a clergyman with the Seventh Day Adventist Church. He acknowledged to himself that he hadn't been as good of a Christian as he wanted to be. He also pictured in his mind the many things he still hoped to accomplish in his life.

He realized that "whatever was going to be was going to be," but resolved to live. "I was going to try my damnedest to stay alive," he told Robertson. He asked God to help him. He held on to the belief that "God would do everything the best," but Bryan didn't think that his death would be the best. This firmly-held belief became his motivation.

With his new found mobility, he attempted to reach the highway, his only hope of gaining assistance, he believed. However, when he moved, darkness covered his visage. He was only able to ambulate 5 or 10 feet at an effort, and then only by stooping, clutching his chest, and repeatedly falling to the ground to regain strength. He attempted to push himself further but was too weak to do so. He told Robertson that he was certain that he never lost consciousness during the whole ordeal.

Hartnell achieved the gravel service road, but had not gone very far away from his former girlfriend. Suddenly, a pick-up truck approached and a man with a heavy coat emerged. His attacker had returned, Bryan thought. Then he noticed an emblem on the driver's jacket.

Park Ranger Dennis Land would report that he was patrolling with Sergeant William "Bill" White—a veteran who had been a member of the Lake Berryessa ranger staff since 1959—near the Pope Creek Bridge when the emergency call had interrupted them. He had deposited his partner at the marina to speak to the witnesses and summon backup, and then headed for Twin Oaks Ridge. When he found Hartnell in the grass on the right of the dirt pathway to the lake, he noticed the blood on the young man's back and abdomen.

With Land's arrival Hartnell realized that the fisherman had not abandoned the couple. Their savior had motored to the marina for help. That boatman, Ronald Henry Fong, who had traveled to Lake Berryessa with his nine-year-old son for a fishing trip, later reported that he told the couple that he was going to get help, left over their pleas to take them with him, and returned after about 25 to 30 minutes. When he first heard their cries, he thought it was a "gag." He noticed through his binoculars one person was resting against another, and one of whom had a large amount of what looked like blood on his back.

The injured man cried out to the ranger, "Help me. Help me!" As Land identified himself, Hartnell changed his message: "Don't bother with me. My girlfriend is hurt much worse."

Land gathered Hartnell into his truck, attempted to make him as comfortable as possible, and drove down to the water to where Shepard remained. When they approached her, Land and Hartnell observed that Ranger White had already arrived by boat with four others. They were offering Shepard assistance. Rangers Land and White had reached the victims by land and by water.

To Hartnell, it seemed that the rangers were not in a hurry. He estimated the Land's arrival at 90 minutes following the attack. White and Land wrapped the couple in blankets and tried to quiet them as they waited for the ambulance.

Though the couple was anxious to get to a doctor, it was another 15 minutes before the ambulance appeared. Hartnell estimated the wait at 60 minutes. Fong also remained there with his son until the couple was transported.

The officers reported that as they waited Shepard was in particular distress. She cried out to them, begging for something that would kill the pain or knock her out. Ranger White suggested that she scratch some other part of her body in an effort to distract her from the anguish. It worked for a few minutes, but soon she was crying out again. He noticed that, surprisingly, the victims weren't bleeding anymore despite the fact there were so many knife wounds. It was a very bad sign.

The journey to the Queen of the Valley Hospital proved to be a tortuous and agonizingly slow ride as they traced the serpentine highway that separated Napa from Lake Berryessa. Hartnell later estimated that the journey took an hour. If only an ambulance had been stationed nearby, he later bemoaned, Cecelia may have survived.

Robertson asked Hartnell a few final questions before wrapping up the interview.

"Did he swear or use profanity?"

"No." Not any more than Hartnell used himself, nothing that stood out to him.

"Did he search you?" Robertson continued.

"Heck no." Hartnell found the man totally unprofessional. He didn't even take the quarters or his billfold.

Robertson was perplexed. "Why did he stab you when you weren't fighting him off or anything?"

Hartnell could think of no good reason. Maybe he got nervous, he considered.

Robertson left his card with Hartnell, telling the injured man that he would be visiting him quite a bit. He assured him that there was a guard on his floor for his protection. Because Bryan feared that his girlfriend would hear of the attack through the media and become upset, he asked Robertson to arrange for a telephone call to her in Oregon. He wanted to tell her himself.

Hartnell asked whether any clues had been found in the attempt to identify his assailant. Robertson said they had, but advised him that a lot of work was required before they could get the guy. Hartnell reiterated that the hooded man had said that he was heading for Mexico.

Hartnell held no animosity toward the stranger. He told Robertson that he did not want this to happen again to anyone. At the time, neither man could guess that decades would pass with no arrest in the case.

After Robertson departed the hospital room, Charles Sims, the Official County Court Reporter took a brief statement from Hartnell, but the patient was still heavily sedated so Sims was unable to go into the case in any great detail.

ᘯ

Earlier that day, at seven in the morning after too few hours of sleep, the lead detectives were back at the crime scene, this time accompanied by Detective Hal Snook, Captain Donald Townsend, and Sergeant James Munk. Narlow and Lonergan aided Snook in tracking footprints from the car to the attack site.

The investigation was in full gear.

An hour later, Narlow and Lonergan received a report from the Park Headquarters that a dentist and his son wanted to speak with them about a possible suspect in the attack. The four gathered at the Spanish Flat coffee shop at 9:12 a.m. The dentist and his 16-year-old son, David, both of Los Gatos, related their potentially relevant experiences of the previous day.

The two had parked their car at approximately 6:30 p.m. a couple miles north of Park Headquarters, they explained to Narlow and Lonergan. While making their way to the beach, David had noticed a man hiking in the area. The lone male adult was approximately five feet ten inches tall with a heavy build. He was wearing dark trousers and a dark shirt that had some red in it, according to the teenager. The shirt had long sleeves. The man carried nothing as he strolled along the side of the hill, halfway between the lake and the road, but when he spotted David, he abruptly turned around and started walking up the hill, to the south of and away from the dentist and his son.

To David at the time the man was just out walking. Nothing suspicious.

The father and son had noticed no car, and only saw the man from a distance of about 100 yards. Also present, according to the dentist, was a man with two boys who were shooting BB guns in the area. The dentist was unaware of whether the three had seen anything or not.

The detectives considered the geography of the area. They estimated that the dentist and his son had been approximately eight-tenths of a mile north of the attack scene. Because there were four water-filled coves across that distance, they concluded that the pair had not seen the man who had stabbed Hartnell and Shepard. They apparently didn't believe there was time for the assailant to drive or walk to the second location. Evidently, the officers accepted the attacker's claim of 6:30 p.m. written on Hartnell's car door.

By 10:00 that morning, the lead detectives were back at the crime scene to aid Snook in locating and collecting additional evidence.

Earlier, at 8:00 a.m., Snook and Lonergan followed footprints from the vehicle to the attack site and back. They made plaster casts of a heel print at the bottom of the first hill. A complete print was taken from the junction of the path and the dirt service road, located about 50 feet from where Land first found Hartnell. Another footprint—this one discovered on a sandy patch of ground approximately 100 feet from the site of the stabbing—was photographed and cast because of its crisp record of instep detail. The detectives placed cardboard beer flats over suspected prints, showing the direction of travel. The distance from the place Hartnell parked his car just off Knoxville Road to the attack site on the shoreline was eventually established at 510 yards.

Snook noticed an abandoned green bottle near a stump on the suspected approach route. He tagged it and placed it into evidence. It was processed for latent impressions, yielding lifts numbered 44 to 48. In 2012, testing of its glass surface yielded negative results for "touch DNA" when a grant for DNA analysis became available to the Napa County Sheriff Department's Cold Case Unit. When funding ran out later in 2012, the unit was disbanded.

The detectives collected numerous soil samples: from the location where attack occurred, from behind the tree where the attacker reportedly stood to don his hood, and from the parking lot area beside the victim's car—at the passenger side where the assailant evidently crouched to write. All of the potential useful evidence was carefully marked as it was gathered.

Snook ordered aerial photographs of the site. These were captured by Napa Register photographer Robert McKenzie. Special Deputy

Harold Moskowitz of the Napa County Sheriff Department's Aerial Squadron piloted the aircraft.

Following what he described at the time as a "thorough crime scene search" that included taking general photographs of the area, Snook returned to the NCSO, arriving at approximately 5:00 p.m. He took custody of the following items brought from Queen of the Valley Hospital by Brambrink and Munk: shoes and socks, trousers, a shirt, a t-shirt, a pair of shorts, a belt, a wallet, a key, a pair of glasses, playing cards, and additional items, all property of Bryan Hartnell's; and, from Shepard, a dress, a slip, a pair of panties, and a bra.

In their thoroughness, the lead detectives interviewed Ranger Sergeant William White that afternoon at 1:20, questioning him about his participation in locating and aiding the stabbed couple. White stated that he had been on routine patrol around the lake just before 7:00 p.m. on September 27, when he received a call from Park Headquarters that instructed him to proceed to Rancho Monticello Resort on Lake Berryessa, where someone was reporting a possible stabbing.

He was met at the resort by Archie White and his wife Elizabeth "Beth" White—neither related to Ranger White—and Fong, the fisherman, with his accompanying son. Together they raced in one of Archie's quickest ski boats to the beach site where the attack had been reported. Once there, they discovered a female writhing in great pain from multiple stab wounds.

At almost the same time, he noted, Dennis Land arrived at the scene in his truck, which was bearing a male with his own set of stab wounds. White then radioed Park Headquarters requesting an ambulance and a sheriff's deputy.

Ranger White repeated for the detectives what Hartnell had said to him at the scene, though his words would be at odds with Hartnell's. He claimed that the male victim had heard the suspect say that he was an ex-convict from Colorado (not Montana) en route to Mexico. White also relayed that Hartnell had heard the hooded man say, "I'm going to have to stab you." Hartnell claimed to have replied, "Stab me first; I can't stand to see her stabbed first." If Ranger White accurately recounted what he had heard from Hartnell, the stab victim must have quickly forgotten this portion of the dialogue, for he never repeated it during the many interviews in which he later participated: those at the hospital, those after his release from the hospital, and those during the decades following the attack. Hartnell consistently reported that his assailant had named the state of Montana, not Colorado, and he remained silent about any request to be the first to encounter the knife. He would repeatedly recall across the decades that he never had any warning of the stranger's brutal knife attack. He explained that he was never in fear of his life—believing that he had successfully dulcified the man who was robbing him—until the blade entered his back. It was also reported that Hartnell told his attacker, "I'm chicken. Stab me first," but the victim denied it, calling the suggestion "preposterous." The lack of congruence between Hartnell's narration of events and White's statement was not surprising to the investigators.

In an emergency, during a state of confusion, the details that witnesses report seeing and hearing do not always agree. There is usually a fair share of contradiction because eyewitness testimony is among the least accurate information that a detective can gather. The detectives realized that it was quite possible that Ranger White was reporting as dialogue what a stunned Hartnell was thinking out loud to himself as he attempted to make sense of his horror-filled experience. White may also have been affected in a way that altered his own memory while he mentally processed the sheer brutality of the attack.

Ranger White also reported that Cecelia Shepard could not see the assailant's face due to a hood, but added that she had seen clip-on sunglasses used to cover the man's eyes. He indicated that he had observed a great deal of blood near her groin area.

A later interview with Archie and Elizabeth White revealed that Archie was the owner of a boat repair shop at Rancho Monticello Resort, where the couple lived. They had been called into action by Ronald Fong, the man captaining the boat that had passed near the couple on the beach to the south of the resort. A couple was covered in blood, a desperate Fong had reported once he arrived at the resort. The two had been robbed and stabbed. When Elizabeth called Park Headquarters, Ranger White had arrived a short time later.

Once the four had achieved the attack site, the Whites explained, they observed a woman on her elbows and knees. She was wearing a blood-stained sweater dress and was rocking in pain. Elizabeth attempted to comfort and calm her. Elizabeth shared what Cecelia had said to her: "'He was a man with a hood... his face was covered... He was wearing black pants. It hurts. It hurts.'" After Cecelia had regained her composure, she added that the assailant had asked for money but didn't take any, wore clip-on glasses on the outside of his hood, and had a black pistol. Archie had heard Hartnell tell someone that the assailant was wearing gloves.

Narlow and Lonergan drove back to the NCSO following his interview with the Whites. Upon their return, an administrator from PUC contacted Narlow at about 4:20 p.m., advising him that three girls, students at PUC, may have observed the knife-wielding man at the lake. The administrator described the Caucasian male seen by the girls as six feet tall, about 40 years of age, and wearing dark clothing. The attack on Hartnell and Shepard may not have been the assailant's first foray down to the water at Lake Berryessa that day.

The three young women, one named Joanne and two named Linda, had been at the lake between 3:00 p.m. and 4:30 p.m. the afternoon of the day Hartnell and Shepard were stabbed. While parking their car, and while sunbathing, they had noticed a dark-clothed man in the vicinity. Narlow assigned Detective Sergeant Ray Land to travel to Anguin to check out the girls' story.

The lead detectives spent the rest of that day—and into the evening—reviewing notes. Narlow also issued another APB, this one for a late model, blue Chevrolet that the three girls had seen driven by the man in dark clothing.

⁊

The investigation continued on Monday, September 29. Narlow and Lonergan interviewed numerous citizens in the morning, and sought information from officers in other departments concerning this and other, similar, crimes. Land, after questioning the three PUC girls, reported back to Narlow that their observations could in fact be relevant to the case. Land had already asked the girls to report to the NCSO. Narlow and Lonergan started a preliminary suspect list. This list, over time, would be subjoined with additional names—many through a linkage to other attacks—eventually growing to hundreds of pages listing thousands of people.

At 2:45 in the afternoon, the young women arrived at the NCSO as promised. Detective Lonergan interviewed Joanne, a 21-year-old from College Place, Washington, who was born June 4, 1946.

Joanne related that she and her two girlfriends, both named Linda, had parked their car on Knoxville Road, two miles north of the well-frequented A&W Root Beer stand. After she exited the vehicle she was driving, she noticed a man in a late model, silver and blue, 2-door Chevrolet sedan, which he had parked behind her vehicle. She glimpsed the driver, a white male, but she did not see him exit his car. Approximately thirty minutes later, the man was observing the girls from about 40 or 50 feet away while they sunbathed at the water's edge.

Because the lake was not visible from the parking lot area, he had exited his car. She estimated that the man was six feet tall, and a muscular 200 pounds, if not 210. She described him as nice looking, wearing dark pants and a dark pullover shirt. He appeared to be staring at them in their bikinis, but whenever they made eye contact with him, he always looked away. She estimated that they were at the lake for 45 minutes before walking back up the hill and leaving. She described the man's car as conservative, not something a teenager would drive. It bore California plates.

Detective Snook interviewed the first Linda. Born June 29, 1947 and living on Sunnyside Road in Sanitarium, California, she stated for the record that they had left Anguin at 2:45 p.m., traveled through Pope Valley to Lake Berryessa, and stopped two miles north of the A&W Root Beer stand (Sugar Loaf Park). While there, she saw the strange man drive into the parking lot area from the south of the girls. He then backed his 1966 or 1967 light blue Chevrolet up until their bumpers almost touched. She noted that it was a 2-door car with California plates. The rear lights were long, not round. She could not see into the car since the back window was tinted to a dark, near-opaque, shade. She added that another vehicle from Anguin was also present at this time: a car with Arizona plates whose two occupants she knew, Miss Denise Brown and Mr. Wayne Haight.

Linda saw the stranger again when she was sunbathing with her two friends. He had gotten out of his car and walked across the beach from south to north at a distance of about 20 feet from the girls. She estimated his age at 28, his height anywhere from six feet to six feet, two inches, and his weight between 200 and 225 pounds. She described his face as having round eyes, thin lips, and a medium nose. His eyebrows were straight, his black hair styled, and his ears appeared small to her. He was well built and nice looking in her opinion. He had a white tee-shirt protruding at the back from under his black, short-sleeved sweatshirt which was bunched up in the front. Linda was also able to recall his dark trousers. When the girls left at about 4:30 p.m., Linda added to conclude her statement, they saw no sign of the stranger or his car. He was not seen entering his car, nor was the vehicle ever spotted again by her.

Captain Townsend interviewed the other Linda. Born in 1948, her birthday was July 8. She resided on Howell Mountain Road in Anguin, and was employed as the secretary of the college press. The 21-year-old also took notice of the late-model Chevrolet that the man had driven, sky blue in color with long, not round, rear lights. She stated that the girls had parked at about 2:55 in the afternoon, and had seen the man in his car. About thirty to forty-five minutes later, she spotted him again about 45 yards from the beach.

The second Linda described the man as stocky, about six feet in height, wearing a black, short-sleeved sweatshirt and dark blue slacks. She said he appeared to be about 30 years of age. His straight, dark hair was neatly combed. His skin color was neither dark nor light for a Caucasian. He wore no glasses on his nice-looking, round face. He had a white belt around his waist at the back that could have been a tee-shirt hanging out behind him. She did not observe him as he exited his vehicle.

The information the girls provided was carefully recorded in case anything they said would be of use in the investigation. It seemed possible to the investigators that this was the man who had stabbed Hartnell and Shepard. But it was also possible that this was a totally unrelated event. Like the information provided by the dentist and his son, this incident was intriguing. It could be used to propel the investigation forward; just as likely, if followed too closely, and it did not record the activities of the perpetrator, it could steer it seriously off course.

In time, a police artist would create a composite picture of the lone hiker who had been spotted at the lake by the girls. A second composite, an alteration of the first by Napa Register photographer Robert McKenzie, was created with the approval of the girls. The second crude sketch of a very round-faced, dark-haired man was the one that was circulated and shown to potential witnesses. Soon tips began to pour in—to the switchboards of the police and the sheriff's departments of both Solano and Napa Counties—necessitating an investigation into each new piece of information. Any fact, however small and seemingly insignificant, the investigators knew, could be the big break they were seeking and lead to the identity of the assailant.

The public began to get increasingly involved in the hunt for the killer. They took it as a personal challenge to support the police effort in any way they could. Concerned citizens telephoned, sent letters, and visited law enforcement offices, offering up numerous tips and suggestions. What had begun as just a trickle of individuals who thought they had seen something, or felt they could aid the police in their work, would in time become a torrent, then a deluge, engulfing not only the Vallejo Police Department (VPD), the NPD, the Solano County Sheriff's Office, and the NCSO, but every law enforcement agency even tangentially participating in the investigation.

Suspects were turned in for sexual perversions, acts of violence—or the mention of violence—and erratic handwriting. Some, it appeared, found their names on a police officer's blotter simply because they were guilty of being a son-in-law, an ex-husband, or an ex-boyfriend of a spiteful accuser.

The VPD received information about a man named Michael, who in 1969 had been charged with manslaughter in the traffic deaths of two people on Highway 37. He was 30 years of age, five feet ten inches tall, and weighed between 180 and 200 pounds. He worked at Union Oil in Rodeo as an inspector, talked constantly about the Zodiac case, and discussed two supposed Zodiac murders he claimed that the police knew nothing about. He owned two guns: a 9mm automatic and a .45 caliber automatic.

The investigators learned that he had never had a girlfriend. He usually walked with his head down, knew the Lake Berryessa area very well, and had made claims that the Zodiac would never be caught. When excited, he was known to put his thumbs to his nose and scream.

On October 15, 1970, Michael was finally contacted with a request for samples of his printing. He was told that his name had been supplied to the department. Michael was very surprised, and also upset that the police would come to his home. After he was read his Fifth Amendment Constitutional Rights, he said that he'd prefer to speak with his lawyer.

Four days later, he entered the police station to provide writing samples. He also brought along two 9mm handguns, for which he was issued receipts. One of these belonged to a friend, but he was told that it too would be examined. The guns were spirited away to a storage locker. The handwriting was collected and sent to the CII along with the guns.

Meanwhile, the composite picture proved particularly helpful in garnering public interest. Its palpable gaze and vague shading worked magic on the public's imagination. It was brought to the investigator's attention that a composite picture of a suspect on a wanted poster from another crime resembled the Lake Berryessa picture.

A copy of the Lake Berryessa composite picture was sent anonymously to the VPD bearing a Vallejo postmark with writing on it that indicated that the picture resembled a man named Mitch who "works at Mare Island." He was described as chubby, soft-spoken, 190 pounds, and just under six feet tall. He liked to hunt. Mitch was quickly identified as Mitchell, a 33-year-old swing-shift worker from Napa.

A security officer at Sears Roebuck in Concord turned in to the police a high school acquaintance who he believed resembled the Lake Berryessa composite. Lynch traveled to Concord and retrieved from the man a photo from a George Washington High School 1959 yearbook, as well as a handwriting sample.

A biker with a heavy build from Benicia, who was six feet, six inches tall and well known to the BPD came under careful scrutiny. His forearm bore a tattoo, possibly home-made, of a crosshair symbol. He had been arrested on a marijuana violation.

A letter signed "a good citizen" claimed that its writer had extra-sensory perception (ESP). It instructed the police to go to 56 Beach Street, the writer "getting" the name Jerry, and maybe a last name, "Simpson." But the ESP proved faulty when investigators discovered that Beach Street started its numbering at 1100. Beachwood Street began in the 700 block. Many well-meaning tips similarly evaporated in significance when officers dutifully followed up on them.

The VPD investigated a man who had been convicted of accosting couples in a lover's lane, and doing so with a hood over his head. None of his attacks involved guns or knives, but he had to be checked out just the same.

On October 3 at 6:15 p.m., a woman contacted the VPD because she suspected that her relative, named Keith, a resident of Montana who was planning a trip to the Bay Area, may have been responsible for the attack at Lake Berryessa. He had left his home on September 21 and was due to arrive in Vallejo by bus on September 26. For no apparent reason, he arrived on October 1 with no explanation for the lost days.

Keith was an ex-mental patient who exhibited strange behavior. He talked about killing people, he carried a gun, and he complained that the Sheriff's Department was always after him. He had mentioned the Montana State Prison in Deer Lodge to his relatives as a place where he had sought employment. The woman thought Keith matched details of the composite photo that was being circulated.

At 9:40 p.m. that evening, Mary and Freddie of Benicia went to the Vallejo Police Station to report an incident that had occurred at the Redwood Inn. About 10 months previous, they explained, they met a man named Jimmy who had returned from Vietnam 4 or 5 month earlier. He bought four or five rounds of drinks for everyone in the bar—until the bartender refused any more money from the man—and rambled on without making much sense. At one point, he grabbed Mary by the throat as she was returning from the bathroom, and threatened to kill both her and Freddie. The couple had forgotten the experience until they saw the composite, which reminded them of the six feet one inch, 180 to 190 pound man who had brown hair and brown eyes. He appeared to them to be in his 20s.

On October 6, an anonymous telephone call suggested that a Gary could be responsible for the attack at Lake Berryessa. When Lynch called the telephone number of the address provided, no Gary lived at the address. The call was answered by Paul who was immediately summoned to the station. Paul was quickly cleared. He had a beard, a mustache, long sideburns, and long hair, and in no way resembled the composite photo.

The police developed several suspects during arrests.

A 29-year-old painter named George was arrested on November 6 for public intoxication and booked at the Solano County Jail. He resembled a circulating composite picture. While still drunk, he claimed to be the Zodiac. The next day the VPD investigated, taking him to room 27 and reading him his Constitutional rights, the Miranda warning. He understood his rights under the law, he said, after he was advised as to why he was being questioned. He proved to be cooperative and polite, and readily agreed to talk.

He had no memory of his claims the previous day. He was out on bail from theft charges, he admitted. He lived in Sonoma with his wife and two children, aged three and five. Regarding the Zodiac, he had read stories in the paper, but had no independent knowledge of the case. Handwriting samples were gathered, and finger and palm prints collected, Mulinax taking the collection to the CII three days later. Though he was six feet tall, weighed 180 pounds, had sandy-blond colored hair with a hairline similar to the composite picture, and wore thick horn-rimmed glasses, he was eliminated on the basis of the handwriting samples.

A security guard known to the VPD was arrested and, in a drunken state, claimed to be the Zodiac. Alcohol may have been responsible for many similar false confessions.

On November 8, at 2:20 in the morning, VPD Officer John Hoffman brought a man named Robert into the station who he had found parked on the north end of Blue Rock Springs Park. The 48-year-old janitor from San Francisco had fallen asleep exhausted after having driven from San Leandro. He had been visiting a long-time friend in Sonoma, having dinner with him following a day of work (he worked the 7:00 a.m. to 3:30 p.m. shift). His clothing was curious and provocative. He wore a new, gray, ill-fitting suit; a white shirt; a blue-and-white checked tie; a reversible vest; brown shoes; and a black fedora hat.

After leaving Sonoma around midnight, he had missed the turn-off at Blackpoint, found himself on Highway 37, and turned onto

Columbus Parkway. He got sleepy so he stopped at the park for a nap—and never got out of his Dodge. He presented an Arizona driver's license. He had in his possession an envelope with writing and printing on both sides. Hoffman noted that the printing included 14 symbols, which Robert called "keystones." To Hoffman, they did not appear to be similar to those sent by the Zodiac. The man claimed to have no interest in horoscopes, and though he spoke five languages— French, English, Portuguese, Spanish, and Italian—he never worked in any but menial jobs and had never married. He was a member of the Church of Christ. He didn't smoke, drink, or carry a gun. He had never been in the military, and had never been arrested. After a photocopy was made of the unusual envelope, Robert was released at 3:40 in the morning.

Lynch went over to Arkansas Street to check on a lead. He learned that the man had an arrangement of stars, including the little dipper, painted on the ceiling of his home. Laughing at his discovery, the detective came to learn that the man worked for the Times Herald.

In response to the attack at the lake, Napa officials issued a warning against parking in lonely spots. The city was hoping to prevent a repetition of the past. The threats applied to the whole North Bay area now, not just to Vallejo. Napa Chief Investigator Donald Townsend noted, "a boy and girl alone seems to be his fancy," adding that the allegedly mentally ill person "must get his sex gratification from the act of killing."

In time, more manpower was added to the investigation. Deputy District Attorney John Cooley and Investigators Phillip "Bucky" Steward and Dave Hall were called in to assist the Sheriff's Office in the hunt for the apparent madman.

એ

Narlow and Lonergan received a sobering telephone call from the Napa hospital at 7:45 on the evening of September 29. They had already heard the news at 4:00 p.m. from Captain Joe Page, Chief Napa County Coroner. Cecelia Ann Shepard had been pronounced dead. Page asked Dr. De Petris to perform the autopsy the following day. Shepard's remains were transported to Morrison Funeral Home in St. Helena. The felonious case had just become a homicide, NCSO case #105907. The detectives sought an assailant who was now responsible for Shepard's death. Even as the investigation into the lacustrine attack changed in nature and severity, a significant piece of forensic evidence provided investigators with a direction:

Also at 7:45, Monday evening, Officer H. B. Schotte contacted Narlow and Lonergan with information on the shoe pattern they were seeking. Earlier in the day, Sergeant Robertson had canvassed a dozen Napa shoe stores, including JC Penney, Montgomery Ward, and a Government Surplus store—all on First Street, Main Street, or in the Bel Aire Mall—in an effort to find a shoe that could make the same impression as those preserved in the plaster casts. No matching shoe was found, though Robertson concluded that the shoe they were seeking may be foreign, may contain a neoprene sole and heel, and could be 10½ EE in size. Where Robertson failed, Schotte succeeded.

He brought to the investigators a retired Air Force Master Sergeant currently employed at Travis Air Force Base as a flight line mechanic. The guest proceeded to show the officers a pair of Air Force boots called Wing Walkers. This Government Issue footwear was dispensed to Air Force mechanics, but was also available to their families. Additionally, any civilians who worked at an Air Force base could secure a pair. They were supplied to every employee at Lackland Air Force Base in Texas.

Narlow and Lonergan inspected the soles. Bingo! It was the shoe for which they were searching. It matched the casts in every way, including the circular design pattern, one and one quarter inches in width, on the outside of the instep. Printed inside the design were the following matched words,

"Avon
Oil Resistant
Super wear
AUYNA"

Narlow and Lonergan decided to keep the new information about the shoes under wraps. They retained the pair provided to them by the flight mechanic for comparison purposes and swore him to secrecy.

☙

Tuesday, September 30 would prove to be yet another frenzied day of investigative activity. At 8:10 in the morning, Narlow received a call that provided one more piece of information about Bryan and Cecelia's trip to Lake Berryessa. An 18-year-old PUC student named Marilyn, living in room B3 of Andre Hall, informed him that on the Saturday of the stabbing she was with a 22-year-old fellow PUC student named John. They were parked on Knoxville Road about one mile south of the Lake Berryessa Marina. While stopped, the couple had seen Hartnell drive past in his white Karmann Ghia. Bryan had waved and had shouted out his window, "Hi, John." The time was 5:15 p.m. Marilyn reported that they had not seen the vehicle prior to this sighting, and they did not see it again.

The police report filed by Narlow noted that Hartnell had been seen driving south. Either the direction had been recorded incorrectly or Hartnell at some point had turned his vehicle around. Hartnell would state that he had approached Lake Berryessa with Shepard from the south, but he later also described looking for a particular location on Lake Berryessa which may have entailed driving back and forth, north *and* south.

Both Lonergan and Narlow observed the autopsy of Shepard's body, conducted from nine to noon at Morrison Funeral home in St. Helena. Dr. Wilmer A. De Petris conducted the grim procedure, assisted by Dr. Dwight G. Straub. Also present were Sergeant Butler, Captain Joseph Page, and the funeral home's owner. Butler photographed the body before, during, and after the autopsy. Lonergan took notes assiduously. Shepard's corpse was recorded as 100 pounds and five feet five inches. The cause of death surprised no one: shock and loss of blood caused by two main stab wounds. De Petris concluded that the multiple stab wounds led to severe internal and external hemorrhage, which in turn caused brain anoxia and ultimately severe brain damage.

According to De Petris, the weapon used against Shepard was a 9 to 11 inch, bayonet-style, heavy, sturdy blade, measuring perhaps an inch across. It may have been sharpened on both sides. Her liver had been sliced by the knife. A secondary wound to her liver was present, possibly inflicted during surgical efforts to save her. Several suture defects were also noted by the pathologist. The emergency room personnel had done all they could to repair the damage done by her attacker—but in the end it was not enough.

The lead detectives spent most of the rest of the day and evening answering phone calls from citizens who had possible knowledge of the crime.

The next morning, on Wednesday, October 1, Narlow and Lonergan traveled to Travis Air Force base in Fairfield to investigate the origin of the shoes that made the footprints at Lake Berryessa. They were able to make significant headway in this part of the case. Armed with a sketch made from a plaster cast of a footprint, the detectives met with Colonel Bender, the officer in charge of base security. Lieutenant Colonel Laverick from the Office of Special Investigation was also present. To receive more information on the newly discovered Wing Walker shoes, they were directed, with the help of OSI Special Agent Donald Santini who had been assigned to assist them, to Base Supply. Base Supply did not have any Wing Walkers in stock, but steered them to the sales store. Once they arrived at the sales store in their circuitous journey, the detectives learned that for a purchase to occur, a buyer had to fill out a requisition form which was then provided to the sales store. Each purchase would require a signature of the buyer. Unfortunately, the store did not keep a record of shoe sizes.

The supply personnel were able to locate a pair that matched the crime scene impressions, a 10½ R Wing Walker boot. For the civilian equivalent, the identical shoe measured a 10½ D. Made by the International Shoe Company in Philadelphia, Pennsylvania, the boots were shipped to Ogden Utah, from where they were dispensed to various installations. The uppers were manufactured by the Weinbrenner Shoe Company in Morrill, Wisconsin; the soles by Avon in Avon, Massachusetts. Over 100 pairs of that size of Wing Walker had passed through Travis in the previous 13 months; however, no specific record of purchasers was available. The requisition forms were either not preserved or they lacked the needed information.

Later that day, Lonergan received a disheartening telephone call. He learned from Santini that 500 to 1,000 additional pairs of Wing

Walkers had been sold as surplus. The haystack in which the detectives hoped to find a needle had just increased in size by a magnitude of 10. The special agent who had called added that there was a list of individuals who had purchased these shoes, albeit a lengthy one. In fact, Narlow soon learned that 103,700 pairs had shipped to West Coast Air Force and Navy installations since 1966, out of more than one million pairs manufactured under a government contract.

෬

On the afternoon of October 1, Narlow and Lonergan met with Sergeant Jack Mulinax and Sergeant Duane Nilsson of the VPD to exchange information on the attacks that each of their two departments were investigating. The Napa detectives learned that the cipher mailed by the Zodiac had been broken by two independent efforts. The Harden's, a school teacher and his wife, in Salinas, and the FBI in Washington, D.C. had each decrypted the message from the Zodiac's 3-Part cipher, the detectives were told.

Also on October 1, in a letter marked urgent, the FBI field office in Sacramento notified the FBI's D.C. headquarters of the stabbing. Noting the similarities to previous attacks, the airtel stated in part, "MO and message left by assailant is identical to individual responsible for previous murders committed in nearby Vallejo." It added that the VPD had developed an excellent suspect from San Antonio, Texas. In asking that the suspect's fingerprints be examined and compared to latent impressions in the Zodiac file, the letter requested an expedited response due to the wide range of publicity, concluding with a phrase that would be used often in communications in the case, "ARMED AND DANGEROUS."

The reply came on October 6. In a letter, the FBI confirmed receipt of the radiogram—a message routed by amateur radio operators through a radio network—from Vallejo Chief of Police Jack E. Stiltz, sent October 1, and the teletype from the Sacramento Office, also dated October 1. This letter was itself a confirmation that supplemented an October 2 radiogram reply. The latent fingerprints gathered in the Zodiac case did not match the Texas suspect, but with the caveat that the fingerprints compared may not have belonged to the named suspect. It was possible that dactylograms from a person with the same name had been compared, rather than those of the intended suspect. Without computers to file, store, and retrieve information, mistakes could occur, especially when dealing with a person possessing a common name.

Later that month, in a letter to Stiltz dated October 24, the FBI concluded that the suspect's handwriting was not a match to hand-writing in the Zodiac case. Though there was an insufficient amount of comparable known standards, there were characteristics noted that suggested that the suspect from Texas probably did not create the Zodiac writing. The material that had been supplied for comparison was photographed and returned.

On Thursday, October 2, Lonergan and Narlow searched finger-print cards, a tedious process at a time before computerized records and computer searches were available technologies. They also fielded calls from citizens attempting to assist in the investigation.

The funeral for Cecelia Ann Shepard was held that afternoon at 2:00 p.m., at Pacific Union College's sanctuary. It was conducted by Robert W. Olsen, chair of the College's Department of Religion and former roommate at PUC of Shepard's father in the 1940s, Robert H. Shepard, a professor at the Seventh Day Adventist college in Loma Linda. Morris Funeral Chapel in St. Helena was in charge of arrangements.

Not to miss an opportunity to collect suspects, Detectives Narlow and Lonergan were careful to position themselves so that they could observe everyone who attended the gathering and everyone who spoke to the victim's family. Sometimes, a murderer will attend the funeral of their victim; more than once, a criminal has been appre-hended through careful observation of a service, because either the perpetrator looked out of place or the perpetrator's actions appeared suspicious to others. Three police officers, Detective Sergeant Harold Snook, Sergeant Thomas Butler, and Detective Ronald Montgomery, took photographs of everyone who entered and exited the church, and many group photos as well.

Narlow and Lonergan also attended the much smaller graveside ceremony at St. Helena Cemetery, which was held soon after the church service. No one stood out during the day's memorialization, and the photographs netted no suspects.

The next day, Friday, October 3, Detective Lonergan interviewed a patient at the Napa State Hospital for possible involvement in the murder. Another odd person had been brought to his attention. At an imposing six feet two inches and 225 pounds, the 20-year-old man had received a weekend pass from his institution, providing him freedom at the time of the attack at Lake Berryessa. He had been discharged from the Air Force the previous January for psychiatric problems. His doctor thought he was capable of the attack on Hartnell and Shepard. As Lonergan interviewed him in the presence of others, however, his innocence became apparent. The patient talked in a very quick tempo, much faster than the assailant at Lake Berryessa was reported to have spoken. Also, his mother confirmed his alibi. Suspicion of him was finally eliminated when it was revealed that he had no access to a car the previous weekend when the felonious assault had occurred.

Narlow and Lonergan spent the rest of the day reviewing the ever-increasing amounts of evidence, and adding to the seemingly endless number of reports.

☙

Also on October 3, Captain Donald Townsend requested by phone the services of the Latent Fingerprint Section of the CII at the California Department of Justice in Sacramento. Townsend hoped that the latent prints that were collected could be matched to one of the suspects in the case. He delegated this work to a specialist who might find a match if one existed. Narlow had separately requested the services of CII to aid in the investigation. He was assigned Special Agent Mel Nicolai, who would work closely with the VPD and the Solano County Sheriff's Office.

Three days later, Raymond Olsen, a latent fingerprint examiner, traveled to the NCSO with Supervising Photographer Vern Meusen, both of the CII. Together they met with Townsend, Narlow, and Snook to review the details of the case. CII Supervising Special Agent Kenneth Horton, CII Special Agent Nicolai, and Napa County Undersheriff Tom Johnson also attended the meeting.

Townsend requested that his guests make copies of the prints that had been collected in the case to compare them to four suspects.

He also asked that they retain the copies in order to compare them to any other suspects that were generated in the future. Before leaving, the specialists received from Snook 35 cards bearing 45 latent prints, one eight by ten inch photo of a latent impression, the names and birthdates of the four suspects, a photo of the passenger door of the Karmann Ghia, five sheets of paper with writing, and one Charlie Brown greeting card that also bore some writing on it. The last three items would be also passed on to the Questioned Documents Section of the CII.

Unfortunately for the investigation, no perpetrator was found. The fingerprints of the four suspects did not match; neither did the other suspects supplied by Nicolai and the Special Services Section of the CII. Several of the latent impressions appeared to *The Examiner* to represent prints made from palms, which the bureau did not at that time collect or store. As requested, the copies were retained for future comparisons, with the promise that should any positive identification be made, the Sheriff's Office would be immediately notified.

Upon his return from his trip to Napa, Olsen provided the samples of handwriting and the picture of Hartnell's car door to Questioned Documents Examiner Sherwood Morrill in person. The date was October 7. He carefully placed the photographs in the Bureau's files for future reference, and then responded to the Sheriff's Office with a letter in which he returned the latent impression cards. As a courtesy, he also sent copies of the latent impressions for future use.

Morrill, after carefully scrutinizing the material, was finally able to match the writing on the door of Hartnell's car to the handwriting on the three July 31 letters that contained the cipher pieces. The person who wrote the 3-Part letters was also responsible for defacing Hartnell's Karmann Ghia.

On October 6, the CII in Sacramento created a case summary. It expressed concern about the wide publicity the murders were receiving. It concluded that the Lake Herman Road, Blue Rock Spring Park, and Lake Berryessa attacks were all perpetrated by the same person, someone who had also made the calls to the police after the July 4 attack and the September 27 knifing. Three Northern California crime scenes comprising four murdered victims were now tied to the killer known as the Zodiac. Despite the Bureau's best efforts at accuracy, the Lake Berryessa slaying was errantly listed as occurring on the weekend of September 20 and 21.

Three days later, the Sacramento FBI Field Office requested that the FBI in Washington, D.C. check its latent fingerprint files for a particular, named suspect. The October 14 reply eliminated the suspect due to the lack of a match, but noted that the suspect had no palm prints on file.

At 2:00 p.m. on October 9, Narlow and Lonergan met with representatives of the Solano County Sheriff's Office, the CHP, and the VPD. The accumulated list of attacks was discussed with all details: December 20 on Lake Herman Road, July 4 in Blue Rock Springs Park, and September 27 at the edge of Lake Berryessa. Now that the three incidents had been linked forensically by handwriting, by the evidence provided in the killer's letters, and through the car door writing at Lake Berryessa, the offices were eager to share and exchange details of their work. While each of them may have been operating with a limited amount of information, together they were confident that enough clues would emerge to suggest a course of investigation, if not reveal the killer outright.

On October 23, the Sheriff's Office received another letter from the Latent Fingerprint Section of the FBI Identification Division. The news was not encouraging. Snook was notified, in reference to his October 10 letter, that prints that he had sent to the FBI—five photos of latent impressions that evidenced "seven latent fingerprints, three latent palm prints, and one latent impression, which is either a fingerprint or a partial palm print, appear in the submitted photographs and are of value for identification purposes"—did not match three named suspects. To do a thorough analysis, the FBI required inked impressions of a suspect's fingers that included the sides, the tips, and the lower joint areas, as well as palm prints. These were not routinely kept in the FBI files. Additionally, two of the named suspects may not have been the individuals previously indicated, some confusion existing over the names and addresses.

The FBI further found no identification records for Hartnell or Shepard. They conducted no laboratory examination on other items submitted, informing Snook that should they be required, the items would have to be resubmitted to the Laboratory. The FBI also explained to Snook that no modus operandi (MO) file was maintained in the Identification Division. Not until the 1980s would law enforcement agencies share criminal MO details with one another so that peregrinating killers could be quickly identified by the specifics of their criminal activities. The VICAP (violent criminal apprehension program) computer software would in future cases be responsible for collaring many criminals who carried out their violence across law enforcement jurisdictions.

Hartnell was released from the hospital on November 9. He returned to PUC to continue his studies. Narlow and Lonergan traveled to Anguin the next day to interview him one more time. With the details the detectives had gathered from the joint meeting, as well as their early investigative efforts, they hoped that the survivor of the Lake Berryessa attack could provide additional information. Unfortunately, no fresh insights into the assailant or the incident could be siphoned from the recuperating victim.

If on September 27 investigators were concerned that the Zodiac had moved beyond the Vallejo area and the confines of Solano County to expand his reach into Napa County, they would be startled by his next location. If they were worried that his pace was picking up— quickening from a seven-month interval to an idle period of a mere twelve weeks—they would be shocked by the length of time it took for him to reappear.

The Zodiac struck next in the metropolitan city of San Francisco exactly two weeks later.

6 | PRESIDIO HEIGHTS

"I am the murderer of the taxi driver"

Paul Stine was a conscientious, hardworking student. As the days grew shorter in October of 1969, his schedule was full. Son of Milford Stine and Audra Busby—both born in Oklahoma—Paul juggled marriage, studies, cab driving, and part-time insurance sales. He was pushing his way through the Ph.D. program in English at San Francisco State College so that he could someday land a job as a professor. On the side, he drove for the Yellow Cab Company in and around San Francisco to help support the family finances, working the 9:00 p.m. to 5:00 a.m. shift beginning in the summer of 1969. He and his lovely wife, Claudia, resided at 1824 Fell Street in the North Panhandle district of San Francisco.

At 8:45 p.m. on the evening of Saturday, October 11, Stine set out in his cab. His first and only paid fare of the shift led him from Pier 64 to the San Francisco International Airport. Soon after, his dispatcher sent him to pick up a customer on 9th Street. While he drove in that direction, a man with a crewcut hailed him for a ride. His second passenger approached the cab somewhere near the intersection of Mason Street and Geary Street, in San Francisco's downtown Theater District.

Stine realized that the location to which the man was head-ed—Washington Street near Maple Street, in the tony Presidio Heights district—could be easily reached on his way to his assigned customer, so he admitted him into his cab, marked his trip sheet, and started the meter. Collecting one fare while traveling to the location of another was a popular way to reduce vacant miles and maximize income. Additionally, driving to such an exclusive area almost guaranteed a generous tip.

Stine would not make it to the next paying customer, however, and the dispatcher had to reassign the 9th Street call at approximately 10:00 p.m. Stine's final passenger was a killer; the destination, the scene of a grisly murder where Stine's life would end, on the north side of Washington Street in San Francisco's rarefied Presidio Heights district.

ℰℐ

So named for the Presidio, an army installation it abuts to the north, the Presidio Heights district is a small, affluent San Francisco neighborhood bounded to the south by California Street and the Laurel Heights district, to the west by Arguello Street, and to the east by Presidio Drive. In the words of *San Francisco Chronicle* reporter Paul Avery in 1969, it is an "area of posh homes." Its palatial mansions—many valued today between $10 million and $20 million, with smaller ones fetching $2 million or more, even after the real estate collapse of 2008—line parallel streets that carve the neighborhood into squares. Driving at high speeds is discouraged throughout the hilly region by the many stop signs, most intersections being four-way stops. Many of the houses are so large, and the property so valuable, that very little land is reserved for front- and backyards. The topography is elevated enough that the residents can look down on surrounding communities if they have the view, and more than a few of the structures stretch for that opportunity with three or more stories and windows on every side.

The quickest route to the passenger's destination from the corner of Mason and Geary was a westward drive on Geary Street, turning north on Highway 101, then westerly on California Street, and turning north onto Divisidero Street, before continuing west along Washington Street.

On Wednesday, October 15, *The San Francisco Chronicle* reported that the passenger sat in the front seat of the cab, a fact reiterated in official FBI reports of the crime. The police determined from the cabby's trip sheet that Stine's destination was the corner of Washington Street and Maple Street. But the mention of that intersection raised questions.

One of two enduring mysteries of Paul Stine's murder (not including the unknown identity of the perpetrator) relates to the final minutes of the victim's life. For some reason, Stine stopped his cab at an intersection one full block west of the intended destination. The killer sent a letter—received October 13, 1969 by *The San Francisco Chronicle*—confessing to the crime of murder "over by Washington St. and Maple St.," even though the murder did not occur there. Stine was found dead in his cab just feet from the corner of Washington and Cherry Streets, one city block beyond the destination listed in the driver's way bill. The reason for the discrepancy has never been made clear, though there were several theories of why Paul Stine ended up where he did.

Some officers believed that the cab driver simply overshot the intersection. In that case, the passenger may have said, "Just pull over here." Because Stine did not survive the attack, no record of a conversation exists, and any words exchanged are known only to his killer. However, law enforcement had to admit that it was equally likely, had Stine driven past the intersection of Washington and Maple, a ubiquitous four-way stop, that he would have stopped his cab, backed up, and deposited his passenger at the proper location.

An alternate theory posited that Stine was shot while driving, requiring the gunman to grab the steering wheel and attempt to gain control of a wild, careening cab, with the final resting place one block farther down the road. This would have required a horrible blunder: a passenger who would shoot his victim while the vehicle was still moving or still in gear. But the distance between intersections and the ordinary stop at which the taxi finally came to rest suggested to many that the extra block was not accidental, and not accomplished by a driverless car.

The actual explanation may have been as simple as an unexpected interruption. It is entirely possible that, as Stine drove his passenger toward the corner of Washington and Maple Streets, the killer spotted something near the intended destination, and chose instead to carry out his planned violence a mere one block farther along Washington.

Washington and Maple *was* the perfect intersection for a killing. It may have been the planned murder scene all along. The trees standing guard at that intersection were high and thick. Potential witnesses in the surrounding homes would have had difficulty observing a killing, with branches and leaves obstructing the view of the street from many windows. The perpetrator would then have been only one block from the Julius Kahn Playground on the grounds of the Presidio itself, the destination to which the killer is suspected to have absconded. If he had killed Stine at the corner of Washington and Maple, he would have escaped his crime quickly and anonymously, and the cab with its dead driver would not have been discovered as quickly as it was. Perhaps a pedestrian or someone in a parked car had spooked the assailant, compelling him to move the death scene one block to the west. In fact, one police report stated that a man walking his dog, a potential suspect in or witness to the murder, was stopped by the police not far from that corner in the aftermath of the shooting.

Because the killing occurred where it did, one block west toward the Pacific Ocean, there were witnesses. The cab stopped in front of a residential home at 3899 Washington Street, in full view of inquisitive eyes. Just before 10:00 p.m., three teenaged children of a prominent San Francisco physician—aged 13, 14 and 16—looked out of the second-floor window of their spacious home at 3898 Washington Street on the southeast corner of Washington and Cherry. They had front row seats directly across the street from the crime scene, and observed the events unfolding below. Though they claimed they did not hear anything, something drew their attention, and they watched in disbelief as the man with a crewcut sat in the passenger seat with the cab driver's body draped across his lap. They had no idea that the passenger had just placed a handgun against Stine's head and pulled the trigger.

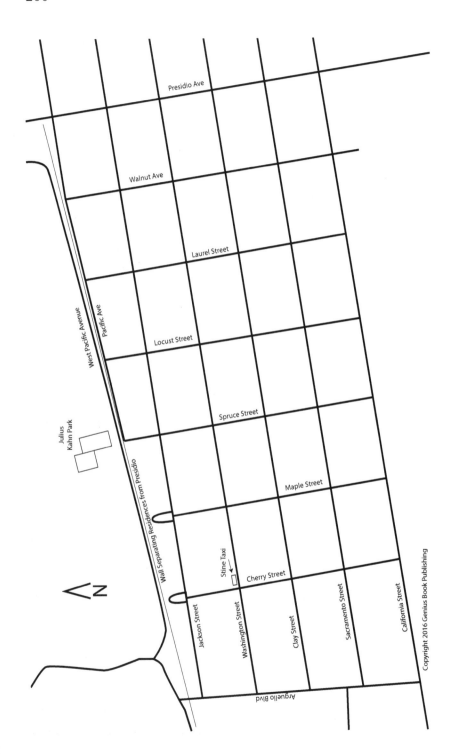

Presidio Ave

Walnut Ave

Laurel Street

West Pacific Avenue

Pacific Ave

Locust Street

Julius
Kahn Park

Spruce Street

Wall Separating Residences from Presidio

Maple Street

N

Stine Taxi

Cherry Street

Jackson Street

Washington Street

Clay Street

Sacramento Street

California Street

Arguello Blvd

Copyright 2016 Genius Book Publishing

The evening was dark and cool. Even though it was only 18 days since the end of summer, San Francisco was gripped by unseasonably cold temperatures. That was not an uncommon situation for a city surrounded by water on three sides. By the time the teenagers observed the taxi, whatever warmth the day had seen had already given way to the brisk ocean breezes. Pedestrians needed a coat, or were forced to clutch loose-fitting clothing around their bodies.

One of the teenagers—the 16-year-old—grabbed a telephone and contacted the San Francisco Police Department (SFPD).

The passenger appeared to rifle through Stine's pockets and wipe down the inside of the vehicle with some kind of cloth, even reaching toward the driver's side of the front seat. The youths watched his movements as he emerged out of the passenger side and began wiping the outside of the cab, probably with the same cloth. As he circled the cab, he stopped at the driver's door and appeared to reach back into the vehicle. Almost casually, he left, making his way north on Cherry Street.

The Chronicle, partly dramatizing the event and partly guessing, recorded that the gunman "dashed" down Cherry Street. A California Department of Justice report stated that he "walked nonchalantly." SFPD Officer Armond Pelissetti, apparently gaining his information from the youths, described him as "ambling or walking down Cherry Street in a northerly direction." His report recorded that the man "fled (walking) north on Cherry St." The killer himself wrote about events that had occurred when he was "walking down the hill." A simple matter of ambulation became a point of contention when different sources began to characterize its manner in wildly divergent terms.

The San Francisco newspapers reported on the apparent robbery. The take: one fare of less than $5 for a total haul of between $10 and $11. Also stolen were Stine's wallet with all of his identification and the keys to the cab. The meter was left running.

Stine's death was reported by the police at 10:11 p.m., according to the City of San Francisco's death record. The City was notified at 10:28 p.m. The time of death was set at 10:00 p.m., though Stine probably died a couple of minutes earlier. Subsequent investigation placed the time closer to 9:55 p.m. The SFPD notified Stine's next of kin—specifically his wife, Claudia—by telephone at 1:20 a.m., the identity of the driver having been confirmed by Michael S. Conway. The body was photographed and the deceased's fingerprints were taken. These prints, preserved to compare with, and possibly eliminate, any prints that would be lifted from the interior or exterior of the cab, were forwarded to the CII of the California Department of Justice in Sacramento. The investigation into what appeared to be a routine robbery began with careful attention to protocol.

Investigators retrieved a pair of men's black leather gloves, size 7, from the interior of the cab. It remains unclear to this day whether these were worn by the assailant (who may then have felt the need to wipe away his fingerprints from the cab once he had taken the gloves off), were left by the killer as a red herring to indicate a hand size different than his own, or were deposited by someone else and had nothing to do with the murder whatsoever. Like the mysterious wristwatch with the broken strap recovered at the Bates crime scene three years earlier, these curious pieces of evidence provided more questions than answers. And, like the peculiar series of murders, they offered more possibilities than solutions.

The subsequent investigation identified the murder weapon as a 9mm semi-automatic, possibly a new model of Browning. The slug removed from Stine's brain and the shell casing recovered from the cab once comprised a 9mm Winchester Western cartridge. *The Chronicle* mistakenly identified the caliber of the bullet that was fired as a .38.

In time, Dr. John C. Lee, MD conducted the autopsy. He noted that Stine's clothing included underwear, shoes, socks, shirts, pants, and jacket, much of the clothing still smeared with blood. The cause of death was obvious: a gunshot to the head with massive blood loss. An entry wound was apparent in the front of the right ear. Black marks were observed on the upper surface of the wound, indicating that the cabby had been shot at contact range.

Stine's stature in death was five feet nine inches tall and 180 pounds. The coroner recorded his dark features, including brown eyes and brown hair. His blood alcohol level measured 0.02%, well within the legal limit to drive, but possibly a sign of irresponsibility for a professional driver. In death, Stine was exposed for consuming a beer, a glass of wine, or a cocktail prior to going on duty. But only one.

The Coroner's Office released the remains on Monday, at 11:24 in the morning. Stine's body was cremated less than 24 hours later with appropriate Protestant obsequy. Paul Lee Stine, born December 18, 1939, had died as the result of a homicide on October 11 at approximately 10:00 p.m. The 29-year-old's Social Security number, SS 572 50 3862, was retired; his wife, Claudia, would never again feel the warmth of his embrace; his doctoral studies would remain unfinished.

℗

SFPD Patrol Officer Armond Pelissetti, badge #1879, along with his partner for the evening, SFPD Patrol Officer Frank Peda, #212, the first officers to the crime scene, arrived at 9:58 p.m. In response to the telephone call from the 16-year-old witness, they had been radioed by dispatch and notified that a cab driver had been robbed and/or possibly assaulted. With the patrol car's flashing lights and siren's wail, they made their way promptly to the scene, ready to provide order, save a life, catch a criminal, or do whatever else their services required. Pelissetti parked his patrol vehicle in the middle of the intersection at Washington and Cherry Streets facing the cab—an aggressive posture meant to take control of the situation—and jumped out from behind the wheel. As the three teenagers cautiously ventured into the street toward the silent cab, approaching as close as 15 or 16 feet, he quickly herded them back to the alcove of what he correctly assumed was the mansion they had exited. He meant to both preserve the scene of the crime and protect their lives from an assailant who may have still been lurking in the vicinity.

Pelissetti reviewed the teenagers' statements with them. They reiterated that they had seen the passenger sitting in the front seat of the cab—in his words, "mid to passenger side"—with the motionless driver slumped partially over in his lap, while he apparently searched the pockets of the victim. It was an obvious criminal attack, though the witnesses never heard the gunshot. To the youths, the passenger appeared to be wiping the dashboard with a cloth—possibly a handkerchief—as he leaned over to the driver's compartment. The assailant, according to the youths, exited the vehicle from the passenger side front door, then circled the cab as he continued to wipe it down. After he had attended to the driver's side front door, he reached back into the cab, then fled walking north on Cherry Street, toward the Presidio military grounds and out of their wide-eyed view.

The excellent look that the killer had given the youths prompted the investigation to assign a police artist to sit down with them and create a composite drawing of what they had seen. A picture of the assailant was released on October 13, two days following the attack. Its details would be challenged almost immediately, requiring an alternate, possibly more accurate, version to be drawn.

Once he was sure the youths were safe and the cab secure, Pelissetti crossed the street to view the grisly crime scene with Peda. The officers peered inside the 1968 Ford Custom to which Stine had been assigned, and found the victim slumped over the front seat with his upper torso on the passenger side and his head resting on the floor board, facing north. The death notice at the City of San Francisco would describe the body as lying in a "semi-supine" position. There was gore everywhere. Pelissetti later described the scene: "The car was full of blood."

Pelissetti immediately called for an ambulance—a code 3 signifying an emergency that required lights and siren, though the officers were fairly sure that Stine was beyond medical attention ("99.9[%] certain he was dead," Pelissetti would later recall)—and summoned other law enforcement agents for an immediate search of the area.

The officers took a description of the assailant from the teenagers, noting that the witnesses had observed across a clear line of view from a distance of about 50 feet, and passed this on to dispatch, which in turn broadcast it. The initial reports had stated that the robber was a "Negro Male Adult" (NMA). Either the youths had incorrectly described what they had seen or the dispatcher had not heard them correctly. However the miscommunication occurred, Pelissetti raced to the radio (years later he would describe his rush, "I couldn't get to the radio fast enough") to let everyone else know that the perpetrator was Caucasian, and not Black.

Inspector Walt Kracke of the Homicide Division arrived at the crime scene, followed 5 or 10 minutes later by SFPD Detectives Dave

Toschi and Bill Armstrong. Toschi had been called at home, Police Operations telling him at 10:25 p.m. that a Yellow Cab driver had been shot to death. Pelissetti briefed Toschi because it appeared that the latter was taking the lead in the case. He assured the detective that no one had contaminated the scene.

Starting that night, Toschi skillfully marshaled the SFPD forces in a quest for a killer that would cost him great personal and professional frustration, nearly a decade of his life, and not a little shame and embarrassment when he was removed from the case under a cloud of suspicion nine years later.

David Ramon Toschi, born July 11, 1931, was no stranger to publicity when he took command of the investigation into Stine's murder. He was both colorful and charismatic, serving the SFPD as an officer from 1952 to 1983. As actor Steve McQueen prepared for his role as the indubitably cool but rogue police lieutenant Frank Bullitt in the movie *Bullitt*, he copied Toschi's trademark style of wearing the shoulder holster for his Colt Cobra upside down (with the barrel of the pistol pointing up, not back) for easy access. Toschi's improvisation became part of the veteran performer's image. In 1971, Clint Eastwood portrayed "Dirty" Harry Callahan, a character in the movie *Dirty Harry* based loosely on Toschi. Four sequels would follow. Years later, Mark Ruffalo played the detective in the 2007 movie *Zodiac*, based on Robert Graysmith's 1986 book of the same name.

Toschi's fall from grace happened unceremoniously when he was demoted to pawn-shop detail at 4:00 p.m. on June 29, 1978 after it was revealed that he had sent fan letters of support, signed with pseudonyms, regarding a fictional serial that featured him as a character. His superiors had concluded that he was more interested in his own publicity and perpetuating his likeness in the fictional serial than the job at hand. He was also suspected of being the creator of a dubious 1978 Zodiac letter, a possible act of self-promotion or an effort to revive a flagging case. Following his retirement from the SFPD in 1983, Toschi found work as the head of a security detail.

Shortly after the reports of the murder reached the SFPD, they notified the Military Police Headquarters of the Presidio, informing them that a killer was on the loose and may have fled into its jurisdiction.

The Presidio of San Francisco, or simply "the Presidio," was originally named El Presidio Real de San Francisco, which translates to "The Royal Fortress of San Francisco." Built in 1776, the former military base is now a 1480-acre park. It was established by New Spain, passed on to Mexico, and then to the United States of America in 1848. When in 1989 Congress elected to end the property's status as an active military base, it had been garrisoned continuously for 210 years. It was transferred to the National Park Service in 1994. Today the Presidio comprises a mix of public and commercial uses, and is governed by a Trust which has kept the land financially self-sufficient since 2005. It was designated a California Historical Landmark in 1933. By the time that Stine was attacked, it had only been listed as a National Historic Landmark for seven years, and been added to the U.S. National Register of Historic Places for less than three years. It would forever be linked to the murder of Paul Stine and the Zodiac serial killer after the murderer fled toward its grounds.

When ambulance #82 arrived, Steward Dousette examined Stine and pronounced him dead at 10:10 p.m. Inspector Kracke summoned canine units and a fire department spotlight vehicle to assist in the search for the perpetrator of this horrendous deed. The city's entire stable of dogs—seven units in total—was pressed into service. With the emergency notifications out of the way, the officers made the next set of calls intended to handle the scene in a professional manner: they notified the crime lab, the coroner, Yellow Cab officials, and a tow truck company. LeRoy Sweet, the Assistant Traffic Manager of the Yellow Cab Company, responded and provided the victim's name, "Paul Lee Stine," and the initial victim identification. He further mentioned that Stine had begun work at 8:45 p.m., and that the last dispatch given to him was at 9:45 p.m., a call for a ride from 500 9th Avenue, Apt 1, the unanswered fare reassigned to another cab at 9:58 p.m. The only other ride that Stine had driven that evening, Sweet reported, was a trip from Pier 64 to the San Francisco International Airport.

Pelissetti's report listed the victim incorrectly as Thomas L. Stine. This was later amended to the correct name, Paul L. Stine, but not before *The San Francisco Chronicle* reporter received the inaccurate name, the dead cabby identified as T. L. Stine in its Sunday paper, its first issue following the attack.

Once assembled, the police conducted "an intense search," according to the police, of the Julius Kahn Playground, the location to which the perpetrator was last seen heading, located on the south side of the Presidio grounds and adjacent to the Presidio Heights district, as well as the grounds themselves. They were assisted by the seven canine units. Also participating were additional officers from the Richmond district and several CHP units. The quest uncovered nothing. SFPD Chief of Inspectors Marvin Lee commented on the officers' thoroughness, "A mouse couldn't have escaped our attention." Sergeant Falk and Lieutenant Kiel were two among many lawmen who aided the efforts.

Nearly an hour after his arrival at the scene, Pelissetti observed that the meter in the cab was still running. He recorded that the cost of the ride had reached $6.25 at exactly 10:46 p.m., in case the information would later be needed to determine a time of death, or in some way flesh out the timeline details.

His report described the killer as a white male in his early 40s, and five feet eight inches tall with a heavy build. He had reddish-blond hair worn in a crewcut. He was wearing eyeglasses, dark brown trousers, a dark blue or black "parka" jacket, and dark-colored shoes. He further should have many blood stains on his person and clothing, and could be in possession of keys to the Yellow Cab as well as the victim's wallet. Last seen, as far as Pelissetti was aware, walking north on Cherry Street, the assailant was to be considered armed and extremely dangerous.

Dr. Henry W. Turkel, MD, a physician acting as coroner, responded to the crime. Officers Schultz and Kindred took charge of the deceased. The SFPD Crime Lab representatives, named Dagitz and Kirkindale, arrived and took photographs of the scene. All of the physical evidence that had been gathered was retained by the crime lab for identification purposes. Once the photography was complete, the automobile, Yellow Cab #912, license plate Y17-413, was towed to the Hall of Justice, and impounded for the SFPD Homicide Department to scour for latent fingerprints.

Detective Bill Armstrong notified his office at SFPD, Room 100, of the attack, and provided the officers with a description of the assailant, advising that it should be broadcast to patrolling officers continuously throughout the evening. The initial reports of the crime lab's investigation disclosed that the victim had no U.S. currency in his possession, no wallet, and no ignition key. The assailant must have taken these. A complete inventory of items removed from the scene was not yet available because all of the victim's property was in the possession of the coroner. Stine's belongings were later received by Michael S. Conway, as authorized by Stine's wife. The cabby's clothing was placed in SFPD box 570 by property custodian M. O'Malley.

c/o

Pelissetti and Peda were not the only policemen to respond in the initial minutes following the shooting. SFPD Patrol Officer Donald Fouke, #847, watched over the eastern side of the Richmond District, east of the Presidio, when he was summoned to the crime scene by the original broadcast of a robbery in progress. His usual partner was not working that night, though years later Fouke could not recall the reason that he was assigned instead to SFPD Patrol Officer Eric Zelms, #1348, his teammate for the evening. Because they were heading north on Presidio Avenue, and had just passed Washington Street, they were able to make a quick U-turn and hurry west to the scene.

As they approached the intersection of Jackson Street and Maple Street, moving at an estimated speed of 40 to 45 miles per hour west on Jackson, Fouke noticed a man walking east on the north side of Jackson Street. He slowed his vehicle. The pedestrian was a Caucasian and not "Negro" as the broadcast had described the gunman. They did not think that the man they observed was responsible for the attack on the cabby. Fouke considered him merely a white man walking in an affluent neighborhood, which was nothing out of the ordinary. He sped past to arrive at the crime scene as quickly as possible, just around the corner to the left. He later reported that the man went east on Jackson and north on Maple, heading into the Presidio grounds. With its four foot drop in elevation, and limited road access, the grounds was a great escape location for a traveler on foot, especially when pursued by a vehicle.

Recalling what he saw years later, Fouke described the pedestrian. He wore a three-quarter length or Derby Jacket (a fashion icon native to San Francisco), with elastic at the waist and the cuffs. The collar was turned down as it usually is on this type of coat. He had a crew-cut haircut, and wore rust-colored pants which were unusual at the time, since they were older and out of fashion. His feet were clad in engineering boots that were tan and possibly low cut. Fouke also believed that he had seen the man's eyes, but could not recall a color. He believed that the man had bowed his head down when confronted by the headlights of the police car. He may have been the killer avoiding police contact, or simply a pedestrian reacting to the bright light.

Fouke noted that the pedestrian walked with a "lumbering gait, stumbling along like a semi-limp." On seeing the man, he slowed the car to perhaps 25 miles per hour from a speed of between 40 to 45 miles per hour before accelerating past him. He estimated that there was a mere 5, 10, or perhaps 15 seconds between the moment they noticed the stranger and the time they lost sight of him.

When observed, the man had turned toward the entryway of one of the residences—possibly 3712 Jackson Street—Fouke explained years later, though he never saw the stranger get to the top of the concrete stairs or enter the home. Even though he remembered the address explicitly years later, he claimed to not have told anyone, and it wasn't listed in any report. His first explanation, when challenged many years later, was that he assumed that the man did not live there so it was immaterial to the case. When asked whether this was important enough to report, he claimed that he thought—"all these years"—that he *had* written it in the record. His two descriptions of the man's movements—that he turned north on Maple to enter the park at the road's end and that he went up concrete steps toward a front door—were never reconciled. Nor was the discrepancy between thinking the information immaterial for a report *and* thinking that he had included it in a written record.

Fouke, reminiscing about the event, was adamant, "we never stopped him; we never talked to him." Others would come to believe that Fouke did in fact stop and talk to the pedestrian. Fouke's claim, firmly maintained for decades, would become a point of contention in the case, and emerge as a second enduring mystery of the attack, the unknown reason for Stine's drive of one additional block being the first. Investigators and armchair detectives have argued for decades over whether or not Officers Fouke and Zelms stopped and spoke with someone as they drove to the scene of Stine's death.

After regaining speed, the officers turned left onto Cherry Street and arrived at the cab one short block later, according to Fouke. They were halted there by Pelissetti, and informed that the perpetrator was a Caucasian male. Fouke responded by mentioning the initial broadcast, and then swore. "*That* was the suspect," he yelled. Realizing that he had seen Stine's killer moments earlier, he turned the vehicle around and raced back toward the Presidio.

He and his partner scoured the area for the man with a crewcut they had last seen as they drove along Jackson Street. They searched near Julius Kahn Playground and the area where Maple Street fed into the Presidio. There was much thick foliage in which a fleeing assailant could hide. They found nothing.

Fouke wrote no report that evening. Discussing the investigation years later, he stated that he did not file a report on what he had witnessed until a full month after the attack. He was prompted to do so when he saw a composite picture of the killer posted in the Richmond District Police Office, he claimed. Noting that the man he had seen resembled the composite, he set about writing an intra-departmental memorandum, also called a "scratch." It was dated November 12 and was forwarded to the Homicide Division and added to the official files, not as an amendment but as additional information to detail and clarify events. When asked about his report, he told an inspector—it may have been Toschi, he wasn't sure—that the man he'd seen was older and heavier than what he had seen in the composite.

But this delayed report, combined with Fouke's later explanations, only raised more questions about the unusual events surrounding Stine's murder.

❦

Pelissetti's description of his own actions that evening, once the scene was secure, markedly contradicted the information provided by Fouke. According to Pelissetti, when Fouke and Zelms arrived at the scene, it was Fouke who called out to *him* to see whether *he* had seen anybody (and not vice-versa). He had replied, "no." He was firm in his recollection: Fouke had not mentioned to him that he had seen anybody or had stopped anybody.

Narrating events decades later, Pelissetti claimed that he retraced the escape route of the killer. He crept north along Cherry Street using all the self-preservation tactics he had acquired in his training. He wisely feared that the assailant could be around any blind corner or behind any car—and there were many alcoves and parked vehicles along Cherry Street. He didn't want to end up like Stine and get his own "head blown off."

When he arrived at Jackson Street, one block to the north, he explained, he had to decide whether to continue north or turn to the west or east to further his pursuit. Because he could see no one scaling the wall to enter the Presidio (where Cherry Street dead-ended into it), and seeing no one when he looked to his left or right, he made the arbitrary decision to turn right onto Jackson Street, proceeding east, paralleling the south edge of the Presidio. He was on the east side of Cherry and the road descended to the east, so east seemed the natural choice.

Navigating one block farther, he achieved Maple Street, and had another decision to make in determining which direction to continue. He was one block north of the taxi's original destination of Washington and Maple Streets. By this time, he realized that his chance of catching someone was essentially nil, the murderer likely far away in an unknown direction. He turned to the right, and as he did so, he noticed a middle-aged man walking his dog. (This man in time would be identified as a wealthy entrepreneur and a possible suspect in the killing.) The man was older and thinner than the gunman Pelissetti sought and had no blood on him—residue of the crime that would have almost certainly have been present on the perpetrator. When asked whether he had seen anybody, the man with the dog replied that he had not.

Pelissetti recalled that when Fouke spoke to him that evening, the other officer did not mention that he had seen or stopped anybody on Jackson Street. Pelissetti claimed that when he communicated with him in the days after the incident, however, Fouke admitted to him that he *had* both stopped and interacted with someone. Pelissetti was as adamant as Fouke on this point. According to Pelissetti, if Fouke was now saying otherwise, he was not correct. The scratch written by Fouke did not comport with what the officer had told him in the subsequent days of investigation, he insisted. His memory was clear: Fouke told him that he had stopped a stranger, and that that stranger had told Fouke he had not seen anyone in the area.

Years later, Pelissetti did not believe that Fouke had seen the killer. He believed that Fouke had stopped and talked to *someone*, but that person was not the murderer, and had merely said "no" when asked if he had seen anything. The area was well lit, Pelissetti explained. Had the man on Jackson Street been the killer, he would have been covered in Stine's blood, and it would have been obvious to anyone who stopped him. Pelissetti was certain that it could not have been the murderer who Fouke had approached.

To further complicate matters, the murderer himself told a third variation of events. It was the killer's tale that would, in time, be widely reported and repeated, achieving the status as the accepted version, despite being of highly questionable veracity flowing from a dubious source. Though it would be no stoop for a killer to lie, it *is* possible that his version was more accurate than those of the two officers; however, the details he presented suggested that he was being deceptive.

On November 9, the Zodiac serial killer sent his longest hand-written communication, the 6-Page letter, which was actually seven pages in length due to the additional writing on the back of the sixth numbered page. In it, the writer claimed to have been stopped by two officers, and when asked if he saw anyone acting suspicious or strange, he directed them around a corner. Their tires "peeled rubber" as they left, he added. This small portion of writing was a significant one, specifically marked for publication by its author.

In it, the killer detailed his account of events:

```
"Ps. 2 cops pulled a goof abot 3
min after I left the cab. I was
walking down the hill to the
park when this cop car pulled up
& one of them called me over
```

```
& asked if I saw any one
acting supicisous or strange
in the last 5 to 10 min & I said
yes there was this man who
was running by waveing a gun
& the cops peeled rubber &
went around the corner as
I directed them & I dissap-
eared into the park a block &
a half away never to be seen
again."
```

On the face of it, the killer's claim is difficult to accept as fact. The Zodiac may have shown his hand by writing that he sent officers peeling rubber around a corner, betraying that his version of events was actually, at least in part, fictional. When Fouke and Zelms were driving west on Jackson, once they passed the cross street of Maple, there were only two corners for them to "peel" around. At Cherry Street, they could turn either left or right—and Fouke claimed that they drove left, though not with squealing tires. Left would—and did, apparently—take them to the scene of the crime, of which they would have been aware that night, having already been summoned to that exact location. For the Zodiac to send them around *that* corner would be absurd. There would be no reason to accept a stranger's tip that a gun-wielding assailant was sprinting *toward* the scene of the crime.

But turning right was no better.

Cherry Street, like Maple Street that parallels it to the east, becomes a dead-end into a wall surrounding the Presidio. Peeling rubber around that corner to the right would lead the patrol car into a 50-foot cul-de-sac north of Jackson Street. Fouke would not have raced around *that* corner because of the words of a stranger either, well aware that it led nowhere. Apparently, the murderer was also a liar, though his falsehoods do not prove that Fouke was telling the truth or remembering events correctly.

Even if Fouke was mistaken in his later memories that he saw the assailant climb the stairs of a home on Jackson Street, the killer's claim remains improbable, if not impossible. A month after the events, the officer wrote in his scratch that the killer had turned north on Maple Street and headed toward the Presidio, moving with a "shuffling lope." If that is correct, Fouke must have witnessed this feat from a spot east of Maple. From this vantage point, had he encountered the killer, there were two additional corners around which he could have sped at the urging of the killer. But these, like those of Cherry Street, also make no sense. A right turn on Maple, like a right turn on Cherry, would dead end within yards. A left turn would lead Fouke and Zelms to achieve the crime scene from the east, something that contradicts the statements of both Pelissetti and Fouke, both of whom agreed that Fouke and Zelms arrived at Stine's cab coming south on Cherry Street. Consequently, wherever the killer may have been spotted along Jackson Street, he lied about directing officers around a corner.

Marvin Lee, SFPD Chief of Inspectors also challenged the writer's claim to having words with the officers when he was quoted by *The Chronicle*, "…it is preposterous that he was stopped and questioned by officers. That just didn't happen."

In another unusual claim, Fouke wrote in the scratch that he did not know whether Zelms had seen the man walking along Jackson Street. He maintained that upon hearing the correct race of the perpetrator, he had turned his car around and sped toward the Presidio. Had he not questioned his partner as to what he had seen, a natural discussion topic while racing after the man? Or had he by this time, a month following the attack, forgotten whether or not Zelms told him that he had seen the man?

So there remain three versions of events. Fouke claimed to have seen the killer but had not stopped nor interacted with him. Pelissetti believed that Fouke stopped—and spoke to—someone, but it was not the murderer. And the Zodiac, claiming credit for the attack in a subsequent letter, wrote that he had been stopped by, and been spoken to by, two cops, directing them on a fool's errand around some corner. No less than two of these three tales must be inaccurate.

Conflicting narrations are commonplace, detectives know. Eyewitness accounts of events are notorious for being faulty and unreliable. People can make mistakes, deceive, and be deceived. And in this instance something more may have been at play: the killer had every reason to obfuscate. He may have believed that his liberty depended upon it, and he apparently enjoyed taunting police officers, having done so numerous times previously in letters and phone calls. The officers too may have had reasons to exaggerate or minimize their role in the aftermath of the attack—or even provide false information. One or both of the officers may have been trying to cover up a very embarrassing event.

Fouke had every reason to fabricate his account. If he had spoken to the killer, it was necessary for him to explain to the department—if not history—why he did not capture him. If he hadn't spoken to him (or could claim that he hadn't), he could blame dispatch and the faulty initial reports for the murderer slipping through his fingers. As a result of his failure to seize the Zodiac that night, his misrepresentations may have been deep and prolonged.

His lies may have included his participation in the creation of the pictures following the attack. The original composite picture, created from the description given by the three teenagers, was made available on October 13, a mere two days after the attack. The amended version was released five days later, based on a second interview with the teenagers (and possibly also with input from Officer Fouke and/ or Officer Zelms). The new drawing depicted an older man with a heavier jaw. Its accompanying description stated that the assailant was "35-45 Years, 5'8", Heavy Build, Short Brown Hair, possibly with Red Tint, Wears Glasses. Armed with 9mm Automatic." The poster listed the items police held for comparison: "Slugs, Casings, Latents, Handwriting." Fouke's claim that his November 12 scratch was produced in response to his viewing of the composites in the Richmond District Police Office might be incorrect, and possibly disingenuous. The intra-departmental memorandum, produced nearly one month after the revised version of the composite was created, was more likely the result of the new version of events provided by the killer.

Without a doubt, the killer's new letter with its writer's claim of being stopped by two police officers would raise many questions for investigators. A quick survey of officers on duty that night must have led to the inevitable acknowledgment, "Yes, Officer Fouke saw someone." If asked where such an incident appeared in a report, he would have been flummoxed. Even on the day of the event, he believed that he had seen Stine's murderer. He spoke with Pelissetti about it, he claimed; he informed communications; he may have been responsible for the newspaper report that someone was seen running into the park, which became the impetus for the search of the Presidio grounds. Though he had told people about what he had seen, he himself had written down nothing. The scratch appeared to be a rectification of that oversight.

The second enduring mystery surrounding Stine's murder is the question of whether Fouke and Zelms actually stopped and spoke with the killer that night. The encounter has been reported as fact by some, the source for that information being the killer's written words. But Fouke adamantly denied it, and Zelms is no longer alive to provide his account of the story. It has been rumored that Zelm's widow has shared that her husband when alive told her that he and his partner did, in fact, stop near, and speak with, the Zodiac.

If the two officers did interact with the assailant in the manner that the killer suggested—and maybe even if they did not—Fouke's scratch was a document of protection, a CYA (cover your ass) made to prevent the SFPD, particularly Officers Fouke and Zelms, from looking foolish. It's one thing to omit a written statement about seeing a killer; it is a much more egregious error to have had the opportunity to apprehend the Bay Area's most wanted man and not do so. The SFPD, like the law enforcement departments in all of the locations that the Zodiac had already struck, was soon frustrated and embarrassed over its inability to identify and capture its quarry.

It is also possible that Fouke spoke to an inspector soon after the event. Fouke claimed that he was approached by one after he had filed his scratch. If he was mistaken in the timing, it may have been in the days following the attack that he reported that the man he saw was older and heavier than the composite picture that was being circulated. That inspector, whether or not it was Toschi, may have used the new information to amend the composite picture—create a second one—without Fouke's knowledge. When contacted many years later, the artist who drew the original composite pictures could not specifically recall events surrounding his work on the case.

It is also possible that Pelissetti was overly influenced by the Zodiac's written words. In reading the 6-Page letter, he may have implanted in his own mind the events as written by the perpetrator. That would explain the supplanting of a memory—if that is what happened—and Fouke's recollection would then more accurately depict what had occurred that night.

The scratch added some additional information not available in the other written reports of October 11. In it, Fouke claimed that the suspect was seen turning north on Maple Street, a dead end road leading to the Presidio Park. This would imply that Fouke himself was the source of the information that led the police to conduct a thorough search of the Presidio grounds. If true, it casts doubt on whether he saw the killer ascend a flight of concrete steps on Jackson, as he later maintained. The scratch also contained a more detailed description of the suspect, only slightly at odds with the visual word picture provided by Pelissetti (whose description was apparently based on information collected from the teenagers, and possibly from Fouke as well). Fouke described the footwear of the man he saw as tan engineering boots, possibly low cut (later the "possibly" was removed and the boots were described by Fouke as "low cut"). Pelissetti's description was of *dark*, low cut shoes.

The San Francisco Chronicle's Sunday, October 12 description of the assailant was similar to that of Fouke. It identified a white man, about 40 years of age, 170 pounds, with a blond crewcut. *The Chronicle* maintained that he was wearing glasses and that he had dark shoes and dark, gray trousers and jacket.

The police reports do not contain the whole story, however. Pelissetti did not mention his trek down Cherry Street to Jackson Street and east to Maple Street. Fouke wrote no timely report, waiting a full month after the event to explain his actions. Zelms, who penned no words of his experiences, was killed on the job in the months following the attack. What exactly these officers did and saw may never be resolved.

Pelissetti later left room for his own fallibility. Years after the events, when pressed, he admitted that he may have been wrong about what Fouke had said to him. He could not categorically eliminate the possibility that the officer did *not* stop somebody. His doubts—suggesting that he acknowledged his memory might be faulty, he might have been wrong about what Fouke said to him, or that the other officer's version of events might indeed have been the correct one—were evident when he admitted, "hard to say if he [stopped someone] or not, point of conjecture."

Contributing to the officers' contradictory stories, likely, was the apparent banality of the evening. By all appearances, it was a routine robbery, botched to be sure, but in that era cab robberies occurred weekly in San Francisco, and assaults on cab drivers were not uncommon. In fact, three months later, on January 25, 1970, San Francisco cab driver Charles B. Jarman was shot behind the right ear and died. His wallet and ID were similarly removed from his person.

Initially, there was nothing to tie Stine's murder to the series of assaults on couples in the North Bay. It had little in common with the Zodiac attacks of the previous 10 months which took place in desolate rural areas, targeted couples as victims, occurred at romantic settings, and included no taxis. The attack on Stine was characterized in initial police reports and in the newspapers as a common robbery that included a homicide. The items missing from the cab seemed only to confirm that it was an armed robbery gone awry: Stine's wallet and the cab's keys provided the perpetrator a motive of financial gain and a disabled car that could not be used in a pursuit. The police initially did not notice, or discounted, the missing tail from Stine's black and white striped shirt.

It wasn't a Zodiac attack until the Zodiac declared it a Zodiac attack.

The Stine letter

A letter arrived at the formidable gray building that housed the offices of *The San Francisco Chronicle* on Monday, the first day of mail delivery following Stine's murder. Carol Fisher Cots opened it. The "Stine" letter began with the familiar, *"This is the Zodiac speaking,"* and included a small swatch of Stine's bloody shirttail. Instantly, the routine attack took on an important historical and criminological context. The murder of Paul Stine was not a botched robbery or some unfortunately accident. It was another in a series of ruthlessly calculated attacks. It was not a surprise that officers struggled to recall exactly what had happened, provided different versions of events, and minimized (or exaggerated) their involvement in the case. Until the arrival of the new Zodiac note, the investigation was nothing out of the ordinary.

The now high profile murder case soon elicited strange reactions from its participants, as these types of cases invariably do. The limelight can urge officers to claim to have done things they know they should have carried out, or deny doing things they know they should not have done. The glare of publicity affects the general public too, causing some to shy away from its light, others to exaggerate their own importance, and still others to seize its promises of fame and fortune with bald-face lies.

Because the killing of Paul Stine occurred on a Saturday night, and the Stine letter arrived with the next delivery of *The San Francisco Chronicle*'s mail on Monday, it is not clear when precisely the missive was posted. It could have been placed in a mailbox soon after the attack; it could have been mailed early Monday morning. It was postmarked in San Francisco on October 13, the day it was both picked up and delivered.

The envelope containing the Stine letter was addressed in a familiar, slanted scrawl, "S.F. Chronicle/ San Fran. / Calif. / Please Rush to Editor." It was posted with two Roosevelt stamps affixed sideways to make the former president appear to look downward. In the space usually reserved for a return address, its creator had drawn a small crosshair symbol, or gunsight.

Upon its receipt of the letter, *The Chronicle* immediately contacted the SFPD. Toschi and Armstrong were initially unaware of the missing piece of Stine's shirt. The murder was being investigated as a robbery gone wrong so the cabby's clothing had been packed away in the morgue, the missing shirttail not deemed important enough to notify the police. Eventually, Criminologist John Williams matched the swatch of cloth that arrived with the letter to part of the missing section of the victim's shirt. He noted that there remained additional outstanding material from the garment, removed from the scene but not included in the Stine letter.

Investigators carefully examined the new note, which comprised three paragraphs on a single page. Each paragraph was completely unrelated to the other two. What the author had written was essentially three ideas, each expanded to several sentences. There was no transition material to join the disparate thoughts, and no suggestion that the three themes had anything to do with one another.

Surprisingly, none of these paragraphs was indented; the Zodiac would never indent any of his paragraphs, though he was perfectly capable of indenting bullet points, which he did in several other letters. If any of his communications cried out for indentation, it was this one. The paragraphs were differentiated by a return of the author's pen to the left margin whether or not there was room for additional words on the previous line. The killer was apparently aware that he had three ideas to relate, and was cognizant of the necessary breaks between them, but would indent none of them.

The first paragraph answered the question, *who am I?* It presented the second use of the iconic phrase *"This is the Zodiac speaking."* And the last time that the words would be followed with a period (or any punctuation). From then on, all future uses of the phrase would appear as a title, absent any punctuation mark at the end. The killer then elaborated on his identity by claiming responsibility for the death of not only the cab driver, Paul Stine, but also the brutal murders that had occurred in the "north bay area," apparently those in Solano County—the two on Lake Herman Road and the one in the Blue Rock Springs Park—and Cecelia Shepard on the shore of Lake Berryessa.

To ensure that there was no doubt to his claims, he had deposited in the envelope a bloodied piece of Stine's black and white striped shirt, which he had collected at the scene of the crime, macabre proof by anybody's standards. (Because black dye is frequently manufactured from extremely dark blue pigment, *The Chronicle* may be forgiven for its report that the shirt was "blue and white." Later reports changed the description to "gray and white." The Napa Register described the garment as "gray and white.") The shirt piece had been ripped from its owner and not cut with a blade.

The second paragraph explained how the killer could have been captured after the attack, had the investigation followed a different course of action. The writer counseled that the police should have waited for him to emerge from his hiding place. He apparently wanted the police to feel great shame at their incompetence, and by contrast, great admiration for the murderer who successfully eluded capture while remaining in the area during the massive search. Additionally, he may have been overcompensating, lying to cover up for his cowardice in having left the area just as law enforcement was assembling.

The third and final paragraph was a clear threat. Obviously intending to send the city into paroxysms of dread, he outlined his plan to kill "school children."

The Stine letter in its entirety reads as follows:

```
This is the Zodiac speaking.
I am the murderer of the
taxi driver over by
Washington St & Maple St last
night, to prove this here is
a blood stained piece of his
shirt. I am the same man
who did in the people in the
north bay area.
The S.F. Police could have caught
me last night if they had
searched the park properly
instead of holding road races
with their motorcicles seeing who
could make the most noise. The
car drivers should have just
parked their cars & sat there
quietly waiting for me to come
out of cover
School children make nice targ-
ets, I think I shall wipe out
a school bus some morning. Just
shoot out the frunt tire & then
pick off the kiddies as they come
bouncing out.
    [crosshairs symbol]
```

The connecting link between the three paragraphs of the Stine letter, if there was one, was the word, "I/me." The mailing reinforced the idea that the Zodiac enjoyed talking about himself, bragging about his exploits, and offering up threats of what he could and would do. The murderer of couples was now responsible for the killing of a cab driver, and was threatening to become a mass murderer of Bay Area children.

The effect was devastating. Fear swept the area, as if a dark, heavy pall had descended.

Initially, due to the incendiary nature of the words, the final portion of the letter was withheld from the public. *The Chronicle* agreed not to immediately print the last paragraph at the request of the SFPD. No one wanted to be responsible for the panic that was sure to result. At the same time, no one wanted to withhold crucial, potentially life-and-death, information from those who needed it. *The Chronicle*'s story about the letter was published on Wednesday, October 15. The threat was made public two days later in newspapers, on the radio, on television, and across the wire services.

When the final paragraph did get released, the law enforcement agencies implemented plans to thwart the threatened attack. Because the Zodiac had perpetrated death in Solano County, Vallejo, Napa County, and now San Francisco, the entire Bay Area had to heed the killer's warning. Each catchment area dealt with the threat in its own way. Some used officers in unmarked police vehicles to keep an eye on the children, other regions assigned police cruisers to tail buses during the morning and afternoon commutes, still others sent aircraft aloft to scan for a sharpshooter. Some communities provided armed guards to ride shotgun or rerouted their buses. Instructions were given to bus drivers in the event the shooting occurred: 1) Do not stop. 2) Tell the children to duck down. 3) Drive fast to flee the area. And 4) Honk the bus's horn to attract attention.

The San Francisco Chronicle, in an article by Paul Avery, noted that in the Napa Valley Unified School District alone, there were 10,000 students who rode the bus. Transporting that number required 64 buses logging an estimated 4,000 miles daily for its 24 elementary schools, 3 junior highs, and 1 senior high school. No one was taking the threat lightly. Buses even had to be checked for a bomb before each run because Santa Rosa received a bomb threat by telephone that suggested one might be found. Several Cessnas from the Napa Aero Club were patrolling the hundreds of miles of roadway.

Other security measures were withheld from the public. They were being kept top secret.

Pierre Bidou, a BPD detective who responded to the December 20, 1968 attack at Lake Herman Road, noted that great fear in Benicia persisted for months, escalating after each new attack. A 10:00 p.m.

curfew had already been instituted for the residents. The entire Bay Area was on edge, especially in places near previous attacks.

Thankfully, the killer never followed through on his threat, and in fact rescinded it in a future letter.

On Tuesday, October 14, at 9:00 p.m., Toschi and Armstrong traveled to Napa and met with Narlow and Townsend at the NCSO. This was followed by a more substantial gathering among area investigators on October 20 at the SFPD offices.

The incomparable Walter Cronkite, in his October 22 broadcast of the CBS evening news, introduced to the American people the pariah of the San Francisco Bay Area. The killer had now achieved a nation-wide audience.

The Yellow Cab Company, on January 27 of the following year, offered $1,000 in reward money for information leading to the arrest and conviction of the persons responsible for the deaths of cab drivers Charles Jarman and Paul Stine. If the Zodiac was keeping track, he would have realized that this raised the total amount of money that had been placed on his head, first started by the now-expired Jensen-Faraday Reward Fund, to $2000.

❧

When Special Agent Mel Nicolai of the California's Department of Justice summarized the Zodiac case, adding the murder of Stine to the other attacks, he listed the following items of evidence that had been collected in the investigation of Stine's murder:

- 2 portions of victim's shirt (white with black stripe), which had been sent in two subsequent mailings by the killer.
- Hand printing from the killer's various letters.
- Latent prints.
- 9mm bullet and casing (the spent casing found on the passenger side of the cab had been fired from a weapon different than the one used in the crime at Blue Rock Springs Park).
- Black leather men's size 7 gloves.

Missing from the scene were Stine's cab keys and black leather wallet, as well as the tail to his black and white striped shirt. Investigators did recover seven keys and one ring. The cab also contained one checkbook, some miscellaneous papers, an auto registration, and a motorcycle registration.

SFPD homicide case #696314 (including robbery cases #692895 and #687697) was heralded on wanted posters, listing Toschi and Armstrong as the investigating officers along with their business address and phone number: 850 Bryant Street, San Francisco, 94103, (415) 553-1145. Captain Marvin Lee of the SFPD, soon after the attack, explained that the crosshair symbol meant "the center of the universe" or "the sign of the Zodiac." He called the killer a psychopath and "a very, very seriously mentally deranged" person who was nevertheless legally sane. He was, according to Lee, a "very, very sick, and very dangerous person," one who attacked with "no remorse" and "no justification." Lee added that he was an "Absolutely ruthless, completely merciless killer," noting, "he thinks killing is just killing," He declared that the killer, due to his callous nature, was going to be "a serious problem for us."

Problem or not, the FBI's expansive resources were quickly ushered into a seat at the investigation. In an airtel dated October 17, the San Francisco Field Office sent the Washington, D.C. Bureau two copies of the Stine letter for comparison to material previously sent, observing that Napa, Vallejo, and San Francisco were all investigating the series of murders. Based on the bayonet-like knife used at Berryessa, military boot impressions deposited at the scene, and 9mm bullets in two attacks, it speculated that the perpetrator may have had a military background. It also sent copies of the Stine letter with its envelope, and copies of the wanted poster, to the field office in Sacramento. It further promised to remain in close contact with the SFPD and to furnish any laboratory and latent fingerprint examinations requested.

Washington, D.C. replied to the San Francisco Field Office in a letter arriving a week later from the FBI Crime Laboratory. The lab noted that most of the letters in its possession were copies. Since some were created after the letters had already been treated for fingerprints—and even clean copies are difficult to study—handwriting comparisons were not possible. However, the specimens it compared were probably the work of one person, it concluded.

On October 22, the San Francisco FBI Field Office requested via airtel that its headquarters check the fingerprints on file (either from a fingerprint card or a photograph) against a suspect that the SFPD had developed. The reply came the next day: no records of the suspect were located for comparison. Some of the prints lifted from the various crime scenes included palm prints, or latent impressions that appeared to be palm prints, in addition to several impressions from fingertips and lower joints. As fingerprint cards did not normally contain these details, the FBI was unable to make use of these impressions when it compared collected prints to known prints in its files.

Over the ensuing months, a flurry of communications crisscrossed the country between the FBI in Washington, D.C. and its field office in San Francisco. Both offices made use of new technologies, including radiograms, quickly notifying each other of new developments. Since the information was sometimes garbled using the then advanced communication tools, and instant confirmation was not yet available, hard copies of each request and each report had to be subsequently mailed. Again and again, San Francisco sent Washington sheets containing the latest slate of suspects. The FBI located suspect fingerprints from their files when it could, and compared them to the latent prints collected from the Zodiac crime scenes. Again and again, the FBI responded: no fingerprint match and no palm prints of suspect available for comparison.

In an intra-departmental memorandum sent on October 19 from the San Francisco FBI Field Office to the VPD, the fingerprints on file in San Francisco were carefully described:

"All of the latent prints in our case were obtained from a taxi cab. The latent prints that show traces of blood are believed to be prints of the suspect. The latent prints from right front door handle are also believed to be prints of the suspect. These prints are circled with a red pen.
The other latent prints many of which are very good prints, may or may not be prints of the suspect in this case;"

Also on October 19, *The San Francisco Examiner* ran a story on its front page that was directed squarely at the Zodiac. It invited the elusive murderer to turn himself in, promising him medical and legal assistance, noting, "You face life as a hunted, tormented animal…" The paper vowed not to trace any call made by the killer so that he could have an unfettered opportunity to tell his mysterious story. It explained, "We offer you no protection, and no sympathy," and inquired, "How has life wronged you?" The killer never again wrote to *The Examiner*, which led to speculation that he was deeply insulted by this paper's attitude toward him and the tone of its approach.

On the next day, October 20, the Attorney General of California, Thomas C. Lynch, called a meeting in San Francisco for 27 detectives from seven agencies to share information about the serial killer operating within each of the jurisdictions represented. The three-hour conference that made ample use of chalkboards was conducted at the Hall of Justice. As the Zodiac seminar proceeded through each of the attacks—a couple shot to death in Solano County, a woman killed in the outskirts of Vallejo, a woman fatally stabbed at the shore of Lake Berryessa in Napa County, and a San Francisco cab driver brutally executed with a bullet through the back of his head—each detective, department, and jurisdiction shared with all the others represented, hoping that the synergy would move the case forward.

Lynch himself was unavailable to attend the event as he was in Colorado at a meeting of Attorneys General. He did, however, make a plea to the Zodiac to turn himself in: he will get the help he needs and his rights will be protected, Lynch promised. Following the conference, SFPD Chief of Inspectors Captain Marvin Lee was circumspect in his optimism, "I couldn't say we're any closer to catching the suspect."

Nicolai's 35-page report for California's Department of Justice, dated April 29, 1970, tallied the progress of the case. Suspect names had been provided by citizens, by various institutions, and by law enforcement and military agencies. There was no shortage of suspects. Modus operandi files, records from oil companies—sales receipts from September 27, 1969 gas purchases—and CHP citations had all been collected and studied. What the comprehensive document could not share was the resolution to the case; the elusive perpetrator remained at large, "Combined efforts by law enforcement agencies have failed to uncover the identity of the 'Zodiac' killer."

On October 29, the FBI Latent Fingerprint Section sent a note to its San Francisco Field Office reporting on the latent fingerprints gathered from the Stine crime scene. Of the prints, 30 were latent fingerprints, 3 were latent palm prints, and 1 was a latent impression (a fingerprint from the lower joint area of a finger or a palm print). One of the latent fingerprints matched those of Paul Stine, collected after his death. The others were not identified with any suspects. Impressions of lower joint areas of the fingers and palm prints were not contained in Identification Division files because they were not routinely collected when fingerprint cards were created in the 1960s. The latent impressions were preserved on three photographs.

On October 30, Earl Randol, Sheriff of Napa County, sent FBI Director J. Edgar Hoover a radiogram requesting an analysis of another suspect. The FBI replied on November 5 to confirm and supplement a radiogram reply of October 31 regarding the work sheet prepared the same day. Once again, no fingerprint match, and no palm prints available. However, the person referred to by FBI may or may not have been the same person as requested, the report cautioned.

The next day, Jack E. Stiltz, Chief of Police of the VPD, wrote Hoover, requesting that the FBI check yet another suspect against collected fingerprints in the case. The reply on November 12 was predictable and familiar. The sets of latent prints were not identical, and palm prints from the suspect were unavailable. The work sheet of November 7 revealed the same. No match.

That same day, the FBI reported back to its San Francisco Field Office what their tests regarding two suspects—one from St. Paul, Minnesota, the other from Brady, Texas—had concluded. Available prints did not match any prints from the Zodiac files, and palm prints from the suspects were unavailable. The tests had been requested four days prior by the San Francisco FBI Field Office, were conducted the next day, and the results were also passed on to the NPD so that it was made aware at the same time as the FBI's San Francisco Field Office.

The FBI in San Francisco requested a comparison for two additional suspects on November 3. Though there was confusion about one of the suspects—whether the man named was the same person whose prints were compared—the reply came the next day: no match and no palm prints on file. Four more suspects were named on November 6, one apparently offered up by an eight-year-old. The comparisons were done on November 7.

On November 10, the FBI was notified by its San Francisco office that a military man had been AWOL since the last Zodiac killing (of Paul Stine, October 11), and had been absent from his base at the time of each of the previous murders. So crucial was this lead that the San Francisco FBI Field Office ordered that the man's prints be sent by direct flight from Washington, D.C. to San Francisco. The prints made it aboard a TWA flight, and the envelope had to be passed between captains during a crew change in Kansas City. A representative of the FBI San Francisco Field Office met the plane at the airport to retrieve the prized prints.

In response to victim Hartnell's report that his assailant at Lake Berryessa had claimed two weeks earlier to be a prison escapee from Montana, the FBI expanded its search to include that northern region of the country. Hartnell followed events and offered assistance from his hospital bed. In an effort to identify the person who may have come from Montana, the San Francisco FBI Field Office petitioned Washington, D.C. on November 6 to contact the Butte, Montana Field Office to investigate. In particular, San Francisco wanted to know whether there was a prison fugitive who may or may not have murdered a prison guard during his escape. Since Hartnell was not expected to survive his ordeal, perhaps the assailant was telling the truth about his past, it was reasoned. It appeared to be an investigative lead with great potential, and the FBI meant to follow it. A copy of the composite photo that was created subsequent to the attack at Lake Berryessa was also furnished to the FBI in Washington, D.C.

Butte was finally given the needed authority to pursue the matter on November 13. The Bureau there was authorized to investigate mental institutions and prisons, and also to contact local police officers and sheriff's offices in any city advisable in an attempt to develop a suspect or suspects.

Its Field Office in San Francisco provided three new suspects to the FBI in Washington, D.C. on November 13. In its communication, San Francisco changed the title to "Zodiac" because that was the name the perpetrator gave to himself. It was by this time the only moniker used in the press, shared among law enforcement services, and discussed in casual conversation, so compelling and ominous was the label. One week later, Washington, D.C. responded to the request, sharing from its work sheet filled out the day after the tip, that no match existed for two of the three suspects, one born in Los Angeles, the other in Troy, New York. Yet again, the elusive palm prints were not available for comparison. No prints of any kind were found for the third suspect.

Meanwhile, the SFPD kept a wary eye on crimes committed in the Bay Area with the hopes that the Zodiac might make a mistake. In one promising event, David Odell Martin was shot and killed on November 21 by Officer Thomas Burns, an SFPD sharpshooter, at Martin's residence following a family altercation. Martin's wife, Geraldine, had run from the house, screaming, "He's gone crazy. He's going to kill us." Martin, who had refused to work the previous five years and was a known barbiturate and amphetamine user, injured his 11-year-old daughter when he pressed an eight-inch circular saw blade against her throat, and pricked his wife's neck repeatedly with a knife and a broken Coke bottle. Burns gained entry to the home through a shattered basement window and terminated Martin with a .38 handgun. Though he died proclaiming he was the Zodiac, Martin was cleared through fingerprint examination and other evidence.

On November 24, the FBI contacted the Office of the Provost Marshal in San Francisco in response to a letter earlier that month stating that a Sergeant had threatened a Gunnery Sergeant. The FBI requested that the office check to see if the Sergeant had written any threatening notes. This was but another in a long string of dead ends. The handwriting samples that were eventually collected failed to yield anything, with no connection to the Zodiac writing noted whatsoever.

❧

The Zodiac's action of selecting a victim from a high-profile, well-populated location—and adding Metropolitan San Francisco to his hit list—had set in motion a massive investigation. The SFPD was far more experienced in tracking killers and better able to financially support a sustained effort. Armstrong and Toschi were described by Chronicle reporter Paul Avery as being "head and shoulders" above the other investigators—he could not praise them too highly, he admitted. However, the additional attention and resources would enter the case with a steep cost.

The murders had now awakened public interest, not merely in the North Bay but throughout the Bay Area, around the state, and across the country. With the release of the composite pictures of the Zodiac that were created after Stine's murder, the floodgates of citizen assistance opened. Public participation became a deluge swamping every police department working on the case. The good, well-intended citizens now provided a tsunami of tips, suspects, theories, and even the weakest pieces of circumstantial evidence against a multitude of improbable suspects. The agencies were overwhelmed. Special Agent Mel Nicolai of the California Department of Justice observed, "Everybody had an idea of who it might be."

A 41-year-old Chicago mystic, hairdresser, and psychic, named Joseph, who claimed that he had accurately predicted Senator Edward Kennedy's car accident and the identity of Sharon Tate's killers, told *The Vallejo Times-Herald* that he was receiving mental transmissions from the Zodiac. He believed that the perpetrator did not want to kill again. According to the psychic, the Zodiac was transmitting that the thrill was over, and that he wanted peace. The image the spiritual man received of the Zodiac was that of an elusive, malnourished man, five feet eight inches tall, 135 to 145 pounds, with silky dark brown hair worn in pompadour which he combed forward as part of his disguise. The tipster, who also contacted the San Francisco press, believed that the perpetrator had possessions in a box, that when he felt and saw them hideous things began to happen.

On November 17, Adrian and Darlene approached the VPD. At 11:00 p.m. they reported on a suspect, named Edmund, who was 20 years of age and resembled the composite from San Francisco. According to the couple, Edmund acted strangely, and had access to guns from his father. He lived with an aunt, and had been booked at the Benicia County Jail (BCJ), so his photograph and fingerprints should be available, they believed. While pursuing this lead, investigators found that the suspect had not been booked at the BCJ, but he did have a registered Browning 9mm automatic, serial #T182411, on which the VPD committed itself to make a further check.

Sandra and her girlfriend, Margo, entered the Vallejo Police Station on June 7, 1970. They reported that on the previous night at 10:00 or 10:30 p.m. they were at the Coronado Inn on Highway 37 and had seen a man who appeared to be acting strangely. They thought he resembled the composite picture of the Zodiac. Sandra, who had observed him for a period of time, described him as a white male, approximately 32 years of age, with brown hair receding to the middle of his head and a bald spot. She estimated that he was five feet eleven inches and 180 pounds, had hazel eyes, and wore glasses that had dark brown frames. For clothing, he wore a nylon sweatshirt with short sleeves, dark pants, and black shoes that appeared to be military issue because they were extremely shiny.

The women noted his effeminate actions: he held his glass with his fingers extended in a feminine way and he walked in a "swayback manner." When she danced with him, Sandra learned that his name was Paul, and that he was stationed in Vallejo. He was evasive in his answers to her, but shared that his favorite song was "Proud Mary." He knew that the band had also played at that venue two months earlier. As all three left the Coronado Inn at 1:00 a.m., and Sandra observed that he drove a small, black car, possibly a Corvette. When shown composite pictures from the Stine attack, Margo said that it looked like Paul.

"That's him!" Sandra declared. She promised to contact the VPD if he returned to the Coronado Inn. She provided a picture of the suspect that she had drawn on the back of a photograph.

Sandra telephoned the VPD nine days later to say that she had spotted the black vehicle, and that it was parked on the 500 block of Capitol Street. It was a Volkswagen Karmann Ghia with Florida plates. Further investigation revealed that the VW was registered to a Chief Electrician's mate, named Paul, assigned to the Naval Inactive Ship Maintenance Facility on Mare Island since March of 1969. Inspector Monez of the Mare Island Investigative Division assured the VPD that they could talk with Paul, or meet him if necessary.

On June 17, 1970, a woman received a letter in the mail with two Oakland A's baseball tickets. Wrapped with the tickets was a note stating, "GIFT FROM ZODIAC." There was a slight similarity between the writing on the paper and the printing on the Zodiac letters. By the time VPD Sergeant George Bawart retained the letter, it had been handled by three other people.

∽

While enthusiastic citizens from across the country flooded the professionals tasked with bringing a murderer to justice—forcing them to follow up on every credible lead, however unlikely—the killer changed his tactics. For some reason, following the murder of the cab driver and the release of the Stine letter, the Zodiac serial killer transformed himself into something quite different than what he had previously revealed to the public. The police were initially unaware of his new face. They continued to follow up on all of the new tips, tracking down people who fit the description of what the public thought the killer must look and act like. As Armstrong and Toschi looked back, scrutinizing past attacks and letters; seeking help from psychiatrists, astrologers (due to the name, the "Zodiac"), and handwriting experts; and distributing the composite photos state-wide, the killer was looking forward. He emerged as a moving target.

Long before the investigators realized it, the killer had reinvented himself.

7 | TRANSFORMATION

"So I shall change"

The Bay Area's most infamous murderer now directed his attention to writing. Following the October murder of cabby Paul Stine, his future attacks—if in fact there were any more—would take a back seat to his campaign of correspondence. His need to instill fear would be expressed not through brutal violence as it had been in the past but through the written word in a series of cards, letters, and notes, each artfully designed to taunt, brag, and menace. Whether due to the threat of nearly being apprehended in San Francisco, some form of psychological unraveling, or a combination of the two, the Zodiac morphed from a violent criminal who repeatedly attacked and sent a few strange letters to a cerebral terrorist who sent many written communications and committed few more, if any, strange attacks.

Though the killer had sent numerous letters prior to the murder of the cab driver, all but one of these was part of a group of nearly-identical notes directed to multiple recipients. Consequently, only four unique mailings were sent prior to October 1969: the Confession letters (two copies), the Bates letters (three copies), the 3-Part letters (three in all), and the More Material letter. The latter was the first note that was not copied, but rather sent to one unique location.

After killing Stine, the Zodiac sent many more—and more kinds of—mailings, including lengthy letters, quick notes, greeting cards, and possibly a couple of postcards, totaling as many as a dozen. Never again would he send a letter in multiple copies to more than one recipient.

During the same period, the killer of 5 innocent victims in four separate forays was responsible for few, if any, additional incidents of violence. There would be no trace of his blitz-style attacks or of his hasty departures. The attacks commonly attributed to the Zodiac in his post-Stine phase so disregarded his tried-and-true blueprint that investigators were left to wonder whether he actually attacked or killed *anyone* after October 1969.

While not unknown, it is rare for a serial killer to cease from the act of killing without the intervention of death, capture, or some form of unrelated incarceration. Generally speaking, serial killers continue to murder if at all possible. When a police department encounters the end of a serial-killing sequence without an arrest, law enforcement suspects that the perpetrator is dead, in prison on an unrelated crime, or has moved to a more fertile jurisdiction. Temporary incarceration serves only to heighten the anticipation of renewed killing once the serial killer is released. Even the onset of illness, the challenge of unsettling life events, and the pressures of an active investigation usually offer only a short respite from the murderous intent.

There is no good reason that a serial killer cannot cease from the activity of murder. Perhaps he or she can move beyond the behavior just as the prankster can outgrow his immaturity. Maybe he or she can stop killing in much the same way a hunter of wild game or a career criminal can "age out" and switch to other, more sedate pastimes. Though few, there are examples of serial killers who stopped.

Dennis Rader, convicted in 2005 for ten murders committed between 1974 and 1991 as the BTK (Bind, Torture, Kill) serial killer, is a rarity. He ceased for 13 years before reestablishing contact with the Wichita Police Department (WPD), in Kansas. By that time the case had gone very cold. While no additional murders were attributed to him after that long hiatus, he did threaten to murder again, and may have been in the planning stages of selecting his next unwitting victims when he was finally captured by the WPD. He was at least contemplating a return to his deadly activity, which for more than a decade lay dormant.

If the Zodiac stopped killing, his action like that of the BTK was exceptional. His continued correspondence to news outlets would prove to investigators that like Rader he was not dead, was not incarcerated, and had not permanently left the area. In future communications he would claim many more victims—the last apparent total in a 1974 letter was 37—but after Stine not a single additional death could be conclusively linked to him.

Any examination of the Zodiac's later activity, that which followed the October 1969 murder of Paul Stine, is therefore a study of numerous letters, pitted with a couple of attacks he may or may not have perpetrated. He claimed that he had not ceased killing, promising merely to change the way he operated.

He declared in his 6-Page letter of November, 1969 that all future murders would be staged to look like something else—and he promised not to announce his future victims. Either this was a clever, face-saving strategy to stop killing while leaving the police to forever wonder whether an unusual death could be his responsibility or he did continue to kill—and was never unquestionably tied to any of these well-concealed murders. Either way, his new strategy was unusual and noteworthy.

However it happened, and for whatever reason it happened, a change occurred sometime between the killing of Paul Stine and the writing of the 6-Page letter, which was received the following month. Though some major alterations to the killer's methods were evidenced prior to October 11, 1969, such as with the More Material letter in August, the killer penned the first of many letters that would *not* be copied and sent to more than one location. He also changed weapons from one crime to the next. By the time he had written the longest handwritten communication of his criminal career, the 6-Page letter in November of the same year, a major metamorphosis was complete.

The Zodiac's near capture in San Francisco may have profoundly affected him. He may have felt as fortunate to be out of jail as Mageau and Hartnell were lucky to be alive. He could have been apprehended or fatally shot near the cab had one of any number of things been different that night: had the dispatch broadcast gone out on October 11 that the perpetrator was Caucasian rather than Black, had Fouke and Zelms been a few seconds quicker to the scene, had the perpetrator been seen by adults and not children.

The bold tone of the letters following the incident can be interpreted to suggest that he was embarrassed, and possibly humiliated, by the narrow escape. His egotistical claims may have been overcompensations for nearly being captured, an attack that did not go as smoothly as planned.

Furthermore, he may have been shaken by the Manson Family attacks. In the Southern California carnage, the Zodiac could observe a killer at work from an objective perspective, and it may have been a sobering experience. He may have come to realize that the perpetrators of the two brutal Southern California events would eventually be captured. The December 1, 1969 announcement that the members of the Manson Family responsible for two nights of mayhem were in custody may have confirmed his worst fears. Not wanting to face the same consequences, the Zodiac may have chosen to go straight.

He may have suspected that law enforcement was closing in on him.

Quotes in newspapers following Stine's murder reflected the confidence of the police in the enthusiastic pursuit of their quarry. Marvin Lee, SFPD Chief of Inspectors, in proclaiming the murderer legally sane, declared, "...our knowledge of this man is increasing... I am confident we will get him." He went on to boast of the "considerable evidence of many different kinds" gathered at the crimes scenes and from within the letters. By this time, he added, 20 officers—in San Francisco, Napa, and Vallejo—were working the case full time. He speculated that the perpetrator was a minor office worker who though severely disturbed rarely if ever gave overt signs of being "psychotic." He noted that the police were checking his letters, word by word, for some slip-up that would lead to his capture.

Lee was not alone in his optimism. Two weeks after the attack on the cabby, Chronicle reporter Paul Avery wrote that *all* the investigators expected the Zodiac to be caught. Their confidence was buoyed by the four eyewitnesses who saw him without his hood, and the three who had heard his voice. Avery noted that samples of handwriting and fingerprints that "may be his" were being compared to those of suspects. Additionally, there were tire tracks and other evidence not disclosed by the police. The very next day, Avery added that the police had a reasonably complete description of killer: age 25 to 35, height five feet eight inches to five feet ten inches, white, stockily built, short cropped hair, and heavy-rimmed eyeglasses. The real possibility that the killer would be caught loomed large in the minds of many detectives.

The headway gained by the police may have frightened the killer as much as he terrified the residents of the Bay Area—and forced a change in his actions.

There are at least two other possible reasons for the radical transformation in the fall of 1969. The Zodiac may have experienced some kind of mental breakdown, as a result of his fear, or entirely separate from it. The Belli letter, received in December of 1969, gave investigators the impression that the writer had gone through some psychological change. The oddness of other Zodiac mailings also hinted at a mental unraveling.

Or, the change may have been induced by something in the killer's own personal journey. He may have run his course with the murder of Stine, and achieved, at least for an instant, that to which he aspired. He may have come to realize that his psychopathy had reached its end. The Zodiac's final confirmed murder—committed on a single male—may have caused something in him to click into place, like the final tumbler for a safecracker. Some manner of emotional burnout may have played a role.

Whatever precipitated the change—whether fear, a psychological unraveling, or a loss of interest—what appeared to be a major transformation in the actions of the Zodiac may instead have been the product of a series of smaller changes, a slow evolution over a number of hurdles, brought about by these, and any number of other, forces in his life. Since he remained unidentified, the distant spectators to his crimes could only guess at his motivation. His actions, however, demonstrated that a major change in trajectory occurred sometime during the months of October and November, 1969.

The Zodiac's reinvented persona coincided with the introducing two new ideas: harm to children and the construction of bombs. His future letters obsessed about both. The killer developed an interest in targeting school children on school buses, and he became consumed with the idea of creating public fear with drawings of a bomb-like device. He threatened in the Stine letter to "pick off" school children as they exited a school bus, promised to blow up a school bus full of children (with two different ominous bomb diagrams), and demanded that his diabolical threats be made public, including the publication of the details of his bomb design.

In addition to letters, he also began to send greeting cards, which he adapted with his own wording to supplement the preprinted pictures and messages. After the murder of Stine, and the penning of the Stine letter, he sent his first. Received by *The San Francisco Chronicle*, postmarked on November 8 in San Francisco, the Pen card was the first Zodiac communication that failed to report on a specific prior murder.

The Pen card

The Pen card was the killer's first, but by no means last, use of a greeting card in his public communication. The two Roosevelt stamps were correctly affixed to an envelope that recorded the address in unusually large letters, "S.F. Chronicle / San Fran. Calif / Please Rush to Editor." There was no return address, but on the back the order had been repeated in smaller lettering running diagonally across the entire envelope, "Please Rush to Editor." The mailing was received two days after its November 8, 1969 postmarked date. (It may instead have been postmarked on November 9, confusion existing over the timing of this and the next Zodiac mailing.)

Seizing on the sophomoric humor of the JESTERS branded card put out by Forget Me Not Cards, the Zodiac added a few sentences of his own. In preprinted words, the card itself stated, "Sorry I haven't written, but I washed my pen… and i can't do a thing with it." It was a parody of the old saw, "I just washed my hair and can't do a thing with it," used at the time in pedestrian television commercials and cheap, cliché-driven romance novels. For some reason, he embraced this reference when he selected the stationary. His choice of cards may even have been a jejune reference to a haircut.

After the September 27 attack at Lake Berryessa, Bryan Hartnell reported that his assailant's hair was brown in color and "kind of greasy." It had been visible through an eye hole cut into the hood. This description would almost certainly have been noted by the man who carefully followed his own press. In response, the Zodiac may have shorn his hair in preparation for the attack a mere two weeks later, possibly marking a change in disguise. The card could then be a suggestion that the killer had planned to refrain from violent activity, at least for a few weeks or months, until his hair could grow back. This scenario would explain his gap in writing (as he himself perceived it), the allusion to hair, and his use of an apologetic greeting card. By this time, the crew-cut-sporting Zodiac composite pictures had been well distributed and publicized.

He added the following misspelling-laden sentences inside the card:

```
This is the Zodiac speaking
I though you would nead a
good laugh before you
hear the bad news.
You won't get the
news for a while yet.
PS could you print
this new cipher
on your frunt page?
I get awfully lonely
when I am ignored,
so lonely I could
do my Thing!!!!!! [crosshair symbol]
```

Toward the bottom of the card's inner surface, the writer added six exclamation points to the word "Thing." Below his iconic crosshair symbol he wrote the following enigmatic phrase: "Des July Aug Sept Oct = 7". It appeared to the investigation that the killer was claiming a total of 7 victims, taken on the months which he evidently abbreviated. Because only 5 known deaths had by this time been attributed to him—those of Jensen, Faraday, Ferrin, Shepard, and Stine—investigators wondered whether two additional murders could have taken place in "Aug" (August), the only month in the list for which they were unaware of any Zodiac killings. (When Bates was later added to the list of Zodiac victims, another October date, the number of unknown murders was reduced to 1.) But that interpretation of the words at the bottom of the card was not the only possible interpretation.

After reading about the Zodiac in his local paper—*The Anderson Daily Mail*—a South Carolina man wrote to *The Vallejo Times Herald* and to J. Edgar Hoover, Director of the FBI, in a letter dated November 13, 1969. He noted that the letters "des," as used by the Zodiac in the Pen card (an apparent misspelling of "dec," the abbreviation for December), was actually a German word. Hoover replied in a letter of November 19, thanking the man for his interest. The brief response made no mention of, nor expressed any appreciation for, the actual information supplied.

That year, there *were* two unsolved Bay Area murders that took place in the month of August. Like the victims at Lake Berryessa, both had been brutally stabbed in one location. If these killings could be tied to the Zodiac, investigators realized, the total number of known Zodiac victims would reach 7, and the "Aug" victims he claimed would be identified. Assiduously, these murders were examined as possible Zodiac kills.

On August 3, two friends, Deborah Furlong, 14, and Kathy Snoozy, 15, rode their bikes to a wooded knoll overlooking their homes in the rugged Alameda Valley section of South San Jose. The schoolmates had taken a lunch and planned to spend time alone. Their bodies were discovered that evening, severely mutilated with a total of more than 300 stab wounds, all above the waist. The coroner had stopped counting at 300. The community was shocked by the appalling carnage. But the Zodiac was not responsible.

The Zodiac's knowledge of the murder of these two girls may have been gained through press accounts of his attack at Lake Berryessa. Following the stabbing of Hartnell and Shepard, detectives from San Jose made known their desire to speak with the man described in the composite picture for possible involvement in their case. They observed that the date of the San Jose murders was absent from the killer's writing on Hartnell's car door, and soon concluded that the girls were not victims of the Zodiac.

A knife attack on a third young girl two years later closed the San Jose case. On April 11, 1971, 18-year-old Kathy Bilek went bird watching at Villa Montalvo Park in Saratoga. Her mutilated body—stabbed a total of 49 times—was found the next morning. Descriptions of a suspicious man in the area led to the arrest of Karl Warner, a former classmate of Snoozy's and Furlong's at Oak Grove High School. He lived with his parents three blocks from the homes of the two San Jose friends. The police discovered the weapon used against Bilek at his residence, and links were established between her death and those in 1969. Warner pled guilty to three counts of murder in September, 1971, and was sentenced to life in prison. He was also a suspect in another stabbing in which the victim survived.

Warner was briefly investigated for involvement in the Zodiac murders. Because he had moved to California from Marlborough, Massachusetts in early 1969, he could not have been responsible for all of the Zodiac's victims, and was promptly eliminated from suspicion.

Following the resolution of the San Jose deaths, the Zodiac investigators were puzzled. Either two additional murders had occurred somewhere else (if the common interpretation of the killer's formula was correct), or the Zodiac was attempting to take credit for the San Jose stabbings, murders he had not committed. He may also have been running up his total number of victims to confuse the investigation, they realized. It was a reasonable suspicion that would continue to crop up in the investigation.

A search for the origin of the Pen card led nowhere. The card's ubiquity made it impossible for the SFPD to trace.

Inside the envelope the killer had deposited another cryptograph, this one on a single sheet of paper and not in three parts. It comprised a total of 340 symbols neatly printed in 20 rows of 17 columns. The 340 cipher would in time achieve uncommon acclaim among professional cryptographers, who would wrestle with its hidden content for decades.

The new cryptograph was quickly published. The 408 cipher had been decrypted by the Hardens, a husband and wife private-citizen team. Perhaps other readers would solve this one, the police and the press hoped.

As the FBI Field Office in San Francisco waited patiently for a report on the encryption from the FBI laboratory, a man from

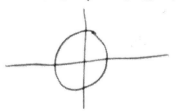

Montana wrote the Napa Police Department (NPD), offering to decrypt the new cipher. He believed that he knew the killer's next victim, and even named a suspect. Further investigation, however, uncovered that the man's suspect was present in Montana during the October 11 murder of Paul Stine, and therefore could not have been the Zodiac. The Montana informant was not the only person to take up the challenge of the new cipher.

Amateur cryptographers by the hundreds worked the symbols, hoping to nudge out a message. Many wondered whether there was a decryption to be found. One of the armchair detectives was convinced that it was decipherable, claiming that "testing shows it is not just gibberish." But not all who made the attempt at decoding the 340 cipher were qualified for the task.

On November 24, a Missoula, Montana resident, who was born in Chicago, sent a message to an FBI special agent, sharing that he knew the name of the agent's husband and daughter. When the special agent called him, she learned that this informant had met her family members through school. He claimed to have solved the Zodiac's message, which in his opinion revealed the name of a victim and the city of Minneapolis.

When detectives delved into his story, however, they learned that he was attempting to involve law enforcement to lend credibility to his questionable deciphering. He had already sent numerous pieces of mail to Vallejo Police Chief Jack Stiltz, and to the homicide divisions of the NPD and SFPD. The Missoula Police Department interviewed him and learned that he believed he had discovered a solution for the cipher and found numerous messages. He was convinced that he himself was a possible future Zodiac victim. He suggested that the Zodiac was in the Bay Area, and was associated with the radio station, KRON. The officers concluded that the man was "letting his imagination run rampant."

Another Zodiac communication arrived on the same day as the Pen card, a letter of 6 pages, though this letter may actually have been postmarked one day earlier than the card.

The 6-Page letter

Postmarked November 9 (or possibly November 8 as there was some confusion about which letter came in which envelope) in San Francisco, the 6-Page letter arrived on November 10, the same day as the Pen card. That same day, a copy of it was sent to the FBI in Washington, D.C., arriving the following day, with the request for a comparison to the previous letters in the case. Even by a quick glance, the penmanship of the new letter looked similar to that of other Zodiac letters, but the FBI Field Office in San Francisco wanted to be sure. Also, San Francisco requested that the Pen card (outside and inside) and its 340-symbol cipher be deciphered. San Francisco wanted to know whether any stray marks, indentations, or deliberately planted clues could lead them to the sender. With unbounded optimism, it requested from Washington a copy of the final solution to the 340 cipher when it became available.

The lettering of the envelope for the 6-Page letter was nearly identical to that of the Pen card: "S.F Chronicle / San Fran. Calif / Please Rush to Editor." The similarities extended even to the diagonally placed "Please Rush to Editor," on the back of the envelope, and the lack of any return address.

Writing for *The Chronicle*, reporter Paul Avery was mistaken when in a November 12 article he mentioned that another piece of Stine's shirt had been enclosed.

The FBI informed its San Francisco Field Office in mid-November that no handwriting had been found for a suspect whose name had previously been supplied to it. Further, the analysis of the cryptograph had not yet been completed, though efforts were continuing. The 340 cipher, so called because of its number of symbols, could not be solved using the key to the 408 cipher because the new cipher contained twenty percent more unique symbols. Though longer in terms of total symbols, the 408 cipher contained fewer unique symbols. The 340 cipher did not give up its solution even when familiar Zodiac words and phrases were run through it, or when it was analyzed by columns, right to left, using even numbered symbols only, and other such ideas. All attempts proved negative, and the FBI eventually admitted in its laboratory report that, "No decryption could be effected…"

In fact, the 340 cipher never would be solved by the FBI, nor by anyone else who ever wrestled with it. When first received, it was examined by the National Security Agency (NSA) and the Central Intelligence Agency (CIA). No result from these agencies was ever made public, or noted in the case files.

The new cryptograph—sent in the aftermath of the 408 cipher's solution—remains on the FBI's top ten list of unsolved but intriguing codes. After nearly five decades, despite thousands of attempts and the use of advanced algorithms, no one has been able to dislodge its hidden meaning. Even with the experience of WWII and the Allied code-breaking achievements, experts armed with supercomputers have been unable to crack it.

Of course, the cipher may comprise a series of randomly placed symbols with no real solution, a reality that the police soon began to consider. This would not be out of character for a killer who claimed in the 6-Page letter to have given the police "bu[s]y work" to have them run all over town. A nonsense cipher, if that is what the 340 cipher was, would indeed chew up hours of investigative time and not a little computer memory.

The new cryptograph contained an odd correction. One of the cypher's symbols, a "K," was crossed out, with a backwards "K" written above it. The correction was cited by several investigators, some in support of and others against proof of a valid decryption. A few believed it implied that the cipher was not gibberish. Others, because the 408 cipher had numerous misspellings and coding errors with no revisions, held that a deviously clever criminal could have amended a non-existent mistake to goad law enforcement into believing that the writer must possess a solution if he took the time and assiduous effort to correct it. FBI cryptologists in the twenty-first century, including Dan Olsen, chief of the FBI's Cryptanalysis and Racketeering Records Units, appeal to a computer analysis of certain rows in the belief that at least several lines of encryption contain decipherable information. So far, none has emerged.

Whether it was decipherable or not, the police danced to the killer's tune, which may have been the Zodiac's ultimate purpose. Law enforcement spent a multitude of hours on a task that to date has not reaped any rewards. The unbroken cipher has only reinforced the idea that the brilliant criminal was in fact cunning, clever, and unstoppable.

There was an intriguing possibility that the police had to confront. The coder may have performed some simple, but unfair—and devastatingly difficult-to-solve—change to the layout or concept of the cipher. If he intended the symbols to be read from bottom to top in a diagonal layout, to be understood to include only some of the symbols, or to be translated into a language other than English, no computer without the specific instruction would be able to solve it for the author's concealed communiqué. Such a twist would provide its creator bragging rights with little chance that the cryptograph might actually be solved.

Additionally, it could have been a different type of encryption. There was no inherent reason for cryptanalysts to believe that its solution was to be found in a simple, homophonic substitution with variations cipher, the type represented in the 408 cipher. The myriad unsuccessful attempts to solve it actually suggest against the possibility of it being in the same format as the 408. Perhaps each character had been substituted with two symbols rather than one, some or half of the symbols being meaningless, or some other clever solution having to do with shapes or other random interpretation. If that was the case, many came to acknowledge, no one was ever likely to solve it without further assistance from its creator.

The 340 cipher remains an interesting challenge for the layperson with an excess of leisure time. A correct solution could be a ticket to fame and fortune—or so some apparently believe. Since a mere high school teacher and his wife cracked the 408 cipher, many people were drawn as if by a magnet to the new cipher. Numerous dubious solutions were suggested in the decades following its receipt; none has impressed professional cryptographers. Eventually, the 340 cipher was forgotten by all but the most determined cipher specialists and die-hard Zodiac enthusiasts.

The FBI reviewed the 6-Page letter and the Pen card on November 18. The next day it reported on its lack of progress in the cryptanalysis. In response to the November 11 airtel requesting comparisons with the two new mailings, which the FBI received on November 10, the Bureau noted that all the writing, with the exception of the

340 cipher, matched the Zodiac's previous letters. Because the page of the Pen card cipher that was supplied to the FBI laboratory was a copy, and not an original, it could not be meaningfully compared to the previous letters.

The individual pieces of the 6-Page letter and the Pen card mailings were assigned laboratory numbers Qc21 to Qc32, the final document being the 340 cipher.

The 6-Page letter read as follows:

```
        1/6
This is the Zodiac speaking
up to the end of Oct I have
killed 7 people. I have grown
rather angry with the police
for their telling lies about me.
So I shall change the way the
collecting of slaves. I shall
no longer announce to anyone.
when I comitt my murders,
they shall look like routine
robberies, killings of anger, &
a few fake accidents, etc.
[a horizontal line the width of the page]

The police shall never catch me,
because I have been too clever
for them.
 I look like the description
    passed out only when I do
    my thing, the rest of the time
    I look entirle different. I
    shall not tell you what my
    descise consists of when I kill
 As of yet I have left no
    fingerprints behind me contrary
    to what the police say
    --

        2/6
in my killings I wear trans -
parent finger tip guards. All it
is is 2 coats of airplane cement
```

coated on my finger tips—quite
unnoticible & very efective.
my killing tools have been bought
en through the mail order out-
fits before the ban went into
efect. except one & it was
bought out of the state.
So as you see the police don't
have much to work on. If you
wonder why I was wipeing the
cab down I was leaving fake clews
for the police to run all over town
with, as one might say, I gave
the cops som bussy work to do to
keep them happy. I enjoy needling
the blue pigs. Hey blue pig I
was in the park—you were useing
fire trucks to mask the sound
of your cruzeing prowl cars. The
dogs never came with in 2
blocks of me & they were to
the west & there was only 2
--

3/6
groups of barking about 10 min
apart then the motor cicles
went by about 150 ft away
going from south to north west.
ps. 2 cops pulled a goof abot 3
min after I left the cab. I was
walking down the hill to the
park when this cop car pulled up
& one of them called me over
& asked if I saw any one
acting supicisous or strange
in the last 5 to 10 min & I said
yes there was this man who
was runnig by waveing a gun
& the cops peeled rubber &
went around the corner as
I directed them & I dissap-
eared into the park a block &
a half away never to be seen

again.
Hey pig doesnt it rile you up
to have you noze rubed in your
booboos ?
If you cops think Im going to take
on a bus the way I stated I was,
you deserve to have holes in your
heads.
--
        4/6
Take one bag of ammonium nitrate
fertlizer & 1 gal of stove oil &
dump a few bags of gravel on
top & then set the shit off
& will positivily ventalate any
thing that should be in the way
of the blast.
The death machiene is all ready
made. I would have sent you
pictures but you would be nasty
enough to trace them back to
developer & then to me, So I
shall describe my masterpiece
to you. The nice part of it is
all the parts can be bought on
the open market with no quest
ions asked.
1 bat. pow clock—will run for
 aprox 1 year
1 photoelectric switch
2 copper leaf springs
2 6V car bat
1 flash light bulb & reflector
1 mirror
2 18″ cardboard tubes black with
shoe polish in side & oute
--

5/6
[bomb diagram]

Bus goes bang car
passes by ok.

--

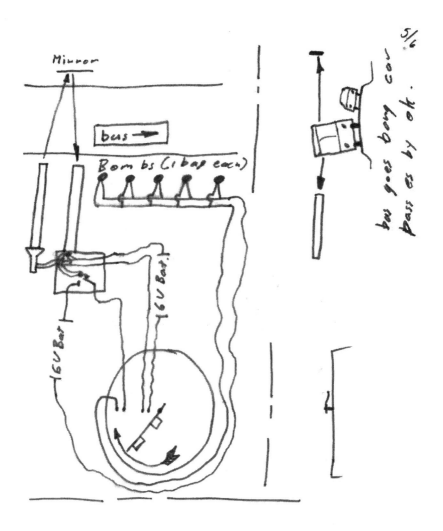

6/6
The system checks out from
one end to the other in my
tests. What you do not know
is whether the death machiene
is at the sight or whether
it is being stored in my
basement for future use.
I think you do not have the
man power to stop this one
by continually searching the
road sides looking for this
thing. & it wont do to reroat
& reschedule the busses bec
ause the bomb can be adapted
to new conditions.
Have fun !! By the way
it could be rather messy
if you try to bluff me.

[large crosshair symbol with points at 1 o'clock,
2 o'clock 4 o'clock and 5 o'clock; and "X"s at 6
o'clock,
8 o'clock, 9 o'clock, 10 o'clock, and 11 o'clock]

         PS. Be shure to
      print the part I
marked out on
      page 3 or I shall
      do my thing [small crosshair symbol]
--

[on the back of page 6]:

To prove that I am the
Zodiac, Ask the Vallejo
cop about my electric gun
sight which I used to start
my collecting of slaves.

There remains some confusion about the precise timing of the
Pen card and the 6-Page letter. While both arrived on November 10,
the FBI laboratory and early reports noted that the card was post-

marked on November 9, and the long letter, November 8. When the FBI evaluated the mailings nearly a decade later, they switched the order, possibly prompted to do so by the SFPD, and matched the Pen card with the November 8 envelope, the letter with the November 9 envelope. Since both arrived together, the order of the two postmarks may not matter for the investigation, expect for one point: the letter with its bomb diagram may have been the "bad news" about which the card warned had it been sent first.

The 6-Page letter in and of itself marked a notable shift in the Zodiac's crime spree. Seven pages in length when including the paragraph on the back of page 6, it was the longest note sent by the killer—and would remain the longest ever received. As such, it contained more information, more new information, and more new categories of writing than any other Zodiac mailing. It was one of only a few multi-page letters the killer ever penned. The writer used many paragraphs to mine the depths of a number of topics, introducing a bomb diagram, a recipe list of bomb ingredients, and details to be used for a bomb's construction, each an entirely new avenue for the killer.

In the very first paragraph, the Zodiac wrote specifically about his metamorphosis: "I will change the way the collecting of slaves." Additional killings, he promised, would be disguised to resemble "routine robberies, killings of anger, & a few fake accidents, etc."

The letter included amended plans to kill children.

```
If you cops think Im going to take
on a bus the way I stated I was,
you deserve to have holes in your
heads.
```

No longer promising sniper fire directed at a bus, he now provided a new plan for a concealed roadside bomb that would detonate when passed by a bus. The letter offered a detailed diagram of such a killing system, as well as instructions to be followed to create the bomb.

He wrote about a disguise that he reputedly wore when killing—and only when killing. He refused the chance to be very specific, taunting instead that he would not disclose the details of his subterfuge. This revelation cast additional suspicion on all eyewitness sightings of the murderer. If he was reported to look a certain way by those who saw him, they may have been wrong in their descriptions due to his physical modifications, whatever they were, in addition to the fact that all eyewitness reports can in and of themselves be very unreliable.

In another innovation, the Zodiac demanded that one specific paragraph of the new letter be printed. He carefully marked it for *The Chronicle* editors. The police speculated that the killer was aware of an editor's need for brevity, and was attempting to control his own press.

The portion selected for publication was a particularly damning indictment of the police activity—if it was to be believed. He claimed that two officers interacted with him following the murder of Paul Stine and then sped away—at his direction—without apprehending him. Why that piece, of all the many paragraphs in the letter, was highlighted may have had to do with its message. No other paragraph so illustrated the killer's apparent cunning juxtaposed against his description of law enforcement incompetence.

In fact, the theme that ran through the entire 7 pages of printing was his brilliance as a criminal. The letter's thesis statement was obvious on the first page, "The police shall never catch me, because I have been too clever for them." This cleverness apparently extended to a picture on page 5 of a roadside detonation device that promised to blast a busload of children. Though the killer had previously threatened children on a school bus—with a sniper attack, in the Stine letter—nowhere had he mentioned, or threaten to use, a bomb.

The U.S. Army acknowledged to the SFPD that in theory the bomb was functional. But, it cautioned, such a creation would not be easily constructed. *The Chronicle* agreed to not publish the diagram for fear it would evoke widespread panic, as the school bus threat in the Stine letter had, and because it was more than likely just a hoax.

The length of the letter, and the depth into which the Zodiac delved with insufferable detail, raised the inevitable question of "why?" and "why now?" Investigators realized that the answers to these questions may have resided in the Stine attack, and in the killer's own fear of being caught. The fact that he was nearly captured on Jackson Street may have led to his extraordinarily rare—for serial killers—retirement from serial killing. The Zodiac may also have been shocked to learn that the SFPD was circulating two composite pictures of him, created with the help of the three youngsters who witnessed events following Stine's murder. It may have been disheartening to him that the SFPD claimed to possess several latent fingerprints. He may have felt threatened by any or all of the developments in the case. In sum, fear may have been the motivating factor in the creation of the letter.

The braggadocio suggested to some that this may in fact have been the case. The Zodiac may have composed his 6-Page letter to bolster his reputation and affirm his now-questioned cleverness and superior intellect. The killer filled 6 pages with boasting and taunting, betraying a truth: he was not a confidently effective criminal, but someone who had been exposed as a craven and ineffectual coward, someone who nevertheless wanted to argue for his brilliance.

His claims of greatness rang hollow. He had been, after all, watched following the murder of Stine, sighted by police officers on Jackson Street, and observed so closely that composite pictures of him could be created and distributed.

Some of the factual content of the letter was also challenged. Lee responded to the Zodiac's description of events in the park by saying, "That is a lot of poppycock." Because the murderer had not mentioned floodlights, and had been wrong about his description of the tracking dogs, Lee was certain that he was nowhere in the vicinity during the search.

As it became apparent that the killer would keep his promise to not announce future victims, the police began to wonder about his new strategy.

The Zodiac's new behavior suggested that letter writing was his cathexis, that which brought him emotional fulfillment. Contact through the postal system began at the outset of his assaults, starting a mere month after Cheri Jo Bates was murdered in 1966. The mail continued throughout the period of known attacks, from 1966 to 1969, and continued even when the murders ceased, if they did, possibly after Paul Stine was killed. Only one attack was *not* followed up with a letter: the murders on Lake Herman Road. But even that brutality was well documented in the Zodiac's next letters of July

31, 1969, in which he claimed credit for not only the murder of July 4, but also his deeds the previous December. The Lake Berryessa stabbing was accompanied by the numbers, symbols, and letters on Hartnell's car door, making it a communication of sorts.

The Zodiac had clearly demonstrated that he could write without the accompaniment of a murder, as he apparently did from 1970 to 1974, but may have been unable to commit murder without writing prior to that date—or at any time. He could write without killing, but could not kill without writing. The letters, therefore, may have been the motivation fueling his attacks, and not the need to murder, killing merely the means to have his letters taken seriously, published, and allowed to create fear. In his own mind, by November, 1969, he may have achieved a place where killing was no longer necessary to accomplish his goals, which he correctly surmised he could then do with letters and telephone calls alone.

Whatever his mindset, the letters would continue even if the killing did not. But first, the case would suffer a significant detour.

8 | MELVIN BELLI

"Please help me"

On October 22, 1969, just before midnight, someone claiming to be the Zodiac telephoned the Oakland Police Department. His demand was specific. He wanted a defense attorney to join newsman Jim Dunbar on KGO TV Channel 7 the following morning, either the famed F. Lee Bailey or a local celebrity Melvin Belli, who had appeared with Dunbar approximately two weeks earlier. He promised to phone into the show if one of these two lawyers was present. His request was immediately taken seriously because the Zodiac was the hottest story coursing through the veins of conversations in the San Francisco Bay area.

The police, the producers of Jim Dunbar's show *A.M. San Francisco*, and Dunbar himself, the determined and inquisitive host of the program, scrambled to comply with the demand. Because Bailey was unavailable—he was already committed to an ongoing court case—Belli agreed to come to the studio. The programming at the station was rearranged so that the show could begin 30 minutes earlier than usual, and a phone line was appropriated for the caller.

In everything, the authorities did what they could to appease their quarry. If he desired an attorney, they were more than happy to comply in the hopes of stopping his murderous spree. If he wanted to share information, they were eager to listen. As long as he was talking, he was not killing; as long as he was communicating, he might reveal enough about himself to be captured. The caller was demonstrating that he knew how to effectively manipulate the police and the press.

By 1969, Dunbar was a well-known and popular personality. His show had graced the airwaves since 1965 and had boosted its station's ratings, and enabled KGO to gain considerable market share. The media personality first drew public attention for his work in radio. In 2006, his skill was recognized when he was inducted into the Bay Area Radio Hall of Fame. Three years later, he received an even greater honor when he was added to the list of inductees in the National Radio Hall of Fame. He retired in 2000, but would forever be remembered for the part his acclaimed television show played in the Zodiac serial killer case.

If the event had been set up on a pretext, a hoaxer wanting nothing more than to disrupt society and stage a big news story, he would be very successful. No one wanted to risk the chance, no matter how remote, that this actually was the infamous murderer, so the show was planned and orchestrated at the pleasure of the mysterious stranger. Everyone preparing for the show hoped he would call again.

Melvin Belli—the caller's second choice—was in 1969 a famed and flamboyant defense attorney who made the Bay Area his home. Chronicle reporter Paul Avery described him as the "world champion publicity hound."

He himself retorted, "I'm no ambulance chaser. I always get there before the ambulance arrives."

More than a minor celebrity, the lawyer had, with his shock of white hair and heavy black eyeglasses, defended Jack Ruby, the man convicted and sent to prison for killing Lee Harvey Oswald, the assassin of President John F. Kennedy. He would later represent the British rock and roll group the Rolling Stones following a murder at their Altamont Speedway Concert of December 6, 1969.

Belli's national profile was nearly that of F. Lee Bailey, the East Coast defense attorney who gained fame for defending Sam Shepard—the trial and aftermath allegedly inspiring the television show the Fugitive. Bailey would later defend Albert DeSalvo, the Boston Strangler, who was killed on November 25, 1973 while serving a life sentence for a dozen murders committed between 1962 and 1964. Much later, he would be empaneled as a prominent member of OJ Simpson's "dream team" defense at the star football player's murder trial.

As the extended television program commenced at 6:25 a.m., Dunbar and Belli made small talk. They pleaded with the audience to not call. Finally, the reserved line erupted 49 minutes into the show.

A man who claimed to be the Zodiac spoke briefly, and then hung up the phone. He did this numerous times. He apparently feared that the police would try to trap the call to pinpoint his location, a process that at the time required several minutes of uninterrupted contact. He must have known that the police desperately wanted to catch the man who had wreaked so much havoc and caused so much pain.

The man kept calling back, but never stayed on the line long enough for the call to be traced. He returned as many as 30 times, providing the name "Sam," at Belli's request, a less threatening name than the "Zodiac." In one exchange, Dunbar commanded, "Tell us what's going on inside you." The caller identified headaches as part of his malady. Taking aspirin did not help him.

The calls went on for three hours, longer than the usual running time of the show. Belli offered to meet with "Sam" at the Fairmont Hotel, a local landmark near where the Zodiac had entered Paul Stine's cab. (*The Chronicle* reported that Belli suggested the steps of Old St. Mary's church in Chinatown.) Instead, at the behest of the man phoning into the show, the St. Vincent de Paul Thrift Shop, located at 2726 Mission Street in Daly City, became the agreed upon rendezvous point. The location was set over a private phone line. The arranged meeting time was 10:30 a.m.

The attorney would never meet the Zodiac—or "Sam"—however. Numerous Paparazzi and more than a cadre of plain-clothed police agents were aware of the new location. Even if "Sam" had intended to meet Belli, he would have been scared off by the entourage. He never showed. A waitress at a candy fountain in the Fairmont Hotel told the police that she had served coffee to a man who resembled the composite picture. She retained the cup and saucer for a fingerprint check.

A green Volkswagen circled the block at the thrift shop several times. It was leased to a former convict. Its driver was not the Zodiac.

Later, at 1:00 p.m. that afternoon, the three living witnesses to the voice of the actual Zodiac serial killer—Nancy Slover, Bryan Hartnell, and Dave Slaight—were transported to the KGO studios by Detectives Narlow and Townsend. They convened around an audio replay of the show. None of them believed that the voice they heard on the tape was the same as that of the Zodiac. Hartnell, the lone survivor of the Berryessa attack, was the most vocal: not only was the pitch of the voice wrong, but the cadence did not match that of his attacker.

Years later, he would explain that the killer's cadence was so distinct that if he ever heard it again, he would recognize it immediately. Hartnell was certain that the Zodiac's voice was older and deeper. "Sam" was not the Zodiac, Slaight and Slover agreed. The voice on the tape came from someone who was too young and too unsure of himself.

It was concluded that the caller was not the killer; it was indeed a hoax. Initially, the police attempted to keep from the public the feedback that the three had provided. They hoped to use their knowledge to prod the real Zodiac out of hiding. Unfortunately for the case, a Napa investigator divulged to the press that the caller was not the Zodiac. The clever strategy the police was developing could never be implemented.

The same caller, "Sam," identifying himself as "Zodiac," telephoned Melvin Belli at his San Francisco home on January 14. He was told that Belli was in Europe at the time, to which he replied, "I can't wait. It's my birthday." He also called KGO TV again on February 5, staying on the line for 20 minutes. But it was still not enough time to trap the call. Nevertheless, the authorities soon learned the name of the hoaxer. On February 18, the FBI's field office in San Francisco notified the Bureau in Washington, D.C. that Toschi had identified the anonymous phone caller who had made his calls from Oakland. The man was investigated, but his fingerprints did not match those in the Zodiac case file.

The only question that remained was whether the original contact with the Oakland Police Department was initiated by the killer, by "Sam," or by someone else. That call was in time identified as also having originated in Oakland, the police suspecting that "Sam" and not the Zodiac was behind it as well. One source reported that the resident to whom that line was registered was investigated and ultimately cleared of any involvement in the murders.

The once-promising lead was a dead end for the case, but one which would resurface. "Sam" never reentered the investigation, but Melvin Belli would. The attorney received an authentic Zodiac letter in December 1969, and was referenced in another the following year. "Sam" or some other hoaxer introduced Belli into the case; the Zodiac meant to keep him there.

An odd, and possibly unrelated, telephone call came into a relief switchboard operator on January 2, 1970, at one minute before 2:00 a.m. A man calling himself Zodiac called the Sacramento FBI Field Office stating that he had just killed someone or something. His voice trailed off so that his final words were unintelligible. The Field Office passed the information on to agencies investigating the Zodiac, including the Napa County Sheriff's Department and the SFPD. Because it was a local call that came directly into the switchboard, it was also shared with the Sacramento authorities as a possible local homicide.

A man claiming to be the Zodiac called Oklahoma City radio station KTOK on October 22. He explained that he left the Bay Area because "it got too hot for me," but it was not the real Zodiac. *The San Francisco Chronicle* reported on this hoax call on December 8. Many people over the ensuing decades made prank telephone calls claiming to be the Bay Area killer.

Belli's recollection of the Zodiac case, and his participation, differed slightly from the police record. In his 1976 book, *Melvin Belli: My Life on Trial*, the attorney steadfastly maintained that he had spoken with the actual Zodiac. Either he did not know about further developments in the case or he valued drama and book sales above factual accuracy. He counted only 13 short calls from the Zodiac during the Dunbar fiasco, and wrote that the initial call had come into the SFPD, not the Oakland Police Department.

He described the Zodiac as a self-aware sufferer of Multiple Personality Disorder (sometimes designated *Dissociative Identity Disorder*), a man who due to his mental illness had more than one personality within a single body. He also claimed that before attempting to meet "Sam" at their pre-arranged location, he had made an agreement with San Francisco District Attorney John Jay Ferdon that the perpetrator of the crimes would not face the death penalty if he surrendered.

Ferdon vehemently denied that he'd ever agreed to such a deal, or any deal, saying that he only promised the man a fair trial: he was unaware at the time whether Belli even represented the "voice" that claimed to be the Zodiac. Belli shot back at Ferdon, accusing him of sabotaging the meeting.

The first reference the actual Zodiac made to Melvin Belli occurred in December with the arrival of a new mailing, the eponymous Belli letter. With it, the killer reached out to the attorney directly.

The Belli letter

In a murder case that contains many unusual pieces of correspondence, the Belli letter stands out. It is among the most curious of all the authenticated postings. Even today, researchers are not sure exactly how to interpret it. Some see in it a cry for help from a criminal whose psychological health is crumbling; others, the mocking taunt of an arrogant sociopath.

Postmarked December 20, 1969, on the one-year anniversary of the Lake Herman Road double murder, the Belli letter was sent with six downward looking Thomas Jefferson stamps. Across the back of the envelope diagonally were the words, "Mery Christmass & New Year." The greeting was missing an R, but had an additional S. It was only the second note to be sent to anyone other than the police or the press. It was also the last. Apart from the missive taunting Joseph Bates, the father of Riverside murder victim Cheri Jo, all previous letters had been specifically addressed to a police department or a newspaper outlet.

This raised the question: why the change? Never before had the Zodiac sent a letter to an attorney or a national celebrity, and he never would again. This one, however, was aimed at the legal community and toward a lawyer who had at the time had achieved rare notoriety.

In the one-page note that arrived on December 23, the Zodiac had written,

```
Dear Melvin

This is the Zodiac speaking I
wish you a happy Christmass.
The one thing I ask of you is
this, please help me. I cannot
reach out for help because of
this thing in me wont let me.
I am finding it extreamly dif-
icult to hold it in check I am
afraid I will loose control
again and take my nineth &
posibly tenth victom. Please
help me I am drownding. At
the moment the children are
safe from the bomb because
it is so massive to dig in & the
triger mech requires much work
to get it adjusted just right. But
if I hold back too long from
no nine I will loose complet(crossed out) all
controol of my self & set the
bomb up. Please help me I can
not remain in control for much
longer.
          [crosshair symbol]
```

This newest mailing was furnished to the SFPD on October 29, and the FBI received its information in an airtel from San Francisco that same day. The letter was accompanied by a striped piece of cloth, which the SFPD lab determined came from the shirttail of the last known victim in the case, Paul Stine. The Zodiac had repeated his macabre act of sending a blood-stained swatch of Stine's shirt.

When it was noticed years later by amateur investigator Ricardo Gomez that the envelope containing the letter and shirt piece was carefully addressed in a font that matched the distinctive number-ing at Belli's residential address, "1228 Mtgy San Fran, Calif.," grave speculation arose that the Zodiac had actually visited the home in person.

The FBI Field Office in San Francisco requested an examination of the Belli letter on December 29, and a comparison to other Zodiac writing. The FBI crime lab received the material on the last day of 1969. The envelope, Qc43, and letter, Qc44, were found to have some distortion, and were not written as freely as threatening letters of the past. Nevertheless, characteristics indicated that all of the threatening letters in this case may have been prepared by one hand.

The identification was bolstered by the letter's reference to a bomb. By this time, no information had been released to the public on the Zodiac's threat made in the 6-Page letter, not the bomb diagram, and not the list of the bomb's components. In order to protect the public from a panic that might ensue from a likely hoax, the SFPD had urged *The Chronicle* to keep the details under wraps.

Apart from the presence of the bloody shirt piece and the reference to a bomb, the match was not an obvious one. The Belli letter stood apart from other Zodiac letters because it was composed with careful, meticulous hand printing. Considerably more time and effort were evident in its creation. The difference between this script and that used in earlier communications such as the 3-Part letters was stark enough to lead some to question its authenticity, despite the enclosed piece of Stine's shirt.

Absent was the hurried scrawl that epitomized most of the killer's other notes. For instance, R's were now carefully detailed, replacing the quick slashes that previously had approached checkmarks. The odd spaces within words were gone. The killer's earlier writing had been messy and uneven, dashed off as though the writer was in a hurry, was uneducated, or was dealing with some deep-seated emotional problems. By contrast, the Belli letter was carefully printed with even letters and straight lines, the lettering you might expect of a detail-oriented adult who labored over each word.

The font of the new letter appeared to be a copybook style, what someone learned in elementary school, having emulated it from a blackboard or a first grade primer. Of all the approximately 20 Zodiac letters, this one was by far the most neatly printed, resembling the accuracy and obvious care that was demonstrated in the two ciphers which had by this point been received, the 408 and the 340. Investigators wondered at the improved quality of the script.

The Zodiac may have felt duty bound to impress the famed lawyer, either out of respect or out of a desire to court favor. By not a small measure, this letter is the easiest of all the Zodiac handwritten letters to read, and it demonstrated that the writer could print clean text when and if he chose to do so.

He may instead have been responding to a November 12, 1969 article in *The Chronicle* in which reporter Paul Avery sarcastically speculated that the "tidy" printing of a previous letter was employed to thwart police investigation. The neatness of the Belli letter may have been a fervent attempt to demonstrate to Avery that his printing was indeed penned in his own handwriting.

In contrast to the deliberate script, the note's message was anything but clear.

The Belli letter was an enigma, its correct meaning open to interpretation. On the surface, the writer cried out for help, three times repeating the phrase, "[p]lease help me." It was an entirely new tone for the killer. The earlier letters screamed with the inference that it was the police who needed help. Filling his letters with bravado and threat, the braggart portrayed himself as strong, intelligent, and brave. These new words by contrast meekly expressed humility and need. The police were left to wonder whether his request for help was a sincere plea or just another in a long line of taunts, now communicated in sarcastic barbs.

In the Belli letter, for the first time, the Zodiac opened the door on the inner workings of his mind, if the letter was an honest appeal. The writer claimed that there was something in him that caused him to murder. It may have been self-revelatory and a cry for help from a victim of obsession, multiple personality disorder, or psychotic thinking. It was troubling to the killer, and an apparent expression of some kind of mental illness. Yet the truth may not be so simple.

If the letter was an honest desire for assistance, it raised many thorny questions. Why, for instance, did he write to a lawyer? The type of help he was seeking, clearly psychological, was beyond the scope of Belli's purview. The Zodiac did not reach out to a medical doctor or a psychiatrist, but to a high-profile trial attorney. If he was after legal assistance or criminal representation, he never requested it.

The communication was also murky concerning what exactly Belli was supposed to do in response to the information. Considering that the Zodiac was not identified, the lawyer could not write or call him, any more than the police could find him and arrest him. Indeed, no further correspondence ever occurred between the Zodiac and Belli, despite the openness that the lawyer presented following the telephone call into the Oakland PD switchboard, and subsequent to the new letter's publication. The attorney expressed willingness to meet with and aid the Zodiac in any way he could. He shared a genuine concern that was well-publicized.

And why did the writer include implied or underhanded threats? Beyond describing his internal turmoil, he explained that withholding one form of attack would make another type inevitable. He claimed to be trying hard to prevent murder number 9 and possibly number 10. Then he asserted that if he held back too long from this/ these murder(s), he would be forced to detonate a bomb that would incur a large body count. Killing one or two people is a very different activity than causing a blast that would demolish a busload of school children. It was not clear why holding back from one would necessitate the other.

The killer claimed that he was in conflict with himself, that there was a force that was attempting to take over him. What exactly was it that the Zodiac experienced that would cause him to murder a single person, or a couple, again? And why, if his resolve remained strong in that matter, would he be required to perpetrate a mass killing instead?

To some, his references to murder appeared to be no more than additional threats communicated under a new banner. Unless the purpose of depositing the piece of Stine's shirt in the envelope was to conclusively identify the sender, its inclusion suggested that the killer was far from being sincere.

The Zodiac's boast of 8 victims was immediately questioned by the police. He had only been credited with 5 murders by this point. The Bates killing had not yet been connected to him, and no other murders would ever be definitively attributed to him in the future. If this were an honest plea for help, some reasoned, the Zodiac would not claim credit for more murders than he actually committed. It may have been the first hint that he wrote quizzaciously.

By this time, the bus bomb appeared to investigators to have been nothing more than a hoax. The Zodiac later offered an excuse as to why he could not carry through with the threat: he was "swamped out" by rain. More likely, the diagram was merely an attempt to scare, not unlike his threat to kill up to a dozen citizens in San Francisco, and not unlike his threat to kill school children by shooting up a bus. None of these scary scenarios ever materialized as an actual act of violence. Future letters would also suggest that no bomb ever existed.

If sincere, the writer's request for help was short-lived. Belli would receive no further mailings. The meek tone would never be repeated. With his next communication, the Name letter sent in early 1970, the Zodiac reverted to his familiar themes of threatening, boasting, and taunting.

The Zodiac's cry for help may have been nothing more than a quote lifted from the Beatles' movie, *The Yellow Submarine,* that had been released in 1968. The phrase "Please help me" occurred in the dialogue as well as in the lyrics of the song "Help" that was prominently featured in the 1965 film of the same name.

The Zodiac would add to his vocabulary the expression "Blue Meannie," another reference to *The Yellow Submarine* in a later letter directed at *The L.A. Times.* Both phrases may have spawned from an idea co-opted from the Manson Family murders, whose twin nights of carnage occurred four months previous to the writing of the Belli letter. The Zodiac may have been fishing for new ways to gain newspaper space and public attention. He may have thought that he could find success by copying the actions of the Manson Family, whose apocalyptic interpretation of the Fab Four provided the fuel for their depravity.

Some detectives realized that the actual meaning of the letter may be no more profound than a new type of threat with a generous helping of mockery. The Zodiac may have been ridiculing the role that "Sam" played in this murder spree when the impostor called into the Jim Dunbar television show. He may have been making fun of anyone who would believe that he himself was in need of help or willing to surrender to the authorities. The letter may have been a tongue-in-cheek response to events that did not include him at all: the carnival that was the Jim Dunbar show where he only appeared to participate. He may have used the opportunity of another letter to threaten the general public by reminding them that he had killed before and would most certainly kill again. He presented his greatest threat to the public when he reminded them in a backhanded way that mass murder might be in its future.

His reference in the letter to something attempting to gain control of him may have been in response to Dunbar asking "Sam" what was going on "inside of [him]." The letter itself may have been in reaction to Belli's words following the Dunbar broadcast when the attorney claimed that the Zodiac was "sick, sick, sick."

It appeared to many that the Zodiac was neither serious about wanting to change his ways nor under the influence of an alter ego that was driving him to murder. He was up to the same old shenanigans: ridiculing, threatening, and taunting, which he had provided in all of his previous communications. If the letter was created and sent during a time of personal insight and sincerity, that sincerity left, never to be seen again, and the insight, however fleeting, did not provide a vision of health over the next four years.

Belli responded to the letter, even though he was in Europe at the time of its arrival. In a telephone call to reporter Paul Avery from Rome on Sunday, October 28, he made an appeal for the Zodiac to contact him. He added that he was willing to meet the killer anywhere at any time. He told *The Chronicle* that he was certain that the Zodiac would reach out him.

He was wrong; the Zodiac never did.

The Zodiac's true feelings toward Belli emerged in a message sent in April of the following year. In the Dragon card, the killer mocked the attorney with the words, "Melvin Eats Blub[b]er." He may have soured on the attorney, but by mentioning him, he revealed that Belli was still on his mind.

Melvin Belli's path would cross that of the Zodiac case at least one additional time. Two years after the debacle of a television show, a good suspect emerged from Southern California. The famed lawyer was invited to give a lecture in order to draw out the man. Charles Ashman, at the time a young law student who police thought might be the Zodiac, was seated in the front row of the lecture, surrounded by police officers posing as fellow students. When the presentation concluded, the suspect eagerly approached Belli to speak with him in person.

Belli did not want to beat around the bush, and boldly confronted him. "Are you the Zodiac?" he queried. Shocked, the young law school student denied being the killer, or ever having killed anyone. He was soon eliminated from suspicion based on other evidence. He went on to be, in Belli's words, "one of the best Constitutional lawyers I have ever known."

9 | MODESTO, CALIFORNIA

"I gave a rather inter[e]sting ride"

The fertile soil of California's Central Valley extends from the rolling coastal hills of California's Pacific shoreline to the jagged Sierra Nevada mountain range on the east side of the state. Measuring as many as 60 miles by 450 miles, the desert plateau comprises more than 14 million acres. Sprawling Sacramento, its largest city, presses against the north boundary. The smaller towns that punctuate the landscape stand out amidst regimented orchards, sweeping ranches, and plenty of ground left fallow. The level plain accommodates long, straight highways for direct, if uneventful, travel. In the summer, ground temperatures frequently linger in the triple digits. At night, an ominous darkness descends, especially in the empty, quiet places.

At approximately 11:15 p.m. on Sunday, March 22, 1970, the realization came upon 22-year-old Kathleen Johns that she was being followed. She was driving westbound along Highway 132, close to the northern end of the valley. She was very vulnerable—alone with her 10-month-old daughter, Jennyfer and in the advanced state of pregnancy with her second child. She did not know that area well, even though she had in the past hitched rides through its vastness with truckers. The car behind her, which had not attracted her attention up to this point, began flashing high beams at her.

She contemplated the meaning of the gesture. Again and again, over the distance of several miles, the driver of the strange vehicle attempted to alert Johns to something. One police officer recorded that the pursuit began in the city of Modesto; another, that it started near Interstate 5, a 30-minute drive from Modesto. Johns herself claimed that she first became aware of the vehicle near Modesto. *Somewhere* on Highway 132 between Modesto and Interstate 5, a strange driver wanted Johns to maneuver her car off the highway.

At first the young mother refused. She continued along Highway 132, even as the flashing of the other car's lights became more and more insistent. Johns thought herself no fool to stop for a stranger along a darkened highway, and advanced toward the promise of a safer region. Finally, after an estimated 15 minutes of driving, she capitulated. Within sight of I-5, the well-traveled Interstate that is a major artery extending the length of California to the north and the south, she slowed her 1957 Chevrolet station wagon to the side of the road to determine the cause of the stranger's concern.

What exactly had happened that night remains a dark mystery within an already enigmatic case. Kathleen Johns and her infant daughter may have encountered the Zodiac serial killer along a dark, lonely stretch of highway. They may have been abducted and driven around for more than an hour in the rural farmland of California's Central Valley by a threat-breathing captor. Or maybe the two did not encounter the Zodiac, were not kidnapped, and did not face any threats whatsoever. The many differing accounts of the young mother's experience do little to clarify events.

The Kathleen Johns incident, of all the Zodiac attacks and suspected Zodiac attacks, is the most difficult to reconstruct from eyewitness testimony, police reports, and interviews. The truth has suffered as a result of sloppy record keeping, vague descriptions, and changing stories. The contradictions are legion, and the points of agreement are not central to the case. The details of what occurred in the life of Kathleen and her daughter that night depended on who was relating the story—and when. There exists variation in location, in dialogue, in actions, and in the order of events. Johns was, according to one account or another, a creative liar with ulterior motives, a kidnap victim, a hysterical woman, an uncooperative witness, or the victim of an attack by the infamous Zodiac serial killer.

In follow-up interviews during the course of her life, Johns proved herself to be fickle and very impressionable, evidently changing her story in an effort to please those with whom she spoke. As many details slipped out of her memory over the years, she appears to have replaced them with accounts of her ordeal that she found in books, watched in movies, or read in newspapers. She had a difficult time disagreeing with others, and was often easily convinced by investigators and researchers who encouraged her to endorse one pet theory after another.

Other significant activities in Johns's life may have affected her ability to precisely remember the details of her experience. In the 1970s, she would later explain that her domestic situation was very unsettled. Within two and a half years of the incident, she had given birth—Jody was born three months after her ordeal outside Modesto, on June 18—divorced, remarried, and traveled to Germany. Because of her changed last name, she dropped out of view of police investigators. The turbulent relationships in her life and her move overseas pressed the unusual event to the back of her mind.

At the time, Johns failed to comprehend the full magnitude of the Zodiac's horror in California. The police and the public were still seven months away from learning that the killer had a history in Southern California that predated his attack at Lake Herman Road, outside of Vallejo. Until then, the case would not receive substantial coverage beyond the San Francisco Bay Area. By the time the story engulfed the south of the state, Johns was on her way out of the country. The kidnapping—if that is what it was—remained a disconcerting but minor event in her mind and in her life. It was not until the early 1980s, nearly a decade after her encounter, that police officials began to challenge the initial reports.

In an authenticated letter sent by the Zodiac four months after the incident, the killer claimed responsibility for the enigmatic attack. While neither explaining his actions nor attempting to prove his involvement—as he had after many of his previous attacks—he merely referred to the odd event as "a rather inter[e]sting ride for a couple of ho[u]rs that ended with my burning her car where I found them."

If the Zodiac wrote the truth, and Johns did encounter him that night, she was very fortunate to be alive because most of the victims who were attacked by him did not live to tell of their experiences. And those who did survive were severely damaged.

By the spring of 1970, Cheri Jo Bates, David Faraday, Betty Lou Jensen, Darlene Ferrin, Cecelia Shepard, and Paul Stine had all been murdered. Though Michael Mageau and Bryan Hartnell had each survived a clash with the killer, they were both left with what their attacker must have assumed to be mortal wounds. Their predicament proved barely survivable, and they miraculously lived. But not without severe emotional and physical effects.

If Johns encountered the Zodiac, she and her daughter were the only female victims to survive, and the only victims of either gender to remain physically unscathed.

Regrettably, the police reports failed to shine a focused light on what exactly happened during the apparent attack. The officers tasked with interviewing Johns and recording events were careless with details and generous with factual errors. The existent police files do not present a consistent, cohesive narrative, with discrepancies between reports being numerous. Even if Johns provided conflicting pieces of information during her interviews with the officers, the reports failed to illuminate it because of their own inaccuracies, contradictions, and vague wording. It is not at all clear whether Johns was the victim of an encounter with the Zodiac, was kidnapped, or was reporting on events that never happened the way she claimed they did.

If a crime had been committed, the perpetrator apparently benefited from his choice of a victim and the location of his actions. Johns proved to be antagonistic to law enforcement, and was easily dismissible by gormless officials in backwater police jurisdictions. The officers could not even agree on whether any illegal activity had occurred.

When all of the police reports are cross-indexed with Johns's later words, a probable narrative emerges for the first half of her most unusual night. But the tale must be told with numerous significant variations. For instance, there remains disagreement as to exactly where Johns, at the behest of the stranger, stopped her station wagon.

Sergeant Charles J. McNatt, badge #7425, in his report for the Patterson Police Department, recorded that Johns entered I-5, was passed by the strange driver, and then pulled over to the side of the highway soon after Highway 132 merged with the Interstate. Deputy Bauer, writing a statement for the San Joaquin County Sheriff's Office (SJCSO), case 70-7475, placed the location at Highway 132, one-quarter mile west of the delta. Deputy Jim Ray Lovett, #160, of the Stanislaus County Sheriff's Department hedged his bet by being vague in his description, placing the stop somewhere in the vicinity of Highway 132 and Interstate 5, noting that Johns was unfamiliar with the area and was unable to give a more precise position. Each of these descriptions would later prove to be either inaccurate or unnecessarily vague.

In all likelihood, the place where Johns pulled off the road, consistent with her later description of what she observed after she parked her car, was just east of Bird Road, still on Highway 132. Johns claimed that she could see a service station ahead of her. She reported feeling comforted in the presence of its welcoming lights. The station, a Richfield at the intersection of Highway 132 and Chrisman Road, still in operation today under a different name, was in fact easily visible from a vehicle parked just east of Bird Road on Highway 132. (The line of sight has since been broken by the construction of an overpass.) This location is precisely where Johns's disabled car was recovered several hours later, according to Reed & Son Towing Company which took possession of the station wagon with California license plates HOJ 518 in the early hours of March 23.

The different locations provided by the officers' reports later became fodder for speculation. Some investigators wondered whether the station wagon was moved at some point after Johns left her vehicle. Because she pulled over in one spot, it was reasoned, and the car apparently found in another, her vehicle must have been relocated in her absence. In all likelihood, the discrepancies were due to the sloppy reporting of a rural area and the careless description of a remote highway. It would have been prohibitively difficult for the assailant to have moved the vehicle, and as details bear out, also highly incredible.

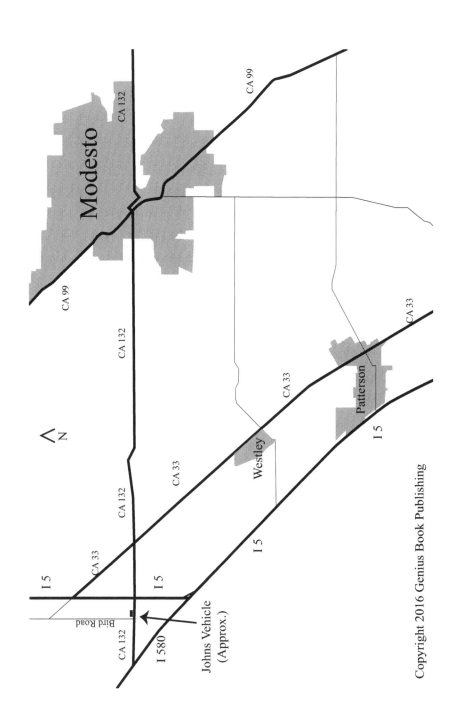

Copyright 2016 Genius Book Publishing

The strange car passed Johns as she pulled off the road, slowing down as she slowed, and then backed up. As he drew his vehicle alongside of hers, the driver of the alerting car told Johns that there was a problem with her rear wheel. He claimed it was "wobbly," and offered to fix it for her.

It was a plausible story. Johns's car, which had been purchased on the street in San Bernardino, was old and in poor condition. The young mother never knew when something else would go wrong with it.

She had no reason to doubt the man's words. Living in a world that was much safer or more naïve than California today, she gratefully accepted his offer of assistance without suspicion. She remained seated and observed what occurred next.

The stranger emerged from his vehicle—described by Johns as a tan-colored late model, possibly a Pontiac or a Buick, "a big, old car"—carrying a tire iron. She reported years later that he returned to his 2-door car to retrieve the tire iron from the back seat after approaching her car on foot. He proceeded around the back of her station wagon to a point where Johns lost sight of him, and began working on her right rear wheel. She could hear him doing something mechanical in nature for about one to two minutes, she later estimated.

Lovett reported that the man labored at Johns's *left* rear wheel, but that description would contradict other reports, suggesting that the officer was inattentive to details, may not have been listening carefully during his interviews with Johns, or was inaccurately parroting details fed to him by McNatt. Years later, Johns admitted to thinking it was the left rear wheel that needed work, without knowing exactly why she believed that it was that wheel. Perhaps Lovett heard and recorded Johns's words correctly, and it was the young mother who was mistaken.

Once his effort was completed, the stranger circled to the driver's side window and assured Johns that her car was now fine and safe to drive. She thanked him as he walked away, but received no response. He climbed back into his vehicle and drove ahead on Highway 132. Johns later described his motion as "slow." She was certain, recalling the incident decades later, that at that time the stranger had not seen

Jennyfer—who had awakened at the noise of the "repair"—and was likely also unaware that she was pregnant.

When Johns attempted to reenter the highway, she did not get very far. Almost immediately after moving forward once again she heard a thump and felt her car lurch. She knew something had happened, but was unaware that her right rear wheel had separated from the axle, effectively rendering her vehicle inoperable. The station wagon was now completely immobile. Lovett reported that Johns at this time exited her vehicle to determine what had occurred, but years later Johns believed that she had stayed in the car "for the most part."

The stranger had not gone far. Seeing her predicament—or anticipating it—he made a narrow U-turn (according to one report) and, returning to Johns's car, offered to drive her to a service station. He may instead have backed his car up rather than performing a U-turn, Johns declaring decades later that she had seen the brake lights of the car as it backed up toward her.

The stranger now suggested that the problem was beyond his ability to fix.

It was a bald-faced lie. In truth, he had unscrewed the lug nuts, effectively sabotaging the wheel. When the station wagon was later located and examined, only two nuts remained, one of which was loose to the point of falling off. The assailant, under the guise of aiding Johns, had removed three of the nuts and loosened the remaining two. At the side of the road, Johns later recalled, he said something to her about the lug nuts being stripped. He never mentioned to her that he could have very easily fixed her car by replacing the hardware he had just taken.

Johns was now at the mercy of the stranger.

For the benefit of the police reports, Johns would describe her "repairman" as a white male, approximately 30 years of age, five feet nine inches, and 160 pounds. He had dark hair and sported black, plastic-rimmed glasses, which she later characterized as "Superman glasses." He wore a dark ski jacket, possibly navy blue in color, and dark blue bell-bottomed pants. She added that he appeared to have some acne pitting on his face.

Over the years, however, her estimates of the stranger would grow and become more specific, and possibly more fanciful. Recalling events decades later, she described him as being, "big" not fat. She noted that she herself was five feet nine inches, and that he was bigger and taller than her. His haircut and attire spoke to her of being military. He had spit-shined shoes, navy blue pants that may have been wool, was very neat, and appeared more clean-cut than any of the people in her coterie. His voice was slow and monotone—in her opinion, cold and emotionless. She detected no drawl or accent.

The young brunette, in response to the stranger's offer, collected a few items from her crippled car, carefully lifted Jennyfer, who in two months—on May 18—would celebrate her first birthday, and eased into the bucket seat of the stranger's 2-door automobile. Johns later estimated that it took her about five minutes to gather some things for her daughter, including diapers, though she admitted to being a very bad judge of time. There were no other cars in the vicinity as the man maneuvered back onto Highway 132, ostensibly headed toward the gas station a mere 500 yard ahead on the right. Instead of stopping at the station, however, he drove past (or may have driven into the station and then out again).

The realization overtook Johns that something was wrong.

What occurred next—the conversation in the car between the driver and Johns—is another portion of this highly enigmatic event that comes in conflicting versions. In subsequent years, Johns would share that she felt that her life was in grave danger. She claimed her driver menaced her with such threats as "you know you're going to die," "I'm going to kill you," and "throw your daughter out of the window."

The police reports recounting Johns's words to various law enforcement personnel that night tell a story that is completely at odds with this later description. According to Lovett's report, Johns stated that the man was "quite friendly with her," did not make any threats, and did not make "a pass" at her, as though her greatest fear was of a young man making a sexual advance. He also noted that she never asked the driver to stop nor asked to get out of his vehicle. Lovett concluded that there may not have been a kidnapping.

Years later, Johns guessed that her ordeal in the stranger's vehicle took about two hours. Lovett recorded her earlier estimate of one to one-and-a-half hours. Because she was unfamiliar with the area, Johns was unaware of exactly where her chauffer had taken her, though she claimed to remember the city of Tracy because he had pointed it out to her. She believed that she had been driven around country roads with no apparent goal. The stranger appeared to know where he was going because he hadn't hesitated, but had traveled rather slowly, suggesting to her that he may not have had a specific destination in mind.

According to one account, as the Richfield station on Chrisman Road shrank in the distance behind her, Johns wondered to herself what the man was doing. She sat in silence. At first, she suspected that he had merely missed the station. Her captor, however, passed by several additional service stations over the ensuing hour or more.

Nearly three decades after the incident, Johns recalled passing a couple of exits on a highway before he took one, suggesting that they may have entered Interstate Highway 5 at some point. But she was certain that they drove on two-lane roads for the most part. When she finally mustered the strength to question him about his actions, which she eventually did on more than one occasion, he simply changed the subject and continued driving, according to Lovett's report. In the words of another officer, Johns had the stranger saying that a station was closed, or that it was not the right station. In the report filed by McNatt, the man was mostly silent during the ride, but when Johns asked what he did for a living, he claimed that he usually worked for a few months at a job, and then when he was between jobs he drove around, mostly at night. Johns, also according to McNatt's report, asked the driver whether he helped others. The man was said to have replied, "When I am through with them, they don't need my help." Lovett wrote that the driver had made some weird statements, including, "when I get through with them, they won't need any help." Years later, Johns recalled glibly stating something like "Hell of a way to help others" to elicit his unusual response. She also remembered that the stranger had asked where she was headed, and claimed to know the area when told.

In a 1998 interview, Johns shared that when the man first spoke, after approximately 10 minutes of driving in silence, he calmly and coolly said, "You know you are going to die." She recalled that he looked like he wasn't "there," not even making eye contact with her.

She took no action for more than an hour. She thought about punching her driver or scratching him; however, she opted to do nothing, believing that he might just be spouting empty threats. She committed herself to reacting if he tried to lay a finger on her or her daughter.

As she sat, Johns noted that the car was very messy. She remembered observing clothing—men's and children's—gum wrappers, children's toys, miscellaneous papers, and a scrub pad for dishes, all strewn about haphazardly. He may have been living in the vehicle, she realized. He never smoked during the drive. She observed no drug paraphernalia; she didn't recall seeing any butts or marijuana joints. She saw no weapons. Though Jennyfer was awake for the drive, it amazed her mother that she did not make any noise, an unusual practice for the normally vocal and lively infant.

Then the ordeal ended abruptly.

Johns escaped her captor when he slowed his vehicle somewhere near Interstate 5, though the exact location was never recorded. They were on a rural road paralleling the highway to her right. As he made a "Hollywood stop," that is, slowly rolling through a stop sign—one account has the driver attempting to wrongly enter the highway through an exit ramp before stopping and backing up the car—Johns suddenly opened the car door and, clutching Jennyfer, dove to freedom. She picked herself up off the ground and hustled over to a drainage ditch, as many as 100 yards away according to one version of events, and lay down to hide. She concealed her daughter underneath her belly. In another account, this one by the SJCSO, Johns ran across a field and up an embankment.

Lovett attributed the risky escape to Johns's feelings of "becoming quite frightened," noting that she feared that the driver might do some physical harm to her.

There are more than a few versions of the driver's response to Johns's flight. In one account provided by Johns, as reported by Lovett, the stranger simply closed the passenger door and drove away. McNatt, sharing what Johns told him immediately after the event, wrote that the man waited for the woman for about five minutes before pulling the door shut and driving off. According to the SJCSO report, after Johns jumped to freedom, the suspect turned the car's lights off, moved a few feet forward, stopped, and waited five minutes before he turned his lights back on again and left.

By the late 1990s, the story had apparently grown and become more dramatic like the fisherman's tale that improves with the telling. Johns now claimed that the stranger exited his car and searched for her with a flashlight. She did not look back, but was aware that she was not gaining any distance from him as she ran. She saw evidence of a flashlight the man was using to track her, and heard him yell, "Get back here," using profanity. She believed he was as close as 30 to 40 feet behind her. In contrast, McNatt was adamant in his report that the stranger had not exited his vehicle.

Following the man's departure, a semi-truck driver on Interstate 5 responded to the commotion at the side of the road. She may have flagged him down, Johns confessed. He jammed on his brakes. Still reeling from her apparent abduction, the young mother refused help from this male. She stood at the bottom of the hill, below the highway, telling him not to come any closer. She was unwilling to trust another man after her upsetting ordeal in the stranger's vehicle, so she waited until a woman could assist her. One soon stopped—Lovett reported that Johns hailed the female driver—and offered to take her to the local police station.

The name and identity of this Good Samaritan have been lost to history, though it was recorded that she was from Missouri. She did not stay long at the side of Interstate 5, and she did not linger after dropping off Johns. The woman first drove the victim to Westley, a small community to the northwest of Patterson and west of Modesto. Years later, Johns could not recall this diversion—or any conversation with the woman. When no police station was found in tiny Westley, they proceeded to Patterson.

At some date in its history, the small town of Patterson, California, which claims the title of "Apricot Capitol of the World," became host to a police substation. Founded in 1909, the town now boasts 20,000 residents, but is not large enough to support a full police force, and does not have the staff to man an office around the clock. Its location—situated back from a lonely stretch of Interstate 5 and surrounded by miles of farmland—is too distant for quick aid from the nearest police departments. An outpost was organized and staffed to deal with any local problem that could not accept a delay. Today, the substation is open only during normal business hours, an arrangement that suits the present needs of the community.

A little more than three hours after first being accosted by the stranger in the 2-door vehicle, Johns was seated inside the Patterson Police Substation, located in Patterson's downtown square, sharing her story with Officer McNatt. The tale she related was quite incredible, and may have raised the officer's doubts.

Once McNatt calmed her down (his claim), she told him how she had been kidnapped and how she had arrived in Patterson, 87 miles to the east of San Francisco and 18 miles outside of Modesto.

Johns explained that she had departed San Bernardino in Southern California on Sunday. She was headed for Petaluma, her Northern California hometown situated along Highway 101. She planned to visit her mother, who she believed was dying. Recalling events many years later, Johns explained that her mother regularly manipulated her with the news that the woman who gave her life was approaching the end of hers, an effective strategy to entice her daughter—and on this occasion also her granddaughter—up for a visit. This was her third or fourth such visit to see her mother "one last time."

The trip would take at least seven hours even if the highways were clear. When Johns drove through Modesto, along Highway 99, she was only a couple hours from her destination. She opted for an evening drive, she explained years later, as the roads were mostly empty, and the darkness and the sound of the engine's purr enticed her daughter to sleep quietly.

McNatt listened to Johns as she described to him the events that had transpired: how she was urged to pull over, how the assailant had disabled her car, and how she had been transported for one to two hours, finally ending up in front of him in Patterson.

While still talking, Johns noticed a wanted poster on the wall of the substation office. She pointed at it, and notified the officer that the person pictured was the one who had just kidnapped her. She may have become agitated at the recognition of the sketches. McNatt reported that she "started to scream and became hysterical again." Johns later denied any hysterics.

McNatt asked Johns if she knew the man on the poster. She replied that she did not. She had never seen the poster prior to that night. Relating the experience years later, Johns claimed that the officer suggested that she should have known, and the implication angered her.

The poster contained the black and white composite drawings of the Zodiac serial killer that were created following the murder of Paul Stine. It comprised two separate sketches, the first made with the help of the three teenaged witnesses who observed Stine's killer from across the street; the other, a modified version of the first drawing, was produced a few days later. Johns related that the amended version looked more like the person who had given her the ride. When told who was pictured in the poster, Johns again became hysterical, according to McNatt.

Though Johns did not know the significance of the poster or the background of the suspect, McNatt certainly did. The Zodiac had become the talk of the area. To the officer, the Zodiac case was big news, a story with a recent tie to nearby Modesto.

Joe Stine, the 34-year-old brother of Presidio Heights murder victim Paul Stine, was a mechanic in Modesto. In response to the slaying of his cab-driving brother, he penned an open letter to the Zodiac, details of which were published in several area newspapers, including *The San Francisco Examiner* and *The San Francisco Chronicle*. The surviving Stine, concluding that the Zodiac was a coward who had no reason to kill his brother, challenged the murderer to show himself in Modesto. He proclaimed that he was not afraid of his brother's slayer, boldly listing the address of his place of employment—the Richfield Service Station at 706 Sutter Street—the precise time he started work (7:00 a.m.), and even the route he took for his daily lunch. The bachelor who lived with his mother was a mere five feet seven inches and 165 pounds, and carried no weapons. He maintained that he had no need of a gun because he was in great physical shape.

Many residents in the valley thought the surviving Stine was more than a little crazy to taunt a killer and place himself at such great personal risk. The people held their collective breath, waiting to see whether the Zodiac would strike in Modesto in answer to the challenge.

McNatt wondered whether the stranger's appearance in Johns's rear view mirror was the killer's response to Joe Stine. A cowardly Zodiac may have traded the opportunity to attack a well-prepared and courageously willing male for an easier target. He may have only been able to muster the courage to threaten a vulnerable woman traveling far from home late at night.

After calming Johns down for a third time, McNatt broke off the interview and called for backup. He may have been frightened himself. Perhaps he, and not Johns, had become hysterical at the prospect of a Zodiac attack. He immediately reached out to the Stanislaus County Sheriff's Office in Modesto to summon another officer for assistance, and promptly whisked Johns out of the building.

McNatt must have felt susceptible to attack in the tiny police substation of a small town. If the Zodiac were to follow Johns there, perhaps neither of them was safe.

Deputy Lovett responded to McNatt's call. In his report (file #062677), he noted that he received the call at 2:30 a.m., requesting that he rush to Patterson. He recorded his arrival in Patterson at 2:50 a.m.

Contradicting these details, McNatt wrote in his report that it was at 2:30 a.m. that the hysterical Johns had been brought to his office, and that it was not until sometime later that he had contacted Lovett. According to McNatt, Lovett was not summoned until Johns calmed down, shared some of her story, saw the poster, became hysterical, and calmed down once more. McNatt's interactions with Johns prior to the call to Lovett would have taken at least a few minutes, possibly 10 or 15. (At a future date, Johns estimated that she was in the substation for 20 minutes before spotting the poster.) A reconciliation of the timelines represented in the two police reports is therefore impossible. For Lovett's record to be correct Johns had to have been brought to Patterson *before* 2:30 a.m., or McNatt had telephoned Lovett immediately upon Johns's arrival *at* 2:30 a.m.

There was an obvious discrepancy in the timing of Johns's arrival and Lovett's summoning. It would not be the last discrepancy.

Immediately after calling Lovett, McNatt transported the mother and daughter in his car to a local diner, half a block down the street, today operating under the name "Mil's."

Recalling events years later, Johns complained about how uncomfortable she was. She was very pregnant, sitting in a dark room, with nothing to do for "hours." Jennyfer was hungry and crying, and no one offered them anything. According to one account, Johns sat in the front window of the closed restaurant, peering out toward the police station.

Fortunately for all involved, the Zodiac never showed himself in Patterson, just as he had passed on the chance to attack in Modesto. When daylight broke, the Johns were taken back to San Joaquin County, to where her station wagon had been located.

Johns evidently did not get along with McNatt. A personality conflict and a mutual mistrust may have contributed to any misunderstandings that morning. According to McNatt, Johns was hysterical when she was brought into his office. Three times in his report, he described Johns as being hysterical or becoming hysterical again. In an interview conducted years later, however, Johns vehemently denied being upset even once, repeatedly criticizing the officer's attitude toward her, "I never got hysterical."

For her part, Johns did not offer assistance as an eagerly cooperative citizen. She bore an obvious anti-police attitude—not an uncommon trait at the time. She admitted to owning a black-light and smoking marijuana, and was sympathetic to, if not a full participant in, the anti-establishment spirit that flourished in the 1960s. She was not nice to the older, by-the-book veteran officer, she later confessed.

The cop and the victim may also have been dragging from the lateness of the hour. Shift work for the police officers and a nighttime drive for Johns may have lowered their defenses, raised hackles, and played tricks on their memories.

McNatt reported that Lovett, upon his arrival in Patterson, also interviewed Johns—or received a briefing from *him*, noting vaguely, "the same story was related to [O]fficer [L]ovett." Not long after his arrival in Patterson, Lovett alerted the SJCSO and departed to search for Johns's abandoned vehicle. He reported locating it on "Maze Boulevard" (the name of Highway 132 as it traverses the town of Modesto), two miles east of Interstate 5.

But the car had been torched, its interior completely consumed by fire.

Lovett recorded that he returned to Patterson at that time and transported Johns and her daughter to Tracy.

The car fire told police that Johns's escape had not ended her assailant's activities that night. After Johns fled his car, the stranger apparently returned to Highway 132 and located her station wagon where it had been disabled. He—or someone else—burned the abandoned vehicle beyond recognition, possibly making use of an accelerant.

He departed, leaving behind the station wagon's flaming shell. In a standard crime report of the SJCSO, Deputy Bauer described what he found when he went to investigate the station wagon that was described to him by Lovett. The vehicle's interior was completely charred, the arson performed while the owner was "hauled about the county." With information possibly supplied by other departments, Bauer too noted that the car's owner had been picked up on the pretext of being taken to a service station for car repairs. If Johns's captor had not set the vehicle ablaze, it had been done by an associate of the assailant or by another stranger in an unrelated—and highly coincidental—act of vandalism

The SJCSO ordered the station wagon towed. Bauer received a report that the hubcap was missing, likely removed from the scene by Johns's assailant. It was eventually located and taken to ID to be checked for fingerprints. The SJCSO contacted the Country Club Fire Department who in turn notified the rural fire department in Tracy for a possible arson investigation. Whether the firemen moved on it or not, the SJCSO declared that it would file arson and kidnapping charges against the perpetrator if he were ever identified.

He never was.

The SJCSO also contacted the San Francisco Police Department (SFPD) and requested fingerprints of the Zodiac, knowing that San Francisco had some on file. When advised of Johns's statement, Inspector Tyrell of the SFPD Homicide Division asked that a full report be sent to his office, attention Inspector Armstrong and Inspector Toschi.

Reed of Reed & Sons Towing took possession of Johns's 1957 Chevrolet station wagon at the location of its immolation. Upon close inspection, he noticed that the right rear wheel was held in place by only two loose lug nuts. (McNatt reported that no lug nuts were in place; Lovett, that one remained.) He removed two other nuts from the right front wheel and tightened all four on the back wheel to correct the problem. He transported the charred wreck to his shop on Highway 50 in Tracy.

ↈ

Two friends, Bill Horton and Fredrick Beamon, witnessed events they believed may have been related to the apparent abduction. They read an article about Johns and contacted Sergeant Hall of the Stanislaus County Sheriff's Office. Hall passed the information to SJSCO Deputy Ambrose who wrote his report from Hall's statement:

While driving on Highway 132, near Highways 33 and 580, in the general area of Johns's encounter with her captor, Horton and Beamon noticed a white, 1959 Buick stopped at the side of the road. The driver motioned for them to pull over. The two continued on, ignoring the request because they felt uneasy about the situation. They had not thought again about the odd event until reading about Johns's experience.

When Deputy Ambrose and Deputy McKay, both of the Stanislaus County Sheriff's Office, later attempted to contact Beamon at his residence in Modesto, his mother, Teresa Watson, told them that her son had left the house on March 22 and had not been back since. He was supposed to be at the home of his friend, Bill Horton, she added. Ambrose offered his business card with instructions for Watson to have her son contact him as soon as possible.

The two detectives attempted to reach Horton, but were unsuccessful in locating him.

The detectives then traveled to Reed & Sons Towing to examine the blackened hulk that was once Johns's station wagon. When they rummaged for the ignition key, which they believed had been abandoned on the front seat—Bauer had observed it there after the fire had been extinguished—they could not find it. Reed had not seen the keys, but mentioned that a couple had been to the lot on March 23 to inquire about the car. Perhaps they had taken them. Johns, with the help of her husband, Robert, who had driven up from their home in San Bernardino, had apparently recovered the key.

Years later, Johns would clarify the end of her time in the Central Valley following her strange encounter. She explained that one of her cars around that time did not need a key, and she didn't think she even possessed one. The vehicle could be started by hot-wiring the ignition. She and Robert had been by the wreckers to see the station wagon and to recover their belongings. Because she had spent much of the day in the San Joaquin County Sheriff's Department speaking with a variety of officers, she was not able to get to Reed & Sons until after dark. Even though all of Jennyfer's worldly belongings had been in that car, nothing of the vehicle was salvageable. The couple returned to San Bernardino that night, without staying over in the Central Valley, and soon put the whole bizarre affair out of their minds.

It wouldn't be until the 1980s, more than a decade later, that Vallejo and San Francisco detectives would track her down and begin to question her again about the events of March 1970. By that time, the information she provided and the initial police reports were irreconcilable. Though officers wanted her to say that her "captor" was some guy from Vallejo, according to Johns, she was simply too unsure of any identification. Suspect photographs were paraded in front of her by law enforcement agents and former law enforcement agents as late as 1998.

Johns passed away of natural causes on June 1, 2002.

಄

It remained a topic of intense debate whether or not the man who picked up Johns was the Zodiac serial killer. There was good reason to believe that he was, but there was equally compelling evidence to suggest that it may not have been. Johns believed she had a direct encounter with the serial killer, and the Zodiac himself, in a letter sent subsequent to the event, claimed responsibility for the attack, including the torching of the car. However, Johns may have been mistaken, and the Zodiac was entirely capable of lying.

Arguing against an authentic Zodiac encounter was the reliability of both Kathleen Johns and the Zodiac. Both represented questionable sources of information. The Zodiac had great motivation to lie, since any obfuscation promised to help preserve his freedom. Any incorrect information that the killer could provide—and he had already supplied some on previous occasions—would hamper the investigation with fallacious leads and burden prosecutors with problems if and when he was identified. Johns, for her part, was suspected of exaggerating and embellishing over the years. Nowhere in the three police records, for instance, was there even a hint that the young mother had received a death threat, a rather important detail for all of the officers to have mistakenly omitted from official reports, if that is what Johns at the time had claimed. Lovett's filing from that day even questioned whether a crime had been perpetrated.

Johns's claims may have morphed and grown with each telling. Many investigators discounted her words, acknowledging that eyewitness accounts are notoriously unreliable. Sergeant Bawart, recalling events years later, suggested that there was something wrong with her story. It appeared to him that she had covert motives, that she was possibly attempting to gain sympathy from her husband or that something similar was in play. And even if she was being fully honest with law enforcement, she still may have been mistaken to equate her captor with the Zodiac.

Investigators had to consider a wide range of possible explanations for the evening's odd events. The entire episode may have been a misunderstanding between Johns and a helpful citizen. It may have been a kidnapping enacted by a bizarre but seemingly innocuous stranger who was not the Zodiac. Perhaps the Zodiac claimed credit for something he did not do, an action that he was known to perform on at least one other occasion. Or maybe Johns's understanding of the incident was the product of a woman under so much psychological pressure and family stress that she saw and heard events in a much different light than they actually occurred, though the police realized that the burning of her vehicle *did* suggest that her "captor," whoever he was, offered at least some threat to her.

The actual survival of Johns and her daughter also suggested something other than a Zodiac event. Surprisingly, both victims lived. If Kathleen Johns was to be believed, the driver had at least an hour in which to attempt, or even commit, murder. He did not do so. No previous Zodiac encounter was longer than 30 minutes, most over in a matter of minutes; no previous Zodiac encounter occurred without a murder; no previous Zodiac encounter involved an invitation to ride in the killer's car; and no previous Zodiac encounter occurred without the use of a weapon. It may be difficult to explain Johns's experience as a Zodiac attack when it appeared to resemble no more than a long drive, without the use of a weapon, in the perpetrator's vehicle, and in which no one was left for dead.

But maybe it *was* the Zodiac who Johns and her daughter encountered.

If it was the Zodiac, there were some interesting implications for the investigation, the investigators noted. The attack presented additional information and another eyewitness. Those tasked with capturing the famed Northern California killer weighed the new pieces of data, hoping that something would tip the scales of justice in their favor.

If this was indeed an actual Zodiac attack on Johns, the episode represented the introduction of a child into the case. Though the Zodiac referred to his victims on Lake Herman Road and at Blue Rock Springs Park as "kids," all of his previous targets were in actuality at least on the cusp of adulthood, teenagers or older. In the Johns event, a true child—Johns's infant daughter—was present. This may have been a mistake on the Zodiac's part since he may not have been aware that she was accompanying Johns until he pulled them over— or even until they entered his car.

Jennyfer's presence therefore may have even saved her mother's life: it may have been sobering for the killer to contemplate the death of a child, or the pain of a motherless infant. It is possible that he was experiencing sympathy for this pregnant woman and her young daughter. At this point in his serial killing career, his vicious plans to kill innocent school children and his threatened bomb were only theoretical. Confronted with a flesh-and-blood infant, he may have had reason to reconsider his diabolical plans, either from personal revulsion or a fear of public scorn.

This attack also introduced the idea that children may have been a part of the Zodiac's life. Johns had observed pieces of children's clothing in the stranger's vehicle. The killer may have been a father, an uncle, or a deviant with a sexual interest in children's attire.

Perhaps the Zodiac had concealed himself in a family, just as Gary Ridgeway, the serial killer known as the Green River Killer, did in Washington State in the 1990s. More tantalizing but uncertain clues for an already confused investigation.

Armstrong and Toschi apparently placed a low priority on speaking with Johns. They may have read the conflicting police reports in their offices in San Francisco and felt no urgency to follow up. It would not be until four months later that the killer would claim credit for the "attack." By that time, Johns may not have been available for additional interviews. It was a lost opportunity in the highly controversial event.

No mailing was sent immediately after the "attack," nor was any telephone call received. These aberrations from his usual modus operandi have been heralded by some as proof that it was not a Zodiac event. In fact, the Zodiac would not refer to this attack until it was well documented in the press, leading to speculation that he was not involved, but was instead claiming credit for something he had learned about through the media. Fortifying the argument that the event was not the responsibility of the serial killer, the next letter from the Zodiac—received one month after Johns's unusual experience—cast a new diagram, breathed new threats, taunted with a new cipher, but made no mention of Kathleen Johns.

The Name Letter

Approximately four weeks following the apparent abduction of Johns, the next authenticated letter arrived, marking a familiar length of time between a Zodiac attack and a Zodiac missive. The two-page "Name letter" was received by *The San Francisco Chronicle* on April 21, 1970, postmarked the previous day in San Francisco.

The mailing, while saying nothing of the Johns incident, nevertheless presented a variety of new milestones in the killer's crime spree. It contained another new cipher—the first not carefully presented on a separate page and the first not long enough to be considered a serious piece of cryptographic work. It also offered a revision to the bomb diagram first detailed in the 6-Page letter.

Lieutenant Charles Ellis of the SFPD reported to the media on the new letter and its new, 13-character cipher. He noted that the

340 cipher, received the previous year, had not been solved, adding that many experts by that time did not believe that it contained any decipherable information.

In the new note, portions of which were not immediately released to the public, the killer denied responsibility for a murder, claiming that the recent bombing of a police station and the concomitant killing of a police officer was not precipitated by him. The violence had been thoroughly reported in the papers and on television.

On February 17, 1970, a pipe bomb had been placed on the windowsill of the San Francisco Golden Gate Park Police Station. Its detonation killed SFPD Sergeant Brian V. McDonnell, severely wounded and partially blinded Officer Robert Fogarty, and injured eight other officers. The carnage was blamed on the radical left political group the Weather Underground, which courts eventually found responsible for numerous bombing deaths, including as many as 20 public officials and 2 of its own members.

The FBI's San Francisco Field Office requested the authentication of the Name letter on the day it was received by *The Chronicle*. The FBI Crime Laboratory in Washington, D.C. received its copy of the letter two days later, and promptly examined it on October 24. A photograph of the envelope, which bore the San Francisco postmark of April 20, was given the identifying title, Qc45; photographs of its two pages, Qc46 and Qc47. Hand printing characteristics noted by the laboratory indicated that these were prepared by the person who had written the other threatening letters in the case.

A further request was made to the FBI in Washington, D.C. for handwriting comparisons and a deciphering of the brief encryption. *The Chronicle* planned to mention the letter in print on October 22, but agreed to withhold certain facts. While the FBI found characteristics that showed the letter authentic, it was unable to decipher the message: "No decryption could be effected for the cipher text portion…"

The new cipher, a mere 13-characters long, was hardly a sincere effort of honest communication. Such a short message would necessarily provide numerous solutions, each of which could be argued to be the intent of its author, especially in light of the many spelling mistakes and errors of coding in the 408 cipher, the only Zodiac cipher that has ever been definitively deciphered. Since it was reasonable to expect that an error or two would be present in the new encryption as well, and because that probability couldn't be excluded, the number of possible correct solutions to the 13-character cipher was essentially infinite. And no thirteen-letter solution could be proven to *not* be the correct interpretation. In cryptographic circles, ciphers less than 30 characters are considered not inherently breakable.

Throughout the subsequent years, armchair researchers obligingly suggested many, many possible solutions. Some were better than others. A notable possibility was "Alfred E. Newman," the name of the famous mascot of Mad Magazine, a counter-culture humor screed that was popular among the youth of 1960s and 1970s. Only one spelling mistake or coding error needed to be acknowledged for this solution to fit the symbols in a simple substitution cipher. The first three symbols of the cryptograph were also the initials of the named solution: AEN.

The FBI determined that the message was too short to be meaningfully decoded. The bureau realized that with so few symbols, without more input from the killer himself, the true, intended solution would in all probability never be known.

As the first contact after the Belli letter, the Name letter suggested that the killer's apparent cry for help in the previous note was a farce, a temporary phase from which the killer had emerged, or was not the intent of that letter in the first place. The writer's generous use of boasting, threatening, and taunting was consistent with virtually all of his previous and future letters.

The first page of the new letter read as follows:

```
This is the Zodiac speaking
By the way have you cracked
the last cipher I sent you ?
My name is --

[13 symbol cipher]

I am mildly cerous as to how
much money you have on my
head now. I hope you do not
think that I was the one
```

who wiped out that blue
meannie with a bomb at the
cop station. Even though I talked
about killing school children with
one. It just wouldnt doo to
move in on someone elses teritory.
But there is more glory in killing
a cop than a cid because a cop
can shoot back. I have killed
ten people to date. It would

This is the Zodiac speaking
By the way have you cracked
the last cipher I sent you ?.
My name is ——

A E N ⊕ ⊗ K ⊠ M ⊙ ↲ N A M

I am mildly cerous as to how
much money you have on my
head now. I hope you do not
think that I was the one
who wiped out that blue
meannie with a bomb at the
cop station. Even though I talked
about killing school children with
one. It just wouldnt doo to
move in on someone elses teritory.
But there is more glory in killing
a cop than a cid because a cop
can shoot back. I have killed
ten people to date. It would
have been a lot more except
that my bas bomb was a dod.
I was swamped out by the
rain we had a while back.

```
have been a lot more except
that my bus bomb was a dud.
I was swamped out by the
rain we had a while back.
```

The second page of the missive presented a revised bomb diagram. Like the first drawing, it outlined an explosive system designed to detonate when passed by a school bus. It incorporated a new provision: a second circuit designated as a "cloudy day disco[n]nect." Apparently, if the sky was overcast, the second circuit would prevent the bomb from being activated. Otherwise, without it, the new diagram implied, on a cloudy day the system would detonate as soon as it was set and would not wait until a bus drove past.

The second page included the following words:

```
The new bomb is set up like
this
```

[new bomb diagram]

```
PS I hope you have fun trying
to figgure out who I killed
 [crosshair symbol] = 10 SFPD = 0
```

The writer's mention of "being swamped out by the rain" launched an investigation into lower lying regions of the Bay Area, the police figuring that if they could find the spots where rainwater pooled, they might be one step closer to identifying the killer. The police also wondered what the killer might have meant by referring to someone else's "ter[r]itory." Did the Zodiac believe he had a specific area, geographic or otherwise, in which he operated?

The killer's claim to ten victims also had to be explored. It provided the investigators with only two possibilities. Either the Zodiac had killed additional victims of which they were not aware, or he was padding the score, falsely claiming victims who did not exist.

They later questioned why he would deny responsibility for one killing—that of Sergeant McDonnell—if he was willing to claim credit for other murders that he had not perpetrated. And why mention a murder that happened two months prior while remaining

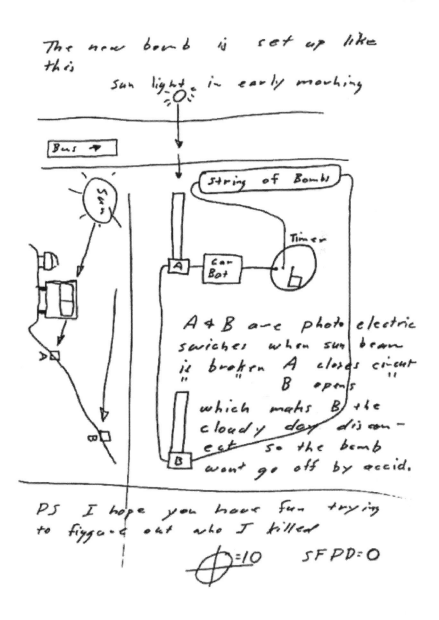

The new bomb is set up like this

Sun light in early morning

Bus →

String of Bombs

Timer

A

Car Bomb

A & B are photo electric switches when sun beam is broken A closes circut B opens which maks B the cloudy day discon- ect so the bomb wont go off by accid.

PS I hope you have fun trying to figgure out who I killed

⊕=10   SFPD:0

silent about the kidnapping of Johns, if in fact he was involved in the latter?

The letter seemed to communicate something about the killer, but investigators could not pinpoint anything specific that would further their quest. If the killer was aware of investigative techniques and used this knowledge to cover any leads, he was also very skilled in tantalizing those tasked with capturing him, and doing so in a way that was not very helpful. He may have offered up large servings of fake and vague clues. One way or another, he aided little in police efforts to catch him.

Many of the reports filed by law enforcement at the time bleakly concluded with the words, "The investigation continues."

The Dragon Card

The killer sent a most unusual communication one week later. Following through on his theme of setting a bomb by a roadside to kill children in a school bus, the Zodiac now provided a means by which the people of the Bay Area could avert the disaster. If two specific actions were taken, he promised, the bomb would not be detonated.

Why law enforcement should believe him and trust him at his word was never even intimated. Even if the offer was disingenuous, however, the police had to take it seriously. They were as committed to preserving life as they were to capturing the Zodiac.

The Dragon card followed closely on the heels of the Name letter, and was postmarked April 28, also in San Francisco. The FBI Field Office in San Francisco received it from *The Chronicle* on April 30, and in turn notified Washington, D.C. of its receipt that same day. San Francisco requested an analysis on May 1, but the lab did not receive its copy of the items until May 4. The envelope was labeled Qc48, and the front and back of the card, Qc49 and Qc50, respectively. The SFPD advised *The Chronicle* to make some mention of the letter to "placate" the killer. The newspaper obliged with a brief story on May 1.

On May 7, the FBI lab reported on the card, noting that some of the previous samples of the killer's writing had been distorted and were not written as freely as others. Nevertheless, all of the samples were likely composed by the same person, it concluded, "Hand printed characteristics were observed, however, which indicates that all of the threatening letters in this case, including Qc48 through Qc50, were probably prepared by one writer."

Also on May 7, an additional request was made of the FBI Laboratory. Because latent prints had been developed from the Dragon card and its envelope, it was asked to make fingerprint comparisons.

The prints—one latent fingerprint and six latent palm prints—were likely deposited prior to delivery by the United States Postal Service or from being handled by the office staff of *The Chronicle*. The lab attempted to find a match, but no identification was effected.

The entire text on the back of the Dragon card read as follows:

```
If you dont want me to
have this blast you must
do two things. 1 Tell every
one about the bus bomb with
all the details. 2 I would like
to see some nice Zodiac butons
wandering about town. Every
one else has these buttons like,
[peace symbol], black power, melvin eats
bluber, etc. Well it would cheer
me up considerbly if I saw
a lot of people wearing my
buton. Please no nasty ones
like melvin's
  Thank you.

[crosshair symbol]
```

The card exposed the killer's childish sense of humor. Two goofy-looking miners were pictured on the front, one riding a mule, the other sitting on a dragon. The caption of the "get well" card declared, "Sorry to hear that your ass is dragon." To this, the killer added in his own hand printing, "I hope you enjoy your selves when I have my B l a s t." followed by a crosshair symbol and "P.S. on back." Except for the Zodiac's words, the back of the card was blank.

The Zodiac was evidently making the promise that he would not detonate a bomb if two conditions were met, two conditions that the killer must have prized. The first demand was to publish his bomb diagram with all of its details. While some information about the Name letter had been passed on to the public, the diagram of the bomb on page two was never printed in newspapers. The bomb diagram from the 6-Page letter the previous fall had been similarly withheld.

The killer had demonstrated no willingness to discuss his demands. He provided no means of communication. If the police wanted to negotiate with him, they would have to do so through the media. Or they could accept his terms as stated.

The irony of the first demand was not lost on the police. If they continued to prevent the publication of the bomb diagram, the public would have no fear because they would never know about it. On the other hand, if they released the sketch to the media, the public could unnecessarily be in fear of a threat that the killer promised to never enact should it be broadcast. Evidently, the intent of the bomb diagram was to scare, and not to be used as a blueprint for an actual device that would kill. Perhaps the bomb did not exist, and the only leverage that the killer felt that he had at this point in his campaign was to terrorize the Bay Area residents with his diagram. Or perhaps he was so proud of his drawing that he wanted it communicated to the world, even if its concepts were never used. Law enforcement wrestled with the implications of the killer's words.

The second demand was for the citizens of the Bay Area to wear "some nice [crosshair symbol] buttons." It was never clear what he hoped to achieve by having his button worn "about town," even though he said that it would "cheer [him] up," possibly suggesting that he was suffering with depression or some other kind of mood disorder such as a bipolar disorder.

The specifics of what the buttons were to look like were not provided, but examples of buttons produced by several groups *were* offered: a circled "Y," known as *ban the bomb* or a peace symbol; "Melvin eats blubber" (a probable dig at attorney Melvin Belli in an allusion to buttons worn by English teachers at the time to promote the novel *Moby Dick*, "Herman Melville eats blubber"); and those worn by the Black Panther political party.

In light of the horror of his killings, and his threat to use a bomb if his demands were not met, the Zodiac's signoff was particularly odd. In great kindness and with polite manners, he ended, "Please no nasty ones like Melvin's / Thank you." It may have been an expression of sarcasm, the police realized.

The second demand was evidently as important to the killer as it was perplexing to the general public. It was never enacted (did he really believe that anybody would proudly display a button that glorified an odious killer?). Undaunted, he renewed his request in three subsequent letters. For him, it was no fleeting fantasy or throw-away line. The public's failure to heed his words soon became the justification for the killer to "punish" the people of the Bay Area.

At the request of the SFPD, the card was withheld from the public for one day. SFPD Police Chief Alfred Nelder then told *The Chronicle* to publish information about the bomb threat. No mention of any bomb appeared in the press until May 1, 1970.

Nelder's reasoning behind the change? The bomb threat was likely a hoax, and in light of the Zodiac's new promise to kill if the bomb details were *not* made public, he weighed the chance of public panic over against the killer's new threat, and decided to share the information. When Paul Avery reported on it, he made sure to include the U.S. Army's assessment that such a far-fetched device would be extremely difficult to construct.

Neither the police nor the public created or wore any Zodiac buttons.

The investigators realized that with the two demands the Zodiac's mind may have been opened a crack to provide a brief glimpse into his soul. By giving ultimatums to the public, he may have unwittingly provided some clarity to his motive for the gruesome murders and his sinister campaign of terror. But what exactly was to be accomplished by fulfilling his requests remained a mystery, possibly another hoax by a killer who'd already proved himself dishonest. He may have been possessed only with a desire to spread fear, with the added goal of gaining notoriety.

The puzzling request for Zodiac buttons was reiterated with the next letter, the Map letter, sent approximately two months later.

The Map letter

Postmarked in San Francisco on June 26, 1970, the Map letter was, like the two previous letters received that year, addressed to *The San Francisco Chronicle*. Curiously, the single, hand-written page was accompanied by a piece of a map illustrating a portion of the Bay Area. The letter included a new cipher, the fourth sent by the killer. The mailing was turned over the SFPD on June 30, on which date the San Francisco FBI Field Office notified Washington, D.C. of its arrival in an airtel. The missive, map piece, and envelope were collectively labeled Qc51 by the FBI Crime Laboratory.

On July 8, the laboratory gave up its attempts to crack the encryption it had received on July 2: "No decryption could be affected for symbols on Qc51."

The new cipher contained 32 symbols, 26 of which were unique, the laboratory noted. A close inspection revealed that a mere three symbols occurred more than once, and these were each used twice. The only similarity to the first two Zodiac ciphers was the length of the row: 17 characters long. Many possible words were run though the encryption, particularly those used in previous communications, such as "with," "east," "west," "miles," "yards," "feet," "bomb," and "kill," but there were no significant hits to any of these potential cribs.

On July 15, the FBI in Washington, D.C. concluded that the hand printing on Qc51 was probably done by the Zodiac, "Hand printing characteristics indicate all threatening letters, including Qc51, probably one writer."

The text of the Map letter read as follows:

```
This is the Zodiac speaking

I have become very upset with
the people of San Fran Bay
Area. They have not complied
with my wishes for them to
wear some nice [crosshair symbol] buttons.
I promiced to punish them
if they did not comply, by
anilating a full School Buss.
But now school is out for
the summer, so I punished
them in an another way.
I shot a man sitting in
a parked car with a .38.
[large crosshair symbol]-12 SFPD-0

The Map coupled with this
code will tell you where the
```

```
bomb is set. You have untill
next Fall to dig it up. [crosshair symbol]
```

[32 symbol cipher: 17 symbols on the first line,
15 on the second]

This is the Zodiac speaking

I have become very upset with
the people of San Fran Bay
Area. They have <u>not</u> complied
with my wishes for them to
wear some nice ⊕ buttons.
I promiced to punish them
if they didnot comply, by
anilating a full School Buss.
But now school is out for
the summer, so I punished
them in an another way.
I shot a man sitting in
a parked car with a .38.

—12   SFPD—0

The Map coupled with this
code will tell you whoe the
bomb is set. You have antill
next Fall to dig it up. ⊕

C △ J ! ▊ O K ⅃ A M ⸕ ▲ Ω O R T G
X ⊙ F D V Ɩ ▊ H C E L ⊕ P W △

The Zodiac's claim of having killed again was in all probability spurious, the investigation concluded. SFPD Officer Richard Radetice had been fatally shot by an unknown assailant as he sat alone in his police car on June 19, 1970, mirroring the Zodiac's words, "I shot a man sitting in a parked car with a .38." Though the weapon used *was* a .38, despite the boast of the letter the death was never attributed to the Zodiac. An arrest warrant had already been issued for Joe Wesley Johnson, an ex-con who witnesses said was responsible for the slaying of the officer.

The killer's words may instead have found their origins with *The Chronicle*'s October 12, 1969 story that wrongly, in the immediate fog of violence, attributed Stine's death to a .38. But the killer's deception was not the only clue found by the police.

The Map letter included a different kind of evidence for the investigation. The inclusion of the piece of a map was the first time that the killer had presented geographical detail in such specificity. Where in previous letters he had referred to directions, where in phone calls he had indicated distances, here he sent a piece of a map and indicated that it was to be used as a tool. Written on the map was a crosshair symbol centered on Mount Diablo, a prominent landmark located in Alameda County of the East Bay. The numbers "0," "3," "6," and "9" appeared at the cross intersections with the circle around the symbol going clockwise from the top. Next to the "0" at the top of the crosshair symbol, the Zodiac had written, "- is to be set to Mag. N."

The purpose of the map, the killer explained, was to aid in locating the bomb he had repeatedly threatened to place at some roadside site to kill children. With the solution to the new encryption in hand, he promised, the police could use the map to locate the bomb which the author claimed had already been set to detonate. By this time, with so much written about a bomb that was never proven to exist, the police had their doubts.

Because law enforcement did not believe there was a bomb, they did not spend undue effort in either the cipher's solution or the map itself. Killers have been known to send maps to law enforcement authorities, directing agencies to the location of a body, a dump site of several corpses, a kidnap victim, or stolen property. Usually, they

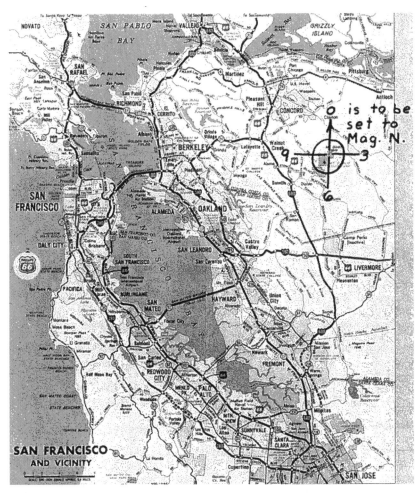

provide clear instructions and are helpful. Never in the history of criminology, apart from this note has a map been used in conjunction with a cipher to indicate the location of a bomb. The pieces were scoured for prints—just like all the previous mailings—but none were recovered.

Investigators were led to wonder whether their quarry was beginning to unravel on some emotional or psychological level. On the heels of the Dragon card with its silliness and bizarre requests, this new mailing might further document the killer's descent into madness, a depth deeper than already evidenced in his appalling attacks. Regardless, the police had to look beyond the writer's mental state in their search for clues.

The Map letter was the third communication of 1970. Like the two preceding notes, it provided new information. It contained instructions and taunts from the killer, and as a result it offered new evidence about the type of person who would utilize such unique ideas. Of the killer's imagination and creativity, there was no doubt, but this letter further contraindicated that he was communicating on the level and being honest with investigators.

The police now had in their possession three unsolved Zodiac ciphers. The evidence was mounting that they were being played by a killer who was more interested in controlling the police than in providing them with sincere clues. Despite the success in deciphering the first, the "408," cipher, a consensus began to build that the remaining three likely contained no useful information and possibly no real solutions, especially the final two ciphers that were short and embedded within the text of letters.

Though longer than the previous cryptograph, the 32-character cipher was even less useful. Because only three symbols were used more than once, and each of these being found only two times in the cryptograph, the mathematical probabilities became apparent: nearly any 32-character solution could fit the cipher. And any solution was no better than any other solution, especially in light of the Zodiac's history of spelling mistakes and coding errors. Even if it could be determined to be a homophonic, single substitution cipher with variations, as was the 408 cipher, the number of unique symbols ensured that almost any conceivable 32 letter combination making a sentence or a phrase would be equally likely—or unlikely—to be a correct solution. If the assumption was not correct, and the cipher was not homophonic, all bets were off, and the solution could be absolutely anything.

What the Zodiac had provided was more than likely not a cipher but gibberish. The mathematically inclined were savvy enough to refuse more than a cursory glance, and wonder whether there was some other direction to tackle its enigma, one that would provide success. No satisfactory solution was ever proffered.

Johns letter

The end of July saw two new Zodiac mailings. Postmarked on July 24 and 26 and addressed to *The San Francisco Chronicle*, the two letters, the Johns letter and the Torture letter, were forwarded to the FBI Crime lab in Washington, D.C., first by a request for an examination in an airtel on July 29, then through photocopies of the letters themselves sent two days later.

The identification label, Qc52, was assigned to the July 26 envelope, and Qc53 to the July 24 envelope. The Johns letter, the first received and shorter of the two, was labeled Qc54; the Torture letter, Qc55. The material was combined in a single mailing to the FBI in Washington, D.C.

The SFPD supplied the two newly arrived Zodiac letters to the FBI in San Francisco, after lifting from them some latent fingerprints. Elimination prints had been taken from any employees of *The Chronicle* who may have handled them. The FBI in Washington, D.C. examined the documents to compare handwriting, and was easily able to match them to the previously received Zodiac letters, noting that some of the letters contained some distortion and were not written as freely as other threating letters, and that most of its samples were photos so they were not as clear as originals. The lab concluded that all appeared to be from the same hand and declared them authentic on August 4, "All threatening letters, including [the two new ones], were probably prepared by one person."

The Johns letter was one of the shortest of the Zodiac letters. After the initial *"This is the Zodiac speaking,"* the body of the handprinted missive comprised a mere two sentences, the whole text not even filling the single sheet of paper on which it was written. In it, the killer finally claimed credit for the attack on Kathleen Johns, but never attempted to provide convincing proof. All of the information in the letter had already been reported through numerous media sources.

The text of the Johns letter was as follows:

```
This is the Zodiac speaking

I am rather unhappy because
you people will not wear some
nice [crosshair symbol] buttons. So I now
have a little list, starting with
the woeman & her baby that I
gave a rather intersting ride
for a coupple howers one
evening a few months back that
ended in my burning her
car where I found them.
  [crosshair symbol, centered on page]
```

The note contained the killer's first reference to *The Mikado*, a light, comedic opera by Gilbert and Sullivan. By claiming, "I now have a little list," the Zodiac was alluding to the song "I Have a Little List" from that opera, first performed in London in 1885. This reference, along with several future Mikado quotes, led investigators to question why the opera drew his attention.

Subsequent investigation included the interrogation of people who acted in, worked for, or habitually attended performances of *The Mikado*. It also led to speculation that the hood worn by the perpetrator on September 27 of the previous year was a physical representation of one of the characters: Ko-Ko, the Lord High Executioner who sang the referenced song. Perhaps the Zodiac was dressing in the costume of Ko-Ko, and identified himself as some sort of executioner.

Why the Zodiac referenced the opera has never been fully explained. All investigation into the Lamplighters and other drama troupes who were performing it during or around the period of time that the attacks occurred led to nothing. Another clue floating in the dark: intriguing, perplexing, but ultimately offering no clear direction.

The letter made references to the enigmatic attack on Kathleen Johns four months after the actual event, leading some to consider this a false claim. Had the Zodiac read about the incident attributed to him and only now claimed it? Or did the killer attempt to remain true to his word in not announcing his attacks, waiting with this information until he found he had little else to offer the public?

The next letter left no doubt about the murderer's interest in *The Mikado*.

Torture letter

Arriving with the Johns letter, and posted immediately on its tail, the Torture letter was one of the most unusual of all of the Zodiac's communications. Almost nothing could be gleaned from a face value reading of the text, despite its length of five pages. The theories on the meaning of the letter proved as diverse as its myriad subject matter. Readers have noted that it could be further evidence of its author's psychological unraveling, clever hints at some kind of veiled message, a diversionary tactic to trick investigators into believing he was legally insane, or evidence that the killer was sadistic at his core. Or maybe none of these theories described the letter's true intent.

The writer first described tortures that he would commit on his "slaves," a euphemism first introduced in the solution to the 408 cipher to describe the people that he had killed. On the surface, the threat itself made no sense. To the sane individual, it was crazy to contemplate performing a torturous act on an already deceased person, which amounted to no more than a threat to desecrate corpses (to which he had no access). By this time, he had claimed 13 "slaves" or victims, though investigators had only been able to tie him conclusively to 5 deaths (later adjusted by some to 6 when information linked him to Bates's murder). What he meant by the additional numbers was open to speculation: people he had killed who had yet to be identified, a false level of murders to mislead investigators and instill additional fear and uncertainty in the general public, or something else.

Detailing 5 tortures that he would enact on his "slaves" if the people of the Bay Area would not wear his "buttons," the Zodiac wrote the following on the first two pages of the Torture letter:

```
This is the Zodiac speaking

Being that you will not wear
some nice [crosshair symbol] buttons, how about
wearing some nasty [crosshair symbol] buttons.
Or any type of [crosshair symbol] buttons that
```

```
you can think up. If you do
not wear any type of [crosshair symbol]
buttons I shall (on top of every
thing else) torture all 13
of my slaves that I have
wateing for me in Paradice.
Some I shall tie over ant hills
and watch them scream & twich
and squirm. Others shall have
pine splinters driven under their
nails & then burned. Others shall
be placed in cages & fed salt
beef untill they are gorged then
I shall listen to their pleass
for water and I shall laugh at
them. Others will hang by
their thumbs & burn in the
sun then I will rub them down
with deep heat to warm
--
them up. Others I shall
skin them alive & let them
run around screaming. And
all billiard players I shall
have them play in a dark
ened dungon cell with crooked
cues & Twisted Shoes.
Yes I shall have great
fun inflicting the most
delicious of pain to my
Slaves

[half-page-sized crosshair symbol] = 13

SFPD = 0
```

Far from instilling fear, the threat of torturing dead bodies—his previous victims—made little sense to investigators. His verbiage increasingly began to fall on deaf ears, becoming mere words, especially since he never carried through on his promises to snipe a school bus or to bomb school children. His ideas staged a theater of the absurd when more and more outrageous boasts were communicated but never enacted. The killer was raising into a large pot at the poker table, but the public was now calling his bluff.

The prose degenerated into near nonsense on the second page, in which he summed up his plans, "Yes I shall have fun inflicting the most delicious of pain to my slaves."

The final three pages of the torture letter presented an almost exact quote of part of *The Mikado*, with liberty taken on much of the spelling and some wording:

```
As some day it may hapen
that a victom must be found.
I've got a little list. I've
got a little list, of society
offenders who might well be
underground who would never
be missed who would never be
missed. There is the pest-
ulentual nucences who whrite
for autographs, all people who
have flabby hands and irritat-
ing laughs. All children who
are up in dates and implore
you with implatt. All people
who are shakeing hands shake
hands like that. And all third
persons who with unspoiling
take thoes who insist. They'd
none of them be missed. They'd
none of them be missed. There's
the banjo seranader and
the others of his race and
the piano orginast I got him
on the list. All people who
eat pepermint and phomphit
--
in your face, they would
never be missed They would
never be missed And the
Idiout who phraises with in-
thusastic tone of centuries
but this and every country but
his own. And the lady from
```

```
the provences who dress like
a guy who doesn't cry and
the singurly abnomily the
girl who never kissed. I don't
think she would be missed
Im shure she wouldn't be
missed. And that nice impriest
that is rather rife the judici-
ial hummerest I've got him on
the list All funny fellows, com-
mic men and clowns of private
life. They'd none of them be
missed. They'd none of them be
missed. And uncompromiseing
kind such as wachamacallit ,
thingmebob , and like wise , well-
-nevermind , and tut tut tut tut ,
and whatshisname , and you know
--
who, but the task of filling
up the blanks I rather leave
up to you. But it really does-
n't matter whom you place
upon the list , for none of
them be missed, none of
them be missed.

[two-thirds-of-a-page-sized crosshair symbol]

PS. The Mt. Diablo Code concerns
Radians & # inches along the radians
```

The FBI located the origin of the three-page quote that closed the Torture letter, and on August 10 sent a printed copy of the song sung by Ko-Ko in Act 1 of *The Mikado* and a portion of the song sung by *The Mikado* in Act 2. The Johns letter and the end of the Torture letter appeared to quote *The Mikado* Act 1; the second page of the Torture letter could be an allusion to Act 2 because of the presence of five similar words, including "billiard."

The FBI did not find a new cipher in either of the letters, "No code or cipher material was found in specimens Qc52 to Qc56." The FBI noted that the mention of the "Mt. Diablo code" within the text of the Torture letter was probably a reference to the Map letter, Qc51, previously submitted.

The FBI did an extensive search of the documents for finger-prints, collecting eight latents from two of its pages. In a subsequently filed report, it noted that a pattern could be determined from the arrangement of fingers that had touched the pages. Not only did law enforcement have individual prints, they knew which prints came from which of his fingers—but only if the lifted prints were actually his, a fact that could not be confirmed.

The Torture letter may have been evidence that Zodiac needed to clarify his allusions in the Johns letter. Arriving with the previous missive on July 27, though postmarked two days after the Johns letter, it was a clear recitation of Gilbert and Sullivan's *The Mikado*. Fearing that his veiled reference—communicated in just a few short words—would fall on uncreative ears, he may have felt the need to spell it out for people who had no understanding of the light opera. Accordingly, he quoted, in parts word for word, a large section of the opera, the song, "I Have a Little List."

The Torture letter provided the only indication that the killer might be interested in torturing other people. He did not mention or even suggest as much in other letters. Furthermore, all his actual attacks were sudden and quick. There was no hint given in the manner of his murders that he was even remotely interested in, or inspired by, the suffering of his victims, many being dispatched quickly and with an absence of the prolonged agony that would accompany the work of a sadist who reveled in the effects of his violence. His rapid departure from the scenes of his attacks further evidenced a lack of interest in his victims' pain.

While his letter celebrated torture, he himself had ceased killing, it appeared. His messages had degenerated into a veritable word salad. They appeared to many to be nothing short of nonsense. *The Chronicle* decided not to publish these last two letters, in their words, "just to see what the Zodiac would do." By this time they suspected that they were actually encouraging him to write by publishing his material, a vicious cycle they meant to interrupt. The Zodiac's interest in *The Mikado* would not be made public until the first anniversary of the killing of Paul Stine, a date nearly three months away.

❦

By the summer of 1970, the investigation was no closer to capturing the Zodiac than it had been at any time in 1969. But neither was the Zodiac capturing the public imagination as he once had. The citizens of the Bay Area were becoming weary of his bizarre threats, and began to believe that he may have ceased killing. A stalemate had been reached as cat and mouse toyed with each other, even as they played a deadly game with citizens' lives and a perpetrator's freedom.

The next move forward would be made by the killer, not in the form of another violent attack but through a successful effort at regaining control of the media, with the hope of a return to a once familiar place on the daily newspaper: the front page.

To remain relevant, the killer would have to look beyond Northern California. To open new markets for his threats, and locate newspapers who would publish his words, his campaign of crime would in time move south. But first, it may have moved west to the California-Nevada border.

10 | LAKE TAHOE

"pass LAKE TAHOE areas"

The next Zodiac attack may not have been a Zodiac attack. It may not have even been an attack.

On September 6, 1970, 25-year-old Donna Lass went missing. She was employed at the time as a nurse at the Sahara Tahoe Casino in Nevada, and assigned to aid any guest or employee with a health concern. Last seen at 2:00 a.m. caring for a patient at the casino's first aid station, the pretty, blonde-haired, blue-eyed nurse simply disappeared following her shift and was never heard from again. She made her last entry into her logbook at 1:50 a.m. in the early hours of Sunday. No one witnessed the departure of the petite young woman—she was five feet three inches and 135 pounds—and no hint of her whereabouts has ever surfaced. Today, little more is known about her fate than was known the week she vanished.

The following day, a telephone call was placed to the bustling casino, and another one to Lass's landlord. An unknown male stated in both calls that Donna would not be returning due to a family emergency.

There was no family emergency, however. It was a cruel hoax, likely designed to give someone a few extra hours to cover up for a crime or escape the area. There was no male who had a close relationship with Lass to justify a legitimate call on her behalf. That caller alone may know what happened to the young nurse.

Lass's vehicle, a new 1968 convertible, was later discovered at her apartment complex at 3893 Monte Verdi in nearby Stateline, California. Lass had rented her new home, but had not yet fully moved into it. The circumstances of her disappearance baffled police and confounded her family. She may have been sighted on September 7, according to a newspaper account. A witness believed that Lass, born November 3, 1944, was accompanied by a blond-haired man. The two were seen walking near the unit recently rented by Lass.

The young nurse left behind her cherished vehicle, a bank account with $500 in savings, and her entire wardrobe. A careful inventory of her possessions revealed that the only items missing were her purse and the clothes she was wearing. Her credit cards remained unused, and there was no sign of any struggle in the apartment.

Her family members employed Private Investigator John Miller of Des Moines Iowa, and offered a $500 reward to aid in locating her, a desperate strategy that over time would cost more than $3000 and revealed no reliable details of her fate. When no additional evidence of her whereabouts emerged, they ruefully acknowledged that she must be dead.

The investigation into Lass's disappearance soon beat a path to the young nurse's former roommate and former co-worker, Jo Anne Goettsche, who had been invited to Tahoe to spend Labor Day with Lass in her newly rented apartment. She traveled the distance from the Bay Area on September 4, she claimed, but not knowing Lass's address, she was unable to make contact with her friend. She visited the Sahara only to learn that Lass was absent. Incredibly, she returned home to San Francisco without meeting up with her friend. According to Goettsche, Lass liked her job and planned to work through the winter in Lake Tahoe to save enough money for a trip to Europe.

The reason Lass's apartment was so clean, investigators speculated, was because she was expecting company. They may not have realized that she had just rented the space, and hadn't had time to soil it.

Initially, no consideration was given to Lass being a victim of the Bay Area's infamous Zodiac serial killer. The nature of her disappearance argued against her inclusion into the case, even if it had been suggested at this stage. In all of the previous Zodiac attacks, the victims were found almost immediately. Not only were they not hidden or missing, on two occasions the perpetrator actually telephoned the police with precise directions to the victims' location. (And no call was necessary after the murder of Paul Stine, the Zodiac evidently witnessing the police response to the scene.) The Zodiac furthermore never ventured outside of California (to kill as the Zodiac, as far as anyone knew), and Lass was last seen in Nevada. The Lake Tahoe area is not near the San Francisco Bay area, the Zodiac's usual hunting grounds, being a three-hour trek from San Francisco under favorable driving conditions. Unlike many previous Zodiac victims, Lass was not known to frequent Lover's Lane areas.

With the arrival of a strange card in the mail, everything changed. Lass's name was added to a list of possible Zodiac victims, despite the fact she worked in the Lake Tahoe area of Nevada, *outside* of California, despite the fact that she was never located, dead or alive, despite the fact that the card may not have originated with Northern California's most notorious serial killer, and despite the fact that the card presented no clear claim of credit for *any* attack.

A concrete connection between the Zodiac and Donna Lass has over the decades proven very elusive. Those who see in the circumstances of the missing nurse the work of the serial killer do so with very tenuous evidence. For Lass to have been killed by the Zodiac implies a number of facts that remain unknown and, at this point in time, apparently unknowable. It is not known, for instance, whether in fact she is dead. If dead, it is unknown whether she was murdered or was merely the victim of a tragic accident. She may even have purposefully left the area and made a new life for herself in some other place. Leaving your identity behind without telling anyone is an activity protected by the Constitution of the United States. Lass may well have utilized her Constitutional freedoms to relocate, for whatever reason.

However, while it is no crime to leave a difficult situation—or any situation—Lass was not the flighty type. Her friends and relatives described her as happy and dependable. It would have been out of character for her to leave in silence. She was sociable by nature, and deeply loved her family. Her relatives soon believed that she was dead. She would have contacted them if she were alive, they were convinced. The police suspected that she had been abducted and murdered, but they could not prove it.

Police Chief Ray Lauritzen of South Lake Tahoe, after his department took up the case, believed that Lass was no longer alive because it was not in her character to drop out of society as so many other young people were doing at the time. He described her as a good girl, not given to drugs and alcohol, and not the type of person who would cease communication with her family.

A reward of $10,000 was later offered for clues to Lass's whereabouts, a fund that would forever lay unclaimed. The newspaper quoted South Lake Tahoe Police Lieutenant John Crow saying that the case was still open but that all leads had been exhausted. No new information about her surfaced, and Donna Lass was eventually declared legally dead by a court decree when no new information about her surfaced.

Despite the differences between the Lass case and known Zodiac events, the young nurse may nevertheless have been a victim of the Zodiac serial killer.

A criminal *can* change his modus operandi (MO). Killers, including the Zodiac, can and do change many aspects of their attacks for a variety of reasons. They attempt to avoid detection so they will incorporate into future missions anything they can devise to increase the likelihood that they will elude capture. As they attempt to draw as much pleasure as they can while following their individual, twisted fantasies, they will often change as they experiment with new and varied ways of carrying out their assaults. They also learn from their mistakes.

If Lass was his victim, the Zodiac deviated from his usual patterns by venturing outside of the Bay area, by concealing a body (apparently), and by never overtly claiming credit. In one way only was it consistent with previous Zodiac attacks: her "demise" occurred at dusk or later on a weekend.

It may be only coincidental that prior to relocating to Stateline, Lass lived in San Francisco and worked at the Letterman General

Hospital, not far from the site of Paul Stine's murder. But it may suggest that the killer, if Lass was a Zodiac victim, had a strong connection with that neighborhood. The first time the Zodiac utilized a cab instead of driving his own vehicle and the first time a "victim" was targeted outside of California, the evidence led to the Presidio Heights District of San Francisco. Some armchair investigators would examine this link and develop a Zodiac suspect, but no conclusive evidence against him was ever established, not as the Zodiac and not for being responsible for the disappearance of the young nurse.

The Zodiac may have boasted about an attack on Lass. If he did so, his communication was veiled and cryptic. A postcard that *may* have come from the Zodiac *may* have referenced Lass. Like so much else in the Zodiac case, this communication—and the Lass disappearance itself—was open to interpretation.

The next two mailings included in the case files made no mention of Donna Lass, and gave no hint of the petite nurse's fate.

The Crack Proof card

Postmarked October, 5, 1970, a newly received postcard began, "Dear Editor: You'll hate me, but I've got to tell you." It contained other messages affixed to the card which, like the opening, were clipped from newspapers, including the date, "Mon., Oct. 5, 1970" and "I'm crackproof, What is the price tag now?" The FBI Field Office in San Francisco sent a photographed copy and a Xeroxed copy of the postcard to the FBI in Washington, D.C. They arrived October 15.

But the FBI was unable to find any hand printing, or anything else of significance that would enable them to compare this card to previously received Zodiac material. In its October 29 report, it was unable to conclude very much. All of the lettering was cut from the Monday, October 5 edition of *The San Francisco Chronicle*. A red cross had been affixed to the card, created from thin red paper. (It was not stained with blood, contrary to several reports.) The address on the front of the card, to which it was sent, "*The San Francisco Chronicle*," had been carefully excised from a copy of that newspaper and pasted to the card, giving no clue to its creator.

The FBI labeled the message side of the card Qc57, and the address side Qc58, reviewing the mailing on October 16. Nothing that would indicate the card's source was found.

As a possible Zodiac card, it has been a detective's problem child ever since its arrival. It may have been created and sent by the Zodiac. It may not have been. The Zodiac himself appeared to claim credit for it when, in a subsequent letter, he declared, "Like I have always said, I'm crack proof," implying that it was he who had previously made that boast. But he may instead have been attempting to co-opt the authoring of a phrase that had already been widely reported in the media. Investigators wondered whether the card was a hoax.

The Crack Proof card made no specific threats or claims, but appeared to use several sentences to boast of the Zodiac's continued killing. "Some of Them Fought It Was Horrible" was created out of headlines that already included single quotation marks around the words, and "The Pace isn't any slower! In fact it's just one big thirteenth" utilized several pieces of published material patched together. The cryptic information provided no direction for investigators, pointed to no specific victims, and may have been an empty taunt.

It also may not have come from the Zodiac, though it did contain the word "Zodiac" cut from a newspaper, and had a crosshairs symbol similarly borrowed from some media. There was no iconic phrase *"This is the Zodiac speaking,"* nor any familiar hand printing (or any writing at all) to link it to the Zodiac case. It may have been a meaningless hoax, and that is what investigators eventually suspected, even though they initially believed that it was an authentic Zodiac communication.

Chronicle reporter Paul Avery took the one-year anniversary of Paul Stine's murder, October 11, 1970, as an opportunity to write about the mysterious card, and for the first time share with his readers the Johns letter and the Torture letter, which had both been withheld from the public.

Once the information was released, the Zodiac's interest in *The Mikado* intrigued many, and led to speculation that his costume at Lake Berryessa was an attempt at parading himself as Ko-Ko, the Lord High Executioner, the prominent character in the light opera who sang the song quoted in the Torture letter. In time, the costume and the light opera became conflated into one single item, many coming to assume that they understood the meaning of the event at Lake Berryessa.

ᕯᕯ

On October 21, the Cincinnati Post and the Times Star Newspaper contacted the SFPD (who in turn passed the information on to the FBI), notifying them that a man had been arrested on a murder warrant by Butler County, Ohio. The suspected serial killer was booked in Cincinnati and charged with the murder of a 16-year-old girl whose body was mutilated with a superficial Z cut into her abdomen. Her left nipple had been excised. The suspect, who was also being investigated for his participation in other murders, had been in the San Francisco Bay Area in August, 1970, during which time two black prostitutes—23-year-old Brenda Vance on August 4, and Janice Smith, aged 22, on August 30—were found murdered in California while they were plying their trade. Both victims had been brutally executed with severe blows to the head. Smith was mutilated extensively, including the removal of her left nipple. Vance exhibited numerous burns to her torso and breasts. Investigators believed that they had each been moved at gunpoint to an abandoned dwelling before being callously murdered.

The man suspected in all of these killings was unwilling to discuss any other case until he was tried on the local murder. Regardless, the FBI opined that he might be willing to discuss his activities with Zodiac investigators, provided that there were no objections from the Butler County Sheriff's Department. Accordingly, the FBI requested that their Cincinnati Field Office contact the Butler County Sheriff's Office for major case prints, a photograph of the suspect, and the needed permission to interrogate him.

Notes passed between law enforcement agencies at the time of this possibly unrelated murder spree revealed new details about the FBI's participation in the Zodiac case. The Feds now attributed 7 murders to the Zodiac (possibly including the 2 San Jose stabbing victims). They had an extortion case against the perpetrator of the Zodiac murders, but noted that the "U.S. Attorney has indicated preference for prosecution by local authorities on murder charges."

On October 22, the FBI granted its Cincinnati Field Office permission to conduct a limited investigation into the new suspect. Prints had already been collected and were in custody. Unfortunately, the investigation could not immediately proceed. The Sheriff of Butler County refused to allow the interrogation of his prisoner because the suspect had been charged with first degree murder, and the Sheriff feared that an interview might prejudice the case he was building.

The Halloween card

The Chronicle received yet another mailing from the Zodiac serial killer in 1970. Addressed to "Paul Averly, S.F. Chronicle, 5th—Mission, S.F.," and postmarked October 27 somewhere within the city of San Francisco, a Gibson Greetings Cards Halloween card arrived on October 29. It was immediately turned over to the SFPD homicide detectives, who forwarded it to the CII in Sacramento. Handwriting expert and Questioned Documents Examiner Sherwood Morrill authenticated it the day after its arrival at *The Chronicle*. The FBI Field Office in San Francisco immediately sent a copy of the card and its envelope to its D.C. headquarters.

The stunningly visual document would become a notorious piece of evidence in the case because of the palpable threats it exuded. It was specifically directed to the attention of Chronicle reporter and columnist Paul Avery, who had by this time written virtually all of *The Chronicle*'s articles on the Zodiac, and who would become embroiled in, and forever attached to, the case.

The same day the Halloween card was received, a postcard which had been postmarked October 17, 1970 in Berkeley and sent to an address in Orinda, was submitted for analysis to the FBI by the SFPD. Like some previous Zodiac mailings, it bore cut out portions of newspapers and other publications. It began with the threat, "Monday, October 12…The Zodiac is going to…" The SFPD knew the card's author, and wanted him investigated as the Zodiac.

For some unknown reason, the FBI Laboratory did not receive the Halloween card until November 2. It recorded the results of its investigation on a work sheet the next day. Nothing of cryptographic significance was noted. It was a generic, ubiquitous greeting card, with the number "14," written on the hand of the skeleton on the

By FIRE

P
A
R

By GUN

SLAVES

By KNIFE

D
I
C
E

By ROPE

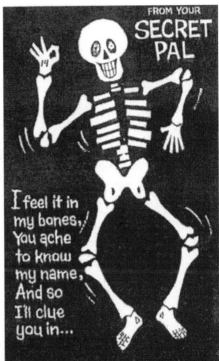

front of the card (which the FBI concluded was probably a claim regarding the number of victims), with several Zodiac symbols added inside and a few strange words and phrases. There were no extraneous markings and no cryptic texts.

The analysis of the three items—Qc59, the Berkeley postcard, Qc60, the Halloween card envelope, and Qc61, the Halloween card—came on November 12. There was no hand printing to compare in any of the three because the postcard was typed or created with cut-out portions of a newspaper, the Halloween card was artfully drawn rather than printed, and it contained too much distortion for a comparison to be effected. However, the Halloween card and its envelope *did* reveal enough detail to demonstrate some similarities to previous Zodiac letters.

The FBI forwarded the Halloween card and the postcard to its Cryptanalysis Unit for further evaluation. The postcard was eventually dismissed as a probable hoax.

The Halloween card may have been further evidence of a killer's psychological degeneration. Another jejune taunt in the form of a greeting card, this one marketed as a friendly jest to a friend or family member for the season of Halloween reinterpreted by the killer into a horrific threat. Much of its content remained mysterious and strange; what exactly the sender was attempting to communicate was not clear. Why the labor was put into supplementing the card with additional words, symbols, and visual enhancements was not obvious. It would have taken the killer considerable time and concerted effort to prepare the mailing, yet all that work was in vain if no clear message was conveyed or comprehended.

None was.

The preprinted words, "From your SECRET PAL I feel it in my bones, You ache to know my name, And so I'll clue you in…" on the front of the Card suggested that it was sent to Avery as a hint to his identity. Inside, the wording continued, "…But, then, why spoil the game?" The killer had previously sent a total of four ciphers, the first one with a cover letter containing the promise, "in this cipher is my iden[t]ity." While no putative encryption is present in the Halloween card mailing, questions arose as to the correct interpretation of many of the pieces of information contained within. What, for instance, did the writer mean by intersecting the large, heavy words "PARADICE" and "SLAVES," what did the many eyes carefully drawn on the interior of the card represent, and how were the vertical words "by fire," "by knife," "by gun," and "by rope" to be understood?

The killer may have been satisfied in sending a visually chilling taunt, complete with skeletons and Zodiac symbols. He knew it would be published in newspapers and shown on television for its emotional impact. Its enigmatic message only served to heighten its palpable threat, and maybe, investigators suspected, that was its intent.

The words added by the Zodiac on the interior, "PEEK-A-BOO YOU ARE DOOMED," "4-TEEN," and the number "14," written on the hand of the skeleton on the card's front, seemed to some a clear threat that the Zodiac had killed again or was threatening Paul Avery as his next target.

Fear led Avery to approach SFPD Police Chief Alfred J. Nelder and request a permit to carry a concealed weapon. He argued that he had gone through the SFPD police academy for a story and had received weapons training. Furthermore, his three-year stint as a war correspondent in Vietnam had caused him to sometimes handle guns. He was awarded the permit. (Avery coincidentally later used the .38 caliber handgun to break up an unrelated mugging in progress.) Avery carried the weapon for about a year by his own estimation. When his fears diminished, he relinquished it.

What precisely the killer was communicating with other symbols, such as the ones written across the bottom of the card's interior and a strange symbol on the envelope's return address, like so many aspects of the Zodiac case, provided a breadth of questions and a dearth of answers.

The envelope was nearly as mysterious as the card. Two identical sentences, "sorry no cipher," intersected one another in its interior, the killer perhaps regretful that he had prepared no new encryption for the investigation. The return address was replaced by a strange symbol that also occurred in the card's interior. Many of the card enhancements were drawn with white artist's ink, leading to speculation that the killer was somehow artistically inclined, or worked in a profession that made ample use of colored markers, white ink, squared paper, and felt-tipped pens.

At the card's receipt, investigators strongly believed that their quarry had killed no more than 5. No other murders could be attributed to him. However, because there were 8 unsolved murders in Northern California at the time, they couldn't categorically state that there were no more than 5 murders committed by the Zodiac. Even though he may have killed out of state or been responsible for accidents that he promised, the SFPD was working with the theory that the killer came so close to being caught after the murder of Stine that he became frightened enough to stop killing.

The San Francisco Chronicle gave front page coverage to the Halloween card and its associated threat on October 31. The story of the graphic card received worldwide attention due to its visual power. In it, many saw a real Halloween horror.

The Pines card

On March 22, 1971, approximately six months following the disappearance of Donna Lass and exactly one year after the Kathleen Johns event, a post office discovered in its system a postcard addressed to *The San Francisco Chronicle*. Postal officials noticed it and fished it out of circulation before it could be postmarked. Some interpreted the card as the Zodiac's claim of taking Nurse Lass as a victim. Like so much else in the Zodiac case, the Pines card spoke with an enigmatic message that was open to interpretation.

Despite the conclusions drawn by some, the card may not have originated with the Zodiac, and even if it did, it may not have referenced Donna Lass.

Addressed to reporter Paul Avery, as the Halloween card had been, the new mailing contained cryptic phrases cut from print media. An Abraham Lincoln four-cent stamp was affixed to a simple five-cent postcard. On the address side, three destinations for the card—"The Times," "S.F. Examiner," and *"San Francisco Chronicle"*—corresponded to the three papers that had each received one part of the three-part 408 cipher. These were apparently cut out of newspapers and affixed to the card. In case there was any question as to the identity its author, its creator had drawn crosshair symbols on both the front and back of the card. Above the crosshair symbol on the address side of the card, its creator had written "Zodiac." The four other handwritten words ("Attn. Paul Averly = Chronicle") included a spelling mistake: Avery had been spelled with an added L, "Averly," exactly as it had been on the envelope to the Halloween card. Avery interpreted the mistake as a taunt, and suspected that the killer was playing with the reporter's ego.

A large picture adorned the front of the card that was later identified as coming from the promotional material of a condominium village, named Forest Pines, at the time under development on the Nevada shore of Lake Tahoe. The ad, portraying an artist's rendition of houses among the trees at a project at Incline Village, had appeared the previous Sunday in several Northern California newspapers, including *The Chronicle*. Construction of the development had just begun.

Two phrases covered parts of the picture, "Sierra Club" and "around in the snow," both clipped from other media. To some, this was a clear indication that the Zodiac wrote about Lake Tahoe in general, and specifically Donna Lass, the only unsolved "murder" in the area. A punched hole in the top right corner of the card further suggested to some that Lass's body ought to be in the vicinity of the indicated location. Below the picture, but also on the front of the card, a number of words and phrases cut from newspapers were affixed: "Sought victim 12," "Peek through the pines" (in quotes), and "pass LAKE TAHOE areas."

The card was immediately turned over to SFPD inspectors Toschi and Armstrong. After some tests, it was forwarded to the Questioned Documents Section of the CII for further study.

Morrill confirmed for the CII on March 25 that the several inked words—only five on the address side of the postcard—belonged to the writer of the previous Zodiac letters. In his professional opinion, he believed that it was created and sent by the Zodiac. But it may not have been, others noted. Some opined that it was written by someone who wanted the Donna Lass disappearance linked to the Zodiac murder spree. Many people at the time had a motive for conflating the two cases, some of whom were still investigating the Zodiac crimes and others who yearned for Donna Lass to be found.

The Zodiac case was flagging. The killer had not killed (as far as anyone could determine) in nearly a year and a half. The Lass-related card may have been sent to revive a stalled investigation. Perhaps a law enforcement official wanted to highlight the Zodiac to further his career. SFPD Inspector Dave Toschi would in the late 1970s be accused of sending fake fan letters that promoted him. He would also be suspected of sending a forged Zodiac letter in 1978 to reignite the case.

The search for Lass had also lost steam. A devoted friend or family member, facing a desperate situation—a lack of new leads in the disappearance of a loved one—may have devised this ingenious effort to draw in outside help. The result was as much as any family member could have desired. The Pines card brought a new energy and renewed intensity to bear on the Lass mystery, a quest that persists to this day for a few amateur investigators.

At the time, the police also realized the possibility that the postcard was entirely unrelated to either Donna Lass or the Zodiac serial killer. It made no direct claims about the woman, not mentioning her name or any circumstances of her disappearance. In fact, a very specific interpretation was required to relate it to that case, one only achieved through great effort with a specific understanding of the vague hints conveyed by the card. It may instead have been another in a long line of cruel hoaxes the case has spawned.

If Lass was not a Zodiac victim, hers would not be the only "murder" that someone attempted to embellish with the Zodiac's infamy.

In April of 1970, Robert Michael Salem, a renowned designer and manufacturer of hurricane lamps, was found dead in his posh 745 Stevenson Street workshop-apartment in San Francisco. As the police entered the home, they noticed that Salem's killer had written near the body using the victim's blood, "Satan saves Zodiac." A crucifix symbol appeared drawn on a wall, and also on the stomach of the corpse.

It was in all probability a copycat trying to throw off detectives. Salem had been stabbed with long knife and nearly decapitated. His left ear had been taken from the scene. The house was thoroughly ransacked, and some money had been removed. His murderer had lingered at the scene long enough to take a shower. He had also turned the home's thermostat up to 90 degrees and then departed through the front door. *The San Francisco Chronicle* reported that it was San Francisco's 40th murder of 1970.

Even as early as October 1969, people were committing crimes and pawning them off as the deviant work of the Zodiac. Daniel Williams, a 24-year-old Martinez teacher who taught at Salesian High, a private Catholic high school in Richmond, California, reported receiving crank calls from someone claiming to the be the Zodiac. The teacher was threatened directly, and then he found a lethal dose of arsenic in an opened can of soda in his house. The police took the threats seriously but doubted that the Zodiac was in any way involved. *The Chronicle* reported on these eerie events on November 8, 1969.

എ

An article in the Sacramento Union, dated March 27, 1971, noted a possible link between the Lass case and the murder of two women in the state's capital. The Sacramento Sheriff's deputies disputed the claim that the Zodiac was responsible for the slayings of Judith Ann Hakari, 23, and Nancy Marie Bennallack 28, but Lieutenant Jerry Saulter, the Executive Officer of the Patrol Division, acknowledged that it was a possibility.

Hakari was a nurse who, like Lass, went missing after work on a weekend night. Her car remained at her apartment. Her body was found seven weeks later in a shallow grave near Weimar, outside of Sacramento. Benellack was found dead in her apartment on October 26 with her throat slashed. She had resided less than 200 yards from Hakari. Sheriff's Inspector Stanley Parsons noted that if the Zodiac had killed Donna Lass, there was a possibility that the killer was also responsible for the deaths of Hakari and Bennallack.

He would later walk back that statement, acknowledging that there was no evidence that the Zodiac was involved in any of the three deaths being investigated.

Any search for Lass in Tahoe, after the receipt of the tantalizing Pines card, would have to wait for the spring thaw. Police Chief Lauritzen, quoted in a Sacramento Union article on March 27, admitted that "we don't know where we're going to begin." There was four to five feet of snow already on the ground, and the flakes continued to fall at a steady pace. Only two feet of the white stuff was observed at Incline Village, the site pictured in the postcard, but a police visit to the area suggested a wait for the search until warmer weather.

The card appeared to reference a wooded area within Incline Village, indicated by the hole punched in the picture. It was explored and excavated numerous times in the succeeding decades, never shedding any light on the mysterious disappearance of Nurse Donna Lass.

11 | THE END

"He plunged himself into
the billowy wave
and an echo arose from
the su[i]cides grave"

The Zodiac eventually ceased his brutality, or at least, the evidence suggests that is the case. *When* exactly is a point of contention, and difficult to attribute to a particular date. Following the disappearance of Donna Lass in September of 1970, no additional attacks or missing persons were ever tied with any degree of certainty to the Zodiac serial killer, just as Lass herself was never unquestionably linked. As far as anyone knew, Paul Stine was the killer's final victim. But there may have been more.

It is not uncommon for investigators to harbor uncertainty about the total number of victims attributable to a serial killer. In fact, it may be the exception when a killer's exact body count is known or generally agreed upon. Gary Ridgeway, Seattle's Green River killer, was convicted for his part in 49 murders, but later confessed to nearly twice as many—and the true count may be an even larger number. Ted Bundy, who killed in Washington State before embarking on a cross-country spree, was charged with 30 murders. He once intimated that his actual number of victims was more than 100. Even though the Zodiac boasted of many more deaths than the 6 that can be tied to him, elevating the "score" in his letters over time to 37, the final two confirmed Zodiac letters—The L.A. Times letter and the Exorcist letter—appeared to offer some kind of closure for the perpetrator, even if the number of total victims remained unclear.

The remainder of documented information about the Zodiac comes to us from the content of letters, but it is not at all clear which of the many letters suspected to be from him actually are, and which of them are clever hoaxes or from other anonymous sources. Following the receipt of the graphics-laden Halloween card, the press received only two more undisputed letters from the serial killer. Other mailings of questionable provenance continued to arrive; consequently, the murderer's literary terminus is as unclear as the end of his killing.

The penultimate authenticated Zodiac communication, The L.A. Times letter of 1971, was sent one week prior to the arrival of the disputed Pines card—the mailing that appeared to implicate Donna Lass as a Zodiac victim. Like the Pines card, The L.A. Times letter would broaden the scope of the investigation and draw other deaths into the orbit of the serial killer.

The L.A. Times letter

On March 15, 1971, The L.A. Times letter, postmarked two days earlier in Alameda or its environs, entered the offices of the Los Angeles Times, the newspaper boasting the largest daily circulation on the West Coast. The envelope bearing two Roosevelt six-cent stamps was addressed, "The L.A. Times, Los Angeles Calif, Please Rush to Editor, AIR Mail." The other side of the envelope had "AIR Mail" in lettering larger than the front. The one-page note inside, scrawled in the now very-familiar Zodiac handwriting, offered very little specificity, and threatened to continue if the perpetrator were not caught.

By this time, few were taking the Zodiac's claims and threats very seriously. To the general public, the killing appeared to have stopped, and the letters were becoming stranger and less relevant. No one dared to dance in celebration, of course, for fear that it might provide the serial killer a motive to kill again. But as the public dreaded additional murders, none came.

This new letter appeared to have been composed in response to current events. Paul Avery, *The Chronicle* reporter who had written numerous stories about the Zodiac case and had received the eerie Halloween card from the Zodiac, received a series of tips, anonymous at first, but then signed, informing him that a murder in Southern California resembled a Zodiac hit. The connection between Cheri Jo Bates's death and the Zodiac was now being established.

The international attention given to the Halloween card had led Phillip Sins to make the connection. Sins first contacted the Riverside Police Department (RPD), but was rebuffed with his theory. He then contacted Avery and implored the reporter to investigate the similarities.

Avery contacted RPD Captain Irvin L. Cross and requested information on the Bates case. Within hours of receiving it, Avery was on a plane to Southern California to research the murder. He was most intrigued by the apparent "Z" on the bottom of two of the three Bates letters.

It was the press's first indication that the murder of Cheri Jo Bates was connected in any way to the Bay Area's Zodiac serial killer. Suddenly, all the evidence gathered in the wake of Bates's murder—the two Confession letters, the three Bates letters, the desktop poem, the latent prints, the cigarette butt, and the watch discovered near the crime scene—had to be incorporated into the Zodiac crime file. It greatly expanded the scope and understanding of the case.

Avery convinced Captain Cross and Sergeant David Bonine (the chief investigator of the RPD) to reopen the case in relationship to the Zodiac, since they could not prove a case against their local suspect. On Thursday, November 12, 1970, Avery hand-carried the carefully sealed Riverside handwriting evidence with a preserved chain of custody to Sherwood Morrill, the Questioned Documents Examiner for the CII in Sacramento.

The following Monday, November 16, the same day that Morrill confirmed that the Riverside handwriting was the work of the Zodiac, Avery authored a long article in *The Chronicle* about the Zodiac's murder in Southern California. Avery later speculated that the Zodiac never mentioned this murder (until he was exposed) because he must have made some mistake down there.

Two days later, Toschi and Armstrong, along with Ken Narlow of the Napa County Sheriff's Office, met with Captain Cross and ergeant Bonine at the Riverside Police Department in Southern California. Together, the investigators compared notes and shared that little information each had about their respective murder investigations. As a follow-up to the meeting, they scheduled handwriting comparisons, fingerprint comparisons, and a broader search for suspects whose activities had brought them in contact with both the northern and Southern California victims.

Some Riverside detectives would never be convinced that the murder of Bates was the work of the Zodiac. They felt confident, and would continue to feel in the following decades, that they knew who was responsible for the death of Cheri Jo Bates. They believed that they merely lacked the convincing proof that was required to bring local youth whom they believed was Bates's killer before a court of law. Cross in particular believed the local suspect was responsible, a position he had steadfastly held since 1968. The Press-Enterprise had run several stories declaring the department's firm belief.

News of the possible Zodiac connection to the murder of Cheri Jo Bates sent investigators scurrying to see whether any of the Riverside City College records contained a match with known Zodiac hand printing.

When the media reports linked the crimes, the killer emerged from his silence. Not to be outdone—and predictably on the move to control his own press—the Zodiac appeared to have been prodded to put pen to paper once again. The reason he wrote to the Times, rather than his usual San Francisco newspapers, the Zodiac claimed, was because the Southern California paper did not relegate him and his letters to "the back pages," an obvious dig at Bay Area papers who were not printing his material—or covering his story—to the degree they once had. Possibly the motive was attention, drawing it to himself once again with a new note to a new audience. If he had once hoped to keep the Bates murder from the notice of the authorities, now that it had been discovered, he may have felt that he had to get ahead of the story.

The new letter dripped with braggadocio. Beginning with the familiar, "This is the Zodiac speaking," he claimed that the "riverside activity" was merely one of "a hell of a lot more down there." The Zodiac was able to successfully regain control of the case because now investigators had to consider the possibility that he had committed some or many of the unsolved murders in Southern California. The necessary follow up may have been a fool's errand.

Notable on the page was a colloquial use of language not widely present in previous letters. The phrase "fiddle and fart" ridiculed the inactivity of the police, who were called "Blue Meannies." Either the killer was showing the true colors of his vernacular or he was now masking his identity with words and phrases that could be employed by a hippy, a member of the Manson Family, or someone involved with one of many other 1960s counter-culture groups.

On a single page, the Zodiac had scrawled,

```
The is the Zodiac speaking
Like I have allways said
I am crack proof. If the
Blue Meannies are evere
going to catch me, they had
best get off their fat asses
& do something. Because the
longer they fiddle & fart
around, the more slaves
I will collect for my after
life. I do have to give them
credit for stumbling across
my riverside activity, but
they are only finding the
easy ones , there are a hell
of a lot more down there.
The reason that Im writing
to the Times is this, They
dont bury me on the back pages
like some of the others.
SFPD—0 [crosshair symbol]—17+
```

The murdered Cheri Jo Bates has languished in the category of "possible Zodiac victims" by many researchers who are unconvinced that the Zodiac was responsible. Despite the fact that copious pieces of internal evidence link the Confession letter to the other Zodiac writings, despite the killer's claim of responsibility, despite the fact that many police officers were quite certain that the writer of the

Confession letters was also responsible for the killing of the coed, and despite the authentication of the Bates letters and the desktop poem as genuine Zodiac communications, the Zodiac may have claimed credit for a murder he did not commit. He may have had nothing to do with the communications either, a fact held by some, though Sherwood Morrill has positively identified the Bates letters and the desktop poem as matching Zodiac's writing. If the Zodiac falsely claimed Bates's murder, he took a great risk in taking responsibility for the death before 30 days had passed. Had someone else been arrested as her killer, the Zodiac would have ended up looking rather foolish. Bates's killer was not identified following the sending of the Confession letter; he never was identified.

Even as late as the 1980s, many in the RPD refused to consider the Zodiac responsible for Bates's murder. The police department was following up on a suspect, and the Bay Area authorities were attempting to tighten the noose around the neck of their suspect, named Arthur Leigh Allen. Since Allen was not responsible for Bates's murder, it could not have been a Zodiac killing, the logic went. When neither the Riverside youth nor Allen panned out as good suspects in the murders for which they were investigated—and the evidence against each of them proved very weak—many authorities once again began to consider the links that conflated the killings into a single case.

☙

No one remembers why the case's main suspect was brought to the attention of law enforcement in the first place.

On October 6, 1969, Detective Lynch first contacted Allen at the suspect's place of employment, Elmer Cave School in Vallejo. He could not recall years later what circumstances led him to interview Allen. Upon questioning Allen in relation to the Lake Berryessa attack, the balding 35-year-old explained that he had gone skin diving at Salt Point Ranch on September 26, and had not returned to Vallejo until between 2:00 and 4:30 in the afternoon of September 27. He stayed home the rest of the day, though he could not recall whether or not his parents were home at the time. He was a part-time student at Vallejo Junior College, and worked part time as a custodian at Elmer Cave. Living with his parents at 32 Fresno Street in Vallejo, the corpulent suspect was six feet one inch tall and 241 pounds.

Over time, other pieces of circumstantial evidence would link Allen to the Zodiac serial killer crimes, much of which the suspect himself offered to investigators Toschi, Armstrong, and Mulinax during a surprise interview on August 4, 1971 at Allen's new place of employment, the Pinole refinery of Union Oil of California. A former friend, Donald Cheney, reported to the police that before the attacks in the Vallejo area, his friend had shared with him that he (Allen) was planning to become a killer. Cheney claimed that his friend indicated to him that he would use the name "Zodiac"—coined from a watch that had been gifted to him by his mother—and attack random victims who would be impossible to connect to him. The diving watch included a crosshair or "Zodiac" symbol on its face in addition to the printed word "Zodiac."

Cheney's claims were cast into suspicion when it was revealed that the suspect had been accused of making inappropriate sexual advances toward Cheney's own child. Investigators had to consider that Cheney invented the story to frame his former friend. Nevertheless, George Bawart of the Vallejo Police Department (VPD) created a document listing 30 links connecting Allen to the Zodiac crimes. None of the 30 points were anything more than circumstantial.

A search warrant was executed on Allen's Vallejo home, but nothing conclusively tied him to the murders. In 1991, when Mageau was shown a photo lineup of men that included the suspect, he first picked out Allen as his attacker, indicating an 8 out of 10 level of confidence in his selection. However, Mageau then pointed to another photograph and said that his attacker had a large head like the man in that second photo. It was not deemed a conclusive identification.

Allen was exhaustively researched and investigated. His handwriting—of either hand, in case he was ambidextrous—did not match that of the Zodiac letters, his fingerprints matched none collected in the case, and warranted searches of his home and trailer provided no forensic match. He was subjected to interviews, multiple handwriting tests, and background checks. A partial DNA profile of the killer was obtained from authenticated Zodiac letters in 2002, when technology enabled small quantities of old saliva to be detected and sequenced. It excluded Allen, whose brain tissue had been preserved following his death in 1992. Most investigators, however reluctantly, looked beyond the case's prime suspect, realizing that there was no more proof that he was the Zodiac than there was evidence that he was the assassin of President John F. Kennedy. Some investigators steadfastly refused to entertain the possibility that Allen was not somehow involved in the series of murders, the circumstantial evidence looming large in their minds.

ભ

In The L.A. Times letter, the Zodiac opened a can of worms when he claimed there were additional victims in Southern California, "There are a hell of a lot more down there." Although the boast could have been a red herring, there *were* unsolved murders in Southern California—many unsolved murders—that could have been the responsibility of the Zodiac. One attack in particular paralleled the Zodiac event on the edge of Lake Berryessa.

On June 4, 1963, 18-year-old Robert Domingos took his 17-year-old fiancée, Linda Edwards, to a remote beach on the Pacific Ocean, near Santa Barbara. They skipped school on the annual "ditch day," two days before graduation, to spend some time alone. The next evening, the couple was found dead of gunshot wounds. Domingos suffered 11 shots; Edwards, 9. Both died from massive damage and blood loss as a result of the Winchester Western .22 caliber Super X copper-coated long rifle bullets, fired from a semi-automatic. Their hands were bound with cords. Edwards' bathing suit had been sliced to expose her breasts. Their bodies had been dragged to, and stacked into, a small shack located away from the beach. Their assailant had apparently unsuccessfully attempted to burn down the shack with matches to conceal any evidence in the murders.

After the link was established between Bates murder and the Zodiac killings in Northern California, this double murder came under increased scrutiny. The similarities to the Zodiac attack at Lake Berryessa, September 27, 1969, were obvious. Both had been carried out on a couple, in a remote area, alongside water, with possibly pre-cut lengths of cord, and with a gun and a sharp instrument present. Similarities to other Zodiac attacks were apparent in the use of the Winchester Western bullets—the same type used to kill Faraday and Jensen on December 20, 1968—and the use of fire, also employed after the apparent attack on suspected Zodiac victim Kathleen Johns. The couple's last minute, unannounced trip to a secluded location followed the same unplanned itinerary as the attacks at Lake Herman Road, Blue Rock Springs Park, and Lake Berryessa.

The investigation acknowledged that it may not have been a Zodiac attack. Arguing against it was a lack of follow-up letter or telephone call, a lack of a specific claim of involvement, and a moving of the bodies, all of these details being substantial differences between this attack and those of known Zodiac killings. Until the case is solved—and more than five decades have already passed—investigators believe that it will in all likelihood remain a suspected Zodiac double murder.

But the Zodiac was not the only serial killer operating in California in that era. In 1972 and 1973, seven female hitchhikers went missing in Sonoma County, part of San Francisco's North Bay. Six of the victims turned up dead, each dumped nude into a creek or a ravine close to a roadway. The series came to be known as the Santa Rosa Hitchhiker murders due to the similarities between the deaths.

Maureen Sterling and Yvonne Weber were 12-year-old students of Herbert Slater Middle School. On February 4, 1972, after leaving the Redwood Empire Ice Arena in Santa Rosa, they hitchhiked on Guerneville Road. Their bodies were discovered on December 28 on Franz Valley Road. Already dead, they had been tossed down an embankment. The badly decomposed corpses would not reveal a cause of death.

Kim Wendy Allen was last seen hitchhiking to school on March 4, 1972 at the Bell Avenue entrance to Highway 101. The Santa Rosa Junior College student was 19. Her body was located the next day twenty feet off Enterprise Road in Santa Rosa, also down an embankment. She had been raped, her hands and feet bound. The cause of death was ligature strangulation that lasted an estimated 30 torturous minutes.

Thirteen-year-old Lawrence Cook Middle School student Lori Lee Kursa ran away from home November 11, 1972. She was last seen on November 21 by friends in Santa Rosa. She may have been observed while two men aggressively pushed her into a van. Her body was found in a ravine off of Calistoga Road in Santa Rosa on December 14. She was known to have hitchhiked in the past.

Carolyn Nadine Davis was last seen hitchhiking on July 15, 1973 on Highway 101 in Garberville. The 14-year-old's remains were discovered on July 31 almost exactly where Sterling and Weber had been located seven months earlier. Surprisingly, the cause of death was listed as strychnine poisoning.

On December 22, 1973, Theresa Diane Smith Walsh hitchhiked at Zuma Beach in Malibu. The 23-year-old was planning to go to Garberville for a family Christmas. She was found six days later in Mark West Creek. She had been tied with rope, sexually assaulted, and strangled.

The seventh victim's remains were found off of Calistoga Road in Santa Rosa on July 6, 1979. The approximately 19-year-old woman was never identified.

Two additional possible victims—Lisa Smith, 17, of Petaluma, and Jeannette Kamahele, 20, of Santa Rosa—were eventually added when the two young women went missing, March 16, 1971 and April 25, 1972, respectively. Their bodies were never found.

The Santa Rosa Hitchhiker murders became part of a much larger set of killings that occurred across a region as far north as Redding and as far south as Monterey, including several in or near San Francisco. In 1975, the FBI reported on a total of 14 homicides between the years of 1972 and 1974, claiming that they were all conclusively linked. This case was never solved. Though some have attempted to link these murders to those of the Zodiac serial killer, no compelling evidence has ever been uncovered to conflate the two cases. And obvious behavioral and circumstantial evidence strongly suggested that at least two separate killers were independently responsible for the carnage.

Following the receipt of The L.A. Times letter, the Zodiac serial killer disappeared as completely and as mysteriously as the three men who had escaped the Federal prison on Alcatraz Island on June 11,

1962, shortly before the institution shuttered its cells for good. But unlike Frank Morris and the Anglin brothers, the Zodiac would reappear. He was silent for almost three years. While the investigation metastasized into Southern California, work continued in the Bay Area to collect evidence, investigate suspects, and develop new leads. The Zodiac would not write for another thirty-four months.

Suddenly, in January of 1974, the Bay Area was startled out of its complacency with yet another authentic Zodiac letter.

The Exorcist letter

The last authenticated Zodiac letter, the Exorcist letter, arrived on the 30th of January, 1974. The envelope bore a single Eisenhower eight-cent postage stamp. It was addressed, "San Fran. Chronicle, Please Rush To Editor." Curiously, three stickers had been affixed to the envelope's front, each apparently removed from the packaging that contained the stamp. One said, "USE Zip code;" the other two contained information about the book of stamps. Postmarked Tuesday, January 29, from somewhere in either San Mateo County or Santa Clara County, this new mailing was written in blue from a felt-tipped pen. The letter comprised a single, white sheet of paper. The SFPD processed the letter and retained possession of it, the San Francisco FBI Field Office sending to Washington, D.C. photocopies of the letter, the bottom portion of the letter that revealed a palm print, and the dusted envelope containing fingerprints.

The Zodiac had written the following:

```
I saw & think "The Exorcist"
was the best saterical com-
idy that I have ever seen.

   Signed , yours truly :

He plunged him self into
The billowy wave
and an echo arose from
the sucides grave
   titwillo titwillo
     titwillo

Ps. if I do not see this
```

340

note in your paper, I
will do something nasty,
which you know I'm capable of
doing.

[unidentified symbols]
Me—37
SFPD - 0

I saw + think "The Exorcist"
was the best saterical com-
idy that I have ever seen.

Signed, yours truley :

He plunged him self into
the billowy wave
and an echo arose from
the sucides grave
      titwillo   tit willo
            titwillo

Ps. if I do not see this
   note in your pape-, I
   will do something nasty,
   which you know I'm capable of
   doing

This new letter appeared to present some kind of end for the Zodiac. Letters received after this one differ in two very distinct ways. First, apart from a likely forgery in 1978, they did not claim to come from the Zodiac, and therefore did not contain the familiar Zodiac scrawl, the crosshairs symbol, the word *Zodiac*, or the iconic phrase, "This is the Zodiac speaking." Second, related to the first, they appeared to be mundane, banal letters to the editor with no apparent or implied threat, no claim of past violence, and minor, if any, demands from the author. If they were from the serial killer known as the Zodiac, they were of a very different tone and demeanor, and did not bear the hallmarks of his previous letters. Either he was attempting to slip these past editors so that he could see his "non-Zodiac" words in print, or he was demonstrating that he was no longer a killer or a threat to society. If they were his, he had once again undergone a bold transformation—or eagerly wanted others to believe that he had.

By this time, the FBI could attribute 6 murders to the Zodiac, accepting Bates as a victim on the strength of the Zodiac's 1971 claim to *The L.A. Times* and the similarities in writing style, as well as the behavioral links between Bates's murder and the murders of the other victims. Written and sent while the nation was relishing its love affair with the blockbuster movie The Exorcist, this new note was an apparent attempt to co-opt the attention garnered by the major motion picture. Perhaps the killer emerged from his three-year absence as a direct result of so much praise being lavished on a horror movie. But there was a much more immediate horror in the Bay Area just prior to the letter's arrival.

For two hours on January 28, 1974, two men went on a rampage—not unlike the one threatened by the Zodiac in 1969 in the 3-Part letters—that resulted in the deaths of 4 individuals. This spree was one small portion of a string of racial murders that became known as the Zebra killings, and took place between October, 1973 and April, 1974. All told, 16 people were killed and between 8 and 10 were wounded. Four men were eventually caught and convicted of the murders. The January 28 violence led the headlines and was the talk of the town. The Exorcist letter was postmarked the following day, and received by *The San Francisco Chronicle* the day after that. The Zodiac may not have wanted his carnage of the past to be overshadowed by this recent crime wave, though he never made any mention of it.

The killer *did* reference the new horror film. The churlish tone of the single sentence that began the letter, and comprised its body, suggested that the killer was sarcastically boasting of his own ability to enact a horror. He seemed to deny his own fear of the scary film by condemning it to the category of "sat[i]rical com[e]dy."

Ironically, while the Zodiac classified the frightening movie *The Exorcist* as a satirical comedy, he treated *The Mikado* as some kind of horror. He quoted the latter in threat, and alluded to it in an attempt to dominate his readers, even though the play itself contained no killing, merely humorous threats to kill. No one actually died during its performance. Rather than a horror, *The Mikado* is a love story and a farce that lampoons British high society and its prudish mores and pompous bureaucracy. So the killer interpreted horror as satire and satire as horror.

The design of the letter was as odd as its message. His normally messy writing was juxtaposed against a very complex page layout. Where one would expect a usual tabulation at the beginning of paragraphs, the writer instead provided a sophisticated use of literary presentation. The letter exhibited a structure as if it were created by an editor or professional writer. The first sentence, sans the salutation or iconic phrase that the police had come to expect, concluded with a sign-off that was roughly centered on the page. Its writer may not have known how to spell, but he was evidently well versed in the signatory portion of a missive. "Signed Yours Tru[l]y:" ended with a telling colon. Used correctly, it led the reader to the next section of the letter, defining who the Zodiac was, or at least providing the title he was willing to apply to himself. The Zodiac apparently self-identified with a quote from *The Mikado*, this one nearly perfectly reproduced.

The note ended with a vituperative P.S. demanding that the letter be published, with an accompanying vague threat if it was not. As so many of his previous threats were never carried out, few paid the words much heed.

At the very bottom of the page the writer inked several unusual shapes, including a heavy dot, a dot with a "tail," some thick lines, and what looked like a large "I," roughly the shape of a tiny cucumber. The ambiguous picture has come to form a Rorschach test slide, researchers positing many, many possibilities as to what the shapes must mean. Whether these mysterious markings contained any information at all, such as a visual puzzle, or were presented as a red herring was never established.

Investigators found many perplexing aspects to the letter.

There was no familiar rhetoric. There was no use of the word "Zodiac" nor the killer's iconic phrase, "This is the Zodiac speaking." There was no crosshairs symbol, and where one would be expected, in his running tally of victims, he instead used the simple word "Me." It was a most peculiar Zodiac letter, separated by nearly three years from the killer's last note.

The words "su[i]cides grave" from *The Mikado* quote led readers to infer that the Zodiac had committed a suicide, either literally or metaphorically. The verse, almost exactly a quote from *The Mikado* Opera, was correctly indented from the left margin, each line following an identical indentation. The two lines of the song were correctly divided, the start of the second line flush with the indented left side of the page. The final three words, a three-fold repetition of the word "titwillo" was the only portion of the verse that was transcribed incorrectly. Instead of what appeared, the first word should have been replaced with "Oh willow," and the other two appended with a final "w": "Oh willow, tit willow, tit willow." Yet, even with these shortcomings, a complex layout was apparent. The three words were carefully set in a poetic display, centered on the lines: two words on the first line; the final word centered on the final line.

The P.S. with which the letter closed was indented correctly following the rules of bullet points. It was left justified and the lines of the message were each indented. Even the letter's "score keeping" was slick. It was right justified on the last two written lines of the page.

Investigators did not know how to interpret this new missive. More questions emerged than answers. Why, for instance, after nearly three years of silence, did the Zodiac deem it necessary to write again? What did the markings at the bottom of the page signify, if anything? And was this the last letter that would be received?

From the professional structure of the words on the page, it appeared that the Zodiac was copying from a printed version of *The

Mikado, and not recalling words stored in his mind. All the man hours that the police spent interviewing Mikado actors and members of troupes who staged the play in the late 1960s, as well as the technical support staff for these companies, led nowhere in pursuit of a criminal who may have once again outsmarted his pursuers. Maybe he owned a printed copy of *The Mikado*, but had copied it slightly incorrectly to frustrate the investigation.

Though SFPD experts had declared it authentic, and the document examiner in Sacramento believed that it was from the Zodiac, the SFPD nevertheless asked Washington, D.C., in a letter dated February 14, to compare the Exorcist letter to previous Zodiac writing. The next day, the FBI laboratory declared that all the threatening letters, including a photocopy of this new one, Qc63, along with a photocopy of its envelope, Qc62, were probably from the same hand. Even though certain threatening letters were not written as freely as others, and most of the specimens in its possession were photocopies, some of which were not clear, the FBI laboratory declared the new material authentic, "Hand printing characteristics indicate all of the threatening letters, including [the Exorcist letter and its envelope] were probably prepared by one person." The lab promised to provide cryptanalysis separately.

Also on Valentine's Day, the FBI field office in Sacramento in an airtel to the FBI laboratory in Washington, D.C. requested the examination and analysis of the strange symbols that appeared across the bottom of the Exorcist letter, as well as the courtesy follow-up of a report on its findings to the Sacramento and the San Francisco Field Offices. But no clear interpretation of the marks could be developed. The March 1 reply from the lab suggested that some of them bore characteristics of Chinese or Japanese writing, but they were not complete radicals. The middle portion of the letter was identified as a quote from *The Mikado* by Gilbert and Sullivan. Portions of *The Mikado* had been previously quoted in specimens, the report noted.

Earlier, on February 6, the FBI had prepared for the benefit of its Los Angeles Field Office a summary of the Zodiac case, which now included the Riverside murder of Cheri Jo Bates. All but the murder of Bates were committed within the regions served by the San Francisco and Sacramento divisions, which had, at the prompting of the police agencies of jurisdiction (i.e. the VPD, Solano County Sheriff's Office,

SFPD, and Napa County Sheriff's Office), requested examinations by the FBI Laboratory and FBI Identification Divisions. As a result, the FBI lab possessed several samples of the Zodiac's hand printing, and the FBI identification Division, Latent Fingerprint Section held some latent prints on file, noting that "some or all of these latent prints may belong to the "ZODIAC." The January 29 letter is being processed, and if authenticated, will [be] added to the material held by the laboratory and Identification Division."

The report noted that no questioned writing or latent prints from Riverside had ever been submitted to the FBI lab or to the Identification Division. Apparently, the Riverside detectives felt no need to expand the scope of its investigation or bring in outside assistance. The request was finally made for Riverside to submit its materials to the FBI laboratory for evaluation.

On February 21, the Latent Fingerprint Section provided the FBI Sacramento Field Office with a report on the status of the case. Thirty-nine latent fingerprints, eleven latent palm prints, and two latent impressions (fingerprint or palm prints) previously reported remained unidentified. A number of individuals had been compared but no identifications were effected. Ten additional fingerprints were previously identified with elimination prints. With due caution, the report added, "Unless comparisons are conducted with the known prints of 'Zodiac,' it is not possible to determine if any of the previously reported prints are his." It further noted that it was also not possible to determine which fingers made most of the previously reported prints; therefore, it was not possible to create a composite set of prints that could be classified and searched in the main fingerprint file. Not only did the prints not match anyone, but they did not match one another from crime scene to crime scene: "Comparable areas of unidentified latent prints previously reported on items from different crime scenes, as well as latent prints on different envelopes and letters, were compared with each other, but no identifications effected."

With the sending of the Exorcist letter, the Zodiac went quiet. Or did he?

Another Transition

The Zodiac may have undergone a second metamorphosis following the writing of the Exorcist letter in January, 1974. The killer of 6, and maybe more, may have resurfaced with additional pseudonyms. Eschewing his usual the "Zodiac" as his title, he may have re-established communication under the new monikers "Red Phantom," "A citizen," and "a friend."

In the same year that it received the Exorcist letter, *The Chronicle* was sent three additional strange notes. They were recognized for the oddness that they represented, both in terms of their messages and their anonymity. Carefully fished out from among other pieces of mail by the Post Office, they were each turned over to the police for a closer examination. Sherwood Morrill, by now retired as the Questioned Document Examiner for the State of California, still kept a close eye on the case, and offered his services whenever they were needed. He quickly identified familiar characteristics in the handwriting of their author, and deemed them authentic Zodiac letters, albeit with no reference to the Zodiac, his past crimes, or any future threats. It was as if, opined the retired examiner, he hoped to slip these letters past the editors of the papers and past investigators.

Three 1974 letters

If authentic—and there was much dispute about whether they were or not; few serious graphologists would offer a settled opinion on such short samples of handwriting—the three letters revealed that the Zodiac was capable, and willing, to proffer multiple personae.

SLA letter

The early half of the 1970 was an assuredly radical time in California. One radical organization that arose was the Symbionese Liberation Army which earned media attention through multiple criminal acts. Most notably, the Symbionese Liberation Army or SLA kidnapped and brainwashed newspaper heiress, Patty Hearst.

Postmarked February 3, 1974, the SLA letter was contained within an envelope that bore one Eisenhower eight-cent stamp and the hand printed address, "Editor *San Francisco Chronicle*, San Francisco, California." The FBI labeled the two items Qc64 and

Qc65. The FBI lab's analysis concluded that sufficient characteristics in the writing made it impossible to determine whether the letter and the envelope were written by the Zodiac. At the same time, no clear evidence existed that someone else wrote them. In other words, it may have been a Zodiac letter, but it may not have been.

The short missive stated simply,

```
Dear Mr. Editor,
    Did you know that the
initials SLAY (Symbionese
Liberation Army) spell "sla,"
an old Norse word
meaning "kill."
    a friend
```

What exactly the editor was meant to do with the information was not explained. It was vaguely Zodiac-like in its reference to "kill" and in the author's apparent arrogance. It yielded no fingerprints or other identifying data, so it was set aside as inconclusive, and possibly irrelevant, to the investigation. The investigation noted that the word "kill" was underlined, and a period rather than an appropriate question mark completed the sentence.

If it was a Zodiac letter, it may have been a reference to the Zebra killings of the previous month, or something prompted by the SLA group that was making headlines at that time. It is equally possible that it was sent by some helpful citizen who noticed an interesting, but most likely irrelevant, connection between the name of a terrorist group and an Old Norse vocabulary word.

Badlands Postcard

Three months later a postcard arrived. Postmarked May 6 and hand addressed to *The Chronicle* ("Editor, SF Chronicle, 5th & Mission, San Fran"), the eight-cent Samuel Adams, pre-stamped card read as follows:

```
Sirs-I would like to
express my
consternation concerning
your poor taste & lack of
```

```
sympathy for the public, as
evidenced by your running
of the ads for the movie
"Badlands," featuring the
blurb - "In 1959 most people
were killing time. Kit & Holly
were killing people." In
light of recent events, this
kind of murder -glorification
can only be deplorable at
best (not that glorification of
violence was ever justifiable)
why don't you show some
concern for public sensibilities
& cut the ad?

    A citizen
```

Numerous Zodiac-like details suggested that it might have come from the killer. The reference to killing, the subject matter of a movie—similar to the Exorcist letter—and the generous use of ampersands instead of the word "and" were each very familiar to investigators who had poured over the Zodiac's many letters.

Other details suggested that the postcard may not have been from the Bay Area's most infamous serial killer. The criticism of violence and the concern for "public sensibilities" were entirely new and ironic for such a violent criminal, if it was penned by the Zodiac. Also, the keen sense of spelling, and the correct use of grammar and punctuation, was very unlike the other Zodiac communications.

Like the SLA letter, the Badlands postcard was set aside. Its stunning content—unexpected abhorrence of violence and holier-than-thou attitude—led investigators to question whether it was from the Zodiac, and to puzzle over what it might mean if it *were* from him.

Count Marco letter

The third and final suspected Zodiac letter of 1974 was postmarked July 8. Its envelope was addressed "Editor, *San Francisco Chronicle*, San Francisco, California." The single, white page inside read as follows:

```
Editor—
Put Marco back in the, hell-hole
from whence it came—he has
a serious psychological disorder—
always needs to feel superior. I
suggest you refer him to a shrink.
Meanwhile, cancel the Count Marco
column. Since the Count can
write anonymously, so can I --
    The Red Phantom
    (red with rage)
```

If from the Zodiac, the Badlands postcard introduced hypocrisy: a killer who deplored even the mention of violence. This new letter, if it was from the killer, doubled down. It was an appalling case of irony, the pot calling the kettle black. A vicious and brutal serial killer was accusing a newspaper columnist of having a "serious psychological disorder." Possibly from the irate tone of the words and nothing more, investigators were intrigued by the possibility that this could have come from their quarry. The arrogance and the need to write anonymously were both noticeably familiar.

The missive could have been written in response to one of two (or both) recent columns that Count Marco had published in *The Chronicle*: "Is Being Called Sexy Degrading?" which appeared on Thursday, July 4, 1974, or "Why Older Men Have Trouble In Bed," appearing on the following Monday.

The FBI Field Office in San Francisco finally sent three copies each of the Count Marco envelope, the Count Marco letter, the Badlands postcard signed "a citizen," and the reverse side of the Badlands postcard, in an airtel dated August 16, to the FBI in Washington, D.C., along with a request to compare the collection with the previously filed Zodiac material to determine whether it too was created by the killer. By this time, they were being represented in the press as authentic Zodiac notes. The items were eventually labeled Qc77 to Qc80. The envelope of the Count Marco letter, bearing an illegible postmark, read simply, "Editor, *San Francisco Chronicle*, San Francisco." The postcard, postmarked "POSTAL SERVICE, CA 945 P 8 May 74," was addressed "Editor SF Chronicle 5th & Mission San Fran."

The FBI in Washington, D.C. replied on September 6. The lab was not as confident as the press in the material's origin. It noted that differences of the Marco letter suggested but did not prove that the letter was composed by someone other than the Zodiac. It was not definitively determined whether the Badlands postcard was written by the Zodiac, but "similarities were noted that indicate the card was probably prepared by the writer of the Zodiac letters."

1978 Letter

In early 1978, a new letter purporting to be from the Zodiac arrived at the offices of *The San Francisco Chronicle* to the astonishment of investigators and news reporters alike. If it could be proven to be from the Bay Area serial killer, it was the first time that the Zodiac had communicated in nearly four years. It meant that the killer was alive, not incarcerated (unless of course the letter was cleverly spirited out of prison with the help of an accomplice), and active in promoting himself. It also meant the killing may not have stopped.

But the long gap in writing, and some details of the new communication, gave investigators a reason to be cautious. Postmarked April 24 and received the next day, the one-page hand-printed letter, together with its envelope, was immediately presented to the SFPD to be processed by its laboratory. It was forwarded to the FBI on May 15, with the information that the SFPD lab had already processed it for prints and indentations.

Though it had been more than four years since authorities had last heard from the serial killer, the one-page letter represented itself as an authentic Zodiac communication, complete with the familiar opening line, "This is the Zodiac speaking." Like all of the previous Zodiac letters that were received after the Stine letter, it also omitted the period from the end of the iconic phrase, cum title. In a familiar uneven script resembling the Belli letter, the writer presented a tone and a series of threats eerily similar to that of the Zodiac's body of work. Either the Zodiac had returned from retirement or someone who had a great deal of knowledge about the case had sent a copycat, hoax letter. Either way, it was huge news.

If fake, it was by no means the first phony Zodiac letter. Not by a long shot. For the previous decade, the case seemed to bring out every attention seeker, armchair comedian, and manipulative wag, who each needed to add to the story or simply enhance its mystique. Many forged Zodiac letters arrived at the offices of the press, the police, or even the anonymous citizen. Most were easy to recognize for their poorly copied handwriting, their un-Zodiac-like tone, or their fanciful flights into decidedly non-Zodiac topics; few were as carefully prepared as this one.

Reporters from media outlets that longed for the former, head-line-rich days of dealing with the Bay Area killer swarmed police officials, digging for quotes, insights and, above all, new informa-tion about the murderer. Dave Toschi, now working alone on the case since Armstrong's transfer to fraud detail, was suddenly in great demand for comment. But the renewed attention came at a great cost to the investigator—and the investigation.

Former Chronicle serialist Armistead Maupin was among the first to raise doubts about the new missive's authenticity. Two years earlier, following his use of Toschi as a resource for his Tales of the City fictional serial, he had received fan mail stemming from a col-umn that featured a character based on SFPD Inspector Dave Toschi. The subplot was added to provide suspense to the serial and readers to the column. His suspicions about these fan letters were aroused when he noted typewriter similarities among all of them. This new Zodiac letter bore some similarities to the letters he had received: in particular, it identified Dave Toschi by name. Maupin approached SFPD administrators with his concerns.

The Examiner reported that the Internal Affairs Division of the SFPD had investigated the matter, but Captain John Mahoney, head of that division, declined to comment. The SFPD Chief of Police also refused to give a statement, as did officers in the Intelligence Division who also participated in the investigation. In spite of their silence to the media, the administrators had found malfeasance in Toschi's activities.

Toschi was identified as the writer of the fan mail. When con-fronted, he readily admitted to penning several letters in 1976 in support of Maupin's serial, which debuted with Toschi's namesake character on September 10. In what the investigator later described as "harmless fan letters," he had praised his representation in the author's column. The letters had requested additional escapades featuring the character. Toschi had been exposed promoting himself behind the scenes. Though deeply embarrassed and ashamed, he adamantly denied any involvement with the new Zodiac letter, however, calling it "totally absurd" that he could have written it. A "high" official at the SFPD acknowledged to the press that there was no evidence that Toschi was responsible for creating the 1978 Zodiac letter.

Nevertheless, on July 11, Toschi was relegated to pawn detail, a horrendous purgatory for such a high profile detective who had single-handedly overseen the SFPD investigation into the Zodiac for the previous two years. By the time he was removed from his post, Toschi had run down over 3,000 leads and looked into the backgrounds of over 2,500 suspects. Within 24 hours of Toschi being removed from his position for the fan mail, Deputy Chief of Investigations Clement DeAmicis initiated a secret investigation into him as the possible author of the new Zodiac note.

A hastily-formed Zodiac investigation team—comprising Toschi, Inspector James Tedesco, and Inspector James Deasy—established in April, 1978, had also led to doubt about whether the Zodiac had authored the new note.

But the handwriting experts could not agree. Robert Prouty, chief of the Questioned Documents Section of the CII, said he didn't think the April letter was genuine Zodiac. He explained that there were so many differences that it must have been produced by another hand. Morrill disagreed. Now retired and in private practice, he declared that if Toschi wrote the last letter, he wrote them all, and was himself the Zodiac. He vouched for Toschi's honesty (as well as Armstrong's). In proclaiming the authenticity of the 1978 letter, he agreed with John Shimoda, Director of the Postal Service Crimes Laboratory, Western Regional Office, in San Bruno, and Pleasant Hill handwriting expert David DeGarmo. He thought someone was jealous of Toschi's publicity. With great criticism of Prouty's experience, he vowed he'd no longer be available to do any work for the SFPD.

On May 16, in the wake of the new Zodiac letter, the City and County of San Francisco requested that the FBI lab in Washington, D.C. re-examine the entire Zodiac collection of letters to determine if possible which were authentic and which were not. They also wanted to know the number of authors involved in their creation. In the letter to William Webster, Director of the FBI, San Francisco confessed that there currently was no suspect in the case, believed now to comprise 6 murder victims. It was noted that Sherwood Morrill had previously, before his retirement in 1973, authenticated all of the current collection of letters, including the now-disputed Riverside letters. By contrast, John Shimoda had formed the opinion that the three Bates letters were not the product of the Zodiac, and therefore not done by the same hand as the other authenticated Zodiac letters. The request was signed off by Charles R. Gain, Chief of Police, written by Captain Charles A. Schuler, Commanding Officer of the Personal Crimes Division. Sixteen purported Zodiac letters, as well as an inventory of the Zodiac communications, accompanied the letter.

The FBI lab declared that a match for all letters was "inconclusive." This was due to the range of variations, writing speed, and a possible disguise or deliberate distortion of the writing. Nevertheless, one person may have been responsible for all of the letters, including the three Bates letters and the desktop poem, the lab reported.

Also on May 16, the City and County of San Francisco made an additional request. They petitioned William H. Webster, attention FBI laboratory, to take another look at the Zodiac case ciphers. The first three pieces had been decrypted, of course, but investigators were interested to know if any headway could be made on the other three as-yet unsolved ciphers. The request was from Captain Charles A. Schuler, Commanding Officer Personal Crimes Division (on the letterhead of Charles R. Gain, Chief of Police).

On June 19, the FBI in San Francisco requested that the Behavioral Science Unit (BSU) at Quantico, Virginia develop a behavioral profile of the Zodiac killer—a brand new science at the time. Included was an additional request for a reply, and the instructions that materials were to be returned to the Police Training Unit of the San Francisco Field Office.

The FBI didn't need to be asked to look at the ciphers. The reply to the City and County's request came July 27. The FBI Cryptanalysis Unit had been analyzing the unsolved Zodiac ciphers, especially the 340, since their receipt in November of 1969, without solution.

The Sacramento Field Office of the FBI contacted Washington, D.C., in a letter dated July 12, urging the Bureau to reexamine the 1978 letter in light of the scandal that swirled around Toschi. Attached to the request was a copy of an article from *The San Francisco Examiner* where doubt was raised about the authenticity of the last Zodiac communication. The FBI, receiving reports of Toschi's reassignment due to the phony fan letters and reports challenging the authenticity of the 1978 Zodiac letter, conflated the two issues, questioning whether Toschi had also written the latter. It instructed Quantico, who had been tasked with creating a psychological profile of the Zodiac, to continue the work, but to do so without the inclusion of the new letter. The FBI replied on August 23 that its BSU training unit would continue as urged, excluding the 1978 document.

While many phrases, and the handwriting, bore resemblance to earlier letters, there were problems as well. In tone and in topic, it appeared phony. While some harbored the belief—and maybe also the hope—of its authenticity, handwriting experts with the FBI confirmed the suspicions held by many.

If authentic, the letter added little to the investigation. No new themes, clues, or threats were presented clearly enough to be investigated—a prime reason for doubting its authenticity. It appeared to be a rehashing of old ideas and pet phrases, with a familiar layout on the page, precisely what might be expected of a very good faked Zodiac letter. It did let the authorities know that he was still alive and in the area, exactly what might be expected from a hoax that originated from the pen of someone who did not want the case to be forgotten. If from the Zodiac, after four years of silence it could have been instigated by something in the Zodiac's life or the culture of the day. If something had nudged him out of the metaphoric suicide he presented in the Exorcist letter, it was never identified. On too many levels the new letter screamed "FAKE!"

With the removal of Dave Toschi, the last of the original investigators on the case and the final full-time investigator searching for the Zodiac, the case entered a new era. No longer was anyone tasked on a full-time basis to find the perpetrator, and no one who knew the case from the outset was fully-engaged in pursuing it. From that moment on, the Zodiac was merely another case—one that garnered much attention, to be sure—drawing whatever manpower it could from other, more pressing cases.

But the 1978 letter was not the final letter to be considered authentic communication from the Zodiac. In the early twenty-first century, as production got underway for the Hollywood movie *Zodiac* based on Robert Graysmith's book of the same name, staff at *The San Francisco Chronicle* decided to scour the newspaper's letter files to find anything from the killer that may have been overlooked. To their astonishment, they found a mailing that may have originated with the Zodiac serial killer.

1990 Card

An anonymous card in a red envelope emerged from *The Chronicle's* files. Postmarked in Eureka, California, in December, 1990, it was addressed:

Editor
San Francisco Chronicle
901 Mission Street
San Francisco, California
94103

The festive red envelope contained a greeting card, which sported the picture of a snowman on the front. In a tone reminiscent of the Zodiac greeting cards with their droll sense of humor, this one read, "FROM YOUR **SECRET PAL** CAN'T GUESS WHO I AM, YET? WELL. LOOK INSIDE AND YOU'LL FIND OUT…" There was no additional writing applied to the card, inside or out. Preprinted words inside the card completed the tease from the front, "THAT I'M GONNA KEEP YOU GUESSIN' HAPPY HOLIDAYS. ANYWAY… " Inside was a small piece of paper with a photocopied picture of a metallic key chain with two keys on it, the source and significance of which have never been explained.

Similarly, what exactly the entire mailing was designed for, what it meant to communicate, and at whom it was aimed are questions that suggested no clear answers. *The Chronicle* did nothing but file it when it arrived, for it made no threat, comment, or demand. It pertained to nothing illegal so the SFPD was never notified of its existence. The name, "Zodiac," was not present, nor was the iconic phrase *"This is the Zodiac speaking,"* and no crosshairs symbol was included to give any indication that the Zodiac had any connection to the letter, or to propel its words to anyone's notice. Only when reviewing its files was it found by *The Chronicle*, and only then was it noticed that the limited amount of handwriting on the envelope appeared faintly similar to that of the Zodiac.

When compared to previous Zodiac communications, there was some similarity. The guessing game posed by the card was identical to that of the Halloween card of 1970, and reminiscent of the words of the 1966 Confession letter, "THAT WILL NOT STOP THE GAME." If the message was the same—*try to figure out who I am*—it had been conveyed across two decades.

The occasion for the letter—if it was sent by the Zodiac—may have been the work of a copycat murderer operating in New York City. Calling himself the Zodiac, a new serial killer was collecting victims and reporting on their astrological signs. He was apparently attempting to take "slaves" from each of the twelve signs of the Zodiac. New York detectives suspected that he was asking potential victims their horoscope sign before attacking them. He was responsible for killing 3 and wounding 5 from 1990 to 1993. Though the copycat wrote "Zodiac" on all his communications, the New York investigation was not fooled for a minute.

The real Zodiac, not wanting to share the limelight with an East Coast impostor, may have sent the anonymous card to inform the public that he was still around (on the West Coast), and not responsible for the shenanigans in the Big Apple.

The perpetrator of the New York murders, Heriberto Seda, was caught in 1996, convicted, and sentenced to 232 years in prison for his violence as the copycat Zodiac killer. He will not become eligible for parole until he is 113 years of age.

If authentic, the card provided little new information beyond the obvious that the Zodiac was alive in 1990, present at one time in the area of Eureka where it was postmarked, and possibly cognizant of the copycat killer in New York. If not from the Zodiac, the note could be from anyone with just about any intention, up to and including the idea that some hoaxer wanted authorities to believe that the Zodiac was alive and possibly active. Accordingly, it had limited investigative value beyond any forensic evidence that might have survived more than a decade in *The Chronicle*'s filing cabinets.

❧

The end of the Zodiac's attacks and letters, and the failure of the early investigation into the crimes by numerous police departments, sometimes working together and sometimes conducting parallel efforts, did not signal the end of the case. Citizens wouldn't allow it. Public interest in the killer's acts would, over the ensuing decades, spawn a shelf of books, countless magazine articles, a handful of movies, a journal and, with the advent of the Internet, scores of websites, all haphazardly doing their part to erect a cottage industry dedicated to the mystery of the enigmatic killer. To law enforcement already wearied by incessant public involvement and an avalanche of tips, the case would sit on the back burner, only occasionally generating interest and the needed funds to pursue one new lead or one new test. But the killer would not be forgotten.

The investigation would continue one way or another.

12 | EPILOGUE

"The police shall never catch me"

The story of the Zodiac serial killer refused to follow a tight script. Its twists and turns, coupled with the many unknowns, provided a vast narration of ever-increasing complexity. Even the facts that were known, or believed to be known, were spread across numerous levels of uncertainty. Investigators eventually realized that this was no ordinary case, the perpetrator no run-of-the-mill criminal. There was no conviction, indeed no trial. The killer could not be found. All promising leads went nowhere. The investigation could provide no crisp Hollywood ending and no "happily ever after" conclusion. At each and every phase of the work, the police met unequivocally with insurmountable frustration. The victimized families found no justice.

This was a surprising turn of events because the killer left behind far too many clues to elude capture, many felt. Some of the hints may have been so subtle that they were missed entirely; others may have been shrouded in a disguise as clever as the one the killer boasted that he wore during his attacks. The detectives could not read the tea leaves. The police attempted to follow the bread crumbs of his letters and violence, but were never able to pick up a clear trail. His disappearance, whenever it happened, discouraged the police. The pace of the investigation into the case slowed to a crawl.

As the 1970s drew to a close, there were no more police officers working the case full time. Dave Toschi's high profile exit in 1978 saw the last of the concerted effort on the part of law enforcement to unravel the Gordian knot. There was no lack of interest in solving the most enigmatic of American criminal riddles, both from within police departments and among residents in the communities they served, but budget shortages and other, more pressing current crimes pushed the case out of the forefront, and new murder investigations supplanted the old. Great excitement welled up any time a fresh and promising lead emerged. Unfortunately, these never panned out, and as the years marched past, fewer and fewer of them could be found.

The case finally emerged as the most perplexing unsolved murder spree in American criminal history. It continued to mesmerize. Worldwide, it received second billing only to Whitechapel's Jack the Ripper, who in the late 19th century England tore open the bodies of five prostitutes without being captured. As in the Ripper case, the Zodiac's crimes were never solved, the criminal's motives were never uncovered, and the extent of his violence was never definitively documented. Many of the case details continue to be debated.

No amount of frustration and lack of progress could deter a certain segment of the public, however. Interest in the case has not diminished, and in fact grew to a furor at times. Websites, magazine articles, popular books, a scholarly journal, and several movies about the Zodiac serial killer have staked their claim to the criminological landscape. Each new generation introduced to the case brought forth patrons to the tiny subculture of Zodiologists, those who spend their spare time researching into, cogitating over, and writing about the man who killed, taunted, and then vanished as if into thin air. The hunt became a juggernaut despite the apparent apathy on the part of law enforcement.

The 2007 movie *Zodiac*, based on the book of the same name, provided a lit match for the public's oil-soaked rags. While never a blockbuster, it earned a respectable $33 million at the box office, plus additional DVD and Netflix revenue. As of April 2013, the

Sonoma County Sheriff's Office was still fielding on average more than two tips on the case per week from the public. The Napa Police Department continued to take in stray leads, even providing a link on its government webpage to a "Zodiac Tip Line" with the promise that all information would be considered. The San Francisco Police Department became less accepting of public participation, understandably tepid in its interest following decades of unproductive leads, but tips still poured in to that West Coast department, as they did to the FBI and to a lesser degree other agencies.

The Zodiac himself, whoever he was, may have felt some relief as the years passed and no new attacks were attributed to him. He may have felt free from capture. But not everyone forgot about him. A warren of armchair investigators meant to bring him to justice. First, the details of the case would have to be teased from the case files and participating witnesses, and then a profile of the unknown offender would have to be generated. With or without the aid of law enforcement, the pursuit would continue.

As the faithful kept vigil, the killer's whereabouts remained fodder for speculation.

Some believed he died long ago; others, that he lived with only vague memories of his actions—if he even remembered them at all. Some wondered whether he lived far away and never fully became a participant in the Bay Area culture, his attacks and letters merely a diversion from a sales job, military service, or travels that took him to the area without leaving him there. Others were convinced that he lived among his victims but departed, later residing in another city, a different state, or one of the many foreign countries spread across the globe. The inevitability of the aging process suggested to some that he may have recently died, or was quickly approaching the end of his natural life.

The cautious warned that he may have been hastily and mistakenly cleared on the faulty basis of fingerprint or handwriting evidence, or something else that led to the change of his status as a worthy suspect. Others doubt that his name ever made it into the hands of the police.

Even if the villain's name did not reside in the case files, everyone agreed that he could not have escaped history. If he was never a suspect, merely a common man living a common life who failed to raise suspicions, his name cannot have been lost forever, as perhaps Jack the Ripper's given name may have been. In 1888, records were not well kept, and someone in the impoverished underclass could easily have escaped notice and eluded the meager records available to us today. This wasn't likely in 1969. The Zodiac's true name must be written down somewhere: on a birth certificate, above a grave, or within a list of gun club memberships.

Regardless of his current location, he has not been forgotten. The pursuit continues through the efforts of some. Many still hold out the hope that someday an attic will cough up a few vital scraps of paper, a telling artifact or, if the quest is exceedingly lucky, even a diary with a bold confession. And there remain additional investigative avenues that have not yet been traversed.

The relevant information about each attack has been gathered as carefully as possible for the era, the collection of the strange letters has been compiled and organized as much as is feasible under the circumstances, and the list of perplexing, unanswered questions about the case has been assembled. Work remains in the areas of victimology, behavioral analysis, textual criticism, and the study of any patterns that may present themselves. At any point, a recently devised technology or brand new process may aid in the search.

Skilled detectives caution that a murder investigation proceeds methodically and sometimes very slowly. If a good suspect is not immediately found—and even if one is—evidence must be carefully gathered, closely examined, and humbly evaluated. Conclusions must not be achieved with haste or hunch alone, lest a killer be overlooked or the name of an innocent person besmirched. An investigator's well-trained intuition may point towards him like the unsteady needle of a compass toward a general direction, but should never be relied upon to the exclusion of all of the other information.

The optimists are consoled by the fact that even very cold cases can be—and sometimes are—solved. Occasionally, a solution has presented itself very suddenly. Denis Rader, the serial killer known as the BTK, attests to this from the cold, bare confines of his prison cell. He was on the loose for decades before being collared for his crimes, the murders of 10 innocent victims. Sometimes when little hope remains, a detective's drilling may strike investigative oil, though optimism has been shown to be an effective fuel in the hunt.

More than 40 years have elapsed since the perpetrator last claimed an attack; four decades have ticked by without the arrival of a new, authenticatable Zodiac letter. Nevertheless, there is hope. With historical precedent as an encouraging guide, despite any lack of overt progress, the investigation of the Zodiac serial killer has not ended.

In fact, for many, it has just begun.

Appendix A

Zodiac Attacks

Sunday, October 30, 1966. Cheri Jo Bates (killed). In Riverside, Southern California, after checking out books from the library of Riverside City College, Bates was attacked outside the library, probably under the guise of the assailant assisting with a disabled car (the distributor wire had been disconnected). Stabbed and slashed with a small knife, her body was found in a nearby vacant lot. Signs of a violent struggle were evident. Some researchers do not accept this as a Zodiac attack.

Saturday, December 20, 1968. David Faraday & Betty Lou Jensen (both killed). While parked in a lover's lane area, outside of Vallejo in Solano County, Northern California, the perpetrator approached, probably parking parallel to their vehicle, and caused the couple to leave their car. The couple was shot with .22 caliber bullets outside the car: David, once in the left ear; Betty, five times in the back as she fled.

Friday, July 4 (or Saturday, July 5), 1969. Michael Mageau (survived) & Darlene Ferrin (killed). The couple was shot in her car with a 9mm handgun, close to midnight in a deserted parking lot on the outskirts of Vallejo, Northern California. Their assailant walked up to the car carrying a large flashlight and fired at both victims. Before returning to his vehicle, he fired additional shots. The perpetrator telephoned the Vallejo Police Department 40 minutes after the attack from a pay phone a few blocks from the station.

Saturday, September 27, 1969. Bryan Hartnell (survived) & Cecelia Shepard (died two days later). The couple was stabbed while on the shore of Lake Berryessa, north of Napa, Northern California. The assailant hogtied the couple with pre-cut lengths of plastic clothesline. He stabbed them in the back (Shepard also in the front) with a foot-long knife withdrawn from a sheath in his belt. He wrote on

Hartnell's car in felt marker. More than an hour after the attack, the perpetrator telephoned the Napa Police Department from a pay phone located in downtown Napa.

Saturday, October 11, 1969. Paul Stine (killed). The cab driver was shot in the right ear with a .22 caliber handgun (not identical to the one used in December) while parked in the Presidio Heights district of San Francisco, Northern California (at the corner of Washington Street and Cherry Street). The ride originated in the Mason Street and Geary Street area of downtown San Francisco. Stine's assailant was observed after the attack by youths as he wiped the inside and outside of the cab, and likely also by two police officers as he fled to the Presidio grounds.

Sunday, March 22, 1970. (Possible Zodiac attack.) Pregnant Kathleen Johns and her infant daughter (both survived). The perpetrator caused Johns to pull her car over on Highway 132, near Interstate 5, outside of Modesto in the Central Valley of California, under the guise of car problems. After disabling the vehicle, he offered her a ride to a gas station, and proceeded to drive Johns and her daughter around for an estimated two hours. Johns escaped by jumping with her daughter from the car as it slowed. No weapons were observed or referenced.

Appendix B

Zodiac Victims:

Cheri Josephine Bates (18) (2/4/1948 - 10/30/1966). Bates was stabbed and slashed to death by the Zodiac with a small blade in a vacant lot outside of Riverside City College library. After the violent struggle, Bates likely died very quickly.

David Arthur Faraday (17) (10/2/1951 - 12/20/1968). Faraday was shot once in the left ear with a .22. He had exited his car in a Lover's Lane spot on Lake Herman Road, outside of Vallejo, in Solano County. Faraday was breathing shallowly when he was found, but was pronounced dead on arrival (DOA), at Vallejo General Hospital.

Darlene Elizabeth Ferrin (22) (3/17/1947 - 7/5/1969). Darlene was shot at least four times as she sat in the driver's seat of her 1953 Corvair, on July 4 or 5, 1969. She died at the scene from massive blood loss, though she may have lived long enough to flash her head-lights to summon help. She was survived by her second husband, Dean, and her young daughter, Deena.

Bryan Calvin Hartnell. (9/1/1949 -). Hartnell survived six stab wounds from a twelve inch bayonet-style knife while hogtied at Lake Berryessa, September 27, 1969. He sustained major injuries, and underwent extensive surgery. He was back in school within weeks.

Betty Lou Jensen (16) (7/21/1952 - 12/20/1968). Jensen was shot five times in the back as she fled the vehicle parked in a Lover's Lane spot on Lake Herman Road. She died at the scene outside of Vallejo, in Solano County.

Kathleen Johns (5/30/1947 - 6/1/2002). Johns survived a possible kidnapping on March 22 to 23, 1970. Seven-months pregnant while traveling from San Bernardino to Petaluma with her ten-month-old daughter, Jennyfer, she was coerced into stopping at the side of the road near Highway 132 and Interstate 5. Under the guise of fixing her car, the assailant disabled Johns's vehicle and offered to drive her to a service station. It may not have been a Zodiac attack.

Michael Renault Mageau (10/29/1949 -). Mageau survived the shooting (at least 4 shots), while seated in the passenger seat of Ferrin's car at Blue Rock Springs Park, on July 4 or 5, 1969, just outside of Vallejo. He was hospitalized and underwent extensive surgery before moving to his mother's home in Southern California.

Cecelia Ann Shepard (22) (1/1/1947 - 9/29/1969). After sustaining 10 stab wounds from a twelve inch bayonet-style knife while tied up at Lake Berryessa on September 27, 1969, Shepard died two days later at the Queen of the Valley Hospital in Napa from a severe loss of blood.

Paul Lee Stine (29) (12/18/1939 - 11/13/1969). Shot in right ear with a .22 by his passenger after driving his cab to the directed destination in the tony Presidio Heights neighborhood of San Francisco. Stine died instantly at the scene. He was survived by his wife, Claudia.

Appendix C

Zodiac Letters

Confession letter A. Received November 30, 1966 by the Riverside Police Department. The single page letter, typed in all capital letters, claimed credit for the murder of Cheri Jo Bates, described events, and threatened additional killings.

Confession letter B. Received November 30, 1966 by the Riverside Daily Enterprise. The single page, typed in all capital letters, claimed credit for the murder of Cheri Jo Bates, described events, and threatened additional killings. Identical wording to (A).

The Bates letter A. Postmarked in Riverside, April 30, 1967, and sent to the Riverside Police Department. A single, pencil-written page of loose leaf binder paper stated, "BATES HAD TO DIE THERE WILL BE MORE." A small Z was centered at the bottom of the page.

The Bates letter B. Postmarked in Riverside, April 30, 1967, and sent to the Press Enterprise. A single, pencil-written page of loose leaf binder paper stated, "BATES HAD TO DIE THERE WILL BE MORE." A small Z was centered at the bottom of the page.

The Bates letter C. Postmarked in Riverside, April 30, 1967, and sent to Joseph Bates, father of the victim, at his home. Single, pencil-written page of loose leaf binder paper stated, "She Had To Die There will Be More." No Z was present on this page.

The 3-Part letter (A). Received by *The San Francisco Chronicle* on August 1, 1969, postmarked in San Francisco, a two-page letter, plus one-third of the three-part 408 cipher. Written with a felt-tipped pen, it documented the author's proof of committing the December 20, 1968 and July 4, 1969 murders, and demanded that the cipher part be published on threat of a killing rampage.

The 3-Part letter (B). Received by *The San Francisco Examiner* on August 1, 1969, postmarked in San Francisco, a two-page letter, plus one-third of the three-part 408 cipher. Written with a felt-tipped pen, it documented the author's proof of committing the December 20, 1968 and July 4, 1969 murders, and demanded that the cipher part be published on threat of a killing rampage. It was written less neatly than (A), probably a copy, with slight wording differences.

The 3-Part letter (C). Received by *the Vallejo Times Herald* on August 1, 1969, postmarked in San Francisco, a two-page letter, plus one-third of the three-part 408 cipher. Written with a felt-tipped pen, it documented the author's proof of committing the December 20, 1968 and July 4, 1969 murders, and demanded that the cipher part be published on threat of a killing rampage. Written less neatly than (A) and (B), with slight wording differences from both, it appeared to be copied from (B).

The More Material letter. Postmarked in San Francisco and received August 4, 1969 by *The San Francisco Examiner*. In response to a challenge in the press, the 3-page letter, written in felt-tipped pen, provided additional details of the two Vallejo-area murder scenes. The letter was the first of many to begin with the iconic phrase "This is the Zodiac speaking."

The Stine letter. Postmarked in San Francisco and received by *The San Francisco Chronicle* on October 13, 1969, the one-page note claimed credit for the murder of cab driver Paul Stine, taunted that the police could have captured him that night, and threatened the shooting of school children as they disembarked a school bus. A bloodied piece of Paul Stine's shirt was included in the envelope.

The Pen card. Greeting card, "Sorry I haven't written…" postmarked in San Francisco November 8 (possibly November 9), 1969, and received two days later by *The San Francisco Chronicle*. Written within the card were a vague threat, a demand that a new cipher be printed, and a claim of loneliness. Inside on a single sheet was a 340-character cipher.

The 6-Page letter. Postmarked in San Francisco November 9 (possibly November 8), 1969, and received with the Pen card on November 10 by *The San Francisco Chronicle*. The 6-page letter, written in felt-tipped pen, contained taunts, boasts of cleverness, a bomb diagram with a list of ingredients, and a threat to detonate the bomb to kill school children. The longest of all Zodiac letters, it had writing on the back of page 6.

The Belli letter. Postmarked in San Francisco December 20, 1969, and sent to celebrity trial lawyer Melvin Belli, the one-page, felt-tip-penned letter requested "please help me" three times, spoke of an inner force that controlled, and claimed an attempt to prevent the killings. A second piece of Stine's bloody shirt accompanied the letter.

The Name letter. Postmarked in San Francisco April 20, 1970 and received the next day by *The San Francisco Chronicle*. The two-page letter included a 13-character cipher within its text, and denied that its author committed the bombing of a police station. The second page was a revised bomb diagram.

The Dragon card. Greeting card, "Sorry to hear your ass is dragon..." postmarked April 28, 1970 in San Francisco and received by *The San Francisco Chronicle*. The writing within the card provided two demands that claimed, if enacted, would prevent the bomb detonation: publicize the bomb diagram with all the details and have citizens wear [Zodiac] buttons around town.

The Map letter. Postmarked in San Francisco June 26, 1970 and received by *The San Francisco Chronicle*, a one-page letter, plus a piece of a San Francisco Bay Area map (containing a circle, numbers and letters, centered over Mount Diablo). A 32-character cipher within its text when combined with the Map promised to reveal the location of a pre-set bomb.

The Johns letter. Postmarked in San Francisco July 24, 1970 and received by *The San Francisco Chronicle*. The two-sentence letter (following the iconic title) referred to the Johns attack, and alluded to *The Mikado*, "I now have a little list…" The Zodiac's shortest missive.

The Torture letter. Postmarked in San Francisco July 26, 1970 and received by *The San Francisco Chronicle*, it was five pages in length. The first two pages detailed tortures that the killer promised to enact on his "slaves." The final three pages were a quote, with errors, of *The Mikado* song, "I Have a Little List."

The Crack Proof card. (Disputed authenticity for a lack of handwriting and an unclear message.) Postmarked in San Francisco October 5, 1970 and received by *The San Francisco Chronicle*, it contained only cut-out words from *The Chronicle* of that date, including, "I'm crackproof."

The Halloween card. Preprinted greeting card stated, "I feel it in my bones…" It was postmarked in San Francisco October 27, 1970 and received two days later by Paul Avery of *The San Francisco Chronicle*. It contained drawn material, symbols, intersected words (on the card and within the envelope), and added Halloween material. The writing was drawn in white artist's ink.

The L.A. Times letter. Postmarked in Alameda County on March 13, 1971 and received by *The L.A. Times* in Los Angeles, California two days later. The one-page missive advised the police to work harder, noted that they had discovered his "riverside activity," and bragged of "more down there." He claimed to have written to the Southern California paper because he was not receiving "front page coverage." It was the last communication to use the iconic phrase and symbol.

The Pines card. (Disputed authenticity for a lack of handwriting and an unclear message.) Postmarked in San Francisco, received March 22, 1971, and addressed to Paul Avery of *The San Francisco Chronicle*. With a picture of a Lake Tahoe condominium project under construction on its front, it may have alluded to the disappearance of nurse Donna Lass.

The Exorcist letter. Postmarked January 29, 1974 in San Mateo County or Santa Clara County and received by *The San Francisco Chronicle* the next day, the one-page note written in blue felt-tipped pen contained a review of the movie the Exorcist, a quote from *The Mikado*, a demand that it be printed, and a strange collection of shapes at the bottom of the page.

The SLA letter. (Authenticity disputed for a lack of any reference to the Zodiac and its lack of Zodiac-like tone or handwriting.) Postmarked February 4, 1974 and sent to *The San Francisco Chronicle*, the short note explained that "SLA" was an Old Norse word meaning "to kill." It was signed, "a friend."

The Badlands card. (Authenticity disputed for a lack of any reference to the Zodiac and its lack of Zodiac-like tone or handwriting.) Postmarked May 6, 1974 and sent to *The San Francisco Chronicle*, it decried the violence in a movie ad for the motion picture "Badlands" and requested the ad be stopped. It was signed, "A citizen."

The Count Marco letter. (Authenticity disputed for a lack of any reference to the Zodiac and its lack of any Zodiac-like tone or handwriting.) Postmarked July 8, 1974 and addressed to *The San Francisco Chronicle*, this letter was critical of a columnist and requested that his column be canceled. It was signed, "The Red Phantom (red with rage)."

1978 letter. This is assumed to be a hoax letter due to a lack of content; the name, Toschi, in the letter; and the many questions surrounding the authenticity of the handwriting. Received April 25, 1978, postmarked a day earlier, this one-page letter offered little new information and appeared to be pieced-together ideas from previous Zodiac letters.

The Snowman card. (Authenticity unknown for lack of reference to the Zodiac and a lack of any concrete information.) This unaltered greeting card in a red envelope was sent to *The San Francisco Chronicle*, postmarked Eureka, California, December, 1990. It contained a photocopied small sheet picturing two unidentified security keys held together by a segmented metal key chain of dull silver color.

Appendix D

Zodiac Timeline:

1966
October 30—Riverside Attack
November 30—Confession
letters (2)

1967
April 30—Bates letters (3)

1968
*December 20—Lake Herman
Road Attack*

1969
*July 4—Blue Rock Springs Attack
and Call*
July 31—3-Part letters (3)
August 7—More Material letter
*September 27—Lake Berryessa
Attack, Car Door Writing, Call*
October 11—Paul Stine Attack
October 13—Stine letter, plus
shirt piece
November 8—Dripping Pen
card, plus cipher
November 9—6-Page letter
December 20—Belli letter, plus
shirt piece

1970
*March 22—Kathleen Johns
Attack*
April 20—Name letter and
cipher
April 28—Dragon card
June 26—Map letter, map piece,
and cipher
July 24—Kathleen Johns letter
July 26—Torture letter
October 5—Crack Proof card
(Disputed)
October 28—Halloween card

1971
March 13—L.A. Times letter
March 22—Pines card
(Disputed)

1974
January 29—Exorcist letter
February 14— SLA letter
(Disputed)
May 8—Badlands postcard
(Disputed)
July 8—Count Marco letter
(Disputed)

1978 and 1990 Disputed letter/
card

Index

Made in the USA
San Bernardino, CA
04 June 2019